D1271107

Humanity in Warfare

Humanity in Warfare

Geoffrey Best

New York
Columbia University Press 1980

This publication was prepared under a grant from the
Woodrow Wilson International Center for Scholars,
Washington, D.C. The statements and views expressed
herein are those of the author and not necessarily
those of the Wilson Center.

Printed in Great Britain

Library of Congress Cataloging in Publication Data

Best, Geoffrey.
       Humanity in warfare.

       Bibliography: p.
       1.   War (International law) 2.   War victims – Law
and legislation.   I.   Title.
JX4511.B4   341.6′09   80–15728
ISBN 0–231–05158–1

To the memory and in honour of Pierre Boissier

Contents

Preface

Having worked on and off for ten years towards this book, and put into it thoughts brewing over some years before that, I am unusually conscious of the extent of my debt to the people who have, sometimes no doubt without knowing it, helped me along the road. None of them, I must emphasize, bears any responsibility whatever for the use I happen to have made of their help. Some of them, probably, won't wholly like it. But that is my affair, not theirs. In any case I feel I should be less than honest were I not to try to mention all I can remember, and to thank them as best I can.

First and foremost, I must mention two great academic institutions, one very old, the other quite new. The old one is All Souls College, Oxford. The visiting fellowship it gave me for 1969–70 enabled me to make a start. The new one is the Woodrow Wilson International Center for Scholars, Washington DC. It celebrated its tenth birthday while I was one of its Fellows in 1978–9. My debts in general to the Master and Fellows of the one, the Trustees and Director of the other, are fundamental. Oxford and Washington are hives of intellectual activity and meccas of scholarship. But it is not just the scholars at such places from whose friendly interest one benefits. Those who cope with their fellows' non-intellectual problems are equally to be thanked. At All Souls, for instance, I was endlessly grateful for the friendly help of Norma Potter in the Codrington Library; while it is difficult to imagine what life would have been like at the Wilson Center without the vigilant solicitude of the librarian, Zdenek David, his immediate staff, and Fran Hunter, Louise Platt, Mildred Pappas, Eloise Doane, and the rest. Cambridge, my Alma Mater, must be mentioned too. The Master and Fellows of Trinity honoured me with an invitation to give the Lees Knowles Lectures in the University of Cambridge in the spring of 1970. My theme was 'Conscience and the Conduct of War, 1789–1900'. This book is a regrettably late flowering of what was then, I very soon realized, a rather premature bud.

I turn from the institutions which have supported my work to the people who have most inspired it and whose approval I should most value. The opinion of the one who matters most, alas!, I shall never know: Pierre Boissier, member of the International Committee of the Red Cross and Director of the Institut Henry-Dunant from 1968 until his tragic death six years later. What I owe to that fine and wonderful man I have tried to say in a contribution to the memorial volume published by the Institut in his honour: *Pierre Boissier, 1920–1975* (Geneva 1977). Then there are several schoolmasters, especially Paul Longland and Walter Oakeshott, and some dons at Cambridge, particularly George Kitson Clark, who first gave me to understand how serious a thing it is to handle history, Herbert Butterfield, whom I did not meet till much later but whose lectures and books helped me acquire the relish for the history of ideas I have never lost, and Noel Annan, whose lectures in that field were singularly exciting.

At Edinburgh, and at Sussex, the sources of my bread and butter for most of the time that I have been having war-and-peace thoughts, I happily have found colleagues to enjoy talking this sort of shop with; I may dare to mention particularly Victor Kiernan, George Shepperson, Owen Dudley-Edwards, Gerald Draper, Rowie Mitchison, Maurice Hutt, John Röhl, Rupert Wilkinson, Christopher Chaffin, Marcus Cunliffe and Christopher Thorne. At Oxford I was privileged to begin a late discipleship to Michael Howard, whose importance to me as a beacon of wisdom and knowledge has been second only to that of Pierre Boissier. I must acknowledge much help received from people outside my own institutions: Arthur Marwick and Christopher Harvie of the Open University (before that, of Edinburgh); Norman Hampson of York; Brian Bond and Derek McKay of London; John Keegan, David Chandler and Paddy Griffith of the RMA, Sandhurst, and Andrew Wheatcroft of Hagworthingham, who introduced me to them; Michel Veuthey of the ICRC and Jiri Toman of the Institut Henry-Dunant; Manfred Messerschmidt and Wilhelm Deist of the Militärgeschichtliches Forschungsamt; François Bédarida of the Institut d'Histoire du Temps Présent (CNRS); Sam Williamson of Chapel Hill, Jim Eayrs of Toronto, and John Pocock of Johns Hopkins; Sam Wells (and Sherry), David MacIsaac, Stephen Pelz, Genaro Arriagada, Frank Sayre and John Watson within the Wilson Center during my time there, and Hays Parks,

Dean Allard, Tom Mallison and William O'Brien in Washington's array of all the talents. I must also mysteriously thank a score of distinguished British military men and scholars who kindly took the trouble to answer a few questions I put to them in the early summer of 1978. As they will realize if they do me the honour of reading this book, I did not in the end find it necessary to use anything they particularly told me. But their thoughtful responses (only two never answered) encouraged me a lot.

I have never yet had the misfortune to come across a library or archive which was not more or less pleasant to work in. The libraries of the universities of Edinburgh and Sussex in particular, under their admirable chiefs Dick Fifoot and Peter Lewis, seem to me models of their different kinds. But I have also laboured with not much less ease and profit in other libraries: the British Museum (which has taken to calling itself the British Library), the Bodleian, the Cambridge University Library, the National Library of Scotland, and the Library of Congress. Archives have not lain much in my way (for which I was thankful when the British Public Record Office moved so much out of everyone's way), but I acknowledge a debt in particular to the Liddell Hart Centre for Military Archives at King's College, London, which has graciously permitted me to quote from its papers; as I am grateful to F. R. Scott for permission to use one of his fine *Selected Poems* (OUP 1966) among the epigraphs to Chapter IV. Over the years I have gratefully received modest research grants from the universities of Edinburgh and Sussex, and from the British Academy.

In conclusion, I happily acknowledge how much I feel I have benefited from the comradeship, comments, and sometimes wholesomely acerbic criticism, not just of matters related to this book but also (which is more important) relative to life in general, received from Simon, Edward, Rosie, and Marigold, my children and my wife.

Introduction

Definitions and Connexions

Facts must be faced. Homo sapiens, *the only creature endowed with reason, is also the only creature to pin its existence to things unreasonable.*

Henri Bergson, *The Two Sources of Morality and Religion,* 1932

It is common experience in the history of warfare that not only wars but actions taken in war as military necessities are often supported at the time by a class of arguments which, after the war is over, people find are arguments to which they never should have listened.

George Bell, Speech in the House of Lords, 9 February 1944

The distinction between moral rules and rules that are better described as procedural or customary is not always easy to draw, but war is as a matter of fact an inherently normative phenomenon; it is unimaginable apart from rules by which human beings recognize what behavior is appropriate to it and define their attitudes towards it. War is not simply a clash of force; it is a clash between the agents of political groups who are able to recognize one another as such and direct their force at one another only because of the rules that they understand and apply. Above and beyond this, because human beings have moral feelings and make moral choices, they have these feelings and make these choices when they are at war . . .

Hedley Bull, *World Politics,* Volume 31, 1979

1 The idea of the book

This book is about an idea: the idea that, if there are to be wars, and so long as wars go on, it is certainly better for the warring parties, and probably better for mankind at large, that the persons fighting should observe some prohibitions and restraints on how they do it; the idea, to put it at its briefest, of humanity in warfare.

Such a juxtaposition of concepts bristles with paradox, and of course provokes scepticism. Is not the essence of warfare a denial of humanity? Are not wars often justly condemned as failures of humanity? Are not these concepts and the institutions which typically embody them incompatible opposites? Such serious criticism and complaints have to be met. Fortunately for the writer of this book and, he believes, humanity at large, they can be. The historian has the support of colleagues in many other fields of scientific study and philosophical inquiry in recording that most (though certainly not all) societies and cultures known to us, including most of those of our own day, display some readiness to observe this idea, although the attempts sometimes come to little more than breast-beating about failure to live up to it. The wish to preserve something of humanity in warfare is more commonly met with than success in doing so; yet the measure of success, carrying from war to war and from time to time, is, as the main part of this book will show, not negligible. It seems to me just as reasonable to suppose that all this signifies something fundamental about humankind, as to conclude, as most of us do for lack of convincing evidence one way or the other, that ordinary 'human nature' contains within it the stuff of both social harmony and social conflict, yearnings towards both war and peace. The spectacle is paradoxical; from some points of view, absurd. But the fact nevertheless seems to be that, even in the most unpromising circumstances of war, humanity can often quite surprisingly break through. Expressing myself in this introduction as a man and citizen besides a historian, such breakthroughs seem to me to be worth study, admiration, and encouragement, no less than the accompanying breakdowns are worth study, reflection, and regret.

Historically, this attempt to preserve and exercise some humanity even *in extremis* has normally clothed itself in codes of custom and even 'laws' mutually recognized by both warring parties. It is the purpose of this book to present the history of this idea in that clothing since the middle of the eighteenth century, an age which is, for reasons which Chapter I will make clear, a good time to pick it up. What was going strong by then in Europe and Europe's North American extensions has since spread all over the world and become, not without pangs and problems with which the second half of the book will be much concerned, a truly international possession. Superficial evidence of this universality is offered wherever appears through the dust of conflict a white flag or a red cross; or whenever issues from the mouth of some troubled combatant an echo, no matter how faint or garbled, of the language of the Geneva Conventions.

That white flag, once no more than the conventional sign made by professional European men of war when they wanted a truce, has become known the world over as a sign to be made with reasonable hope that those seeing it will temporarily suspend hostilities and engage in cautious dialogue instead. The Red Cross began its world career in the eighteen-sixties simply as the badge agreed to be worn by those engaged in the single task of relieving the sufferings of the wounded in battle. It has now attained the astonishing status of the only symbol normally accepted throughout all races and countries (some recent regrettable exceptions are not yet proved persistent or deliberate enough to invalidate the generalization) as representing the interests of humanity at large. The Geneva Conventions must share celebrity with the Universal Declaration of Human Rights and perhaps the Charter of the United Nations as the most nearly universally known and seemingly accepted statements about what is due to man from man. These global recognitions are equally the historical product of Europe's imperial expansion and the psychological and moral product of inherent human preference and need; something like a natural readiness – natural at any rate to a large proportion of mankind – to recognize what an excellent recent writer has called 'the moral reality of war',[1] and to worry about it.

2 Why this book is not about 'just war'

Just and Unjust Wars, by Michael Walzer, is the title of the book just referred to. Like most of the serious writing about moral values in relation to war, its language comes out of two related great traditions: the ancient Christian one, substantially founded by St Augustine, and developed to a high pitch of refinement by the close of the Middle Ages, and intermittently resuscitated since then; or the modern, explicitly marxist tradition developed by Lenin and other marxist commentators on the 'imperialist' and 'colonialist' conflicts of the twentieth century. Their shared roots and common channelling through the Enlightenment help to explain why they both distinguish wars that are worth fighting from wars that are not, and likewise lay down such rules for the conduct of wars as will make more likely than not the achievement of the (by definition) 'just' objective pursued. Each invites, indeed demands, responsibility in decision-making, and each is well capable of counselling strict observance of limitations and prohibitions, though neither is absolutely bound to do so. Not surprisingly, therefore, these two related moral traditions are attractive modes or styles for guiding the thoughts not only of committed believers and ideologues within those traditions (whose interests in their war-justifying elements might appear, on close inspection, to be greater than their interest in the war-moderating ones) but also of anyone who is interested in limiting the incidence and the incidents of war. Since I admire some of these 'just war' books greatly and often recommend them, I must now explain why nevertheless I am going to eschew their approaches and their language.[2]

I never thought of writing in terms of 'just' or 'unjust' wars and war conduct, primarily because the world's principal experts on the matter of humanity in warfare avoid such language like the plague. I refer to the International Committee of the Red Cross, by whose example in general and by several of whose officers in particular (above all, he to whose memory this book is dedicated) I have been much influenced. By all means let people approach this matter by way of 'just war' theory if that suits them. For many it may be the way that makes most sense. But the example of the ICRC proves at least that 'just war' thought and language is not indispensable; and there are reasons, to which I shall come presently, for suspecting that it may sometimes be positively unhelpful. The Red Cross has always administered relief to sufferers in wartime without regard to the quality of the causes for which they may have been fighting; for the excellent and explicit reason, that human suffering is human suffering, whether incurred in the course of a 'just war' or not. Privately, members of the Red Cross (*a fortiori*, the ICRC, its permanently neutral and impartial cortex) no doubt have their own views as to the relative rightness and wrongness of the causes invoked by those fighters. Simply as Red Cross members, however, they ought to have no opinions on the matter, their movement's philosophy being that it is better that they should have no such opinion, since to engage in the business of judgement of motives and purposes would be to commit them in an area where it is essential that they remain uncommitted.

Most national Red Cross societies, it must be confessed, understandably tend to fail to maintain such lofty indifference. I shall comment on that inevitable degree of lapsing later. But the ICRC, with its unique position and its special role in the neutral centre of the world's humanitarian concerns, has less difficulty in living true to its principles. Accordingly we observe that it never, never engages in judgement about the rights and wrongs of the armed conflicts amidst which it does its work; as if it knows all too much about the demands made by War, and the indispensability of meeting them, to be able to rise at the same time to the height of the demands made by Justice. Humanity, not Justice, is its *prime* concern. The only judgements it will venture to make, and these only reluctantly and only when it is thought helpful, are as to whether the Geneva Conventions and related laws and conventions about humanity in warfare are being observed or not. It may thus happen (and one suspects that it has happened) that a belligerent possessing what would generally be judged the less worthy cause, may nevertheless have been the more assiduous observer of humanitarian law. This may be another of the paradoxes, the near-absurdities, in which the subject is undeniably rich; I only beg readers to suspend judgement until they have finished the book, in the course of which the grounds for the ICRC's principles will become clearer.

Wars may then be 'just' or 'unjust', in the view of anyone who cares to classify them thus; international humanitarian law and its particular application to circumstances of war go on regardless, and the words 'just' and 'unjust' make no appearance in its earliest, its best-known, and to date its most effective instruments, the Geneva Conventions; nor, for that matter, do they appear in the Hague Conventions and Regulations for Land Warfare, with which we shall later be at least as much concerned. From the practical regulator's point of view, these moral inquiries into the motivations of wars are at least irrelevant. One of the most effective regulators ever was Louis Renault, Professor of International Law at the Sorbonne and France's leading representative at the Hague Conferences of 1899 and 1907, and by all accounts one of the two or three most outstanding men there. Hear what he said in his preface to the French army's manual on the law of war, 1913:

War is not, as some have said, force put to the service of Right in international relations, or an act of legitimate defence aimed at repulsing an aggression or obtaining reparation, or, more simply, an extreme means of defending one's own rights. These definitions should be rejected, because they don't correspond to reality – not all of it anyway. From the point of view where one has to start in order to regulate warfare, war must be seen simply as *a state of affairs*: a variety of acts of violence by means of which each belligerent is trying to submit the other to his will.[3]

I adopt this non-ideological humanitarian standpoint, and am pleased to borrow a fellow-worker's description of it:

> ... judging particular situations on their own merits, weighing the consequences of actions by the standard of the humanitarian view itself ...; it checks the future against the past, [proceeding] from precedent to precedent. ... It becomes possible to define what is right by defining what is wrong ...[4]

One may, then, exercise a concern for humanity in warfare without necessarily and consciously bothering about how any particular war stands in relation to the 'just/unjust' criteria; which, I repeat, is not to say that preoccupation with such criteria may not produce the most valuable of books. But there are other and less innocent practical aspects of the 'just/unjust' debate, as to which its more theoretical practitioners can seem to be inadequately alert.

Every well-informed student of the history of warfare knows that some of the most inhumane wars ever fought have been proclaimed to be 'just' by those who fought them. James Turner Johnson, who has written one of the best books about the history of 'just war' theory, argues strongly that those singularly inhumane 'religious wars' of the sixteenth and seventeenth centuries, usually advanced as examples of how conviction of 'just' cause can evoke horrible behaviour, ought to be classified not as 'just wars' but as 'holy wars', distinct from and (mainly because of their other-worldly frame of reference) more unmeasured than the classical 'just war' proper. Like Walzer, he seeks to rescue the idea of 'just war' from the 'realist' condemnation expressed in A. J. P. Taylor's remark: 'Bismarck fought "necessary" wars, and killed thousands;

the idealists of the twentieth century fight "just" wars and kill millions.'

Whatever justice in war *should* mean, however, several facts about the actual conduct of war and the behaviour of people in war force themselves upon the notice of anyone who seeks to study the observance of humanitarian law. First: conviction of righteousness elides easily into self-righteousness, and self-righteousness is not the best state of mind for moderation, objectivity, and the practice of human kindness. Second: although 'just war' language has for many years been part of the *lingua franca* of international marxism, just as 'holy war' remains part of the *lingua franca* of international islam, it seems in both cases to be taken most seriously by groups and governments whose acts and policies show them to be the most ruthless. Third: belligerent states neither marxist nor islamic have sometimes been led by overmuch conviction of righteousness into policies most immoderate and inept; witness for instance 'unconditional surrender' in world war two, the second phase of the Korean war, the Anglo-French 'Suez adventure', Vietnam. Fourth: courts administering the law of war, and jurists expounding and analysing it, have concurred to maintain that its very existence and viability, precarious as in the nature of the case they must be, depend upon an unstated assumption that each party is neither more right nor wrong than the other *in having gone to war in the first place*; 'all laws of war . . . must . . . assume that both parties are equally in the right.'[5] And fifth: whatever jurists and outside commentators may be saying or deliberately not saying about the merits of any particular conflict, men fighting willingly in it (unwilling conscripts may of course be a different matter) tend to profess that their cause is a just one; something they will, something they psychologically *must* make themselves believe, whether God and his agents on earth really consider it so or not.

The whole fine language about justice in war thus gets dragged through the mire of the battlefield, and is made in practice meaningless; regularly called into use as part of the panoply of emotional self-intoxication so often found necessary (as actual alcoholic intoxication has sometimes been found necessary) to get people fighting furiously, and calculated to cloud judgement about right and wrong. But fortunately for the ultimate interests of humanity, this ferocious, and by any standards immoral, language of war appears to have less than the completely demoralizing effect one might expect. Actual fighting men can very well show by their actual conduct towards their enemies that they don't wholly believe everything they have been egged on or bullied to say; as if, instinctively exercising some dispassionate objectivity about the situation they all find themselves in, they know that the men on the other side have to believe likewise. Much historical evidence, some of it to be drawn upon in these pages, shows that even 'just'-feeling men, unless worked up to an unusually intense level of emotional frenzy or ideological temper, can observe towards equally 'just'-feeling foes all the chivalrous or humane regard compatible with the given situation.

3   *Jus ad bellum* and *jus in bello*

Attempting what I am attempting, then – a history of the laws and customs by which the more developed countries have thought fit to control their conduct of war amongst themselves through the past couple of centuries – it is not difficult to justify a deliberate bypassing of 'just war' theory. But at this point I must recognize and admit that 'just war' categories can only be dispensed with when a work is as precisely delimited as this one. 'Just war' theory, as I have already mentioned, is concerned to evaluate both the causes of war and the conduct of war. The classical terms for these two main branches of the subject (like so much else in international law, derived originally from the Romans, and very useful on account of their conciseness) are, respectively, *jus ad bellum* and *jus in bello*: the law governing your going to war in the first place, and the law governing what you do when you get there. My book is about nothing but *jus in bello*. Its restriction to that branch of the whole great subject does not embarrass me, since it is on its own, without necessary regard to kindred systems, an institution of considerable significance to mankind, and no one has yet written its history. To write its history and at the same time, appropriately intertwined, the history of the causes of wars, would be a colossal undertaking. I am not up to it. But my half of the whole is not without direct relevance to the other. Serious study of the law of war on its own has this therapeutic quality, that it calls attention to its own limitations, and suggests their remedy. One cannot for long contemplate the cruel and pointless aspects of war without reflecting upon the phenomenon of war itself. It seems quite a natural progression, to advance from inquiry into the conduct of wars to the inquiry as to why they happened to begin with; to which the conclusions might be that it was a pity they happened at all. Which of us, thinking calmly about the matter, would disagree with what Thomas Arnold wrote in his interesting 'war and society' lecture of 1842: 'Though I believe that theoretically the Quakers are wrong in pronouncing all wars to be unjustifiable, yet I confess that historically the exceptions to their doctrine have been comparatively few . . .'[6]

Writing neither about the causes of war (a branch of social science by now in a high and exciting state of development), nor about the morality of engaging in wars, the momentous matter with which 'just war' writers are primarily engaged, I close this section of my introductory argument with the suggestion that, although it springs from different sources and flows through somewhat different channels, this empirical humanitarian stream of inquiry in the end joins forces with those others. One cannot contemplate restraint in the conduct of war without being driven to consider restraint in the recourse to war. The law of war on its *jus in bello* side – the side which appears alone in the manuals by which armed forces are supposed to regulate their conduct of operations, and by which international juridical opinion evaluates their faithfulness in doing so – says nothing, dares not say anything, about *jus ad bellum*. But thought about the one is barely separable from thought about the other, and even those humanitarian activists who have most insistently and explicitly kept out of the debate about 'just' and 'unjust' wars may have been doing more about the general war problem than meets the eye. At any rate, this seems to have been, and presumably remains, the covert faith of the ICRC. For obvious reasons it is committed to no particular opinion about war in general (other than implicit acceptance of the lawfulness of wars entirely of self-defence, the only sort of war the Swiss need contemplate) and its influence has always been exerted to damp down overtly pacifistic motions within the Red Cross movement at large. But the general tenor of its preferences is unmistakable, and the implications of the Geneva Convention are equally so. Only a mentally-dulled militarist could study them and be made more warlike; they must make mentally and morally active people less accepting of war.

This attitude was nicely expressed by Gustave Moynier, the

sage jurist who presided over the first forty years of the ICRC's existence. Towards the end of a public lecture in Geneva, one winter evening of 1890-1, he was able to speak more openly than was prudent at international gatherings. From a masterly survey of the Geneva Convention's relative successes and failures in the mitigation of the horrors of war since 1864, he turned to regard it in its wider context and role, as an instrument of pacification, a force for peace. 'First of all,' he said, 'we might note that the Convention has furnished an argument in favour of the brotherhood of men. In subscribing to it, the several factions of civilized mankind have – never before with so much unity – placed themselves under a common rule, formulated entirely in the light of moral considerations. . . . Recognizing that after all they all belong to the same family, men have concluded that they ought to begin by showing some regard for another's suffering, up to a certain point . . . pending the time when a still stronger conviction of their common humanity shall lead them to understand that the very idea of their killing one another is monstrous.' So, he went on, the idea at the heart of the Geneva Convention might be expected to germinate and sprout in the minds and hearts of men, leading them from one restraint upon their violent appetites to another, from refusal to fight in unjustifiable wars (he did not say 'unjust'!) to refusal to let themselves be found fighting wars at all. '*La civilisation de la guerre* – the humanizing of war – could end only in its abolition. *Sursum corda*!'[7] It was a typical conclusion for its epoch, and it was, of course, much too optimistic. Moynier, like so many other believers in progress about that time, had his timescale wrong. But in principle he was right. That closing clarion call might mean a lot more now, outside Switzerland, than it could do in Geneva then.

4 The *jus in bello* vindicated

Scepticism about the value of the law of war is nothing new. Anyone who writes or thinks about it has to make up his mind whether the idea that it is one of civilization's triumphs is a boon or a bane to mankind. The changing terms of its justification from time to time are part of its history, and will be included below. But something ought to be said about it in these opening pages.

There seem to me to be two sceptical criticisms which need to be met: first, that while it does no particular harm, the law of war does no particular good either, and may therefore be discounted as a standing failure; second, that it does positive harm, and had therefore better be abolished as a standing nuisance.

The first line of scepticism has this much firmly to be said for it, that the law of war is obviously more liable than any other branch of law to fall short of its goal. Its mission, strictly speaking, is impossible. It seeks to introduce moderation and restraint into a medium peculiarly insusceptible to those qualities. Definitions and descriptions of war alike agree that parts at least of its essence are passion, violence, and unpredictability. Even the most self-consciously controlled, chivalrous, entirely professional wars have their moments of confusion and nastiness, and most campaigns and wars are nothing like that anyway. Is it reasonable, for example, to get cross when a thirsty, sleepless, over-worked, anxious young officer with death in the air all round him fails to keep sedulously 'within the law' when we know very well that much lighter pressures bend the law-abidingness of even the most respectable pillars of our communities, not to mention their less respectable flying-buttresses? No one should be surprised that the law of war is at the best of times never more than imperfectly observed, and at worse times is very poorly observed indeed.

But this line of criticism goes deeper. At least, it may argue, the codes and systems of law which your accountants, garage owners and dons are expected to observe are generally accepted; no one makes radical criticisms of them, they are in quite good working order, it is clearly in almost everybody's interest to observe them almost all the time, and there is an effective machinery of detection, enforcement and punishment waiting in the wings to help concentrate the minds of possible deviants at critical moments of temptation. Such can be said of any healthy branch of law or legal system. The requirements of the law and the sanction of the law go together. How different, however, must appear the system of international law, especially the branch of it with which we are concerned! The great difference between international law and any system of national law lies in the reality and effectiveness of the sanctions attending breaches of the latter. One famous school of jurisprudence maintains that there is simply no law where there is no sovereign power to enforce it. Anyone can understand that laws without reliable means of enforcement lack much of their value and force. International law by definition has no means of enforcement other than what its participants agree to submit to. There is no international, or rather *supra*national, sovereign. The International Court of The Hague only handles those limited classes of disputes which States choose to allow it to handle. It suits those States' interests to submit thus far to its judgements. The European Court at Luxembourg has gone further. The meber States of the European Comunity have accepted quite a large obligation to conform to its common law; but this expressly excludes matters of national defence and security. When it comes to matters with a military aspect, States are normally at their most sovereign; the attempt to institute an international criminal court, capable of enforcing among other things the law of war, has so far utterly failed, nor is there any present prospect that things will change. Whatever may be the sanctions of the law of war, they do not include a known and inescapable court with some sovereign power behind it. One of Britain's greatest experts on the law of war, Thomas Erskine Holland, a man who as a matter of fact believed profoundly in it and fought for it nobly, nevertheless thought it proper in 1880 to describe international law as 'the vanishing point of jurisprudence';[8] an exercise in legal perspective to which his no less distinguished successor Hersh Lauterpacht has added the observation, that 'If international law is, in some ways, at the vanishing point of law, the law of war is, perhaps even more conspicuously, at the vanishing point of international law.'[9]

Such judgements, even from such men, being possible, we should perhaps not so much complain that the law of war does not work well, as marvel that it works at all. And yet it does work. Almost all international wars, and some major civil wars, since the eighteenth century have been softened by the operation of the law of war. There has often been room for further softening. Even vestigial recollections of the law seem to have disappeared at some bad moments and on some dark fronts. Beastliness occurred even where everyone had apparently been trying to behave well. But the weight of the evidence is unmistakable, that the law of war has done nothing but good, and the implication is clear, that wars where it was not enforced, known, or even dimly apprehended, were the more horrible for their lack of it. Legal precisians who are reluctant to grant this, fail to note how much the extreme weakness of formal sanctions is compensated by ordinary muddled human sentiment and sentimentality; the personal paradox of man's mixed nature within the social paradox of war.

The second line of criticism, the more worried one that the law of war actually does harm, has to be answered in different terms. What is thought (by the critics answered in the preceding paragraph – not by me) to do neither much harm nor much good may at any rate be left where it is. What is alleged to do positive harm had better be abolished. This charge, which has turned up in one form or another throughout the centuries and has obvious attractions for people with particularly passionate or absolute casts of mind, was put by just such a person, Tolstoy, into the mouth of Prince Andrew Bolkhonsky in a celebrated passage in *War and Peace*. It came when he was discussing the war – and war in general – with Pierre Bezhukov.

'Not take prisoners,' continued Prince Andrew, 'that by itself would quite change the whole war and make it less cruel. As it is we have played at war ... We play at magnanimity and all that stuff. Such magnanimity and sensibility are like the magnanimity and sensibilities of a lady who faints when she sees a calf being killed; she is so kind-hearted that she can't look at blood, but enjoys eating the calf served up with sauce. They talk to us of the rules of war, of chivalry, of flags of truce, of mercy to the unfortunate and so on. It's all rubbish. I saw chivalry and flags of truce in 1805. They humbugged us and we humbugged them. They plunder other peoples' houses, issue false paper money, and worst of all they kill my children and my father, and then talk of rules of war and magnanimity to foes! Take no prisoners but kill and be killed! ... If there was none of this magnanimity in war, we should go to war only when it was worth while going to certain death, as now. ... War is not courtesy but the most horrible thing in life; and we ought to understand that, and not play at war. ... The air of war is murder; the methods of war are spying, treachery, and their encouragement, the ruin of a country's inhabitants, robbing them or stealing to provision the army, and fraud and falsehood termed military craft. ...'[10]

This is strong stuff, and anyone who has got far enough outside his conventionally patriotic and aggressive self to be able to look at war dispassionately knows it is 'true'; as also is 'true' so much of what Tolstoy wrote, both in that epic and later, about patriotism and militarism. Yet one is not bound to be persuaded by it. Tolstoy probably put it more fiercely than anyone else; but the argument was not new when he took it up, and as good an answer to it as any I have read had in fact been given, about the time Tolstoy was getting his first direct military experiences, by the British radical MP, John Roebuck. In the course of a searching review of Napier's *Peninsular War*, he thus met Prince Andrew's argument:

> It has indeed been said that, in those who wish to diminish strife, it is unwise to render the intercourse of warring armies less ferocious and destructive. By stripping war of its horrors, it is supposed that we foster a warlike spirit, and invest the horrible business of slaughter with an attractive and deceiving character. If, indeed, we could hope to put an end to all war, by making it terrible, then we might admit the justice of this argument; but of this happy state of universal peace we have no expectation; neither do we believe that we should conduce to its attainment by creating and increasing ferocious habits amongst opposing nations. Cruelty begets cruelty – one atrocity creates another, by way of reprisal – and national animosity is kept alive and heightened by a desire to gratify personal hatred and revenge.[11]

Tolstoy himself evidently came later to similar conclusions. Through Prince Andrew he aired some of his strong thoughts about the war problem, and one cannot doubt that they appealed strongly to the violent and aggressive aspects of his personality. But in the long run he turned away from that radical solution and adopted instead the equally radical pacifist one; no less absolute, and (as those of his admirers who retained some critical faculties at once recognized) no less satisfying to his will towards moral domination, since like the Prince Andrew solution it also disposed, god-like, of the powers of life and death. Most varieties of pacifism are less life-denying than that ruthless form of it espoused by the aged Tolstoy, which, taken seriously, is a way of death rather than life. But Tolstoy's pacifism, like other pacifisms, at any rate contains a solution to the war problem, namely, the belief that the appetite for war will diminish and shrivel in proportion as people offer not resistance and counter-violence but love and non-resistance to those who threaten them. Whether one's admiring respect for this belief and so many of those who adhere to it leads one to be a pacifist or not depends first, I suppose, on whether one thinks this a plausible estimate of probabilities, and second, on how much one thinks it matters if the estimate turns out to be mistaken. 'The pacifist argument that it pays everyone not to have wars runs up against the fact that it would pay some people, in a world where others are pacifist, to make war on the pacifists.'[12]

In between the positions of unrestrained and absolute violence on the one hand, unresisting and absolute non-violence on the other – which are, in not wholly dissimilar ways, consistent responses to the question what to do about the horrors of war – comes the position described in this book: accepting war as a more or less regrettable recurrence in the mixed moral experience of mankind, without abandoning hope of sooner or later reducing its incidence to near-vanishing-point; in the meantime, restricting the extent of its horrors by observing the laws and rules of war, appealing partly to the softer side of human nature, partly to plain self-interest (which may or may not be thought the worse side). Those who adopt this standpoint are fortified by a belief that the law of war has on balance done more good than harm. By definition, they do not expect too much. Richard Falk, one of the United States' most powerful writers about the contemporary law of war, has wisely remarked upon 'an ironic tendency for people to expect law in international affairs to do more for the order and welfare of the comunity than it does in domestic affairs. Perhaps', he speculates, 'law is given special duties in world affairs to compensate for the weak international social structure; when these extravagant expectations are disappointed, the contributions actually made by law to world order are extravagantly neglected.'[13] Among those contributions, as has already been suggested, are several besides – in sum, perhaps, more valuable – the limited role as yet found for the law of war as a body of law, the neglect or contempt of which brings not just unpleasantness but also punishment in its train. With 'war crimes' and their punishment, this book will not be directly concerned. Of course it will include the description and explanation of what have been called 'war crimes' and will take note as far as need be of the decisions made about them by tribunals, both national (as most have been) or international (as were only those of Nuremberg and Tokyo after world war two), but it is emphatically not just about 'war crimes', on which in any

case an enormous amount has been written. Nor does it presume
to enter the immensely important field of international crimi-
nology. Its focus is on the law of war as ordinarily conceived and
talked about in diplomatic conferences, government and general
staff offices, soldiers' barracks, and civilian parlours; not as presumably it is talked about in judges' chambers and in classrooms
of international law; of whose special outlook we must now take
note.

5 A word to the international lawyers

Since this book, whatever other uses it may be found to possess,
purports to include an outline of much of the modern history of
the international law of war, I must now justify to the international
lawyers the liberties I shall take with their language and their
notions. I am an historian by training and profession, daring to
claim to have studied international law no further than to have
picked up a smattering of it along with the other smatterings
necessary for the handling of a theme which, as a matter of fact,
ramifies into rather a large spread of human and social sciences.
Historians, however, have learnt to take that sort of thing in their
stride, and the proof of the pudding, after all, is in the eating; if I
have learnt enough about the history and essence of international
law to make sense in what I say about it, I trust the international
lawyers will give me credit. It is pleasant to acknowledge that most
of the best writers about it have been, and still are, international
lawyers. My debt to them is incalculable. And yet, in the end, I
have felt that this branch of their great subject could not be presented as it deserves unless I present it in a rather broader context
than has been usual with them, using a somewhat looser language.

The law of war is viewed in these pages as the hard and sharp
edge of a broader-based concern with humanity in warfare *and out
of it*; as part of an encompassing international humanitarian law
which, by some contemporary jurists' view of things, is evolving
at present, but has yet some way to go before it is entirely visible
and universally acknowledged. Without being so unhistorical as
to speak of an international humanitarian law for generations
which did not use the expression, it would be no less unhistorical
to fail to recognize that something very like an international
humanitarian law was the theoretical seed-plot, the philosophical
base, from which the jurists of Europe were evolving the law of

war from the sixteenth century onwards. Their law of nations, *jus gentium*, in its origins was expressly meant to establish what justice required in respect of men as individuals as well as of men gathered into peoples or nations. It is no accident that the doctrine of human rights, ruggedly revived within the past two generations and the centrepiece of international humanitarian law in that reviving form, was transmitted towards our own times by way of *jus gentium*, and came into its first modern flowering in the same years as did our law of war.

The law of war's natural roots and nourishment, then, are in the general cultural history which produced it along with other gestures towards maximizing the mutual amenities of mankind and minimizing its pains and hardships. That it should have become somewhat separated from this common stock as it became more systematic and refined, and as it found itself increasingly tied to the rigidities of military thought and practice, is not surprising. Its sense of separateness was also aggravated, through the nineteenth century, by the ascendency of a school of jurisprudence, the positivist school, whose main philosophical business was to pooh-pooh the *a priori* claims of the natural law tradition and to imply that the pursuit of humanity in warfare could have no deeper sources than the self-interest of the States which chose to sign treaties about it. Into the story of this battle between 'naturalists' and 'positivists' I emphatically intend *not* to go, partly because the differences between them seem to matter much more to them, 'insiders', than they need to do to the mass of us 'outsiders'; and partly because in practice this battle has not affected the main humanitarian issue.[14] However great its importance for legal philosophers, that battle has no claim to prominence in the story of a kind of law recognized, talked of, and practised by thousands of laymen for every one jurist professionally concerned; a kind of law most proper to be studied by all, whether jurists or not, who are interested in the possibility of restraining, limiting, and reducing man's inhumanity to man.

The branch of international law which is the subject of this book will therefore be handled in constant recollection that international law itself does not cover the whole of the conduct of States towards one another, nor does it cover the whole of their record in respect of what we are learning with increasing confidence to proclaim as human rights. The cry of 'sovereignty' has covered a multitude of sins. No doctrine has been more dear to the modern national State than that of its sovereignty. It is by virtue of this doctrine that States have always built into their acceptances of international law qualifications designed to safe-guard those expressions of collective consciousness called 'national honour' or 'dignity', 'national interest', 'national security', and above all 'national survival' and everything thought necessary thereunto. Of such matters, States conscious of their sovereignty have insistently denied, as they still deny, that other States can be judges; claiming also, by implication if not expressly, that the power of international law to control what they do by virtue of these claims diminishes in proportion with the directness and im-mediacy of the perceived danger to national existence. To cover this field of policy action, the doctrine of *raison d'Etat* was evolved and espoused. From the sixteenth century onwards it was invoked to justify, within States, departures from the normal course of justice and right; as between States, such variations from apparent legal propriety as the elimination of inconvenient neighbours (e.g. Silesia and Poland in the eighteenth century), and the viola-tion of the rights of neutrality (e.g. Denmark in 1807, Belgium in 1914, Norway in 1940).

International law writers usually look hard in the other direction whenever *raison d'Etat* is around, just as they would insist, before the 1948 Universal Declaration began to make a difference, that what States did in respect of 'human rights' or anything that might be so called was none of their business. Taking the broad view of the subject which we are taking, however, we cannot main-tain so stolid a front. Humanity can suffer from international con-flict, whether for *raison d'Etat* or *raison de* something else. Those parts of a government's policy towards people or peoples which come neatly within the categories of the international law text-books are only artificially differentiated from those parts which do not. The same national (or, maybe, international) culture which produces the one produces also the other; tendencies which colour the one may be expected to colour the other too; and, so far as their evaluation in the light of humanitarian norms is concerned, they must be taken account of together. I shall therefore, after giving due warning, not hesitate to elide from *raison de guerre* (the doctrine conventionally pleaded to excuse departures from the law of war) to *raison d'Etat*, from military necessity to State necessity, whenever the one seems to be in the same case with the other as an expression of a national idea about the use of force. Likewise, when dealing with the painfully important topic of reprisals, which international lawyers carefully (and with very good reason) distinguish and separate from retaliation and revenge, we may need to remind ourselves that the international lawyer's delicate surgery may be less helpful towards the full understanding of them than a rougher socio-political analysis which will identify their common sources and strengths. The concerns of international law are too important to humanity, in this respect at least, to be left to the international lawyers. Unless their categories are enlarged and loosened, at any rate for non-professional purposes like ours, realistic connexions between them and the real worlds of politics, public opinion, and warfare cannot be made, and humanity may be the less well served. Such nonsenses may continue, for example, as the writing of international law books about world war two which, by keeping strictly to the letter of the law as it was when the war began, and leaving out of account such *raison d'Etat* matters as invasions of neutrals and such unclassifiable peculiarities as concentration camps, forced labour and genocide, give the overall impression that Germany had a better record in respect of humanity than the USA or the UK.

Having admitted that in a few respects I shall find it necessary to stray beyond the conventional language and limits of international law, it is pleasant to draw close again to the normal practice of international law in respect of the definition of war. This matters the more because so much of the violence – and a lot of it, armed violence – to which society (if it does not wish to dissolve) has to set limits and controls does not correspond to any conventional definition of war. All war is conflict and violence; but not all conflict and violence is war; and not all conflict is violence, either. Between war according to the classic, deceptively simple definition of it which everyone knows ('the Seven Years War', 'the American civil war', and so on) and the normally non-violent rank-assertion and competitiveness going on in the ordinary life of most societies, there spreads a graduated spectrum of social conflict which many social scientists regard as continuous and integrated. Little Johnny's pulling of little Emily's hair and his getting slapped for it, we can hardly doubt, will have something to do with grown-up Johnny's responses to potential victims and aggressors. For many purposes and in many contexts this unbroken spectrum makes good sense. Even avowed utopian political thinkers some-times leave room for socially beneficial modes of non-violent con-flict in their blueprints for peaceful futures. Non-utopians concur in seeking means for the 'safe' direction and harnessing of con-flictual tendencies. What has been considered thus safe at one period of history may not seem so safe in another. International war was pretty generally regarded as the most natural and proper of such harnessings, positively beneficial from some nations' stand-points, until well on this side of 1914. Experience and reflection since then seem to have reduced the acceptability of the idea of international war, but no net gain to humanity has clearly accrued, other forms of armed conflict and new revolutionary arguments for it having swollen in proportion as the classic old international form of it has shrunk.

Within the last few decades, therefore, the nature of the argu-ment about the use and value of the law of war has changed. Until the nineteen-forties, it applied solely to international wars between the supposedly more advanced countries. The only exception to this rule was allowed in the cases of a civil war between civilized brothers, as in the USA, 1861–5. No attempt was made to extend it to any other non-international war – the doctrine of sovereignty insisted that how States dealt with rebellions and civil disturbances was their own affair – and it was taken for granted that those kinds of conflicts would be the nastier. Not much respect for the law of war could be seen in the Russian civil war of 1918–21 or the Spanish civil war of 1936–9; while the manners in which the British, the French, the Spaniards, the Portuguese and the Dutch put down rebels in their colonial empires, or the Italians acquired one, were every bit as nasty as those in which Paraguayans fought Bolivians, or Japanese, Chinese.

Since world war two however the attempt has been made to extend the law to non-international as well as truly international wars. As shall be described in Chapter V, it achieved a modest early triumph when the Geneva Conventions were up-dated in 1949. Since then it has stayed alive but not much more than that. The ICRC's efforts to strengthen it at the 1977 up-dating met with many setbacks; the continuing cult of sovereignty being the main-spring of them. But the vision remains attractive, of diffusing the practice of restraint in recourse to armed violence, and of extending the exercise of this restraint far beyond its present, mainly international, field of application; somehow or other establishing in the public mind, as well as in the conduct of public business, norms of humanitarian conduct which may pervade the whole field of conflicts and, by gradual influence, reduce them.

Readers who find themselves exclaiming that this is the very nonpareil of utopianism ought to mark that its leading proponents in international debate have been the hard-headed spokesmen, men predominantly with legal trainings, of the ICRC; 'civilians' who know more about the realities of war, probably, than most men wearing military officers' uniforms around the world at present. Nor are their arguments in its support sentimental or mainly philanthropic. The self-interest of men and society is at least as much appealed to as their softer side. But arguments, even of the most convincing self-interest, have never yet done much to dissuade men from passionate rushes into battle. The health of the movement to extend humanitarian law into the field of non-international armed conflicts remains, at the time of writing, uncertain. Until Chapter V, it need not concern us. From now until the end of Chapter IV, the armed conflicts we shall be dealing with will all correspond more or less to what is 'war' in the layman's common usage: i.e. the organized and controlled violence of one political body against another.

This common lay usage goes a bit further than some political science and (until quite recently) most international law, in its readiness to include civil wars and substantial rebellions. It does not go far in the direction of those social scientists for whom formal international war is only one extremity of the spectrum of social conflict we noticed earlier, a spectrum so continuous and integrated that no one part of it can be studied separately from another. Much contemporary 'conflict research' is conceived and carried out in these terms, and valuable no doubt it is for those seeking the profoundest sociological and psychological connexions between the sources of one sort of violence and another. I realize, moreover, that in among these sources must be found also some at least of the keys to understanding the development of conflict restraints and prohibitions, which may be found at every level of society, from the familial upwards. Most of that fascinating area of study will have to be left out of view. The only levels of society beneath this lens are the international and major national ones; our study will be of the restraints and prohibitions observed, or recommended to be observed, in international or quasi-international conflicts, reflective as they must be of moral norms current within the national societies at grips with one another. I could therefore adopt as my own, with hardly any qualifications, this definition of war made early in this century by John Westlake, who, with T. E. Holland, led the British international law field: war, he wrote, was 'an effort by each of two nations to bend the other to its will, by all the means in its power which do not violate neutral rights, and are not ruled out as inhuman'.[16] My only glosses on that would be, first, that by 'nations' we may now have to mean *de facto* nations or peoples short, as yet anyway, of *de jure* Statehood – i.e. the embryo or emerging States represented by plausible national liberation movements; and second, that the ideas about what rights should be allowed to neutrals and what methods of war should be judged inhuman, although they mean most to us and become best known to us after becoming articles of international law, only achieve that status because they have already come to mean something in the cultures of the several nations compiling that law. Any branch of law whose prescriptions go too far beyond the common notions of the society it purports to regulate runs the risk of becoming alien to it and therefore neglected by it. Westlake's definition, just as it stands, suggests, probably unintentionally, that practices allowed by the law of war are less changeable than must actually be the case. If his long life – he was born in 1828 and died in 1913 – had been only a little longer, he would, I guess, have found time to rephrase it.

6 A word to the military

To military readers, of whom I hope there will be many, I have two things in particular to say: first, I hope they will take this subject seriously; and second, I trust they will think twice before taking a dislike to the way I write about it.

No one, I believe, will deny that the subject itself cuts a negligible figure in most military writing, even much of the best of it. This neglect seems to me lamentable, and damaging. It is damaging to the pursuit of truth because it leaves out an element which is in fact always present somewhere – which may indeed usually be traced *everywhere*, once you know where to look for it: in the political and strategic policies of States, in the organization and command of armed forces, and in the minds and hearts of the members of those armed forces, from their ethos and their *esprit de corps* through to their instructional programmes. Governments and their departments of state have to know about the law of war if only because of its clear and firm place in the international law to which they are tied, and armed forces have knowledge of it in their bones at least to the extent that it is in their traditions (where part of its appeal is to their enlightened self-interest).

Yet it is clear that much in the nature of international politics and military life works to obscure the fact of this legal omnipresence and to put it out of mind. Governments, like all other entities subject to a rule of law, now and then experience urgent desires to evade it, and the doctrine of *raison d'Etat* gives them some ground (questionable though many find it) for doing so. So much in the nature of an armed force's life and work is, naturally, directed to the cultivation of a tough and bold approach to its main business and *raison d'être*, the disciplined and controlled use of violence against the violent, that the voice of law – inherently a voice of restraint and prohibition – very easily sounds irrelevant or slightly absurd; probably less so in some military cultures than in others. This is all the more strange and inappropriate, considering that the discipline and the self-control to which soldiers and so on are vocationally dedicated are themselves testimony to the value the military profession places on the principles of restraint and prohibition as such. Few bodies of trained men are more intensively trained to do what they are told to do, and *not* to do what they have been told *not* to do, than professional soldiers. And they are thus instructed, not only because it is a condition of their success in their particular business, but also because it is a condition of their so conducting that business as not to mar the end for which that business was undertaken. The body of law and regulations which defines the purposes and methods of organized military power ultimately is one with, and indivisible from, the moral and legal constitution of the society which supports it, and it is determined by the same general culture; the injunction of economy of force in the conduct of military operations comes out of the same barrel, for instance, as the injunction to discriminate in its use. The law of war is actually much more closely allied to, and knitted in with, the other laws of which the fighting man is more directly and constantly conscious, than he tends to realize. But it seems beyond dispute that, experientially, the idea of law in war very easily goes against the natural grain of a military organization, and fighting men not unnaturally feel it to be an uncongenial intrusion into their workaday affairs. And so not only is formal instruction in the law of war often skimped and taken less than seriously but – here I add the fruits of my own observation to a mass of historical evidence – a common and immediate reaction of fighting men when faced with some embodiment of the law of war seems to say, though perhaps in different words – 'What? That stuff?'

Now, this instinct towards dismissiveness and disregard, which certainly characterizes some military men, seems to me a great pity. It renders the military less true to themselves than they ought to be, and constitutes, in fact, a self-demeaning of their profession which they themselves must, on reflection, regret. Nations call armed forces into being to become their experts in violence, indeed; but it is controlled violence, directed to politically-determined ends (except in certain well-known international episodes of history which are subsequently always seen to have been regrettable), and in principle dedicated to the winning and maintenance of peace no less than of the wars which, by most philosophies of war and peace, are simply punctuations of the more preferable condition. Our law of war historically evolved as part of this general body of ideas, and is in fact one of the main international institutions designed to make them achievable. Respect for the law of war, which has often been a point of honour, pride and self-respect with military men because of its moral, even religious content, is a virtue in a political sense as well; something in which military men have as much interest as everyone else within their country (assuming, of course, that their idea of the State is not, as for example seems to be the case with some recent South American military-political thought, just that of an army writ large).

These things being so, I find myself repeatedly surprised and saddened, and sometimes rather shocked, by the neglect of the law of war element in so much military writing; memoirs, biography, history alike. I look forward to inquiring more closely into this grave matter on a later occasion. Two randomly chosen examples, which just happen to be at the top of my mind as I write, will point to what I mean. The long article in the *Dictionary of National Biography* on the eminent Victorian military writer Hamley, who wrote his army's standard manual of operations *en*

route to becoming General Sir Edward Hamley, although it gives
twelve of its three hundred and twenty lines to his medals and
decorations, says nothing whatsoever about his two vast letters to
The Times in early 1871 about the German conduct of the
Franco-Prussian war, which are one of the later nineteenth century's main documents on the law of war and were noticed as such
by contemporary continental experts. Then there is Norman
Stone's brilliant, learned, prize-winning and altogether very good
book *The Eastern Front, 1914–1917* (1975). It covers almost
everything that could be relevant; 'total war needs total history',
the author is quoted as saying; but do its three hundred pages tell
me anything about the respective armies' policies and practices
when occupying enemy territory, as all of them were doing some
of the time? They do not. That hugely important topic is virtually
untouched, not because Dr Stone could not have found material
for doing so – indeed, some of the material he uses for other purposes would have served as sources for this one too – but simply
because, I suppose, it just did not seem important enough to include. I cannot go on about this now. Suffice it to say that, so long
as the place of the law of war and the chain of considerations which
comes in its wake is not explicitly given its due place in the writing
of military history, so long must those writings be defective in a
major part. I hope this book may provoke interest in correcting
that rather chronic deficiency.

And now for the second and briefer set of my remarks, which
proceed from my observation that the members of armed forces,
being trained and often perhaps in any case morally inclined to pay
careful respect to their superiors in service and State, to believe
loyally in the virtues of their kind and corps, and to avoid at all
costs calling them into disrepute, generally take unkindly to, or
feel discomfort in the presence of, criticism of persons and organizations they particularly respect and even hold sacred. Without
embarking on a long excursus aimed to persuade them that it is
more likely, as a matter of fact, to conduce to their own professional
comfort *and success* if they recognize things as they objectively
are rather than as myth presents them, I will simply ask them to
look at the matter a historian's way; the way of a historian, that is,
in a free country; and to attend briefly to what this historian,
anxious to avoid misunderstanding, wishes to say about himself.

First, I take it for granted that conventional patriotic considerations are out of place in scientific inquiry. Patriotic fervour is no more helpful a condition for discovering the truth about the history of the law of war than could be high blood pressure for running a British car factory. I may or may not be a patriot out of the study (as a matter of fact, I am a patriot, of the kind who believes that it is no service to one's country to pretend that it is perfect), but what matters here is whether I am a historian, and a good one. If my history is wrong, then nothing else in the book or deducible from it can be much use; but please let the history be judged fairly before conclusions are drawn about anything else. Let military or old-style patriotic readers also note, if they find me being rude about one of their heroes or sacred cows, that I am just as willing to be rude about everyone else's, if I know enough about them to know that they deserve it. It seems to me preferable to risk being thought to say things too strongly, rather than risk having people fail to note that I said anything at all.

And finally, let the military reader be explicitly advised of a few things which may not stand out as he reads this book, though most of them could, I believe, be deduced from it: (a) with admiration I acknowledge the extent to which the origins and much of the ancient strength of our law of war lie in the European military tradition itself; (b) with greater admiration still I recognize the extent to which good soldiers, sailors and airmen have made it a point of honour and duty to observe the law even when it is to their own personal risk; (c) although I have to make many elisions in the course of so compressed a book, and despite my referring often to 'the military' and even, when occasion seems to justify it, to 'the military mind', I am well aware of the definitional problems of such usages, and resort to them only *faute de mieux*; and lastly, (d) although I have to use the terms of the subject itself in talking about soldiers and civilians, I do not fall into that most common, flattering and delusive of civilian assumptions, that civilian = good and military = bad. Far from it. So far as one can distinguish them from each other, which at some period of history (as of the contemporary world) is not easy, civilians have often been ascendant in the political leadership under which (unless it is a mere puppet or a political neuter) the military are seen to have done terrible things. Militarism, another term I have to use without always being able to define exactly what is meant each time, may be a nasty thing, but let the military man ponder on my conviction, that there can be no nastier a militarist than a civilian one.

7 A word to my fellow-historians

This book, then, is not written just for people interested in history. Part of its readership, I hope and expect, will be more interested in other aspects of its theme than the purely historical one. This introduction so far has been directed mainly to those people : 'humanitarians', people of philosophical and theological turn of mind who worry about war's rights and wrongs, and people concerned with the unpeaceful side of international affairs, especially the military. I turn at last to those – the great majority of my readers, probably – who will be more interested in this as a history book. I owe to those of them who like, as do I, to know something of the mind and methods of an author, and who perhaps also believe, as do I, that a scholar ought to be explicit about these things, a brief explanation of how I have set about it.

The idea of writing some such book came to me about 1964. When pressed to say why I hankered after a project so remote from everything I had so far done, I could only account for it as a convergence of interests aroused by the Campaign for Nuclear Disarmament, then just subsiding from its heady early years, and by the European Movement, which had got me thinking for the first time in my life about international relations; I recollected also, after many years of forgetting, how much I had been interested in 1946-7 in the moral issues brought out by the 'war crimes' trials. Pressed further by hard-headed interlocutors to justify (as one at Columbia memorably put it) the scrapping of so substantial an investment in one sort of history for a possibly dubious speculation in another, I used to reply that I believed Humanity in Warfare to be a more *important* subject than any I had worked on hitherto; to which I would add, if needled, that I wanted to be working on something directly engaged with the life and struggle of the world around me. I even ran the gauntlet of the 'knowledge for its own sake' school by admitting that I wanted to be doing something 'useful'. That was certainly naive. Opportunities for deeper thought about the 'usefulness' and 'relevance' of historical studies offered by the next few years of campus *jacqueries* taught me to be less rash and presumptuous in my assessment of what scholarly activities were likely to be 'useful' and what not. But I still believe one may strive not to be useless . . .

So I laid plans for an escape from the Victorian historical work-house (of which I have the happiest memories) and, after at last completing *Mid-Victorian Britain* in the summer of 1969, was able to make a start on the international law books. There, I rightly reckoned, was where the substance of the matter would be found. I am glad I started with them rather than with the 'Nuremberg' literature, because the latter, emotionally so stirring, might have encouraged a 'war-crimes' approach which would have diverted me from the broad-based work I had in mind. From international law books of the past two hundred and fifty years, I soon became reasonably adept at the naming of parts. A chronological skeleton began to take shape. At least I could see the order in which things happened.

Some of those writers, 'international lawyers' rather than 'historians' though they undoubtedly were, were good historians too, well able to suggest why things had happened as well as in what order they had happened. I found myself admiring most of all our English John Westlake, the Belgian Ernest Nys, and the American Henry Wheaton. Most, however – and this seems to me to have become increasingly true of this century's writers – have either been not much interested in history, being content with reach-me-down explanations often palpably cribbed from a common store, or, faithful to the mood of their age and class, been more interested in scoring patriotic points than in establishing scientific truth. This branch of scholarship seems to have become extensively national-ized between about 1900 and the second world war. A frightening lesson in the mentality of academic garrisons may be obtained by comparing such prime specimens as the American James Wilford Garner, *International Law and the World War* (1920), Mérignhac et Lémonon, *Le Droit de la Guerre et la Guerre de 1914–1918* (1921), and the four-volume collaborative official survey, *Völkerrecht im Weltkrieg* (1927).

It quite early became clear to me, then, that I was not going to find much of the history of humanity in these necessary tomes. The rest of what I needed would have to be brought to market from other sources; nothing less, ideally, than the history of civil-ization since the eighteenth century. Much of the past eight years has been devoted to scrabbling among the pebbles on that shore.

Progress has been intermittent. Only my critics can judge whether I have been at it for long enough, and worked at it sensibly enough, to succeed in the writing of a book the conception of which has grown so large with the passage of time. I did not realize, when I began, how complicated it would be, how many ramifications into the moral and social sciences there could be. The decision to call a halt to further reading and to write it now may as well be called arbitrary as calculated. No historian can ever really read *everything* relevant to his project unless it is a pretty small one. All of us who tackle the larger themes live with danger. Have we been sensible in our selections of reading matter? Are we historically sensitive enough to know when we don't know, and will it be held against us if we admit it? I shall not hesitate to admit that I know that I don't know, and shall sometimes prefer explicit speculation to loose ends. Now and then I have gone beyond the plentiful basic reading to sink a shaft of deeper inquiry into a particular topic which seemed likely to produce something significant. The locations of these research shafts are visible in the notes. But there are not many of them. There is room for an army of researchers. I can hope for nothing better than to provide some visions of what awaits them.

I have acknowledged fully, I hope, in the Preface, the extent of my major debts to institutions and to individuals other than authors or in capacities other than as authors. A few more or less recent books have overlapped with parts of my theme enough to be of special usefulness. F. J. P. Veale's *Advance to Barbarism*, which I am thankful I early found by serendipity, gave me much encouragement as well as some annoyance. Sydney Bailey's *Prohibitions and Restraints in War*, a model of its concise kind, taught me a lot about the contemporary nuts and bolts. In James Turner Johnson's *Ideology, Reason, and the Limitations of War*, already mentioned, I was happy to salute a kindred enterprise, which has saved me much time in deciding what to say about the period before my mid-eighteenth century start. I long to see his promised follow-up. I am profoundly sorry that it was not until I was two-thirds through the writing that I discovered William O'Brien's excellent 'military necessity' articles of nearly twenty years ago. Michael Howard and Pierre Boissier both mattered to me greatly in different ways. But apart from them, I am not aware of standing on any particular person's shoulders.

Chapter I

The Later Enlightenment Consensus

The things which make men alike are more important than the things which make them different.
Aristotle

In all their invasions of the civilised empires of the South, the Scythian shepherds have been uniformly actuated by a savage and destructive spirit. The laws of war, that restrain the exercise of national rapine and murder, are founded on two principles of substantial interest: the knowledge of the permanent benefits which may be obtained by a moderate use of conquest, and a just apprehension lest the desolation which we inflict on the enemy's country may be retaliated on our own. But these considerations of hope and fear are almost unknown in the pastoral state of nations ...
Edward Gibbon, *History of the Decline and Fall of the Roman Empire,* Chapter 34 (1776–88)

Not only in its means but also in its aims war [in the eighteenth century] increasingly became limited to the fighting force itself ... All Europe rejoiced at this development. It was seen as a logical outcome of enlightenment. This was a misconception. Enlightenment can never lead to inconsistency; as we have said before and shall have to say again, it can never make two and two equal five. Nevertheless this development benefited the people of Europe. ...
Karl von Clausewitz, *On War,* Book 8, Chapter 3 (1832)

In time, my story begins in the later Enlightenment, one of the names by which historians describe that cultural epoch of the middle and later eighteenth century which elided into its successor (no need to linger on the question of its name and nature) about the time of the 'democratic revolutions', themselves largely shaped by it. In space, it begins in Europe and Europe's imperial extension in North America where, in 1776, the 'democratic revolutions' actually began. The naming of historical epochs is an unending game for historians, and the names they choose are determined largely by the characteristics they are looking for. Politically speaking, this epoch is usually called the *ancien régime*: 'When Kings were many, and machines were few, And open atheism something new'.[1] Marxian historians regard it as an epoch of more or less decaying feudalism. All this is true enough. Indeed, the *ancien régime* (except, arguably, in North America) still prevailed, and its rulers and ruling classes continued to run their countries primarily for their own benefit, which, so far as they thought about the matter, they assumed to involve also such benefit as providence had intended for their subjects. In central, eastern and southern Europe its feudal survivals were still going very strong indeed; elsewhere the ambitions and intrusions of 'the bourgeoisie' were affronting the lords of land and lineage and persuading or forcing them to an accommodation. These matters are important and relevant. Social, economic, and political history lies all around us. But it is through the lens of cultural history that it seems most helpful at first to look, because this is the story of an idea which, about the middle of the eighteenth century, was widely diffused among the ruling and (not necessarily the same thing) educated classes of the ancien régime, and was thought to be of great importance for the improvement of the general happiness and welfare of mankind; a matter to which the thinkers of the Enlightenment gave much attention, and as to which they were, more or less, optimistic.

1 The publicists

Ideas are one thing, their implementation is another. Throughout the book, I shall be traversing to and fro between the idea and its observance; between the men of ideas to whom naturally fell the task of refining and elaborating it, and the men of decision and action upon whom fell the responsibility of observing it – military men of course most of all, but above and around them the whole of the later *ancien régime's* political establishment, which was (and felt itself to be) cosmopolitan, homogeneous, and concerned to keep up with the intellectual progress of the age. This is essentially a

story of interaction, an interaction which becomes more complicated as years go by for many reasons which will be sufficiently
stated in due course, but which for one reason in particular must
be stated now : namely, that the relation between the men of ideas
and the men of decision and action seems to have been more direct
and simple at the beginning of this story, then ever it was thereafter.

The closeness of this connexion may be explained largely in
material terms. The groups referred to were relatively small,
cohesive, and interlocking. By 'men of ideas', of course, I mean
only those relatively very few men whose eighteenth-century lives
gave them opportunity to read, think, talk, and write. To say that
they were the only men *thinking* at that time, would be preposterous.

> Full many a gem of purest ray serene
> The dark unfathom'd caves of ocean bear;
> Full many a flower is born to blush unseen,
> And waste its sweetness on the desert air.[2]

Eighteenth-century Europe and its American dependencies may
have been full of mute, inglorious Montesquieus and Grotii;
indeed, the more 'enlightened' and progressive you were in those
days, the likelier were you to believe that this was in fact the case.
Ineluctable however was the fact that historical and social circumstances – 'chill penury' chief among them – kept the circle of the
educated and articulate a small one, at the same time as it was, like
the larger circles of the rich, cultivated and powerful which it
interestingly permeated, a relatively cosmopolitan one, speaking
the same language all over Europe and believing that it was promoting the welfare of mankind by the international exchange of
improving and improved ideas.

Much the same may be said of the men of action with whom we
are most concerned: the commanders and officer corps of the
armies, upon whose capacity for the controlled and well-aimed use
of force ultimately rested the political map of their world. They
too were relatively homogenous and cosmopolitan. A mixture of
hereditary aristocrats and gentry with middle-class professionals
(with even a few famous risings from the ranks), their code of conduct crossed national boundaries just as naturally as did many of
them personally in their military careers. It can hardly be said that

their numbers were small, since the social group we are talking about included all who enjoyed and valued the right to bear arms; a transnational social class whose economic status was often, in the poorer parts of the continent of Europe, much lower than that of the 'bourgeoisie' whose social and political subordination it was therefore the more important for the military aristocracy to maintain. But in their organized military form they and their professional middle-class coadjutors (more prominent, incidentally, in navies than armies) who between them commanded the formal armed forces of eighteenth-century Europe did not compose a very large body of men. Pre-revolutionary armies, however recruited, were compact, professionally-trained, internationally-recruited organizations which cost a lot to maintain and which their masters did not wish to make any larger or more costly than could be avoided. Their armies therefore were not large (except for Prussia's, which, though in absolute terms not big, was exceptionally large considering its population and resources). Since we are concerned with only their officers, who made the big decisions and gave the orders, most of whom must have been able to read and some of whom were interested in ideas, it is not unreasonable to say that here, too, on the other side of our central connexion, we are dealing with a visible social group sharing many fundamental principles and attitudes; the greater part of them, of course, traditional and inherited, but some to some extent open to the influence of changing times and the new ideas pressed upon them by the other group, the men of ideas whose business it was – some of whom, indeed, had purposefully made it their business – to do just that. It was a common article of faith among the men of the Enlightenment, that ideas could and ought to influence action.

The men of ideas with whom, in this early part of the story, we are most concerned were then known and are still best referred to as 'the publicists'; meaning *not* journalists, as the term implies today, but those learned men, philosophers with a practical bent, who specialized in what we now call public international law and international relations; not 'international lawyers' – they were much too close to moral and political philosophy for that, and much of what they wrote was meant for a readership stretching well beyond courts, cabinets, colleges and military academies – but undoubted forerunners of the international lawyers who were to emerge later. One of the first of those (or was he one of the last of the publicists?), the excellent American Henry Wheaton, looked back from 1845 and wrote: 'A mighty importance was then attributed to the study of the writings of the publicists, which strongly contrasts with the almost total neglect into which they have now fallen.'[3] He may have been underestimating the regard for them in his own time. I am sure he was not exaggerating in his assessment of their importance in the preceding century. Their classic predecessors (Grotius above all, but also Pufendorf and the lesser lights) were thoroughly studied and constantly referred to, with all the respect due to pioneer moderns recovering one of the great achievements of the ancient world. The publicists of the eighteenth century itself were read and reprinted with all the respect due to contemporary authorities on a matter engaging the anxious attention of all men capable of reflecting upon the general condition of human affairs and all men actually engaged in conducting their international dimension: how could relations and intercourse between States be improved, and how could war – the rough edge of those relations – be averted, limited, and softened?

It is a feature of the Enlightenment mind (a feature which some may find engaging), that it did not find war attractive or exciting, as did Romantics and Nationalists of succeeding epochs. The 'civilizing of war' – even perhaps its removal from the regular practices of mankind – seemed in the Later Enlightenment a worthwhile and a reasonably practical undertaking. Interest in this great matter was not confined to the publicists alone. It was a common theme with the philosophers and social scientists of the century, whatever their cast of mind; some – Volney, for example – having so simplistic a view of the universe and all that lived therein, that a new age of peace and contentment seemed to be only just around the revolutionary corner; others, like Kant, the most 'pessimistic' about human nature of those I have in mind, understanding matters to be much more complicated, but nevertheless offering reasonable hope that the human impulses towards self-interest and (if it was anything but self-interest in a peculiar form) benevolence would gradually combine to combat institutionalized violence. Abolition of war was, even to the cautious Kant, not beyond belief; but for him and for all others except the instant utopians, what mattered more – because it was a more immediate problem and not, they believed, an intractable one – was the control, the limitation, the 'civilizing' or 'humanizing' of war. Among the familiar disasters from which humanity suffered, war seemed to be the biggest man-made one. Nothing could be done about volcanoes, or, probably, famines, but something could be done about war.

Indeed, men of the Enlightenment maintained, something already had been done about it. It was common form in these mid- and later eighteenth-century years to compare their wars with those of earlier, less enlightened and progressive ages. Mr Jefferson was effectively casting George III as an unenlightened despot when he included, in the list of grievances of the American colonists, that the British monarch had 'endeavoured to bring on the inhabitants of our frontiers, the merciless Indian savages, whose known rule of warfare is an undistinguished destruction of all ages, sexes and conditions.'[4] Things were not like that in Europe now, wrote the French author Rabaut: 'Wars are less bloody than among ignorant and savage people: armies slaughter each other politely; heroes salute before killing each other; soldiers of opposing armies pay each other visits before battles, as people lunch together before an outing. No longer is it nations which fight each other, but just armies and professionals; wars are like games of chance in which no one risks his all; what was once a wild rage (*fureur*) is now just silly (*une folie*).'[5] A much better known but less ironic author, the most influential of the publicists, Vattel, told a like tale. His famous book, *Le Droit des Gens, ou, Principes de la Loi Naturelle, appliquée à la conduite et aux affaires des nations et des souverains*, first published in 1758, repeatedly points out the contrast between what (according to his idea of it) the natural rights of war allow belligerents, and what modern belligerents actually do. 'At the present day, the Nations of Europe almost always carry on war with great forbearance and generosity. These dispositions have given rise to several commendable practices, which exhibit often a high degree of courtesy.'[6] The example which immediately follows reminds us that we are still in the world of the *ancien régime*. 'Refreshments are sometimes sent to a besieged governor; and the besieger ordinarily refrains from firing upon the quarters of the King or general.' It was this sort of aristocratic bias in the laws and customs of war which led some historical observers acidly to deny that the Enlightenment's self-satisfaction about its achievements in the war-taming line were anything but self-deception. Albert Sorel for example easily enough assembled a hair-raising selection of brutal, oppressive and horrific episodes for his dazzling sketch of 'the customs of war at the end of the *ancien régime*'.[7] About the same time an English writer, James Farrer, evidently sympathetic towards the peace movement going strong in those years, blamed the publicists for 'having in fact led us into a Fool's Paradise about war (which has done more than anything else to keep the custom in existence), by representing it as something quite mild and almost refined in modern times.'[8] He blamed Vattel more than anyone else; I suppose, simply because Vattel had been the most widely-read of his kind. Kant, he remarked, was more sensible, in going 'straight to the point of trying to stop war altogether'.[9] No doubt Kant was more sensible than Vattel (and everyone else, probably). But Farrer misrepresented him. Pending the stopping of war altogether, Kant was as desirous as anyone else of his generation to limit and mitigate it in the meantime, and he was, presumably, as pleased as any other reflective person to observe the extent to which war, the demon and monster calling to his mind images of 'bloodshed, the desolation of families, the pillaging, threats of violence, the devastation by fire and sword'[10] – was in fact a monster on a tighter rein than ever before. For my own part, I cannot help thinking Sorel's a bilious sketch. Bellona, the goddess of war, really was to some extent tamed in the later Enlightenment, as the celebrated historian of German militarism, Gerhard Ritter, himself put it in the second chapter of his *Staatskunst und Kriegshandwerk*, 'The Art of Statesmanship and the Craft of War'.[11]

War, then, might be less horrid than it once had been. At some future date it might, perhaps, in the view of some exceptionally optimistic people, be dispensed with entirely. Meanwhile, it was still a commonplace of international experience, and the question for the men of the later Enlightenment, faced with this as with any other disagreeable and discreditable consequence of less than adequately enlightened human nature at work, was, what to do about it? Even in the new world, where the vices of the old could hopefully be held at arms' length and where, after a conflict as nasty as the war of independence, most men must have hoped never to experience war (except against the natives) again, the question had to be asked. 'The United States', President Washington told Congress at the end of 1793 when the international situation was black indeed, 'ought not to indulge a persuasion that, contrary to the order of human events, they will, for ever, keep at a distance those painful appeals to arms, with which the history of every other nation abounds.'[12]

2 Variety within their consensus

Before sketching the later Enlightenment consensus about the restraint of war and warfare, let us examine the credentials of such a description. I have been speaking of the men of ideas of the later Enlightenment as if they were a quite cohesive cosmopolitan group, and I have implied that, on the matter in question, the desirability of mitigating the horrors of war and the possibility, moreover, of doing this, they sang much the same tune. This generalization is based on a reading of the major works of the most important of them, and a random sample of a few others: Vattel, J. J. Moser and G. F. Martens, being by common consent the most important; the sample including Derschau, Hübner, Lampredi, Buondelmonti, Tetens, and de Rayneval; with Kant, Hufeland, Rousseau, Volney, Condorcet, Helvetius and Bentham occasionally called upon in support. Among these thinkers and writers I find a consensus which was also shared apparently, by the thinking part of the propertied public, and the practical conclusions which flowed from that agreement were searching and extensive. Such conclusions could of course be approached from different starting points and along different tracks. That so many different tracks led to the same conclusion says something about the general tendencies of the age in which the trackers lived, and since it was their conclusions, not their starting points or staging posts, that diffused influences upon the world of action, it is not necessary to submit the original tributary streams of thought to the kind of close analysis that used to be dignified as 'the history of ideas'. But a brief parenthesis about them is called for, since some of the central and continuing arguments about the shape of the law of war have roots in them, and their shadow will sometimes fall upon the pages that follow.

First, then, it must be noted that two schools of jurisprudence are here distinguished by experts in that subject: the 'natural law', *alias* naturalist, *alias* ethical school, and the 'positive', *alias* historical school, on the other. The former alone existed until the Renaissance, whose political writers (resting of course partly on ancient authorities) introduced a new pragmatic approach, cast more in terms of what States were actually perceived to do in their relations with one another than of what, from first principles of natural and/or divine law, they ought to do. These two schools may be characterized thus : the former, more concerned to present what international law ought to be, and interested in actual international behaviour only in so far as it shows whether the law is followed or not; the latter, only concerned to present international behaviour as it actually is, and dignifying that by the title of positive international law, whether it corresponds to natural, divine, or any other morally conceived law or not. The theoretical difference is clear enough, and the different definitions of law at stake are of momentous importance. Yet it seems fair enough, for the purposes of this book, to note this difference and at once to pass over it, on the ground that neither school in practice is as inattentive to the substance of the other as their philosophical champions, arguing it out in the histories of law and the textbooks of jurisprudence, seem to expect. 'Naturalists', once they get beyond lists of first principles, mark carefully the points at which the natural law finds lodgings in State practice. 'Positivists' have hearts too, and rarely resist marking the points where *their* international law impinges on the happiness of man. The fact is, they are not so far apart as some of them think, and from a practical humanitarian point of view their interlockings and shared concerns are not at all surprising. Vattel, who appears more than any other publicist in my early pages because he was, it seems, the most practically influential of them all, is usually criticized by philosophically-bent legal historians, even by those who admire him (as many do), for having been mixed-up and inconsistent, part-positivist and part-naturalist.[13] But that is precisely what makes him interesting to us! It helped his book towards unusual direct influence, and it probably partly explains why he was able to do something without which the future of the law of war might have been uncertain indeed : complete its detachment from exclusive connexion with the concept of 'the just war', and plausibly justify its independent existence and moral value, irrespective of whether 'justice' was to be found in a war or not. That there is a fundamental, natural law of nations, by which their conduct towards each other should be guided – he never doubts; but equally he recognizes that something less perfect, derived from the other by imperfect men in an imperfect world, is actually the best that can at any one time be hoped for. He calls the latter 'the voluntary law of nations'. It seems to be the positivists' international law under Vattel's proprietary name. While clearly some belligerents have a just cause and some do not, and therefore, according to classical just war theory, are differently placed vis-à-vis their legal obligations, in practice, argues Vattel, if the law of war is to be enabled to do its softening work, the causes of all belligerents must be counted as equally just (or unjust) *for that purpose alone*.[14] This was a giant stride forward in the development of the law of war. We shall frequently recur to it.

The second cause of fundamental differences of opinion between contributors to the consensus of the later Enlightenment was philosophical variety: at its extreme, the gulf between schools of thought as far removed from each other as Utilitarianism and Idealism. On the one side, those who could appreciate Helvétius and Bentham but would have difficulty with Kant; on the other, those who would appreciate Kant but think Bentham and Helvétius superficial and crude. One would expect to find arguments about human rights and so on embittered by such contrasting ideas about human personality and the ultimate sources of knowledge and truth. Yet I cannot see that it made much difference in practice. To explain why, would require another book. All I feel obliged to do is note that at no stage of my story can I find good cause to judge that one or the other school of thought was more conducive to practical humanity. Each seems equally to have produced men and movements capable of moral aberration and ideological excess. 'In the bombing of London,' wrote L. T. Hobhouse as he read Hegel in 1918, 'I had just witnessed the visible and tangible outcome of a false and wicked doctrine, the foundation of which lay, as I believe, in the book before me.'[15] But what doctrine lay beneath the bombings of Dresden or Hiroshima?

The third cleavage within the consensus was that between the men of the *ancien régime* and the men who were, whether they fully realized it or not, bent on destroying it. Again, a giant gulf; from a marxist point of view, an irreducible ideological one; and yet, their perhaps somewhat different responses to the law of war's demands for sympathetic recognition of common human difficulties do not seem to have amounted to much in practice. No keener advocate of a reformed and extended law of war existed in the seventeen-eighties than that arch-bourgeois Benjamin Franklin; but he got all his ideas about it from the European publicists, whose nearest approach to revolution was to be in the service, some of them, of absolute monarchs; and his most striking appearance in our pages will be as the American manager of a 'model treaty' between the USA and Frederick the Great's Prussia, whose principles regarding the law of war he found exemplary, and with whose collaboration he was glad to reprove the maritime war practices of that arch-bourgeois nation, Great Britain. Aristocratic officers undoubtedly tended to believe that officers of bourgeois backgrounds had different ideas about honour, risks, and sacrifice. The influx of sub-aristocratic types into the officer corps after the Revolution seems, however, to have been accompanied more by the newcomers' adoption of traditional standards than by their radical modification of them; and if it was 'bourgeois' to be calculating about the costs and risks of war but aristocratic to go unquestioningly to war at the sovereign's command, where are we to place Clausewitz? The fact is, that once again we discover that the different parties to the later Enlightenment consensus, divided from each other in many intellectual and social ways though they were, were not significantly at odds in respect of the law of war. British naval war policy was probably the most calculatingly ruthless of any country's during the French wars, but the effects of French land warfare were certainly the most extensively damaging and deadly. Both can, with ingenious enough argumentation, be presented as the products of 'bourgeois' ascendancy, but one is driven to ask, what kinds of bourgeois were Lords Hood, Howe and Nelson, the Emperor Napoleon and his titled satraps? The matter is immensely complicated, and I must leave its resolution (if there is one) to readers sharper-minded than myself. The only quite clear class line I see drawn across the map of violence in these years, is that between the aristocrat and the bourgeois on one side, and 'the people' on the other; the latter's propensities towards violence and unmeasured styles of inflicting it being found both disagreeable and frightening by their propertied superiors.

3 Fundamentals concerning war and peace

And so we return from that excursus about the social and intellectual composition of the later Enlightment consensus, to its substance. What view did it offer of war and of the matter of humanity in warfare? We must begin at the beginning. The view or vision of mankind from which it began has to be classified among the 'optimistic' ones. All political theories have roots in some idea of man and of mankind. The more or less optimistic one held by our consensus men (that consensus, as I have already remarked, allowed quite a wide variety and included Kant, who was not optimistic in the obvious sense at all) had been gathering strength for many decades, as it drew apart from the severer and more literal christian versions of belief in original sin, and as it acquired arms powerful enough (as it thought) to drive away the spectre of Thomas Hobbes. Original sin and Thomas Hobbes were, indeed, to make strong come-backs, with many modern allies, subsequently. Social science has sought in vain for incontrovertible objective evidence that one emphasis or the other is the more 'correct'. My way through the thicket is to conclude that each view in its extreme form does injustice to observable facts, and that wisdom must lie at some prudently chosen (and preferably defensible) place in between; being 'sociable with them that will be sociable, and formidable to them that will not',[16] but believing in the reality of the will towards sociability more than did Hobbes.

The later Enlightenment consensus included some extreme optimists, believing that men were not only perfectible but nearly perfect – a few of whom met their end on the guillotine, which, so far as the 'pessimistic' were concerned, served them right. More central was the conviction that in some real sense mankind was one ('all men are brothers'), and that all nations and States were capable of harmonious collaboration and exchange ('that larger society which nature has established among the peoples of the world').[17] Men and nations alike, however, were so far from fully realizing their own natures and their own interests, that wars between them (i.e. between States, their necessary collectivities) still occurred. The 'inordinate passions and mistaken self-interest of men' kept them from realizing their natural capacities to become citizens of the world. War could not – not for the time being, anyway – be avoided. It was inevitable, because it was sometimes necessary. But the tragic necessity of war must not make men unmindful of their true natures and the nature of the world they inhabit. Essentially 'brothers', men are now and then compelled by cruel force of circumstances to appear as enemies. However:

Let us never forget that our enemies are men. Although we may be under the unfortunate necessity of prosecuting our right by force of arms, let us never put aside the ties of charity which bind us to the whole human race. In this way we shall defend courageously the rights of our country, without violating those of humanity. Let us be brave without being cruel, and our victory will not be stained by inhuman and brutal acts.[18]

War, then, was occasionally inevitable and justified; justified by the failure of every endeavour to come to a non-violent resolution of a dispute about really serious matters. (So little did the publicists consider war over minor matters to be justifiable, they scarcely mentioned it.) War was not to be undertaken for any but grave and respectable causes: causes which would stand scrutiny by observers both in the present and in time to come. Thus the expressions in the American Declaration of Independence, that it was prompted by 'a decent respect to the opinions of mankind'; and, 'Let Facts be submitted to a candid world'.[19] The French revolutionaries were as punctilious as the American. When, 'for the first time since the day of its liberty, the French people found that they might be reduced to the necessity of exercising the terrible right of war', their representatives in the National Assembly felt they 'owed to Europe and to the whole of mankind (*humanité*)'[20] an explanation. Rulers and governments who cared about conscience and reputation would not go to war except as a last resort, and 'unfortunate necessity'.[21]

By what tokens might the candid world recognize the existence of this unfortunate and regrettable necessity? Primarily, when a State's existence or security were at stake. Whether they were whole-hearted 'natural law' men or whether they were incorporating some positivist attitudes, the publicists took their definitions of necessary occasions of war from the old 'natural law' tradition, which had always allowed States (as it had individual men in the state of nature, and by conscious analogy with them) to take up arms when injured in their actual integrity and rights or threatened in their actual or prospective security. Vattel, who seems perfectly representative in this respect, put it thus: States, under the obligation common to all natural entities to act in accordance with their own nature, owe it to themselves 'to preserve and perfect their own existence'; 'perfecting' themselves is their own internal affair and

is what matters most to the people inhabiting them (i.e., as securing to them a good sort of life), but an all-important precondition
is security against assault from without. If, having given no offence
to anyone else, a State is attacked, it may most certainly defend
itself in all ways necessary to that end; unquestionably, defensive
war in such circumstances is as 'just' a kind of war as one can get.
Not less justified is war to avert serious (but certainly not just
imaginary or vaguely possible) dangers. 'A Nation or State has the
right to whatever can assist it in warding off a threatening danger,
or in keeping at a distance things that might bring about its ruin.'
So 'preventive war' could be justified, too. Beyond this, Vattel
followed the regular course of his age by relating both of these
main justifications of war to the 'balance of power': that 'well-
known principle . . . by which is meant an arrangement of affairs
so that no State shall be in a position to have absolute mastery and
dominate over the others.'[22] Alliances and the mere threat of war
were expected to be this happy arrangement's normal way of working, but it might sometimes come to war, which, for such a good
and necessary purpose, was justifiable – because necessary.

What were not justifiable, because they were not necessary in
the same real sense of being necessary to protect and secure the
natural rights of States whatever their size, were above all wars
whose motives lay only in the satisfaction of aggressive or expan-
sionist ambition. The French revolutionaries proudly disclaimed
such wars in Title VI of their Constitution of 1791: 'The French
nation renounces the undertaking of any war with a view to making conquests, and will never employ its forces against the liberty
of any people.' But other familiar types of war were held to be no
less reprehensible in the lust for 'glory', or in mere 'convenience': [23]
for example, resorting to force without giving the laborious and
temper-testing processes of negotiation time to work, or disregarding a small neighbour's rights just because he was a nuisance.

However dreamy or sentimental this kind of language may
sound to a later twentieth-century ear, it must be noted that these
would-be legislators of international relations were not soft-
headed. They understood well enough that wars would occur, like
it or not, for good reasons or for bad; they had no illusions about
the realities of war; they thought it desirable, and not impractical,
to control and limit the nastiness of what they could not altogether
abolish. It went against reason to suppose that the taking up of

arms could not be discovered to be more justified on the one side than on the other in any particular case, yet Vattel and those who followed his lead realized that it would be fatal to the viability of the *jus in bello*, once war had occurred, to carry over from this theoretical difference as regarded the *jus ad bellum*, any practical preferences in respect of the law of war. If the law of war in its *jus in bello* form was to work at all, the rights and wrongs of conflicts had to be forgotten by those managing the conflict itself, whatever might be brought into consideration by the 'other parties' concerned – observant and potentially influential neutrals, for example, 'the opinions of mankind', shifts in political opinion within the belligerents, 'the judgement of history' – as they brought into the calculation the foreseeable consequences of the conflict, the utterly unpredictable consequences (every serious student of war knows about them) and the costs (all sorts : material, psychological, reputational . . .) likely to be incurred by victors and vanquished alike.

Both on the grounds of going to war in the first place, and then in the mode of their conduct of the war, States' and soldiers' pleas of 'necessity' would be assessed, not by reference to their own subjective and/or self-interested criteria, but objectively, in relation to the particular situation itself and to certain absolute criteria founded in a natural law whose business it was to attend equally to the welfare of the individual and the species. The publicists were extremely realistic in the amplitude of their recognition of the demands of 'necessity'. Indeed they made so much room in it that they invited misrepresentation in later, more nationalistic, less peace-preferring decades, when their many recognitions of 'necessity' were too well remembered, their not less emphatic statements of the moral criteria which should guide appeals to 'necessity' too easily forgotten. Those criteria, to put them at their simplest, were : the fundamental unity of mankind, and the natural rights of men; the preferability of the state of peace to that of war; and the general principle (to which we might give the recently-popularized description of 'proportionality') that means were not indiscriminately justified by ends and that the ends at stake (in questions of peace, war, and the conduct of war) were general, universal, and historical; not particular, local, and temporary.

Such principles not, perhaps, seeming ridiculous and unacceptable – at any rate as statements of general truths – to most of us in the later twentieth century, we may give the international theorists of the later Enlightenment a better hearing than they were getting between, say, the eighteen-sixties and the nineteen-thirties when the rejectors of the fundamental unity of mankind and the promoters of international animosity were in the ascendant. The later Enlightenment consensus was cosmopolitan; long before the eighteen-sixties – indeed, already by the middle of the seventeen-nineties – it was running into trouble with 'nationalism'. Nationalism for long retained in Europe a cosmopolitan colouring, sharing the cosmopolitans' ideal vision of a world of peacefulness with just this difference, that nationalists thought it must wait until all nationalities had achieved and come into enjoyment of the political independence naturally due them. But it also contained from the start (as contemporary evidence amply proves that it still does contain) strong spirits of jealousy and rivalry between nations, which were likely to stimulate hostilities between them and to add new strength and zeal to old imperialism. The bourgeoisie, whose pressing towards political power was the prime political characteristic of these nineteenth-century years, proved itself equally malleable in both directions, for peace and war alike. Patriotism did not confine itself to the posture of defence. National pride and self-satisfaction turned easily into aggressiveness and xenophobia. Every new philosophical and scientific movement that could fuel aggressiveness and warfare, did so. The nineteenth century, busy as it was with enthusiastic pursuit of the later Enlightenment's pointers towards ways of peace, became much more interested in war. These are commonplaces, and I mention them only to preface an admission that the priorities of the later Enlightenment do indeed invite contrast with some of those which chronologically succeeded them. The earlier maxims and rules therefore easily came to seem dated and quaint, arguably irrelevant to a more bustling and muscular age.

Their contentions sounded weakest when it came to the perpetual question which is at the heart of the real business of international relations : how generally acceptable, how 'moral', may the means be by which the political map of the world adapts to match the economic map? The later Enlightenment consensus expressed itself strongly in favour of the rights of small States (it was not without significance that many of the publicists were in the service of the same!), reproved wanton or casual aggression, and denounced territorial expansionism. This was a language more evidently appropriate to pre-revolutionary central Europe than to its western and northern coasts, where overseas expansion had for the past two or three hundred years built up profitable systems of empires founded on military and economic might. (Only in Kant, of the authors from whom I compile this consensus, do I find a serious, however terse, recognition of this difficulty.[24]) It was going to sound uncongenial to the ears of successful continental nationalism turned imperialistic, as the French one was already by 1800 and the Prusso-German one was to become not long after. It was a language which might at least be difficult to accommodate to the economic world of the industrial revolution, which demonstrated its power to alter very rapidly and drastically the relative standings of States towards each other. How did wars, founded in circumstances such as these, relate to the conventional categories of 'the just war'? If not precisely, in those terms, just, were they at any rate justifiable? And what kind of necessity, if any, could be invoked to justify them?

These questions are extremely important to us because 'necessity' is a crucial concept throughout our story. It will appear most often in the form of 'military necessity', repeatedly invoked in attempted justification of breaches of the law of war, and to varying extents taken account of in that connexion by all writers of international law books. But we shall have to take it beyond that connexion. The 'military necessity' which blurs some edges of the *jus in bello* is in fact blood-brother of that 'State necessity' concept which blurs the edges of the *jus ad bellum*. Together they are twin progeny of the general concept of 'necessity' *tout court* which finds its place in the analysis and definition of Statecraft. Discussions of 'military necessity' have an unnaturally confined and artificial flavour in many international law of war books because of the restricted field of reference they allow themselves. Many seem bound by their professionalism to seek illustrations, elucidation and philosophical guidance from no wider a field than their own case law (which at once involves them in the dangerously unhistorical business of handling on equal terms like-looking incidents from perhaps widely removed historical situations). Or they refer, perhaps, to one of the very few statements of general moral principle within their own basic documents; which almost always means the 'Martens declaration' in the preamble to the 'Hague Regulations'.[25] Whereas the proper field to which to refer exceptional and morally disquieting departures from a prevalent normal ethic or code, claimed to be justified by 'necessity', is, of course, that prevailing national ethic itself, in all its applications, in society, war, and State alike.

Not only is such an extensive setting of the concept of 'necessity' beyond the normal practices of international law. It is also beyond the bounds of much political thought. For opposite reasons, the Machiavellian and the Hegelian traditions make 'necessity' a thing all of its own: the former, by placing one specially important use of it, State necessity, *raison d'Etat,* beyond normal moral appraisal; the latter, by distinguishing it as a unique, autonomous sort of morality and therefore separate for different reasons from the rest of morality. When 'Machiavellism' and Hegelianism came together in the nineteenth century (further fortified, often enough, by super-heated nationalism and perverted Darwinism too), State necessity was better able to fly above ordinary moral claims than ever before or since.[26] But I find it impossible to write even this empirical history of the law of war without insisting that *every* field in which 'necessity' has claimed freedom should be kept available for scrutiny, because all are integrally related. They are so, firstly, as fields in which the powerful have claimed a licence to use force in ways going beyond, or plainly contrary to, their normal limits; and in which, secondly, those powerful have relied on being declared innocent on appeal to their own constituencies. Rulers/governments have relied on the support of their subjects/citizens; the military have relied on the support of both. The British destructions of the Danish fleet in 1807 and the 'Vichy' fleet in 1940 were domestically *popular*; as were Captain Wilkes's removal of Messrs Mason and Slidell from the *Trent* in 1861, and the German bombardment of Paris ten years later. Such instances could be multiplied ad lib. Behind the definitions of 'military necessity' in the writings of publicists, international lawyers, and military pedagogues, lies nothing other than the amount of licence a society (it may be an international, it may be a merely national one) is prepared to give to force in the conduct of its affairs; from the invasion of a neutral neighbour, at one end, to the killing of an apparent civilian on suspicion of being a saboteur at the other.

Whatever came to be thought about the intrinsic uncriticizable amorality, or the *sui generis* uncriticizable morality, of exercises of 'State necessity' after the turn of the nineteenth century, the men of the later Enlightenment consensus found no difficulty in subjecting all exercises of 'necessity' to a common moral assessment and guidance. 'A lawful end confers a right only to those means which are necessary to attain that end. Whatever is done in excess of those measures is contrary to the natural law ... ; right keeps pace with necessity, with the demands of the situation; it never goes beyond those limits.'[27] Whether it was a question of resorting to war, or of conducting war, they invited rulers and governments to remember that both the resort to arms and the use of arms stood to be appraised in the light of the purposes for which they had been adopted; everything that was necessary to the achievement of those purposes (and was not expressly banned by the customary law of nations) was legitimate; no measure of force was legitimate that was not necessary to those purposes. Napoleon's sentiments were impeccably those of the later Enlightenment when he said: 'My great maxim has always been, in politics and war alike, that every injury done to the enemy, even though permitted by the rules [i.e. customary international law], is excusable only so far as it is absolutely necessary; everything beyond that is criminal.'[28]

With that principle, however, was coupled in the consensus of that epoch this accompanying one, to which Napoleon's practice showed him less attentive: 'The natural law ... forbids us to multiply the evils of war indefinitely.'[29] Montesquieu, earlier, put it thus: 'The law of nations is naturally founded on this principle, that different nations ought in time of peace to do one another all the good they can, and in time of war as little injury as possible, without prejudicing their real interests.'[30] Peaceful relations were the more normal, natural, infinitely more preferable, style for States to adopt towards each other. War was not positively unnatural (if only because it could sometimes be so 'just') but its causes were 'unnatural' in the sense that unjust aggressiveness, annexationism, imperialism, etc. were the kind of behaviour characteristic of the imperfectly civilized and educated. The perfectly educated and civilized would find non-violent ways of resolving their disputes. The very uneducated and uncivilized (who usually appeared in the publicists' pages as 'savage and barbarous tribes' etc.) were supposed to be incapable of finding non-violent ways of resolving their disputes. (The publicists had not the benefit of modern anthropological research.) The quite educated and civilized of later eighteenth-century Europe, whom our publicists felt they were addressing, while not yet able to avoid violent conflicts altogether, should, they hoped, be sensible enough to realize that restraint of violent appetite and passion in this respect as in all others was what was best for health, longevity, sociability, and a good conscience.

Taking war, then, not as autonomous and inevitable but as regrettable necessity and itself contingent, they could remember that, just as they only went to war because a proper state of peace was otherwise unattainable, so would they conduct the war in ways that would not obstruct the restoration of peace. 'Necessity alone justifies Nations in going to war; and they should all refrain from, and as a matter of duty oppose, whatever tends to render war more disastrous.'[31] Not enmity but concord was the natural (i.e. civilized natural) state of neighbouring nations of reasonable, educable men. Hence the publicists' insistence that nothing should be done in time of war which might prejudice or obstruct the return to peace; meaning by peace, of course, a just peace in the sense of being bearable to the vanquished. 'Victorious, France will want neither reparations nor revenge,' declaimed Condorcet when the National Assembly was debating the disagreeable prospect of war during the winter of 1791–2; 'Such are the sentiments of a generous-hearted people (*un peuple généreux*). . . . Such are the principles of the new system of politics it has adopted [i.e. the publicists' complete package]: to repel aggression, resist oppression, forget everything once there is nothing more to fear, and to see nothing but brothers in its vanquished enemies once they have been disarmed or reconciled. . . .'[32] When, a few months later, war had actually begun, and the French Republic was anxiously but proudly contemplating its historic status and heroic responsibilities as the country which, having inaugurated the era of Liberty, now had to defend it against infuriated and fearful Despotism, the National Assembly, at one of the many sessions when the principles of the war were under discussion, received this characteristic draft decree: '. . . the National Assembly, considering that humanity and good-will are the principal feelings which nations ought to have towards one another; that the vicissitudes of their political relations ought never to change these fundamental feelings; that although war may have occurred as an inevitable misfortune, it is the assembly's most sacred duty to soften the evils that follow in its train;' etc.[33] Experience was soon to teach the French that it was not easy, actually, to love their enemies; but they certainly tried admirably, at the beginning of the war, to do so.

The central point of these philanthropic principles, seen in the light of their relation to the principles which justified the resort to war in the first place, was to facilitate the restoration of peace. No different was a large part of the purpose of the law of war, the *jus in bello*, once the war had begun. That is what the rest of this book is about. But since the *jus in bello* will have to be presented as more of a self-contained intellectual system than it actually is, this opportunity must not be missed, to fill out the later Enlightenment consensus of this element of the *jus ad bellum*. Its ideal war was one which interrupted the usual relations of States as little as possible. France and Britain set a striking example of what could be done by giving their explorers, respectively, Bougainville and Cook, safe-conducts to see them safe past each other's warships, war having broken out since their leaving home.[34] Edward Gibbon noted in the second spring of the Seven Years' War, that the customary civilities had temporarily declined: 'the resentment of the French at our taking their ships without a declaration had rendered that polite nation somewhat peevish and difficult. They denied a passage to English travellers. . . .'[35] Samuel Johnson had the same thing in mind a year later when he penned his essay in aid of the London Committee to Relieve the Wants of the French Prisoners of War:

> That charity is best, of which the consequences are most extensive: the relief of enemies has a tendency to unite mankind in fraternal affection; to soften the acrimony of adverse nations, and dispose them to peace and amity. . . . The rage of war, however mitigated, will always fill the world with calamity and horror; let it then not be unnecessarily extended; let animosity and hostility cease together; and no man be longer deemed an enemy, than while his sword is drawn against us.[36]

Vattel, as usual, is particularly instructive and profound. At several places he counselled self-restraint in the drafting of declarations, manifestoes, etc., lest their fiery language raise tempers higher than they need be:

Is it necessary in an age so enlightened to remark that in the documents which sovereigns publish relative to the war they should refrain from all offensive expressions which would indicate sentiments of hatred, animosity, and bitterness, and are only calculated to excite like sentiments in the hearts of the enemy? . . . Let us be proud of our more gentle manners [than those of Homer's heroes, Frederick Barbarossa, et al.], and not look upon a forbearance, which produces such substantial results, as mere idle forbearance.

At the head of the next chapter, where it became his business to define 'the enemy', Vattel went at some length into the obviously crucial point that 'official enemies' are to be distinguished from 'personal and private' ones, and regarded differently:

The Latins had a special term (*hostis*) to designate an enemy State, and they distinguished it from a private enemy (*inimicus*). Our language has only one term for the two classes of enemies, who should, however, be carefully distinguished. A private enemy is one who seeks to hurt us and who takes pleasure in doing so; an enemy State makes claims against us, or refuses ours, and maintains its rights, real or pretend, by force of arms. The former is never innocent of guilt; he is inspired by malice and hatred. On the other hand, it is possible that an enemy State may be free from such feeling of hatred, it may not wish us evil, and may be seeking merely to maintain its rights.[37]

From Kant, who summarized the publicists' arguments better than anyone else, I take an illustration of a third level of concern about the extreme desirability of keeping open a broad, smooth and cool road to the resumption of peaceful relations. 'The attacked State', he wrote in *The Metaphysics of Morals* (1797), 'is allowed to use any means of defence except those whose use would render its subjects unfit to be citizens. For if it did not observe this condition, it would render itself unfit in the eyes of international right to function as a person in relation to other States and to share equal rights with them.' He gave some examples of impermissible behaviour, which are so much of their age as sharply to remind us that, however firm and unchanging the substance of the *jus in bello* may be thought to be, its forms must change all the time. If he had listed torture, mendacious atrocity stories, and use of children as combatants or aids to combatancy, instead of 'the use of [one's] own subjects as spies ... poisoners or assassins ... or even just to spread false reports', we could understand his point perfectly. His conclusion anyway is clear enough: 'In short, a State must not use such treacherous methods as would destroy that confidence which is required for the future establishment of a lasting peace.'[38]

And now for the law of war in its most familiar sense, the *jus in bello* proper. Vattel as usual rests it firmly on its natural foundations. We recur to his distinction between the natural law of nations as it ought to guide the minds of sovereigns (which in principle could of course be collective: 'the sovereign people') if they really understood what was good for them and their species, and 'the voluntary law of nations' (as he called it), which, *faute de mieux*, sovereigns agreed to allow to govern their actual conduct towards each other, the better to avoid the irritant nuisance of 'continual accusations of excesses in the conduct of war' and the peculiarly vitiating vicious spiral of reprisals and counter-reprisals. This was, this is, our *jus in bello*: a mixture of, on the one side, prohibitions of acts which are 'essentially unlawful and obnoxious' such as 'the massacre of an enemy who has surrendered and from whom there is nothing to fear', acts which 'in [their] own nature and independently of circumstances, contribute nothing to the success of our arms and neither increase our strength nor weaken the enemy', and, on the other, permission or at any rate toleration of every act of force against enemy persons or property 'which in its essential nature is adapted to attaining the end of the war, [not stopping] to consider whether the act is unnecessary, useless, or superfluous in a given case unless there is the clearest evidence that an exception would have been made in that instance. . . .'[39]

4 Definitions of 'enemy'

Fundamental to all else was the definition of the enemy. Classical tradition, retained intact by Grotius, the prime proto-publicist of the previous century, had regarded the whole population of the antagonist State as 'enemies'. But Grotius was not representative. Other proto-publicists had attempted to distinguish between those subjects of the enemy State who really were 'enemies', in the sense that they composed the State's human means of making war, and those beyond power of arms-bearing who could not be called 'enemies' in more than a theoretical, titular sense. And Grotius himself clearly favoured making practical distinctions between the two sorts: his adherence to the classical view by no means meant that he favoured classical wars of enslavement or extermination. The publicists and their associated writers about war in the later Enlightenment were similarly split. Not as to the proper practice of war, for they were all of one mind about that; distinction could and should be made in practice between eiemy subjects who were part of his military force and those who were not. But how much distinction could be made, and on what grounds of principles, found them more at odds among themselves than did any other point of common interest. These differences are to be explained, I suppose, partly in terms of the closeness or remoteness of individuals' understandings of the actualities of international relations, wars, and armies; and partly by reference to the extent to which they allowed their common *credo* *i*n the universality of mankind to dictate their prescriptions of the rights and duties of subjects and citizens of nations and States in the here-and-now. Let us see between what poles their spectrum of views was spread.

Approaching one pole, though not, I think, right at it, was Vattel. Readers who have (correctly enough) formed an opinion of Vattel as the prime international humanitarian of the later Enlightenment and therefore as the butt of much 'realist' and 'positivist' sarcasm through the following century may be surprised to learn that the pole of argument near which Vattel stood was the tougher, 'realist' one, the one which allowed the widest possible definition of enemy status. It was as if he had decided that it made more sense to admit that the theoretical band of enemy personnel and property was very wide, insisting at the same time that it was not *necessary* for practice to go towards the theoretical limits; instead of adopting the opposite approach, Rousseau's, of defining a strictly limited theoretical band, and then adjuring practice to stick to it. Vattel, presumably at least in part because he understood what war was really like, laid it down that once war was properly embarked on, the whole populace of the enemy country could not but be regarded as 'enemies'. 'When the ruler of the State, the sovereign, declares war upon another sovereign, it is understood that the whole Nation is declaring war upon the other Nation. ... The two Nations are therefore enemies, and all the subjects of one Nation are enemies of the subjects of the other.'

Nor would he rest content with so general a statement. 'Since women and children are subjects of the State and members of the Nation, they should be counted as enemies. . . . All that belongs to that Nation, to the State, to the sovereign, to the subjects of every age and both sexes, constitutes enemy property.' Only after those swingeing definitions, truly painful to the sweeter-talking Rousseau-ites towards the other pole, did he produce his practical qualifications. Of women and children he immediately added: 'that does not mean that they may be treated as men who bear arms or are capable of doing so'; and in the later chapter where he was surveying in some detail what was 'justifiable and permissible' to do to the enemy in time of war, he enlarged the category of 'non-combatants' in what by then was conventional style to include 'feeble old men, and the sick, . . . ecclesiastics, men of letters, . . . husbandmen [i.e. peasants] and in general all unarmed people'. That such were, in principle, 'enemies', he could not doubt; 'but these are enemies who offer no resistance, and consequently the belligerent has no right to maltreat or otherwise offer violence to them, much less put them to death.' The moment they did offer resistance or become in any other way whatsoever involved in the war apparatus, of course, their title to indulgence disappeared. It disappeared even where it was 'not their fault' but simply by accident of war; being caught inside a besieged fortress, for example, or in the cross-fire between armies. Vattel laid some emphasis on the role of 'accident' in war. It was not the only likeness between him and Clausewitz. He does not say in so many words what the military realists rather relished saying, I think, about the turn of our own century: that, in war, the 'innocent' suffer along with the guilty'; but that unmistakably is his meaning. It also seems clear that he thought this was bound more to affect property than persons. The realities of warfare normally allowed more room for the sparing of non-combatant persons than the sparing of non-combatant property. Armies had to live off the country they were invading or occupying, and 'property' would necessarily be seized. War in any case was a rough business and should not be embarked upon without calculating that many of the risks were incalculable. 'All citizens are exposed to . . . losses, and it is his misfortune upon whom they fall. If in civil society we must risk our lives for the State, we may well risk our property.'[40]

At the other pole in defining non-combatancy stood, unrivalled,

Rousseau. In an early part of *Du Contrat Social* he threw off a definition of surpassing simplicity which has remained a pole of basic reference for many international lawyers ever since, at the same time as it presents for students of Rousseau's thought the problem, that its tenor is startingly inconsistent with most of the rest that he wrote about man, society, and war. It is less the business of a historian to express surprise at what happens in history than to explain it; especially when it is something that has gone on happening for nearly two hundred years. Rousseau's definition is still going strong. Its appeal lies partly in its virtuousness; a fragrant breath of Eden amidst the dust and smoke of conventional war literature. Partly also in the way it is presented in *Du Contrat Social* as a self-evident maxim of systematic political philosophy. On the other hand, largely because of its attractive and high-sounding moral tone, it lent itself admirably to propaganda uses; as we shall shortly see, it became regularly used by the contenders for European hegemony in their struggles with the intervening maritime giant, Great Britain. The vogue of Rousseau's definition has little to do with its intrinsic political sense, everything to do with the political purposes of those who have found it useful, whether theorists of war and peace, or belligerents wielding words as well as weapons.

What did Rousseau say, that had such mighty consequences? In chapter 4 of Book I of *Du Contrat Social* (1762) he said: 'War, then, is not a relationship between man and man, but between State and State, in which private persons are only enemies accidentally, not as men, nor even as citizens, but simply as soldiers; not as members of their fatherland, but as its defenders. . . .'[41]

Passing over without attempting to explain the fact that Rousseau wrote much that was inconsistent with this, I surmise that, swimming with the humanitarian tides of his epoch, and observing (accurately enough) that contemporary warfare was increasingly conducted by relatively compact 'regular' armies, less to the loss and harassment of non-combatants than was the case in earlier times, he was offering in an extreme dogmatic form ('with his usual levity', was how Westlake grimly put it[42]) what the publicists were painstakingly and cautiously groping towards: a juridical definition of non-combatant immunity which should match the practical immunity increasingly achieved and recognize the cosmopolitan aspirations of the age. Rousseau's intention was good –

as always – but his maxim, in that unguarded form, was preten-
tious and imprudent. Not even in 1762 could the interests of
citizens/subjects be so clearly distinguished and separated from
those of their 'States'. True, the relations of governors and
governed could thus be represented in many *ancien régime* countries, and of course a versatile radical critic and reformer like
Rousseau was pleased thus to represent them. His maxim was a
useful enough tool to promote the protection of the ruled against
the vices and follies of absolutist rulers. But already in a few
countries – in the United Provinces, for example, and in Great
Britain, in some Swiss Cantons, and in practice if not quite yet in
theory, in the Thirteen Colonies as well – 'the people' were accustomed to political participation in the determination of their
States' fortunes; and the dominant drift of later Enlightenment
political theory, a drift which Rousseau himself was actively promoting, was to extend that participation wider and deeper. When
the American colonists made their well-publicized break for freedom a few years later, their public language, much of it the conventional language of later Enlightenment progressive thought,
plainly gave *that* bit of Rousseau the lie. 'When in the course of
human events', they began, 'it becomes necessary for *one people*
[my italics] to dissolve the political bands which have connected
them with another. . . .' There followed a catalogue of the political
iniquities of King George III, 'a Prince, whose character is . . .
marked by every act which may define a tyrant, . . . unfit to be the
ruler of a free people.' So it came back to *the peoples* of America
and Britain, whose political involvement was presented as total.
'Our British brethren', said the Americans, 'have been deaf to the
voice of justice and of consanguinity. We must therefore acquiesce
in the necessity, which denounces [i.e. demands] our separation,
and hold them, as we hold the rest of mankind, Enemies in War,
in Peace Friends.'[43] When the French Revolution occurred a bit
later, its language about peace and war was similarly collective. It
had to be. Rousseau's maxim made little sense in relation to it.
Yet it was just then that Rousseau's maxim entered the era of its
greatest popularity: not the least of the many paradoxes in which
this story of the law of war abounds.

The sensitive distinguishing of combatants from non-combatants being the most central theme of this book, a brief summary
of what happened in consequence of the vogue of Rousseau's

maxim will prove a helpful guide to what is to come. It was doubly defective and disadvantageous when adopted and announced as a guide to practice. First. it released the conductors of war from the obligation to justify their infliction of hardships on non-combatants. Rousseau said that wars were between 'States', not 'people(s)'; therefore (if you swallowed this), people(s) were not objects of military operations. But people(s) nevertheless got hurt, often very badly. How else could that be explained by a Rousseau-ite, except as some sort of unavoidable accident or incidental feature of war, more or less beyond your own control and responsibility? Since it was by definition not part of your purpose, it was not among the necessary nasty acts for which you were responsible. Thus a huge realm of civilian wartime experience was, so to speak, lifted beyond the primary range of juridical scrutiny and placed in a secondary category of 'things that just happened in war'. Vattel's approach was likelier to minimize nastiness to civilians because, taking it for granted that some nastinesses would happen (not just because of the realities of war but because the enemy war strength was not to be found in his armies alone, a truth that Rousseau's doctrine obscured), it nevertheless classified all this as 'necessity' which could be intelligently anticipated and responsibly controlled.

A second disadvantage following from Rousseau's maxim lay in its suggestion that there was a sharp distinction between the soldier (or the role of the soldier) on the one side, and the man, the citizen, the patriot on the other. This invited practical consequences that had in them much that was essentially unfair: boosting the protection of the 'soldier' while it undermined the possibility of protecting the citizen or subject who personally engaged, as a good citizen was entitled to, in the defence of his country. Vattel made much more room for the latter. The great majority of the publicists was very well aware of the difficulties made by the general participation of 'the people' in their countries' wars, and their ways of accommodating them were not always very satisfactory (mainly because they were inhibited by *ancien régime* distrust of popular political involvement); but accommodated they had to be, because all subjects/citizens *were* 'enemies' or 'patriots' (according to the point of view) and their participation had to be anticipated and provided for accordingly. Vattel, for one, did this with care and discrimination in Chapter 15 of his Book III. The gist of his argument was that war was mitigated in proportion as the original natural right of whole nations, once at war, to grapple with each other, was modified by custom ('the voluntary law of nations') to confine the grappling to those formally commissioned by the sovereign to undertake it. Such might be few (none but 'regular armies or standing bodies of militia'), they might be many (if 'privateers and partisans' and a *levée en masse* were used); they would still not be the whole people, even if (as Vattel's logic, though not his explicit words, obviously suggested) an intermediate category of semi-combatants were to be inserted between the others, a category of people who at a secondary level of involvement were not personally fighting but were more or less directly supporting those who were.[44] This was complicated but it was practical and useful. It took into account realities both military and political: the military's demand that they should know with some preciseness whom they were fighting in order to go easy on those whom they weren't; and the political fact that representative systems of government spread responsibility and enthusiasm for wars way beyond royal closets. Rousseau's well-meaning but practically useless maxim merely encouraged self-deception among the French, once their Republic, having decreed that its 'public force is made up from the whole people ... all Frenchmen are soldiers',[45] had gone on to its resounding proclamation, on 23 August 1793:

> Young men shall go to battle; married men shall forge arms and transport provisions; women shall make tents and clothing and shall serve in the hospitals; children shall turn old linen into lint; the aged shall betake themselves to public places in order to arouse the courage of the warriors and preach hatred of kings and the unity of the Republic.[46]

Well might non-French polemicists inquire, what price Rousseau now? The curious and instructive fact however is that hardly any but British polemicists did so.

5 The laws and customs of the professionals
The substantive law of war, as the later Enlightenment publicists elaborated it, was much more concerned with non-combatants than with fighters. Here is a notable difference from what the law of war became a century or so later. Following the bellicose and

militarist bents of later times, the law of war in the later nineteenth and early twentieth centuries became preoccupied with
what happened to the fighters, and the interests of non-combatants
were tragically neglected for too long. Since 1945, the tide has to
some extent turned. Protection of civilians is again at the top of
the agenda. This does no more than mark a return to the proportions observed by our publicists, who were less concerned with
what the fighters did to each other than with what they did to the
civilians and the property around them. The fighters, they sensibly
reckoned, could look after themselves.

A large part of the modern law of war has developed simply as
a codification and universalization of the customs and conventions
of the vocational/professional soldiery. How often and how much
in history this class of men has developed such bodies of custom,
capable of being shared with those of like status and calling whom,
for the time being, it was their duty to fight, I do not know. No
doubt it has to some extent depended on shared other values and
interests; religious, racial, socio-economic, etc. The chivalric code
of later medieval Europe is a prime example of such a transnational or cosmopolitan customary law, and it is one of the several
tributary streams from which our modern law of war derives. Not
less so are the aristocratically-derived codes of conduct honourable and proper in officers and gentlemen, which solidified in the
seventeenth and eighteenth centuries; akin to chivalry and well
able to recognize and admire it; like chivalry and the aristocratic
code in its relative freedom from nationalism; but able to survive,
at a pinch, without chivalry's aristocratic connections and ob-
sessions. By the eighteenth century, these intrinsically cosmopolitan bodies of ideas had produced corresponding bodies of customs
and conventions – the word 'convention', so important in our
story, has here its vital source – which, first, did much to make war
less dangerous to the war-minded, and second, incidentally, did
something to make it less damaging to the non-combatants. The
latter effect, which was of course hailed by the humanitarians of
the later Enlightenment as evidence of progress, ought not to be
wholly discounted as such on account of its undoubtedly self-
interested military origins.

As to the former, regulating the conduct of combatants towards
each other, the most obvious and 'solid' usages by the eighteenth
century (in the sense of being thoroughly articulated and uni-

versally admitted) were the elaborate arrangements laid down for 'capitulations' and truces. Capitulation was the technical term for the surrender of the garrison of a besieged fortress. Sieges were the great set-pieces of military science, and perhaps were among the most attractive events in most continental soldiers' experience, on account of the self-indulgent pleasures (plunder, rape, drinking and gorging) which normally awaited the victors at their close. Sieges took weeks or months to conclude, and the military arts of fortification and siege-works were highly developed. The investment of a fortress, the steady construction and extension of the trenches sheltering the besiegers and their artillery, the breaching of the walls, etc. had about it something of the formalized manoeuvring of a courtly dance. Not much ordinary fighting would go on through most of this protracted operation (unless there happened to be an unusual amount of foraying, or of outside interference with the besieging force) and fighting might be avoided altogether if a capitulation were to be signed at the appropriate moment: i.e. when a 'practicable breach' had been made in the fortifications. Whether the commander of the fortress would agree at that point to a capitulation or not would depend on his estimate of his chances of successfully repelling successive assaults or of being relieved before he could no longer do so. Very often there was no such prospect of relief or indefinite resistance, and therefore it became an accepted thing that the making of that practicable breach would be taken as a sign that it was time to call it a day. These capitulations were not surrenders, with all that implies about clear-cut victory. They were prudent agreements between a force that seemed certain to win and one that seemed certain to lose, on terms that gave the former the substance of victory (tenure of that fortified place) without exacting the last drop of blood *en route*, and which liberated the latter in an acceptably honourable way. The formal capitulation, together with the similar rituals of *parlementaires* to arrange truces, conventions, capitulations and so on, perfectly exemplify the gentlemanly and self-limiting sides of eighteenth century warfare. Without any difficulty at all they lent themselves to the publicists' incorporation of them into the evolving law of war.[47]

Equally easy to fit into place were similar usages, not yet so well developed, concerning the wounded and the captured. The capitulation and the *parlementaire* were the *pièces de résistance*, the most elaborately developed and, apparently, universally observed, of the eighteenth century's law of war; but these other usages, developing at the same time and for the same reasons, lent credence to the general belief that enlightened progress really was succeeding in softening the sufferings of *hors de combat* soldiers and reducing the chances of their deaths in or after battle. 'Conventions' had so often been agreed upon before battles to protect what we now would call the 'ambulance men' and 'field hospitals' and to spread their healing work over the wounded of both sides, that their form was on the way to becoming as standardized as that of the capitulation. The taking of prisoners and subsequent exchange, or mere release, of them (instead of killing them, enslaving them, or releasing them only for ransom) were by this time regular practice also.[48]

A third level of usages, less firm again than those just described but strong enough in principle, had to do with weaponry: regulating the means by which, after all the manoeuvring and fancy footwork were over, the men of war actually did their dreadful work of injuring and killing each other. The history of warfare has been repeatedly punctuated by allegations that certain new weapons are 'unlawful', because in some way 'unfair' by the prevailing criteria of honour, fairness and so on, or because nastier in their action than they need be. Our own century is exceedingly familiar with this argument; with excellent cause. No argument in the later nineteenth century was more stirring than that about 'dum-dum' bullets. Red-hot cannon-balls made something of a like stir in the eighteenth. Beneath the historical oddities of these arguments something very serious is at stake: a prudent fear of war's expansive power, and an entirely realistic recognition that an innovation once used is, in the nature of things, if it is found 'to work', very unlikely not to be used again. A plausible case can always be made for what promises to kill more people (assuming they are the right people) more quickly, let alone more cheaply; and history shows that not only is this case regularly made but also that it usually succeeds. We might call that the abstract, pre-ethical, argument of mere technical efficiency. It is as regularly met by the contention we have just been noticing. In an age like the eighteenth century, when science and technology were not, as a matter of fact, making much difference to warfare, this argument was neither frequent nor loud. We shall hear much more of it later on.

6 The sparing of civilians

So much for the law of war as it regarded combatants. They were not unable to look after themselves. But who would look after the interests of the civilians, if the publicists did not? Most of what the publicists wrote about the law of war (apart from what they wrote about State matters like declarations of war, indemnities, rights of conquest, etc.) was about the persons and property of the vast majority of the populations of the belligerent States who were not engaged in combat, and the whole populations of the neutral States who had nothing to do with it. The best endeavours of the publicists were used to limit war's ravages upon them. Yet the resort to war in the first place marked an entry into a realm where limits were vague and wavering, and introduced that form of human relations and social activity which is of its very nature the least illimitable. The publicists knew this. It might have needed a Clausewitz to draw out all the ramifications of the nature and essence of war, but no one could come away from a careful reading of Vattel, Moser and Martens, the prime publicists of the period just before Clausewitz's, without realizing that their understanding of the physical and psychological character of war, though expressed with none of his professional relish, was substantially as forthright and clear-sighted. War's essence, they agreed, was violence; its object (which they indeed dressed in richer moral clothing than he) was to bend the enemy to one's will; it was a form of activity whose very nature tended to baffle men's attempts to control either their own passions or its development and effects. All this was common ground between them and him. Whereas he, however, had lost or never had much serious interest in the possibility of controlling the contents of this box of terrible tricks once it was opened, the publicists, sharing a less despairing or less nationalistic idea of human and social nature, retained hope that the principle of self-interest (they were not relying on anything more elevated than that) would take a sufficiently long-term and wide-angled view to build into the approach to war's violence some grasp of the fact that immediate apparent gains in the present (*this* smart trick successful, *that* battle swayed, even this particular war won) could very likely amount to losses in the future (damaging reprisals, a more ferocious conflict, lost reputation, the brutalization of one's own people, future wars of revenge, etc.).

It was in relation to war's impact on non-combatants and neutrals that the publicists had to go furthest in their refinements of the principle of necessity. In war, once it had started, a whole lot of non-combatant people were going to get hurt. The fact that war inevitably had that effect was not least among the factors that ought to make States (however restricted or extensive their decision-making bodies) careful about starting it. But war was sometimes a necessity. The same necessity which brought States to embark on war justified their using all means towards winning it which were strictly necessary, *and none which were not*. Necessity was a kind of law but it was not unlimited or irresponsible. '*Kriegsraison geht vor Kriegsmanier*' – a German military maxim often quoted, more or less meaning 'to get out of a desperate jam, you can bend the rules' – applied only up to some uncertain point. Necessity itself was subject to, first, those considerations of humanity in the long-term and the wider view which we have just noted, and second, the proviso that what was claimed by the military under the title of 'necessity' should not be mere 'convenience'.

In laying down the law for the protection of non-combatants, the publicists found it impossible to lay down precise guide-lines and inevitably differed somewhat among themselves in their emphases. Apologists for controversial acts of State or war in later generations were to find it convenient to see only the differences of opinion and to ignore the extent of agreed ground of principle beneath. The differences – about, for example, the extent to which 'devastation' of territory was permissible, or how far a besieging commander might bombard the inward parts of a stoutly defiant fortified city – naturally and inevitably flowed from the fact that most decisions about what was necessary and what was not had to be made (as we saw on page 49 above) in the light of particular circumstances. The principle was all-important and fixed, the practical application almost infinitely flexible. While Rousseau's amazing maxim suggested the fixed unlawfulness of any and all acts of war bearing hardly on civilians and their property, the publicists not only believed that to be in principle misleading but knew it to be in practice impossible.

Now for Vattel's discussion of the law of war with respect to enemy property and non-combatant persons. We have already noted his foundation principles, that all persons and property under the enemy's sovereignty were in some sense 'enemy', but that distinction could also be made, and should be made whenever possible, between enemy persons actually engaged in hostilities and those who were not. A similar distinction could be made between property that belonged directly to, and was officially used by, the government, and property that was 'private'. The former was obviously at open risk, because part of the enemy's war-making power; the latter in varying degrees less so, because its belligerent usefulness would vary so much from place to place, and according to its kind. For the publicists it went almost without saying that an invading and occupying power was entitled to 'live off the land' (if only because in most circumstances he would have no choice – one of the harsh necessities of war) at least by means of requisitioning and levying contributions, which were the fairest and least painful ways of doing it. 'Who wills the end, wills the means', wrote a juridically orthodox correspondent in the *Moniteur*, 4 December 1792, apropos of the current dispute about the ethics of General Custine's occupation of Frankfurt;[49] 'Contributions are an ordinary accompaniment of war. Necessity demands it, the publicists acknowledge it.' Subjects of a country at war and in the path of invading armies had no right to expect anything else. They might indeed expect something worse. 'The enemy may be deprived of his property and of whatever may add to his strength and put him in a position to make war', wrote Vattel; further, 'a belligerent lays waste to a country and destroys food and provender, in order that the enemy may not be able to subsist there; he sinks the enemy's ships when he can not capture them or carry them off. Such measures are taken in order to attain the object of the war; *but they should be used with moderation and only when necessary*.' [My italics] Devastations and destructions and seizures motivated by 'hatred and passion' however are clearly *unnecessary* and wrong; doubly wrong, indeed, if they also destroy some of the common property of mankind – its inheritance from the past, or its means of subsistence and enrichment in the present.[50]

'Devastations' gave Vattel and the others more trouble than most of the practices of war that hit and hurt civilians, because typically they hurt them so much. Moser, always cautious, citing many examples from the Seven Years' War, did not commit himself to the judgement that strategic devastations were always unlawful, but implied that they must often be so: 'Certain sovereigns, generals and other officers hold that they cannot be accused of wrong-doing if, when against their will they have to quit some region or place, they devastate it in order to prevent the enemy positioning himself there.'[51] Vattel, judging that devastations were 'savage and horrible excesses when resorted to without necessity', and condemning the French devastations of the Palatinate in 1674 and again in 1689 on those grounds ('In vain did the French court justify its action on the ground of protecting the frontiers. The devastation of the Palatinate contributed little to that end, and the evident motive was the vengeance of a cruel and haughty minister'), found two grounds on which so drastic a measure of warfare might be justified: first, when there was a 'necessity of punishing an unjust and barbarous Nation, of putting a stop to its cruelty, and preventing acts of depredation' – so long as the punishment fell on the right people, and not just on the helpless, uninfluential, and 'innocent'; second, when a sovereign determines to create a barrier of wasted territory to protect his frontier against an enemy whom it is otherwise impossible to check. Vattel cited Peter the Great's devastation of 'more than eighty leagues of his own territory' in order to slow down and weaken Charles XII's invasion in 1709. The battle of Poltava could not otherwise have been won. 'But violent remedies should be sparingly applied, and their use is only justified by reasons of proportionate gravity. A Prince who should, without necessity, imitate the conduct of the Czar would commit a crime against his own people; and if he were to do the like in the enemy's country, when not impelled by necessity or strong passion, he would become the scourge of mankind.'[52] Gérard de Rayneval, an experienced French diplomat who retired from the public service in 1792 and in his retirement wrote an admirable treatise, *Institutions du droit de la nature et des gens*, concluded that devastation of enemy territory could sometimes be justified when retreating before superior forces; but, he continued, it is likely to be more dangerous than it is worth; 'it is sure to exasperate the enemy; it makes him thirst for revenge, and leads him to make reprisals if he gets onto your own territory. Therefore, only the most extreme necessity can make a general take upon himself the responsibility of ordering it.'[53]

I have given enough examples of the later Enlightenment publicists' reasonings about civilians in wartime to indicate their general drift and tenor. They may be summed up thus: civilians and their property would suffer in wartime, partly because it was in the natures of war and the war-waging human beast that they would suffer, partly because there were good philosophical reasons why they should share the suffering; but military discipline, political good sense, moral self-respect, and humanitarian sentiment concurred to enjoin that this suffering and damage should be kept to the necessary minimum, which was a great deal less than would be caused by military indiscipline, political imbecility, cynical egoism, and sheer self-indulgence and callousness. The commonest heads of their discussion of this matter were: plunder, the soldier's ancient right and expectation, but increasingly deplored, deprecated, and so far as they dared, prevented by the officers; requisitions and contributions; devastation; and the treatment of civilians in fortified or defended cities – was it lawful to bombard them in order to expedite surrender, as some military opinion favoured? Should civilians be allowed to leave cities before sieges or bombardments began? etc. From this small and particular beginning in respect of the bombardments of eighteenth century fortresses, great debates about the fates of civilian thousands, even of whole national populations, were later to develop. With them to look forward to, we may now leave the topic of non-combatants in land war and turn in conclusion to the rather different scene of war at sea.

7 Sea war and the neutral

War is war, whether it is waged by land or sea (or air). It is a peculiarity of the history of the law of war that so many participants display strong tendencies to treat sea war and land war as different things. Noticing or feeling correctly enough the practical differences resulting from the dissimilarity of the physical and geographical media in which they take place, picking up (if they were continental Europeans) the ancient notion that 'the high seas' were in some sense the common preserve of all peoples, and in many cases responding instinctively to the calls of their personal or national experience, the tendency has naturally been for some 'experts' on land war or sea war, with national constituencies perhaps hanging flatteringly on their lips, to pontificate about the one kind of war familiar to them in virtual isolation from the other.[54]

Such writers have included many international lawyers, whose outlooks became 'nationalized' along with almost everyone else's as
the nineteenth century turned into the twentieth and Europe's
militarized nationalism reached out to embrace its nemesis. We
shall see in due course what intense differences of opinion then
developed between the 'Anglo-American' and the 'Continental'
schools of thought, and we shall not need to go beyond national
political factors to explain them. But in the later Enlightenment,
the situation was different. Some publicists indeed were beginning
to display faint foreshadowings of that later split, but land war and
sea war seem still to have gone together in their minds and writings. Inasmuch as the increasingly separate treatment of them
later was no more than a gesture of convenience, making manageable by matter-of-fact division an accumulating mass of material
(treaties, conventions, case law, etc.) that otherwise threatened to
become unmanageable, it was harmless enough. To the extent
however that it went beyond that to imply – and in some writers'
hands expressly to state – that war at sea was juridically, philo-
sophically, different from war on land – perhaps for no deeper
reason than that Rousseau's egregious maxim seemed to make sense
applied to the one but not to the other – the separation served only
to confuse thinking and to raise tempers. War was war, and the
rights of belligerency were the same, whatever the medium, as the
later Enlightenment publicists well knew.

   The different characteristics of war at sea found themselves represented not in any distinction of fundamental nature but in the
kinds of topics to which the publicists addressed themselves when
they handled it. Not much needed to be said about the combatants
in wars at sea; it was taken for granted that their fortunes, in the
event of their becoming wounded, ship-wrecked, or captured,
would be determined by customs and conventions of maritime
warfare exactly analogous to those obtaining in land war, known
among Eurocentric seafaring men the world over. Nothing particular needed to be said about the principles of combat at sea,
which differed from those governing combat on land only in the
larger room given to the practice of deceptions, the greater demand
made therefore on that fragile though crucial distinction between
permissible *ruse de guerre* and impermissible 'perfidy'. Nothing
much need be said about the persons of non-combatants in war at
sea, the numbers of such being in the nature of things limited, and

their right to be spared barbarous or merely wanton mistreatment universally admitted. But a very great deal had to be said about the property of non-combatants; more and more was being said as the eighteenth century wore on about that special class of non-combatant (as we may for the moment eccentrically call him), the Neutral; and almost everything that was said related to Great Britain.

The prominence in this part of the law of war of Great Britain is nothing to be surprised at. The development of the law naturally followed the examples and to some extent the inclinations of the leading or dominant military powers. In respect of land war, the field of modern instances (*ancient* instances, Greek and above all Roman, were still much quoted) was mainly French, with Frederick the Great's Prussia coming up fast in second place. On land, Britain hardly mattered. But at sea, Britain was all-important. She had become so at the expense of the previous masters of the seas, the Spanish and the Dutch. I do not know whether the proto-publicists of the sixteenth century referred much to Spanish and Portuguese examples. Dutch ones however had become dominant by the later seventeenth. Then it was Britain's turn, vigorously contested by the French and, until 1780, more or less resignedly resented by the other sea-going States of Europe. Hanoverian Britain did not invent the law of war at sea. Like its land equivalent, it had a long history, principally distinguished from the other by its commercial character. The law of sea war was, for obvious reasons, mainly about commerce, as land war law for equally obvious reasons was not; and neutrals came into the picture much more than on land. When evolving the law of land war, publicists only rarely needed to consider the rights of neutrality: what drastic necessities might justify a belligerent in demanding safe passage over neutral territory; what a neutral State should do with belligerent fugitives; what duties a belligerent owed to neutral residents in a combat zone, etc. But belligerents could usually get at each other without finding neutrals in the way, and relations with neutrals had not usually much to do with individual belligerents' war capacities. War on 'the high seas' was very different! In that medium, neutrals were ever present, going about what they considered as their lawful business, some of which might seem to be of decisive significance to one or the other of the belligerents.

The prolonged and bitter controversies that marked the development of the law of war at sea from the middle of the eighteenth century well into the twentieth were more on account of rights of neutrals than anything else. By the Seven Years' War it was generally accepted that a maritime belligerent's rights included that of stopping and seizing his enemies' merchant ships and contents of enemy ownership; also that he could search for and seize as 'contraband' war-supporting goods on neutral ships going to enemy ports; also that he could blockade enemy ports, if he had the naval strength to do so, and stop all shipping, enemy or neutral, going in or out. This may seem much; but it was not enough for the British, who, in order to put the tightest possible screw on their oceanic competitors and to wring the maximum commercial advantage out of their wars, claimed (not all at once; I am kaleidoscoping demands made during the half-century 1750 to 1800) these additional powers: to seize neutral goods in enemy ships and enemy goods in neutral ships, to enlarge the contraband list to include foodstuffs, and to stop neutrals taking over and covering by their own flags the enemy's colonial trade. The controversies thus provoked by Britain's aggravating claims were heightened by their encountering more or less coincidentally the diametrically opposed claims of those who – some of them consciously and some, I surmise, not so – were seeking to introduce Rousseau's maxim and an advanced version of Smithian free trade principles into maritime warfare, which seemed to them to demand the entire freeing of 'private property at sea' from belligerent interference and the removal of general economic pressure (as distinct from the special lawful matter of contraband) from warfare almost completely. This school of thought attained amazing peaks of popularity and influence in the later nineteenth century, only to be shocked to death by the first world war. Its first protagonists, like its last, were American. Its most constant foes were, of course, the British.

The resolution of this armed argument lay, inevitably, in the definition of neutral rights. What one maritime belligerent chose to do to another was not generally something affecting them alone. Neutrals were generally affected and they insisted on being heard. Their arguments and complaints, moreover, carried some weight, even before they ganged up on Britain in the (to the British, exceedingly unwelcome) 'Armed Neutrality' of 1780. Neutral trade, neutral shipping, neutral sympathy, and, in matters of the law, neutral connivance, were not without their uses even to the monarch of the waves. British self-interest therefore dictated some accommodation with neutral rights, even though it might never be as self-denying a one as the champions of neutral rights thought proper. There had hitherto been much difficulty in finding in the idea of the 'neutral' rights as clear as those in the idea of a 'belligerent', chiefly because of the continuing strength of the 'just war' idea; neutrality by definition having somewhat of a seedy aspect when self-conscious righteousness was on the march. By the middle of the eighteenth century the question of neutrality was engaging much attention and several publicists established their reputations with books about it (above all Hübner and Lampredi). But it was the omnicompetent Vattel who more than anyone else defined in generally acceptable terms what the rights of neutrals really were.

Vattel's definition (which seems to be virtually that put upon neutrality ever since) is of less relevance to our inquiry than the solution he offered to the crucial question, how to adjust the rights of neutrals to those of belligerents? As usual, he appealed to 'the law of necessity'. However unmistakable neutral rights might be, and however firm their claim to recognition, they were no firmer than the claims made by belligerents to recognition of *their* rights. Nature and necessity therefore dictated an accommodation between the two. Vattel's argument reached its sharpest point when it approached the touchiest (politically speaking) part of the subject: the right of belligerents to search for and to seize contraband. Neutrals, he observed, are not obliged to cease trading impartially with both sides in a war; 'if they do no more than attend to their commerce, they do not thereby declare themselves against me; they merely exercise a right which they are under no obligation to sacrifice to me. On the other hand, when I am at war with a Nation my safety and my welfare require that I deprive it, as far as is in my power, of everything that will enable it to resist me and do me harm. Here the law of necessity comes into force. . . .' Neutrals would not like it, but it was for belligerents to make up their minds, whether they preferred to antagonize the neutral or materially to strengthen the enemy. Once the declaration of war had been properly notified, neutrals, 'if they choose to expose themselves to the risk of carrying [to my enemy] articles useful in war, . . . have no cause for complaint in case their goods fall into my hands, just as I do not declare war upon them for having attempted to carry them. They suffer, it is true, from a war in which they have no part; but that is an accident. I am not opposing their right; I am merely exercising mine; and if our rights conflict and mutually injure each other, it is the result of unavoidable necessity. Such conflicts of rights happen every day in war. . . .'[55]

Vattel then went on to describe how 'there seems to be a fairly general agreement among European Nations' as to the rules that had to be observed 'in order to set bounds to these inconveniences and to allow as much freedom to the commerce of neutral Nations as is consistent with the rights of belligerents'. What he described proved to be, during the following fifty years, unsatisfactory to both sides of the evolving confrontation; less, on the one side, than embattled maritime belligerents (the British first and foremost, but in their wake the French) thought their right, and less, on the other side, than the increasingly bold and confident neutral interest thought theirs.

The first blast of the trumpet seems to have been sounded by Frederick the Great, espousing what I will call the arch-neutral side in what the old law books called 'the case of the Silesian Loan'. The foundations of this dispute are too extensive and peculiar to describe here.[56] The important thing is that Britain's pressure upon the edges of the accepted contemporary notion of maritime rights of search and seizure gave the ingenious Prussian a golden opportunity to do what continental would-be hegemonial powers were to do repeatedly thereafter: pose as the champion of neutral rights against British arrogance. By 1752, the essentials of this case were being stated by Prussia in these terms: the sea is free to all mankind, and belligerent rights in sea war are to be interpreted minimally, not maximally; 'Free Ships Make Free Goods' – a famous formula on the maritime side of our story, claiming that enemy property on neutral ships, provided only that it was not contraband in nature, was safe from seizure; and a strictly minimal definition of contraband. Britain's rejoinder was unyielding, and included the usual British insistence that the only proper courts for the adjudication of such matters were those ('prize courts') of the belligerents; which, in practice usually meaning British courts, was something that continental countries found especially distasteful, however unavoidable it might be.

The experience of this dispute had no effect on British maritime policy (Prussia, after all, at that date was nothing much for Britain to be afraid of) which reached what many critics thought its highest-ever point of presumption in 'the rule of the war of 1756': the claim that neutrals went beyond their rights when, during a war, they conducted under their own flags a belligerent's colonial trade, from which they were normally excluded. So it went on until, during the war of American independence, the neutral States joined forces in the 'Armed Neutrality', more or less claiming everything that Prussia had been claiming thirty years earlier, and winning from the then hard-pressed British some (temporary) concessions. The Americans, who with the French had mightily relished this spectacle of a united neutral action, the effect of which, whatever its intention, was to join them in undermining the British empire, did not fail to rub in the lesson by incorporating, in their 'model treaty' with Prussia in 1785 – a treaty perhaps more of publicity or propaganda than of calculable commercial value – articles guaranteeing to observe the 'Free Ships, Free Goods' rule towards neutrals in case of wars in which either of them might be engaged, and so clarifying matters as in advance 'to prevent all the difficulties and misunderstandings that usually arise respecting the merchandise heretofore called contraband. . . .' A later article also, incidentally, avowed on behalf of both countries that, if ever they should find themselves at war with one another, they would adopt and practice the most perfect imaginable version of the late Enlightenment's law of war; not merely giving each others' merchants nine months to settle their business before clearing out 'without molestation or hindrance' but also allowing 'all women and children, scholars of every faculty, cultivators of the earth, artizans, manufacturers, and fishermen unarmed, and inhabiting unfortified towns, villages or places in general and others whose occupations are for the common substance and benefit of mankind . . . to continue their respective employments, . . . nor shall their houses or goods be burnt or otherwise destroyed nor their fields wasted by the armed forces of the enemy into whose power by the events of war they may happen to fall . . .'.[57]

It was easy enough for the fledgling United States and machiavellian Prussia, countries which had not the slightest prospect of engaging in hostilities with one another, thus to favour the world with an edifying lecture. But not less philanthropic sentiments appeared also in much early French Revolution proclamation and speechifying. A few examples have already been given. It was, to return to where we began this chapter, the dominant drift of the age: no doubt embraced in its 'Rousseau-an' entirety only by adventurous and unsuspicious spirits, adopted with many a prudent qualification and reservation by those who did not like to go too fast, and presumably despised and rejected, so far as they apprehended it at all, by those whose minds did not rise above particularist national/patriotic loyalties or mere animal vigour. But that the idea of a restraining and moderating law of war, in no matter what form, conservative, Rousseau-an radical, or something in between, seemed in the later Enlightenment no less manageable than attractive, I have no doubt. The evidence for it seems to me indisputable, not only during the decades before the French Revolution but also through the decades following it, when it continued to enlighten and inspire the minds of many, despite the contrary lessons of so much of their experience in the wars which filled the next two decades. Yet at the outset of those wars, the Enlightenment ideal was still alive and well in Europe, and nowhere more than in Paris. It will be the business of the next chapter to show what went wrong.

Chapter II

First Steps in Modern War: Revolutionary, National and Popular

Allons, enfants de la patrie
Le jour de gloire est arrivé ...
La Marseillaise (1792)

La guerre de 1940 ... a été préparée par des sous-officiers
divinisés: du caporal Hitler au sergent Mussolini. Il est probable
que si les guerres napoléoniennes restèrent correctes et ne
s'abimèrent pas dans les atrocités du despotisme délirant, c'est
parce que Napoléon avait fait ses humanités et ne pouvait se
débarrasser entièrement de l'esprit critique et du sens de la
dignité humaine qu'elles confèrent.
Gaston Bouthoul, *Les Guerres: Eléments de*
Polémologie (1951)

Such a scene of slaughter as there was on one hill would appal a
modern soldier. The night came on most awfully wet. . . . The
next morning was fine, and as the sun rose we marched over the
field of battle. Our soldiers' blood was then cool, and it was
beautiful to hear the remarks of sympathy for the distress of the
numerous dying and wounded all around us. Oh, you kings and
usurpers should view these scenes, and moderate ambition!
Sir Harry Smith recalling the fight at Sabugal in
his *Autobiography* (1911)

Ye'll find, Hinnissy, that 'tis on'y armies fight in th'open. Nations
fights behind threes and rocks.
'Mr Dooley' [Finley Peter Dunne] 'On understanding the enemy', in *Mr Dooley's Philosophy*
(1900)

The law of war, as the consensus of the later Enlightenment understood it, took a considerable beating during the Revolutionary and Napoleonic wars of 1792–1815, but not because its exponents rejected it. The publicists of the post-war generation and the steadily growing body of internationalists and peace people showed some tendency to interpret what happened in these war years as a collapse of the later Enlightenment's hopes and a betrayal of its principles. They were more mistaken about the betrayal than the collapse. Experience encouraged second thoughts. Lamentations about the allegedly fallen standards in these wars were heard less often after the wars of the eighteen-sixties. After the infinitely more awful experience of the two world wars of our own century, it is easy enough to recognize how much respect was retained for the law of war by almost everybody who had to do with planning and fighting the wars of 1792–1815, and how valiantly some of them strove to maintain its practice in even the most adverse circumstances. But there can be no denying that circumstances often were extraordinarily and discouragingly adverse.

What happened was nothing like a general rejection of the law of war within the class of men who knew about it, but rather, two great changes in the world around them which made the maintenance of that law more difficult. One of these changes was simply the 'external' one, that there entered into the business of willing and fighting wars classes of people who generally knew nothing about the later Enlightenment's consensus. The other great change, quite different in both nature and effect, was 'internal' to the class(es) who found that consensus congenial: the mental change wrought by that flood-tide of revolutionary ideas that swept through many of the same minds which had helped to conceive and nurture the consensus itself. The revolutionary ideas of that epoch included new ways of thinking about war, about the State, and about 'the people'. They made observance of part of the later Enlightenment's law of war more difficult, sometimes impossible. The frequency of complaints about that difficulty and impossibility is in itself evidence of the seriousness with which the idea continued to be taken. The frequency with which the men making those complaints are found to entertain in at least part of their hearts and minds some warmth of response to those new ideas about the nation, State and war, is evidence of something equally serious: the kind of schizophrenia induced in the minds of men who respected the idea of restraint in war at the same time as they participated more or less willingly in revolutionary, national and popular politics. The main point of this chapter will be to show how the latter made difficulties for the former. (The rest of the book will show how they have continued to do so.)

By exactly what stages and through exactly what labyrinthine instrumentality of intentions and accidents a war, entered into by the French in 1792 with rather limited, pacific and law-abiding intentions, turned almost at once into a war rather unlimited and discouraging to lawfulness, is a field of historical research to which I pretend to make no contribution. Much as I should like to ascertain in detail the development of the armed forces of revolutionary France and their military operations as part of the general history of the great Revolution itself, the proportions of my project require no more than a discernment of major movements and landmarks. It must suffice in these pages simply to indicate the nature of the base from which the French began, before suggesting what were the main explanations of the fact that things turned out so differently from what they – and, I guess, almost everyone else – expected.

1 The Revolution's early preoccupation with legality and humanity

The makers of the French Revolution no more expected or wanted war than most other revolutionaries who nevertheless have found themselves soon involved in one. The more fantastically optimistic of them believed that they were inaugurating a golden age of peace. The more cautious and worldly-wise did not expect, so long as Louis Capet remained head of State (which effectively he did until the flight to Varennes towards the end of June 1791) that France would be any more war-prone or war-provocative than before; they must indeed have hoped that it would be less so, convinced as many of them were that unrepresentative government was a main cause of unpeaceful international relations. Their peaceful intentions and expectations found expression in the first sentence of the section of the 1791 Constitution dealing with 'The relations of the French Nation with Foreign Nations': 'The French nation renounces the undertaking of any war with a view to making conquests, and will never employ its forces against the liberty of any people.' Debates during the winter and spring of

1791–2 on the possibility and prospect of war resounded with
protestations of peaceful intentions. The French people, happily
freed from the bonds of their ancient servitude, had no interest, it
was said, in risking their lives and substance in aggressive or an-
nexationist war. But defend themselves, their country, and their
precious liberty, of course, they must. The necessity for doing so
came in the spring of 1792. After reiterating the just-cited sentence
from the Constitution, the French declaration of war went on to
affirm:

> ... that the war which it is forced to sustain is not a war of
> nation against nation, but the just defence of a free people
> against the unjust aggression of a king. That the French will
> never confound their brothers [i.e. the people of Austria, the
> nation at large] with their real enemies; that they will neglect
> nothing in order to alleviate the scourge of war, to spare and
> preserve property, and to cause to return upon those who shall
> league themselves against its liberties, all the miseries insepar-
> able from war. . . .[1]

In this we see the germ of an idea which was soon to become
troublesome – the distinction between monarchs (bad) and peoples
(good); but the overt principle of the whole was thoroughly consistent with the later Enlightenment consensus, as regards *jus ad
bellum* and *jus in bello* alike.

Equally consistent with the principle of the latter, but going far
beyond any contemporary application of it, was the decree which
followed, a few days later, about prisoners of war:

> The National Assembly, wishing, at the outset of a war under-
> taken in the defence of liberty, to regulate by the principles of
> justice and humanity the treatment of such enemy soldiers as
> the fortunes of war may place within the power of the French
> nation, [etc., etc.] decrees, first, that prisoners of war are safe-
> guarded by the Nation and under the special protection of the
> Law; second, that unjustifiable severities, or insults, violence or
> homicidal assaults committed against prisoners of war will be
> punished by the same Laws, in just the same way as if those
> excesses had been committed against Frenchmen; ... fifthly,
> the upkeep of prisoners shall be provided from the revenues

specially provided for the war, and shall be on the scale enjoyed by corresponding grades of French infantry in peacetime.[2]

Nothing like that was to be internationally agreed for more than a hundred years. Almost as startling was Kersaint's proposal to initiate a radical raising of the standards of maritime warfare by a unilateral abolition of privateers (one of Benjamin Franklin's hobby-horses) which was sympathetically debated.[3] Not until 1856 did anything like that gain international approval.

These virtuous expressions came at the very beginning of the long conflict, in its first, innocent, relatively defensive phase. But no less consistent with the consensus were the sentiments accompanying the outward-going phase which followed hot on its heels. Like it or not (and some Frenchmen and revolutionaries obviously did not dislike it), the French (increasingly committed to republicanism) found themselves pressed by circumstances to export their revolution and to take under their wing revolutionary movements in neighbouring lands. The monarchs of every neighbouring land were showing themselves aggressively hostile; the revolutionary armies did well enough in battle against their punitive expeditionary forces to expedite their somewhat precipitous withdrawals from French and bordering non-French territory; French armies pursuing them found themselves in Belgian and Rhenish territories where for mixed reasons something of a welcome awaited them. Political and military arguments joined to recommend what few if any Frenchmen had anticipated in the spring of that year, that they should move towards encouraging antimonarchical revolutionary movements in other countries of their western world, and offer them such armed assistance as might be within their power.

There was no overt annexationism or empire-building in this, though one cannot doubt that it was a steadily emerging *arrière pensée* in some power-conscious minds. Through the autumn and winter of 1792–3 the French publicly presented their purposes to themselves and to the world (for whose opinion they still had a decent respect) as 'philanthropic'. They sought nothing for themselves, and proclaimed that they could be expected to derive nothing for themselves except the grateful friendship of the people whom they had helped to liberty (plus, as in November they concluded to be only fair, the costs of the liberation). Fighting and foraging now on foreign territory, the commanders of the revolutionary armies and those in Paris who sought to direct them did their best to keep within the good consensus. Dumouriez, advancing into the Belgian vacuum after the battle of Jemappes (6 November 1792), enjoined upon his troops the strictest regard for civilian persons and property, taking practical steps to make that possible by paying for his supplies in ready money, some of which he raised by loans in proper form. Custine, partly from force of circumstances, did otherwise as he advanced more slowly after Valmy (20 September) into the Palatinate and then across the Rhine as far as Frankfurt. He had to enforce requisitions and raise contributions as he went but there is evidence that he too tried to observe the standards of our consensus, even at some risk of being suspected of harshness toward revolutionary heroes. There was an apologetic note in the explanation he offered for transmission to the National Convention: 'Citizen minister, it is painful for me to have to tell you that I have today [2 October] been compelled to take very drastic steps to save Spire from devastation by pillage which was beginning even while our troops were still driving the enemy from its streets.' He described in detail the succession of events, terminating in the summary execution of the ringleaders. 'Order is restored, the pillage stopped, the pillaged belongings restored to their owners. There was no other way to arrest the disorder and to save the honour of the name of France. This severe example has won the approval of the entire army. . . . My soul is torn by all this; but I owed it to the glory of the name of France and I would rather die than see that suffer.'[4]

These two examples of Dumouriez and Custine seem to be reasonably representative of the standards the leaders of the French nation and armed forces were trying to observe in this short second phase of the war. It soon yielded to a third phase of such disagreeable and exploitative realities that its rhetoric of philanthropy rang increasingly incredible, until at last hardly anybody outside France could think it anything but humbug and propaganda. Elements of humbug and propaganda presumably were present from the beginning; the 1792 decision to go to war had seemed positively good to some. But I am persuaded that it would be a mistake to conclude that this language was nothing but persiflage through the early years of the French revolutionary war. In fact prevented by circumstances and by conflicting desires in their own minds from limiting the scope of the war and restraining the manner of its conduct as much as the publicists' consensus dictated, many Frenchmen still looked to that consensus as to a guiding light. One sees it, for example, in the considerable body of opinion that was disturbed towards the end of 1792 about Custine's exactions from the citizens of Frankfurt when some clearly found it distasteful that France should be conducting war in the same way as 'despots' did; in the *'violents murmures'* that greeted representative Garnier's suggestion on 7 August 1793 that the British prime minister was such an 'enemy of the human race' that anyone had the right to assassinate him; in the short shrift apparently given to the *outré* suggestion made six weeks later by the Paris department member Lullier, that in order adequately to prosecute the war against the British, 'one hundred thousand men should be landed on the shores of England and left there, after burning their boats, so that, forced to live by despoiling the inhabitants, they would avenge the many wrongs that these perverse neighbours have inflicted on us'.[5] One sees it in the dislike sometimes felt by the soldiery for revolutionary ideologues' rigid or fanatical approach to matters which the conventional wisdom of armies took more casually; by Sergeant Bricard, for instance, recording on 8 thermidor, year II (mid-1794) how he and his comrades grumbled about the local political commissars (thus I translate the *'représentants en mission'*) when they sent back to the enemy for reimprisonment three French soldiers who had been freed on parole; and by the French soldiers' famous turning of a Nelsonian blind eye to the Convention's decree of 26 June 1794 that no quarter was to be given to British or Hanoverian soldiers.[6] One sees it in the desire recurrently expressed in debates, that the French nation should show its moral superiority to the British in war by eschewing the use of reprisals. It was taken for granted that perfidious Pitt would run readily to reprisals, but the French, liberated and raised to a higher moral level, ought to resist that ancient temptation.[7] A few days after Lullier's suggestion, representative Couppé protested against a form of words in a decree which gave the impression that, in withdrawing from the extreme ideal position of forswearing reprisals altogether, the French were abandoning their *'principes philanthropiques'*. 'By this decree', he said, 'the Convention did not mean that our country should renounce all ideas of humanity, nor set itself on the road towards emulating its atrocious enemies by massacring, as they do, civilians young and old, and wounded left on the battlefield.' Barère, as tough a war-maker as you could find, agreed. 'We do not wish to conduct ourselves barbarously, nor make war like cannibals; we wish simply to give up those principles of universal philanthropy which get in the way of our military operations, and of which our enemies take advantage.'[8]

As a last example of this persisting pursuit of lawfulness in the French conduct of their war, I instance another of the consensus concerns which was recurrent through its early years : the concern to keep its scope precise and limited. The political stance of the Revolution in its early philanthropic and liberationist phases chimed conveniently with Rousseau's maxim about the only lawful wars being between States and not between peoples. '*Guerre aux châteaux, paix aux chaumières*', the war-cry famously coined by Chamfort and worn out by repetition, easily elided into, for example, '*Guerre aux tyrans, paix aux peuples!*' (as it was put at the head of the capitulation of San Sebastian in the summer of 1794).[9] 'The times are past when we used to fight Nations', proclaimed Custine as his troops entered the Rhineland in late 1892; 'Now we have to do only with despots and their satellites. With one hand, the soldier offers to the people the symbol of peace; the other, he uses to drive his sword into the breast of their oppressors.'[10] In a debate in the Convention on 16 October 1793 Saint-Just defended the Committee of Public Safety against the accusation that its measures of economic warfare against the British were tantamount to 'nationalizing the war' – i.e., turning it from a war against the ruling elite into one against the British nation. No one apparently wanted that. It was not considered a proper way to fight even an all-out war, such as that against Great Britain had already become. Saint-Just admitted, as we have seen others doing, that the days of philanthropy were over ('Philanthropy sacrificed 100,000 French lives and 1,200 millions of money in Belgium') but to 'nationalize' a war was not considered right, even if it were as all-out a war as the war in which they were by then engaged. It was not right, of course, partly because it was not prudent.[11] Our consensus did not deny the identification of moral principle with self-interest. The Committee of Public Safety in the following spring expressed its gratification in learning that the *représentants en mission* with Jourdan's army of the Moselle had taken steps 'to prevent the war from becoming a national one against us [*de se nationaliser contre nous*]. Spare everywhere places of worship, safeguard the homes of the common people, the disabled, children, old folk.' But of course, they continued, you must all the more take it out of their rulers and oppressors, our particular enemies. . . .[12]

Such were among the conscious echoes of our law of war consensus which made themselves heard during these opening months and years of the great struggle. I cannot have uncovered more than a small fraction of all such that must exist. But this is not the only persuasive evidence of the extent to which the later Enlightenment's ideal continued to command at least some men's allegiance. For each conscious echo of the consensus there must have been many less articulate(d) aspirations; the wars' record of instances of humane, chivalrous, and (juridically speaking) punctilious conduct is there to prove it. But these wars offer another record as well. Quantification of such matters is obviously impossible, but the universal impression derived by both participants and historians is that the later Enlightenment's law of war became more often honoured in the breach than the observance. It is my impression that this was much more because 'circumstances' made observance of the law difficult or impossible, than because men's minds had turned against the idea of the law itself. Only to the extent that those 'circumstances' were of their own deliberate making or conscious complicity, might there appear a basis for judging that they cared less about the law than they might have done.

The first category of circumstances bearing upon observance of the law of war which must be briefly mentioned is obvious, commonplace, ubiquitous, and, for all its powerfulness, incalculable. I refer simply to War and the nature of war itself; *le phenomène guerre* as philosophers and social scientists are accustomed to analyse it and all its cultural connexions and resonances, its psychological attractions, its social and political uses and abuses, its natural content of the chancy and unpredictable, the passionate and uncontrollable.[13] This is the basic context within which the law of war has – has to have – its being, and it is of course the major part of the explanation of why observance of the law is never – can never be – better than partial and imperfect.[14] I have to take as read most of the ordinary workings of human nature in politics and the actual history of the French Revolution both in its own country and as a European catalyst. Indeed such basic matters will for the most part have to be taken for granted throughout the book. Given its aim and proportions, not much attention can be paid to such matters here, and with this justification, that being to some extent 'constants', they are less significant elements of the explanation of change than elements which, relatively speaking anyway, demand to be taken into account as 'variables'. Of such demanding historical 'variables', there is no lack. The remainder of this chapter will be devoted to them and their apparent effect. Of the relative 'constants', let us simply note, therefore, before moving on to what is more material to our particular purpose, that the prospect of war, the glamour and excitement and aggressiveness of it, attracted certain types of man in the early seventeen-nineties as it has always done and may forever do; that ancient unquestioning passions of patriotism, national attachment and religious belief called men to fight for causes presented to them by persons whom they trusted or in terms which they were accustomed to follow; that notions of national expansion and imperial splendour must be presumed to have been at work; that war for some at least was 'fun', opportunity, fulfilment, gain. Let us note also that, *as always happens*, Revolution and War, once begun, turned out in various ways to be different from what was expected by those imprudent or vainglorious enough to give indications of what they expected. With the revolution came also (as often happens) civil war; from the war in defence of the revolution, developed war for continental hegemony. And, to conclude this sketch of the 'constants' in play, war was war, as it always is : people got hurt whom it had been no one's deliberate intention or hope to hurt; aims, expectations and hopes changed as time went by; soldiers behaved in the ways customary among their kind and virtually obligatory, one might say, for men of their occupation, helping themselves to food and shelter by the force which came so naturally and easily to them, when food and shelter were not at once provided by their leaders.

Now for the 'variables' – circumstances more local and particular in their incidence, things happening or forces working through these years which belonged to them alone or gave expression just then to 'constants' in peculiarly powerful ways.

2 Nations in arms, first mode: France in and after 1793

First of all, it was of primary importance that the war which developed out of the French Revolution was different in kind (as well as in quantity) from every war that had preceded it for at least the previous century and a half. There is a case for describing as the first of the modern 'total' and 'ideological' wars which have since become familiar. These are historical commonplaces and we need not linger on them. The war did not long remain a limited war of dignified defence. The French (of course I mean the ultimately triumphant party in France) were defending not only their territory and their national dignity, they were defending also their revolution and the interest they had acquired in it. That interest either substantially was, or could plausibly be represented as, something worth fighting, even dying for. For almost all it was 'liberty'; for many it was property besides. Such a cause was not merely one worth maintaining in one's own country. 'Liberty' and its revolutionary accompaniments 'equality' and 'fraternity' were goods it could seem a duty and pleasure to extend to others. So self-evidently good were these principles that, when they failed at once to catch on in neighbouring countries, surprised French revolutionaries ran rather quickly to explain the failure in simplified terms of conspiracies, oppression, and wickedness. Meanwhile, revolutionary fellow-travellers within those neighbouring lands encouraged or positively invited the French to aid their liberation. So the war became, in one of its aspects, recognizable as a modern-style intervention by a revolutionary great power to promote revolution and 'liberation' among its neighbours.

This had already happened by the end of 1792. Here are a few examples of the kind of argument and rhetoric used during that December. 'Our principles are to liberate, that is, to Frenchify (*franciser*) the whole of Europe', wrote a very clever person signing himself 'Ph. A. Gr.' in the *Moniteur*. 'The other governments of Europe have compelled the French to become the entrepreneurs [*sic*] of liberty for every other people.'[15] 'Let the history of our first revolution and our experience since then guide you', the president of the National Convention admonished a Belgian deputation. 'There can be no bargaining with principles; no such thing as semi-justice, semi-liberty. People who cannot deal firmly with kings, will not be able to deal firmly with prejudices. The French nation stands for all humankind . . .'[16] A final example comes from the great session of 15 December when Cambon reported, on behalf of the committees for finance, foreign affairs and the army, their plan for assuring adequate support for French armies in occupied foreign territories. He pointed out the impossibility of any longer pretending, as some gentle souls still liked to do, that the French armies did not march abroad as revolutionaries. On the contrary, he said, we ought to admit it and make the most of it. 'Already tyrants know this; when we enter an enemy country, it is expected of us to sound the tocsin. (Applause.) If we don't ring it, if we don't solemnly proclaim the downfall of tyranny and privilege, the people, accustomed to its chains, won't be able to break them; it will not dare to rebel; merely making speeches to it won't do any good.' At last, in an atmosphere of terrific excitement, Cambon read the Proclamation designed to be made to each liberated people. It began:

> The people of France to the people of . . . ! Brothers and friends, we have won our liberty, and we shall keep it; our unity and our power guarantee it. We offer to help you too to enjoy this inestimable good, which has always been your right, denied you by your criminal oppressors. We came to chase away those tyrants; they have fled before us; show yourselves now to be truly free, and we will guarantee to protect you from their vengeance, their plotting, and their return. . . .[17]

There was more in this Proclamation, especially its final paragraph, than meets the eye, and I presume it was not meant to meet the eye of the peoples thus happily to be assisted towards their liberation. To that almost hidden meaning, we shall soon return. Meanwhile it will suffice to remark that with this was formally instituted what had for several months been maturing, the standard style of French liberationist pronouncement not much parodied in the apocryphal version: 'We have arrived and you are free. Anyone found on the streets after six o'clock will be shot at sight.'

Besides their pride and joy in being 'free' – 'free' both in the socio-economic sense of being freed from the impositions and restraints of feudalism, and politically free because made participants in representative government – the French in the early seventeen-nineties experienced their revolutionary enthusiasm also as pride and joy in their nationality. Historians of nationalism, driven by the multiform character of the subject of their study to differ in many points of interpretation and emphasis, have no difficulty in agreeing that the kind of national feeling that came to possess most of the people of Europe during the period of these wars was new enough to mark an epoch in its history. The forms it took, the springs from which it started and the channels through which it flowed, differed from country to country. There is a great contrast between what we might coarsely summarize as the French kind and the German kind. France, after all, was a political unity, as well as the biggest and richest continental State, and the bulk of French speakers in the world had been living within that political unity for several centuries; to whatever use the French would put this new wave of national feeling, it would not have to be what it soon became for the North Germans, the expulsion of foreign oppressors from their countries and the pursuit of political unification. What was, however, common to those two and most other nationalisms was the strengthening of the sense of community with the rest of your fellow-nationals, and a readiness to fight for what you shared with them. For those French – effectively the great majority – who relished their revolution, this meant of course its achievements and promises. The sense of being French and fighting for '*la belle France*' and for its '*gloire*', as well-remembered military heroes of France had fought for centuries, amalgamated with the sense of having achieved a social and political status worth defending against counter-revolutionaries striving to take it away from you. It might embrace also a missionary sense of responsibility to confer the same blessings on more backward neighbours (not to mention a sense of imperial mission).

Revolutionary ideology and national solidarity thus came together in this revolutionized France of the early seventeen-nineties, and produced the totally new – to the monarchs of the surviving *ancien régime*, new and totally terrifying – phenomenon of 'the nation in arms', *la nation armée*; scrambling through the political and economic crises of its revolution, holding together despite civil war in the west and south and varying amounts of conservative feeling everywhere, first improvising and then classically establishing adequate administrative and economic bases for great power activity; a country where, to use one of its self-descriptive phrases, every citizen was a soldier and every soldier a citizen; and where, in the *Levée en Masse* decree of 23 August 1793 (cited above, p. 59), not just adult male citizens but just about everybody else were prepared for involvement in the national war effort; a '*patrie*' whose '*enfants*' seemed to be potentially available for its military purposes in hitherto unimaginable numbers, and with a hitherto unprecedented spirit and '*élan*'. '*La Marseillaise*' says it all.

The 'total' novelty and consequent disturbingness of a great nation possessed by such a revolutionary ideology was very early discerned by Edmund Burke and adopted by conservative political theorists the world over. Burke had that aspect of the revolution sized up even before it had begun to gather momentum. Philosophical appraisal of its military implications was slower in coming. This was no doubt because those implications were not unmistakably clear until General Bonaparte elucidated them; which was not until the later nineties. What were the respective shares in that revolution of the man Napoleon Bonaparte and the French nation? Less sceptical and perhaps less scientific generations, habituated to military hero-worship, used to attribute all to 'genius'. Pinning perhaps too uncritical a faith in social science, some historians more recently sought to explain the militarily startling phenomenon of Napoleonic warfare by anything but that. My stance in this fascinating controversy is this simple one: Napoleonic warfare must have had something to do with the peculiar talents and interests of the man; but those could have found no such grand outlet, and could hardly have been provided with such massive means, had '*la nation armée*' not been there for him to lead, represent, manage, and exploit. The transformation which war underwent in his lifetime is rightly labelled with his name, for he had more to do with it than anyone else; but at least in its origins and first development it was the natural military consequence of the French Revolution. To some incalculable extent, war, we must suppose, would have taken on many of its new features whether he had been there or not.

Our concern is not with transformation of warfare in general, but with how that transformation hit the law of war. It hit it hard. Not the law so far as it governed the relations of conventional combatants with each other. Those remained very much as they had been throughout the eighteenth century. There were more of them and their sources of recruitment had become greatly enlarged, but in their capacities as uniformed soldiers fighting more or less conventional battles for their kings and/or countries, they seem to have stuck to the rules, and (so far as one can judge at such a distance) to have wished to stick to the rules very much as did their fathers in the later Enlightenment. Little changed at sea, either; later in this chapter we shall see how both maritime belligerents and neutrals continued along the lines already laid down, with no greater change than had to be expected when the stakes of war had risen to such desperate heights. But there was great change, and change for the worse, on land; and it was almost entirely at the expense of that class of persons about whose fortunes in time of war the publicists had been most concerned: civilians.

3 Civilians in the way of war

Civilian sufferings during the revolutionary and Napoleonic wars were enormous, mainly because French armies could not operate without inflicting them. An army marches on its stomach, said – or is reported to have said – Napoleon. He could better have said, armies march on civilian stomachs, for that is what really happened. Supplies were at the root of the trouble. Every army needs to be fed and sheltered as well as clothed, transported, munitioned, and so on. Logistics – the science of military supplies and movements – lie behind all stories of military success or failure. Seeming to be less glamorous and exciting than campaigns and battles, they are ignored in all popular books of military history, and inadequately dealt with, to tell the truth, in many scholarly ones. Martin van Creveld has recently struck a fine blow to remedy that defect. Their importance through this first half of the modern history of the law of war is enormous, because until the later nineteenth century (to some extent, even thereafter) big armies had usually no choice but to 'live off the land'. That was for various reasons. The technical means of supplying armies in the field – i.e. in another country's fields – did not exist before roads became better and more numerous than they were in Napoleon's time. The road that was going to make the biggest difference of all, the railroad, did not yet exist. Only by sea was it sometimes possible for a maritime power to keep an army supplied from home; as the British did Wellington's Peninsular expeditionary force. Apart from anything else, it was a time-honoured, profitable trick, and cheaper, to keep your army supplied from the resources of a country other than your own. Political considerations might make this an unattractive policy, but tradition and national egoism joined to sanction it. The armies of the *ancien régime* lived like this. Their elaborate supply organizations did their best to provide them with most of what they needed, but when that failed, they requisitioned what they could not do without, paying for it if they could and if it was their government's policy that they should, but requisitioning it anyway. And when the campaigning season ended, as it almost always did with the approach of winter weather, those *ancien régime* armies would establish winter quarters, if they possibly could, on enemy territory. They were not positively 'making war nourish war' in the more aggressive and sadistic sense of that famous phrase, but they certainly made war at their enemies' expense so far as they could. The publicists knew all this, and obviously regretted the extent to which civilians – second-class 'enemies', at most – were thus victimized; but they observed with approval the tendencies of contemporary armies to manage their requisitions and billeting in orderly and equitable ways, so that the civilian in invaded or occupied territory was spared the rude self-helpfulness of brutal and licentious soldiery, and the burdens of feeding and lodging the invader were shared more equitably by the whole of the national population, instead of weighing solely on the wretched inhabitants along the lines of march.

The military outcome of the French Revolution was abruptly to change all this. The revolution's characteristic armies were mass ones; the sheer size of the French military manpower potential at once distinguished it from any recent historical precedent or contemporary parallel. The French military administration in the early years of the revolution was in many respects incapable of providing for these armies the logistical back-up they would have liked; but they went on fighting nonetheless, as perhaps no other armies of that date would or could have done. Partly from necessity but partly also, I reckon, because it was congenial to them, these large armies developed an original style of campaigning and fighting; specializing in rapid movement with minimum baggage-trains, and to some extent relying on mass in attack to make up for lack of professional accomplishments. The consequence of all this for the civilian was disastrous. Whatever inhibitions Austrian, Prussian or even British comanders might have had about continuing to campaign after the failure of their normal logistical support-system and therefore necessarily at the expense of civilian populations (and there is some evidence that such inhibitions did affect them[18]), the French seem to have felt none after their prompt production of a casuistical philanthropic cover-up story for what they were doing. Already by the end of 1792, not much more than half a year after hostilities had begun, the shape of things to come was almost transparently clear. The French generals had pushed the invaders out of France and followed them onto foreign and usually 'enemy' soil. The explanation-justification included military logic and liberationist zeal, but it was also in large part economic. My modest inquiries have found nothing to contradict the confession of J. L. C. Gay: 'Our expedition to the right bank of the Rhine [was due] entirely to pecuniary considerations. The treasury of the army was empty. . . . Our incursion into a rich and defenceless country was to procure us the money of which we were in such dire need.'[19] Custine perceived (or was instructed to perceive) as the supreme necessity, the maintenance of his army at foreign expense. So he laid heavy requisitions on the prosperous citizens of Speier, Worms, Mainz and finally Frankfurt. We have already noted how he tried at the same time to prevent pillage. The unabashed counsels of old Marshal Luckner to squeeze the utmost out of these occupied territories, and no bones about it, were apparently rejected as inhumanely retrograde as well as politically idiotic.[20] Custine was trying to keep the business within bounds, as most French generals were to continue to do through the next twenty years. But it was a business so akin to plain pillage and pilfering in both its theory and its practice, that the distinctions between what was by one view of 'necessity' lawful and what no view of law or necessity could excuse were very easily eroded; and during that winter, his and the other French armies in occupation of foreign territory were, in fact, to a considerable extent out of control. They could hardly have stayed together and alive otherwise.

This sort of thing was as painful to the philanthropic and the lawfully-intentioned as the differences in practice between one general and another were politically embarrassing, and it was only to be expected that there should be controversies about it and debates in Paris. Their upshot was the plan adopted on 15 December 1792 for getting liberated peoples to pay the costs of their liberation. Perfectly explicit in Cambon's exposition of it, this purpose was only most dimly perceptible in the operative proclamation to the liberated. Its fine opening flourish, I have already cited (above, p. 86). Its peroration ran thus:

You are, from this moment, brothers and friends; all citizens, all equal before the law, all called equally to defend, to govern, and to serve your country. At once, then, form yourselves into local assemblies; hasten to establish local administrations; the representatives of the French republic will make arrangements with them for the securing of your happiness and the brotherhood which ought henceforth to exist between us.

It is not surprising that not all liberated peoples understood that the first function of these new-formed local authorities was to raise money and supplies for the French forces in their midst. So it was to go on through the remainder of the wars. The political complexion and rhetorical style of the French presence changed from time to time, but in a substantive sense the only change experienced by the local civilian populace would be the extent to which this exortion was regulated and disciplined or pillagey and plundery. The less it was of the one, the more it would be of the other. The system of requisitions which was absolutely fundamental to the operations of French troops outside their own country (requisitions within it were fundamental too, but in a very different way) had 'marauding' for its constant companion till the end. This marauding did not happen because French generals liked it. They knew as well as anyone else of military experience how destructive it was of discipline, how wasteful of resources. They might also ponder upon its sure alienation of the people through whom their lines of communication had to pass. Although familiar and regular enough to be referred to as '*le système de maraude*' or '*le système dévastateur*',[21] it was never explicitly recognized and stated as official policy. It was just something that happened almost all the time; relatively at its slightest when the French military administration was able to organize (usually through contractors) the establishment of 'magazines' along or close to the projected line of march, as for example through some of Napoleon's armies' march from the Channel camps towards Ulm in late 1805; relatively at its horrible worst when the French armies went into countries with no means of keeping alive but what they could wring from the natives, as for example Soult's and Masséna's marches through western Spain into Portugal in 1809 and 1810 respectively. How much self-questioning and serious argument there was about it, I do not know. There certainly was some. Many French officers obviously felt it to be a continual nuisance and embarrassment (as did, in proportionately less degrees, officers in other armies, whom circumstances sometimes brought to similar straits), and I have come across strong expressions of regret about it.[22] On the other hand some officers winked at it more than others. Davout, for example, had a reputation for unbending severity towards disorderly maraudings (matching his reputation for unbending rigour in the orderly levying of requisitions); but Ney, of whom it is admiringly said that he 'loved his soldiers', had a reputation for allowing a lot of it to go unnoticed. 'Masséna, that great warrior whose eyes and brain became clearer amidst the smoke and roar of cannons, closed his eyes and stuffed his ears when anyone tried to talk to him about depredations.'[23] Similar contrasts, of course, would occur right down the scale. The grim facts of the matter have been obscured for subsequent generations by the sentimental folklore of popular militarism, in which the depredations of patriotically uniformed men become as innocent and engaging as schoolboys' apple-scrumping, and it is implied that the terrified civilian cannot mind having his geese and pigs and seed-potatoes eaten, and his doors and window-frames burnt for firewood, by such jolly chaps.

Already it has become clear that 'requisitions' existed more clearly in the heads of law-minded soldiers than they often could in the experience of civilians supplying them. Discussion of this whole topic has been bedevilled by confusion of terms, neglect of distinctions, and failure to establish exactly what happened on particular occasions. For 'requisitions' in kind and for 'contributions' in cash there was legal authority of a kind. But they were only two (or two variants of one) of the several forms in which exactions from the civilian population might grow out of the barrel of a gun, and before going any further it will be well to note what they were. One was crime. Armies recruit criminal along with non-criminal types and do things which tempt non-criminal types to try their hand at crime. What is described as 'plunder' in one book or 'requisition' in another may actually have been sheer crime, against orders and with no justification of any sort. 'Plunder', in fact, was lawful on rare and famous occasions, as an inducement and reward to the assaulters of a defended fortified city. 'Marauding' may or may not have been inexcusably criminal, according to circumstances. If it was the only way an army could keep alive, there was some beginning of a justification of it, but as an activity it was understandably difficult for the victims to distinguish from plunder. Criminality being a more or less unpredictable constant, we need say no more about it. But there was one form of exaction and extraction in which the French specialized, which without being either clearly 'requisition' or 'plunder' or 'crime' might partake of something of the character of each. I mean the purposeful economic exploitation of occupied or subject territory for the combined benefit of the French forces there and the French war effort in general. Since this was not the least of the modes in which the French military presence impoverished and immiserated the lives of enemy or allied civilians, it is worth a special mention here, not least because it is usually confused with 'requisitions' and 'contributions' in the international law books and in such history books as take note of these things.

Like most other characteristics of French military behaviour during these wars, this one, although it only attained its full perfection during the reign of Napoleon, revealed itself in the earliest months, becoming explicit in 1793. Perhaps it was already germinating in the autumn of 1792, as revolutionaries began to debate what rationale they should adopt for the requisitions and contributions which would clearly have to be exacted from occupied territories if the French armies were not to crumble. Cambon's plan overtly confined itself to the conventional principle of requisitions for the supply of the army on campaign. But some of the others who helped produce it may already have looked further. Nearly two months earlier, for instance, Lebrun had written to Custine: 'You must sweep up everything before and beside you the length of the Rhine, while treating the people with fraternity. . . . I believe it would be very nice if you profited by the circumstances to enrich the Bibliothèque Nationale with several great and costly works found in the libraries of the places you have conquered for liberty.'[24] It is the mention of the Bibliothèque Nationale which strikes the novel exploitative note. To seize the plate and precious possessions of bishops and barons and to apply the proceeds of their sale to the maintenance of the occupying army was one thing, not without legal precedent; to send such precious possessions back to the capital as national loot was another, with no respectable precedent whatever.

That was in the autumn of 1792, before France and the revolutionary party had entered their months of most intense anxiety and crisis. The onset of that crisis, which was in part a financial and economic one, of course provoked emergency measures in every field of national life. Military occupation policy therefore became tougher, and its exploitative element more pronounced. The Committee of Public Safety instructed the generals of the republic that, beyond 'taking hostages from among the most notable inhabitants', raising massive financial contributions, and collecting everything materially necessary for their forces, they were to 'seize and take safely to the rear of their armies the victuals, forage, cattle, horses, ropes, iron-ware, hemp, linen, leather, fabrics, woollens, and everything else which, while not being immediately necessary, may be for use later . . .'.[25] The precedent thus set was consistently followed. The Committee's *arrêts* of 25 August 1794 show how far Carnot's administrative talent had already brought the exploiting business to a fine pitch of bureaucratic efficiency. The avowed theory was still that the liberating and unjustly attacked French were only collecting what was due to them from the liberated populations and their former oppressors. The practice was one of efficient financial and economic leeching.[26] Nothing but circumstances and opportunities changed with the coming of the Directory, Consulate, and Empire. The exploitation might be honestly or corruptly administered; the armies which in the last resort assured them might be well- or ill-behaved; the proportions would vary, between what was needed for the troops on the spot and what was to be sent back to France; the form of the exploitation varied, from gigantic contributions raised at one go from rich cities like Genoa, Milan and Hamburg, to long-term programmes applied over a course of years like that in Aragon, where Suchet's good discipline secured the churches from spoliation while, remarks Morvan, the inhabitants worked hard 'for their own advantage and for that of their dominators',[27] or the six-years' squeezing of Prussia. Its most spectacular achievement was Napoleon's 'enrichment' of the Bibliothèque Nationale and the Louvre (and his own family palaces) with art treasures from everywhere his victories had taken him. Those paintings, statues and the like were reclaimed after he had left for St Helena. Memories of the general French exploitation of the resources of occupied territories however stayed fresh for many generations, providing, as our later Enlightenment publicists warned that such deeds would, natural fuel for the counter-nationalisms which the French invasions and occupations did so much to provoke.

4 Civilians as enemies

The civilian sufferings we have just been considering in connexion with requisitions etc. were justified, so far as any contemporary felt it desirable to justify them, as ineluctable necessities of war, inseparable from the fact and nature of war itself. By some definitions of war and of the rights of States at war they will appear to be more justifiable than by others. But one significant feature demands comment. Whether 'really' inevitable or necessary or not, they do not seem to have been deliberately inflicted as means towards winning the war. This point is very important, because sufferings from exactly the same causes were going to be at least part-justified by that argument, half a century or so later, and similar sufferings, deliberately inflicted by different means, were at the same time being justified by that same argument also. The argument to which I refer is that found in Vattel and to varying degrees in most of the publicists, that since the non-combatant population of the enemy State participated in its enemy character (though of course less significantly than did its accredited combatants), pressure could lawfully be put upon them or upon selected sections of them to persuade them to give up the struggle, or to reduce their support for the struggle. Fundamental to this argument was the condition that the civilians in view should possess real, demonstrable influence upon, or value for, the belligerent government. We have already noticed Vattel's qualification, that the infliction of privations and sufferings upon enemy civilians of no political or war-economic significance, just because they were 'enemies', was merely atrocious. But he could not and did not deny that where such enemy civilians did possess significance, they were legitimate objects of appropriately measured military pressure.

This, clearly, was incompatible with Rousseau's much-quoted maxim, which never enjoyed a greater vogue than in France during these wars. It seems to have been lifted to a new and higher place of celebrity when an elaborated version of it was incorporated in the address given by a prominent French jurist, Jean Etienne Marie Portalis, at the 1800 opening of the French Prize Court. No more than Rousseau was he one of the publicists. A distinguished constitutionalist of the first Revolution, he had managed to keep out of harm's way when it became dangerous and, after a brief exile, returned to his homeland to become influential as one of Napoleon's principal experts on legal and constitutional affairs. For whatever mixture of reasons, but no doubt mainly because it suited current State policy, he included in his address a passage incorporating several of Rousseau's phrases almost word for word, and elaborated upon the rest, in a manner otherwise rather redolent of the later Enlightenment. Its provenance and authorship lent it the look of superior juridical status, and the State publicity machine made sure that it became widely known; but in fact it was only Rousseau writ large.[28] So was another version of it, produced a few years later by Talleyrand in another policy-orientated and officially-broadcast pronouncement.[29] French government policy being so publicly wedded to this doctrine, I do not know how far to believe Morvan when he says, at the close of a fine assessment of the bad moral habits bred into the French army by Napoleon's strategic methods: 'Victory once obtained, the Emperor saw to it that the army was well fed, while, at the same time as it put itself into good order again, the expense of it caused to the occupied region affected public opinion and pressed it to demand peace.'[30] One can hardly doubt that a French occupation would thus depress public spirits and encourage war-weariness, but whether contemporary rulers were much moved by such moral effects, and whether it was ever much of a part of Napoleon's conscious intentions that they should be so, I cannot judge. If he was consciously doing this, he was setting an exact model for the Prusso-German occupation policy in Denmark, 1864, and in France, 1870–71.

But whether or not it was covertly (it could not, without extraordinary hypocrisy, have been openly) part of Napoleonic policy thus to turn the screw of land war on enemy civilians, there is no doubt that it was still, as it had long been, part of the British policy for war at sea; just as it was part of French naval policy, even though it may only have become so under British duress and by perhaps reluctant way of reprisal. War at sea was mostly, by definition, economic warfare. The only other belligerent use of the sea was for landing invasion forces on the enemy coast. France several times tried or threatened this during these wars. None of these attempts succeeded; but it is impossible to deny that a successful invasion of either Ireland (the more common target, because of the prospect of instigating a war of national liberation) or England might have had decisive effects. For the British, the facility of moving troops wherever they wished by sea offered less spectacular an advantage. The number they could raise from native soil for foreign service was strictly limited, and although their continental allies were willing to receive subsidies from the British for vast coalition armies, the Russians were not much, and the Prussians and Austrians were not at all, interested in letting these armies be transported far away from the national base. Economic warfare therefore remained Britain's speciality and main recourse in combating enemies for whom the sea-lanes of the world had any importance; and economic warfare, by definition, was war against at least a part of the enemy's civilian population.

The French can have expected nothing else. Their own inclinations were of course strongly for the transposition of the law of war at sea into the gentler mode adumbrated above all by their friends and clients, the newly-freed Americans, but admired also by the smaller maritime, would-be neutral sea powers in general.[31] What might be called the Ben Franklin programme – abolition of privateering, 'free ships make free goods', non-interference with enemy fishing and non-contraband trade, etc. – appealed to their hearts, in the idealistic early months of the conflict, as well as their minds, and moreover could sail smoothly with Rousseau's maxim at its mast-head. Franklin and Rousseau however were not names to conjure with in the British Admiralty or Parliament; nor were governing Britons likely to be anything but puzzled or apoplectic to read this sentence in a revolutionary leader's speech on 12 January 1793: 'If the French republic, in returning to the people of Antwerp the free navigation of the Scheldt [which France had proclaimed a few weeks before], is tearing up treaties made between tyrants, it is only vindicating the principle of property; and its conduct in this is both just and magnanimous, because French interests are not involved.'[32]

By the time Brissot was talking like this, Pitt's government had for several weeks had its mind made up that a country which was thus bidding fair to revolutionize the strategic as well as the political and moral map of western Europe would have to be fought. Already by New Year's Day the Convention had learnt that 'Two vessels loaded with grain, one destined for Bayonne, the other for Brest, have been held from leaving the Thames by order

of the British Government.'[33] Such an embargo was nothing new.
More novel in the armoury of British economic warfare was the
attempt which at once followed, to put upon the French nation the
screw of hunger. The French harvest of 1792 had been poor and
French society was for obvious reasons disturbed, dislocated and
in part rebellious. In November, it was being suggested that
Britain's ally the Netherlands should corner the international
wheat market.[34] Nothing came of that. But on 25 March 1793 the
British and Russian governments agreed to put a complete stop to
the export of foodstuffs from their own ports to France and to stop
neutrals taking food there as well; a programme of blockade in a
broad, loose, legally questionable sense, to which successive
British Orders in Council gave further strength. Since Britain had
sought to do something of the same to France in 1709 (and there
were even earlier precedents), it is doubtful whether Lefebvre is
quite correct in saying that this was 'the first time' that 'the civilian
population of an entire country [had been treated] like that of a
besieged town'; but he is right about the principle.[35]

War at sea thus rapidly became as total as it technically could
be at that epoch of sails and semaphores, with the French responding in kind; destroying British commerce as best they could (i.e.,
by use of privateers, in which they were highly skilled) and incur-
ring the irritation and wrath of neutrals (especially the Americans,
with whom their early good relations rapidly soured) by what was
alleged to be necessary interference with neutral traffic. Such
interference was not at all what the French had originally wanted,
and they sought to excuse it as necessary reprisals forced upon an
unwilling nation by their irredeemably uncivilized foe. French
reprisals, replied the French foreign minister Desforgues, in
almost purely Vattel-ian terms to the American minister, Gouver-
neur Morris, on 14 October 1793,

> . . . will continue only as long as our enemies employ against us
> means disapproved by laws of humanity and by those of war. . . .
> You will see on the one hand, the firm determination of destroy-
> ing several millions of victims, merely to satisfy a spirit of
> vengeance or of ambition, and on the other, the desire of repel-
> ling unjust aggression by severe laws, and a regret at being
> reduced to that extremity.[36]

The propaganda of the Revolution and the propaganda of the

Empire after it (one might add, of the German Empire also, a hundred years later) continued to harp on the advantages to be gained by the trading and progressive nations of the world by 'freeing the seas'; a mixed political and economic liberation, only to be accomplished by the much-harassed smaller sea-going powers' acceptance of the leadership of some continental giant, able to take on Britain, the modern Carthage, at its own game.

The grand climax of this all-out economic war came between 1806 and 1812, when Napoleon's French Empire became dominant enough in itself, and influential enough outside its own borders, to attempt the entire closure of the continent to British trade, and the British responded by attempting to close it to neutral trade. The object was not just to weaken the enemy's war effort by general impoverishment and specific deprivation of essential supplies. It went beyond that, to the hope that the lowering of the bourgeoisie's standard of living, and the immiseration through unemployment and hunger of the lower classes, would depress national morale and exacerbate war-weariness. As with imperfect means in the seventeen-nineties, so with more nearly complete ones in the early eighteen-hundreds, the two imperial antagonists, besides fighting each other in every way they knew how, were acting as if it were an undisputed fact that Rousseau's definition of the proper limits of belligerent activity was wrong, and Vattel's was right. No more disputable, but certainly more deplorable, was the fact that in such a war, neutrals found themselves much involved, damaged and aggrieved.

5 Neutrals in the way of war

For neutrals, this was a return to bad old times from which they had thought themselves just emerging. Historians reading this story of the neutrals' tussle with Britain during these renewed war years cannot escape a sense of *déja vu*. (France, incidentally, was much less involved; after getting into an undeclared state of war with the United States in the later nineties, it had little choice but to sit back in hope of picking such plums as might be shaken off Albion's tree.) The issues in debate were no different from what they had been in earlier eighteenth-century wars, nor had naval technology since then advanced in any way that could radically affect them (as they would be affected by the technical advances that would happen before these issues came into debate again).

On the one side there was 'The Neutral'. He felt much surer of what ought to be his rights than he could have felt thirty years before, and with a brand new armoury of supporting arguments about the progress of mankind and spread of civilization through commerce and enrichment, pressed 'The Monarch Of The Waves' to go much further than of his own volition he would dream of going, or than anyone could make him go without the expenditure of a great deal of blood. On the other side, The Monarch Of The Waves complained that the ultra-Neutrals expected him to fight with one arm tied behind his back. 'Necessity', he claimed – not narrowly 'military necessity' as inferred in traditional books about the law of land war but a necessity in the maritime situation itself – entitled him to expect of neutrals some understanding that their enjoyment of the use of the seas was bound to be diminished when a war was going on; also that enforcement of minimal contraband lists and close blockades, the very least a dominant maritime belligerent might expect, was not also the very most.

Between these two contrasting attitudes, which were much more sharply posed and pressed than any matters of land war law at that time, nothing better than a compromise was to be hoped for; a compromise which, while it might inconvenience a belligerent (who, if he cared at all about humanity, might be expected to put up with it) would not positively disadvantage him (which no neutral wishing to remain neutral could expect a belligerent to put up with); a compromise which, while it could not help damaging neutral interests, would at any rate not endanger neutral lives; and which, while admittedly sacrificing neutrals to the necessities of war, would not shamelessly sacrifice them to the interests of the dominant maritime belligerent alone. To put it in other words: the conflicting interests of the opposed parties were incapable of a solution which would give each what each most wanted. Therefore both had to give way. Since the neutral, faced with superior forces, would *have* to give way if compelled to do so, his reaction in this tussle is beyond moral measurement; the measure of the virtue of the superior belligerent, as of his correspondence to the spirit of the law of war, would be the extent to which he might forbear to lean harder, or more to his own advantage, on the neutral than he had to.

There can be no generally satisfactory end to the study either of the battle of arguments, wits, and menaces between Britain and the neutrals in the wars of 1793–1814 and 1914–18 (for the issues and arguments were strikingly similar in both), or of the question in particular, whether Britain's attitudes and policy were those of which a self-professed maintainer of international law should have been proud. I simply offer a summary of the claims and outcomes. The claims of the most outspoken neutrals, as expressed by Thomas Jefferson on behalf of the United States, and Andreas Peter Bernstorff on behalf of Denmark, went beyond what could possibly be conceded, without reservation, by a maritime great power, and beyond what Vattel's middle band of the consensus required. Jefferson's letter to the American minister in London, Pinckney, after he had received (through unofficial channels; the British government was rudely snubbing that of the United States in those days) a copy of the Admiralty Instruction of 8 June 1793 is worth quoting at length, because it lays so much of the ground-work of this extreme neutral position as it was argued not only through the wars of 1792–1814 but also throughout the hundred years which followed. He began by citing the first article of those instructions, which declared the British government's intention of buying on its own account or of diverting to some friendly country any kind of grain going to France. 'This article', wrote Jefferson,

is so manifestly contrary to the law of nations, that nothing more would seem necessary than to observe that it is so. Reason and usage have established that when two nations go to war, those who choose to live in peace retain their natural right to pursue their agriculture, manufactures, and other ordinary vocations, to carry the produce of their industry for exchange to all nations, belligerent or neutral, as usual, to go and come freely without injury or molestation, and in short that the war among others shall be, for them, as if it did not exist.

Upon that last sentence we may pause. It was a very American sentiment, but Bernstorff was capable of saying the same thing. The extreme neutrals' position with regard to war at sea was to maintain that they should be as little affected by it as neutrals might be by wars on land between States bordering on their own. Referring sometimes to the high seas as 'the common possession of mankind' and so on, they demanded in effect that the physical properties of water should be ignored and that maritime States, whose economies and military characters had been wholly formed by their maritime activity, should de-nature themselves and their environment the moment they switched from peace to war. This was preposterous, but it was psychologically understandable. Maritime powers in peacetime, as a matter of fact, did not experience bordering neighbours in the same way that land powers did. The endless tracts of ocean became in their minds and theories of international relations a medium of existence quite different from what they actually were in a political sense: borders between States irregularly stretched out, filled with water, and more or less forgotten about for most of the time. New-World polymath Jefferson perhaps *ex animo*, Old World politician Bernstorff no doubt disingenuously, wrote as if the element of water made States' relations in some way inherently different from what they were on land, and as if therefore a maritime power at war should behave in some way fundamentally differently from a land power. The remainder of Jefferson's letter formulates this belief beautifully. It expresses among other things the neutral's eternal and very understandable resentment against being involved (no matter how) in wars not of his own seeking or liking. It very properly offers every kind of guarantee of impartial and equal trading. But it goes out on a limb in its underlying implication that nature loves neutrals more than belligerents, and its explicit demand that belligerents should sacrifice their opportunities of winning wars expeditiously for neutrals' sake. This was a limb where only a very powerfully armed and formidable neutral (or coalition of neutrals) could safely venture. It was as if a neutral should take to himself moral credit for not being bellicose, instead of perceiving that he was lucky not to have to choose whether to be bellicose or not. Summing up the American predicament Jefferson wrote: 'This is a dilemma which Great Britain has no right to force upon us. . . .'[37] But Britain, perhaps, had not wanted to go to war at all. A British contemporary might have inquired (of course, in more pompous language): why should the buck stop with Britain?

I take more pains to sketch this ultra-neutral position of the later eighteenth century than I do its opposite, the ultra-belligerent one, because it was the more novel and original, because it was part and parcel of the later Enlightenment's broad endeavour to protect as many categories of persons and properties as possible from the likely effects of war, and because that purpose gave it a kind of moral authority to which those who believed it to be, in its ultra form, untenable and to that extent wrong, had nevertheless to defer. At all events it did the most which any humanitarian doctrine can do in the context of war, by making a moral affirmation to which nothing less than some very real belligerent necessity, perceived as such only after comprehensive moral evaluation, could provide a respectable answer.

The British Admiralty (I am of course dodging the big question of how the making of its policy was shared within the political and administrative structure), holding the ultra-belligerent view which was the natural opposite of Jefferson's, believed that the necessary nature of war at sea permitted almost every interference imaginable with neutral trade in the enemy direction; just as they perhaps had got into the way of assuming that the ways of thought and action which had become second nature to them were in themselves in the nature of things. A prime function of the law of war being to encourage inquiry into the basis of claims or assumptions about necessity in military operations, I find it instructive that this aspect of the naval wars of 1793–1815 passes almost unnoticed in even the best books about it (I am thinking especially of J. Holland Rose, Herbert Richmond, and more recently the excellent works of Michael Lewis and G. J. Marcus). What I surmise to be the assumptions of the Admiralty seem to be among the assumptions of its historians. There is room for a very big book about the British navy and international law 1756–1856, which will begin with the latter instead of just now and then casually glancing at it. The subject is all the more important for Britain's necessarily decisive but always controversial place in that law's 'making', mainly through the decisions of its Prize Courts, which have been a big part of the case law ever since. It seems to need rather a large effort of imagination or perhaps 'de-patriotization' for British naval historians to realize that what seems to Portsmouth so natural as hardly to need explanation may seem so unnatural as to be beyond excuse in Brest, Copenhagen, and Cadiz.

Not wishing to be accused of caricaturing the British naval mind of the age of Nelson and Napoleon, I recommend to impartial inquirers a look at a few volumes of the letters, journals and memoirs of its heroes with an eye especially for the assumptions which sometimes showed in and never lay far beneath their articulated attitudes. These men were, it seems to me, brave, skilful, patriotic, aggressive, often clever, sometimes really likeable characters, of whose presence in the military pantheon any nation might be proud and for whose deeds any Briton who does not positively dislike his country's relatively high standard of living should be grateful. But they generally were not paragons of international legality, nor did the British public expect them to be so. The English and British, as a matter of fact, never had been. Just as, on land, your terrorist may be my heroic resistance leader or liberator, so at sea your pirate may be my heroic patriotic adventurer. The Spanish and French views of the morality of England and Britain as maritime and naval powers should be compulsory reading for all who wish to write the latters' naval history, let alone any work of international maritime relations. I quit the ground of this touchy subject behind the smokescreen of a quotation from a sensible British admiral in a memorandum about 'the salute in the narrow British seas' (i.e., by traditional British understanding of them, from Cape Finisterre in Brittany to Stadland in Norway,[38] which the British navy continued to be instructed to enforce until at least 1805. 'Many now deceased officers of sound understanding and great distinction', he recalled, had regretted those instructions as

... mischievous and ridiculous. ... Nothing has so much contributed to make us hated by other nations as our naval insolence, which on many occasions has been carried to a pitch absolutely insufferable. It was the saying of a very popular Admiral of what is called the old school, who has been dead a great many years, 'Well, commend me to the good old times, when an Englishman never did *right* and would suffer no *wrong*.'[39]

Whether the attempt by naval power to make the French people hungry was unlawful or not is one question; even a not unpatriotically-inclined authority like Hall (who however seems impartiality itself compared with, e.g., Higgins and Colombos) describes the British government's policy and arguments alike as 'indefensible' and as 'excesses [which] cast discredit on the doctrine under the shelter of which they screened themselves'.[40] The French nation however was by its own account of itself 'in arms' against the British (and everyone else) and the French government itself had undertaken the collection and distribution of food. On Vattel-ian principles, the British policy (at least in 1793-4, and supposing that there was then, as Wheaton thought there was not, a realistic possibility of its succeeding) had something to be said for it. So far as the French were concerned, British sea-war policy does not seem to me self-evidently unlawful, and much of the French complaint about it may be dismissed (as may most of the German ones just over a hundred years later) on the ground that they would no doubt have done the same to Britain if they had been able.[41]

But British policy vis-à-vis neutrals was more questionable. Of British policy from the seventeen-fifties onwards, it does not seem unfair to say that it was to lean on neutrals as heavily as they would bear without actually joining the enemy, and more heavily than imperative military necessity required. This, after all, was the crux of the matter. Some degree of interference with their own affairs and prosperity they might not be able to avoid; but to how much such interference would a maritime belligerent choose – for it was in part a matter of choice – to subject them? The very shrewd publicist Tetens, no Anglophobe extremist even though he lived in the neutral country which suffered the most from British interference, Denmark, thought Britain took unfair advantage of the situation and sought to cover itself by stretching the doctrine of military necessity further than it could credibly go. He must have had Britain in view when he drew a fine distinction – a distinction of the sort upon which the law of war entirely depends – between interferences with neutral trade that might be justified on grounds of military necessity and interferences explicable only on grounds of military convenience or commercial advantage. 'Agreed', he wrote in 1802,

> ... it may be greatly to a belligerent's advantage to isolate, so to speak, his enemy in the world of commerce; agreed again, that there may be no way to stop that enemy's trade, protected as it is by naval forces, except by forcing neutrals to cease trading with him; it is nevertheless *not* the case that the belligerent in question may claim such an urgent case of necessity that he may consider himself justified in demanding of neutrals such a renunciation. We witnessed such goings on in the late war, and even more so in wars before that. Reasonable men throughout Europe object to them. Simply to do a bit more harm to your enemy does not justify you in hurting the rights of third parties.[42]

The war of 1793–1814 presented an exact model for that of 1914–18 in its story of British affronts to neutral interests, neutrals' indignant complaints, and a kind of diplomatico-legal catch-as-catch-can lasting the length of the war, with Britain at some points making concessions (which caused die-hards to declare that the Empire was done for) for the sake of international political advantage and moral reputation, and at others successfully avoiding having to make them. After the revival of an Armed Neutrality in 1800 (as in 1780, with Russia at its head), Britain agreed to a series of maritime conventions in 1801 which were, from an international legal point of view, just conciliatory enough to earn Wheaton's praise and the veteran English statesman Lord Grenville's denunciation.[43] In May 1806 the British government made a concession to American opinion; the United States unfortunately not receiving news of it until it was too late perhaps to avert their non-importation agreement. My own (admittedly patchy) inquiry can discover nothing else resembling concession to neutral interests in this sombre area of economic warfare, or conciliation of neutral opinion. The rest of the story goes wholly in the opposite direction. So, for example, we find Jefferson's successor Madison arguing in 1806 that it *must* be contrary to natural justice for a belligerent to retaliate upon its adversary by a measure operating through neutrals unless that adversary had struck at it through a neutral and that neutral had acquiesced; which was not what had happened in that case.[44] Similarly extreme in its pretensions was Britain's proclamation of what other countries called 'paper blockades'; not 'close blockades' of particular ports, which were universally admitted to be lawful, but announcements by Orders in Council that whole tracts of coastline were 'blockaded', thus purporting to legalize the (perhaps selective) seizure of neutral ships attempting to use them.[45] Especially galling to Americans was the British practice, which they would *not* give up, of searching American vessels, not so much for enemy persons or goods, but for British naval deserters or seamen; an extent of interference which can surely only have occurred in the mind of a naval administration habitually dependent for manpower on that odious British pecularity, impressment. These were the kind of misuses of the claim of necessity to cover what was merely convenient, at the expense of neutrals, to which Tetens was referring. The concept of 'convenience' will come before us again.

My description of certain aspects of the British way of warfare so far has clearly suggested that, at least so far as neutrals were concerned, Britain used its mighty naval power more to neutrals' disadvantage than it need have done if there had been any strong desire to pursue the publicists' goal of minimizing the effects of war on non-belligerents. Further, I conclude that the plea of 'necessity' was sometimes used to cover what was really no more, according to the publicists' vocabulary, than 'convenience', self-preservation, the sole authorizer of almost (but not quite) any act of necessity, not being clearly at stake. But at least, a British advocate might have said, there was nothing in all this inconsistent with humanity. Neutrals suffered, yes, to a much lesser extent, but from the same general cause that made enemy civilians suffer. Some enemy merchants, manufacturers, shipowners and bankers found it more difficult than they liked to enrich themselves and their dependents; standards of living were, perhaps only temporarily, depressed; the British no doubt took the opportunity to engross as much as they could of everyone else's trade; but no civilian lives were forfeited, neither was it the intention of the British that they should be.

6 Bombardment and destruction

The British advocate or apologist would have had more difficulty with another area of belligerent activity in which Britain became conspicuous, and at which we must now look: the use of bombardment and burning to put pressures of directly deadly and destructive kinds on enemy civilians; either because bombardments had always been like that, or because enemy civilians were said to share responsibility for the war, or as 'reprisals'. (But 'reprisals' usually covers something else. It is the most deceptive and shifty word in the whole vocabulary of the subject.)

This British prominence in the bombardment and destruction business is the more important for its becoming part of the contention, widespread among continental European writers since the early nineteenth century, that this was a peculiarly and characteristically British (in the early twentieth century it was often expanded into an 'Anglo-American') way of warfare; in particular, the lineal ancestor of British strategic bombing in the second world war. I am rather dubious about this contention, and shall return to it later on. British practice in these respects (and United States practice when the United States got the chance) indeed probably was the most rigorous and tough in the 'civilized' war-making world in the early nineteenth century, but later the Franco-Prussian war was to show that Germany was just as tough, and certain French admirals were to show themselves to be at least as bloodthirsty as, and even more tactless than, their British counterparts. But how this British practice is to be explained – whether because there was something in 'the British (military) mind' which encouraged it, or whether circumstances (i.e., maritime supremacy) simply gave to the British an opportunity which they could not refuse and which no other country would have refused, had it been similarly placed – I will not try to judge.

We may glimpse some of this in the war of American independence. This is not surprising, since that war presents examples of almost everything that one belligerent in those days could do to another.[46] It was a war of national liberation and a war between great European powers; it was 'conventional' in some respects ('regular'-looking armies fighting battles and performing sieges, war-ships manoeuvring and exchanging broadsides), it was 'irregular' in others, involving 'native auxiliaries' in guerrilla or partisan fighting on land, and privateering, its maritime equivalent, at sea; besides being international, it was also in many respects a civil war, and like all such it opened vistas attractive to many for the prosecution of vendettas and feuds. At one end of the moral scale, it boasted all the niceties and refinements of contemporary European conventional warfare; at the other, it grimly displayed the tar-and-feathers, the scalping-knife, the fowling-piece behind the hedge, and the torch in the hay barn. The destruction of buildings, therefore, and the wasting of landed properties were among the things which happened; most often, surely, as incidents of the 'civil war/feuding' between Americans themselves, but often enough as deliberate acts of the British for Ben Franklin *et al.* to feel that it constituted a just cause of grievance.[47]

More glimpses of the same proclivity towards what might be described as 'bomb-ship diplomacy' are offered by Britain's relations with Denmark. The Danes, with their capital city Copenhagen so strategically sited as janitor of the Baltic, thrice experienced British readiness to use this strong arm. On each occasion Denmark's neutrality was the cause of trouble. Denmark, as has already been remarked, was among the boldest and most imaginative representatives of the rights of neutrality. Having a sizable fleet of its own, some room for diplomatic manoeuvring (because of its position between Britain and Russia) and well-fortified harbours, it was in a promising position to press those rights. From mid-1798 onwards the British found its pressure increasingly intolerable. The Danes, for whom the war was opening a gold-mine, began to protect their merchant vessels in convoys, and instructed the naval captains in command of them to refuse to allow them to be searched by the belligerents (i.e., the British). Two years of mounting tension ended in the dispatch of a British fleet to lie off Copenhagen, to add weight to the arguments of the British diplomat in the city as he sought to persuade the Danes of what was good for them. Wrote the admiral in charge to the First Lord of the Admiralty in the midst of all this: 'I feel perfectly easy as I have no doubt of burning or destroying both town and fleet.'[48] The Danish government was persuaded; but for the moment only. Leaning on the Russian end of their diplomatic rocker, they almost at once became members of the second Armed Neutrality, and thus were in line to become the first object of Britain's refusal to accept its demands. In the spring of 1801 it took Nelson's defeat of their fleet, and the clearing of a way for his bomb-ships, to make the Danes see British sense. In 1807 Copenhagen was subjected to the worst experience of all. An unrepentant neutral still, its prospects of remaining so were diminishing towards zero as Napoleon, extending his imperium northwards and eastwards, put Prussia on a lead and came to a settlement with the Tsar. From the British point of view, it was inconceivable that Denmark could avoid incorporation within Napoleon's 'co-prosperity sphere', and inevitable, therefore, that the still useful Danish fleet would sooner or later be placed at the Emperor's disposal. That the British government faced a real emergency (comparable to that caused by the French fleet after the fall of France in 1940) is indisputable, and 'necessity' could be alleged much more plausibly than in 1801. Not the grounds of the action, but its mode is what interests us here. The mode again was bombardment; this time by the army. Copenhagen's sea-wards defences having been made impregnable to warships, the navy's share in this combined operation was to land the soldiers and secure them from interference while they got on with the job. The job took three days to finish. The commanding general's instructions were to avoid alienating the local populace, so far as he could, and it seems as if everything was done to make this operation as relatively painless and bloodless as possible. The admiral described it as a 'sad necessity'. The general didn't like the job and wished the Danes would not compel him to destroy the town.[49] But he was ready to destroy it if he had to; and quite a lot was destroyed before the Danes gave in.

A last glimpse of the British navy at this kind of work may be offered by the war of 1812–14, against the United States. This again was caused by disputes over neutrals' rights. It was a vicious little war, with enough instances of misconduct and destruction early committed by both sides to set going as nasty a spiral of vindictive reprisals as there has ever been.[50] The unravelling of such is almost impossible and always thankless, and I shall not attempt it here. The nastiness derived partly from the employment of militias, who as usual were less disciplined than regulars (still worse were Kentucky sharpshooters and the like), and whose natural desires to burn and loot were ill-restrained; partly from the involvement, again, of Indians; and partly from the intensity of personal dislike and worse, contempt, which many on each side clearly felt for their foes. The Americans were fed up after so long a course of slights and injuries from an apparently unregenerate former despot; the British upper and officer classes, at any rate, despised American democracy and enjoyed the prospect of giving it a lesson.

Admiral Cochrane told the Admiralty in early 1814: 'I will be fully repaid [should he get into trouble for disobeying orders *not* to encourage a slave insurrection] if I can annoy them and bring the consequences of the war home to their own doors. They are a whining canting race, much of the spaniel, and require the same treatment – must be drubbed into good manners.'[51] If anyone gave anyone a lesson, it was the United States' little navy, which proved itself much more formidable than the over-confident Britons had expected. This disagreeable humiliation may in part account for the extraordinary vindictiveness to be found in, for instance, the relish with which Admirals Cockburn and Cochrane set about executing the Admiralty's orders: 'If you shall be enabled to take such a position as to threaten the inhabitants with the destruction of their property, you are hereby authorized to levy upon them contributions in plate and money in return for your forbearance. But you will not by this understand that the magazines belonging to the government or their harbours, or their shipping, are to be included in such an arrangement; these together with their contents are in all cases to be taken away and destroyed.'[52] The outcome of all this was the most concentrated series of deliberate destructions of enemy property during the whole twenty years of warfare: largely 'public', it is true, but including much that was 'private' too. Some at least of the soldiers sharing in these combined operations did not much like what they were being asked to do. Contemplating an attack on Baltimore ('the most democratic town and I believe the richest in the Union'), Cochrane opined to his masters that the place 'ought to be laid in ashes'. If they agreed, would they please, he suggested, drop a hint in the ear of General Ross, 'as he does not seem inclined to visit the sins committed upon HM's Canadian subjects ['reprisals' was of course the justification being offered for these excesses] upon the inhabitants of this State. I do not mean this as any complaint, for a better man nor a more zealous officer does not exist. He is just what he ought to be, and when he is better acquainted with the American character he will possibly see as I do that like spaniels',[53] and so on. According to another soldier, Harry Smith, more than the public buildings of Washington would have been destroyed by Cockburn if this admirable general had not interposed himself. 'Fresh from the Duke's humane warfare in the south of France,' Smith recalled, 'we were horrified at the order to burn the elegant houses of parliament and the President's house . . .'.[54] Indeed it was inexcusable; though more excusable, by the tragic criteria applicable in such matters, than Napoleon's demolitions of large parts of the Kremlin. General Robert Ross seems to have been the publicists' very model of a moral major-general.

7 Nations in arms, second mode: partisans and national resistance

'The nation in arms', as the French presented themselves in defence of their revolution and their country, appeared to contemporaries and has appeared to historians ever since as a revolutionary new phenomenon, however much this or that element of it may have followed some partial precedent. The mobilization of, virtually, the whole manhood of a nation in an atmosphere of consuming patriotic zeal was something with which historians of certain small countries – Switzerland, for instance, and the United Provinces – felt themselves familiar, and of which the earlier phases of ancient Greek and Roman history offered everybody inspiring examples. But that so large and formidable a nation and State as France should manage thus to excite and organize itself for belligerency with apparently (there was of course a lot of propaganda to egg on the reluctant and to bamboozle the dubious) such solidarity and success, was astoundingly new; all the more so when this extreme of belligerent capacity, historically displayed usually by relatively small nations liberating themselves from oppressors or defending themselves against bullies, now adopted the form of a very large nation (France had in fact the largest population in Europe), quite capable of becoming a bully itself.

How 'the nation in arms' in its French form hit the law of war, we have already seen. Such large bodies of troops moving fast and hungrily through allied and enemy territories with hardly any of the 'conventional' backing of magazines and supplies could not but give to civilian wartime experience a bad turn for the worse; aggravated, as has been made clear, by the logically separate phenomenon of French economic exploitativeness. It was not different from *ancien régime* practice so much in nature as in scale; for these French and French-formed armies were a great deal larger, more insistent, and more ubiquitous than the eighteenth-century norm. The other great powers found themselves driven to respond in kind, and their armies in turn attained, though in fits and starts rather than continually, vast proportions; bringing in their wakes also problems and hardships for civilians, only less than those brought by the French to the extent that their leaders were always, until 1814, campaigning on their own or allied territory. When they crossed the French frontiers the Allies were for the most part (the Prussians felt and behaved differently from the Russians, Austrians and British) sensibly anxious not to provoke the French to massive popular resistance against them.[55] All this, but mainly the French share of it, considerably reduced the usefulness to the civilian of the law of war; not because it put him into the firing line but because it impoverished and perhaps starved him. He was however brought right into the firing line as well as the starving line by another aspect of the 'nation in arms', to which we must now turn.

'The people', 'the nation' now also appeared in arms in the form of national popular resistance to French invasion and/or occupation; and this, like the other, was new not so much in nature (for partisan warfare had all sorts of precedents, 'professional' as well as popular) as in scale and collective intensity. Especially in mountainous regions, the tradition of popular warfare had always remained lively, while a variety of ancient laws and customs combined to keep alive also the concepts of universal military service in times of national emergency; embodied, if ever it came to the point, in various forms of militia or *levée en masse*. The big difference between these other machineries of national arming and the French one was that the French revolutionaries took it up with enthusiasm and confidence, while the monarchs of the *ancien régime*, if they took it up at all, did so with doubt and distrust. To put arms into the hands of 'the people' for anything more than the most local and temporary purposes was, for those rulers, desperately worrying. Arms, by their way of thinking, were to be borne and used solely by their loyal aristocracies (who shared their apprehensions of the potential dangers of popular activity) and their reliably disciplined regular armies (whose training, indoctrination, and life-style was calculated to separate them from the people from whom they sprang). Militias of one form or another existed, and there was a certain amount of debate about their usefulness among military thinkers; but *politically* they were indigestible by *ancien régime* institutions, so much so that when the Habsburg and Hohenzollern rulers of the time were forced by the desperateness of their circumstances to make some use of them, in 1809 and 1813 respectively, they did so reluctantly, and went back on their tracks at the first opportunity. Popular arming played a part, but not a very significant part, in the Austrian and Prussian expulsions of the French. It played a much bigger part, however, in the Russian one;[56] and it played the biggest part of all in the first and most famous of them all, the Spanish; from which, between 1808 and 1813, came the word which has ever since been used to describe the whole phenomenon: guerrilla.

Spaniards count it as one of the greatest episodes of their nation's history, that in 1808 they did what no other nation invaded by the French had so far done; they at once began a widespread national resistance, which they kept up until, five years later, the French were compelled to get out. Not quite all Spaniards felt like this about the French. Some, the 'Afrancesados', welcomed the prospects of modernization which French influence offered to bring with it; and there are those who will still argue that it would have been 'better for Spain' had the rejection of French patronage and inspiration not been so total. But total, in the event, it was. The Afrancesados were a small progressive elite, scattered among the middle and upper classes, almost entirely urban. The mass of the people preferred, in effect, to be backward and Spanish rather than progressive and Frenchifying. Finding more than enough leadership from among their own ranks, from the non-Frenchifying upper classes and from the clergy, who heartily participated in and encouraged what they perceived as a crusade against irreligion, the Spanish people put up a resistance, the like of which had not been met by the French before. They even drove a French army to surrender; at Bailén, in July 1808. That never happened again. Spanish conventional forces were, for reasons we need not go into here, not much use. But the Spaniards proved very good at what was more difficult, not to mention unpleasant, for the French to handle: popular resistance mainly by guerrilla methods, after the first grand gestures of implacable defiance; the insurrection in Madrid on the famous 'second of May', the successful defences of Valencia in June and, with unprecedented valour and persistence, of Zaragosa from June to mid-August, all in 1808.

There is no doubt that the Spanish guerrilla war and popular resistance against the French, beginning in the autumn and winter of 1808–9, was effective. It might never on its own have been effective enough to drive the French out. Wellington's Anglo-Portuguese army appears to have been the proximate instrument of that. But it was the guerrillas who prevented the French from effectively occupying the whole of the peninsula and who made their partial occupation of it costly, burdensome and uncomfortable; Napoleon's 'Spanish ulcer', as someone well put it. Whatever its share may have been in the total sum of factors which in the end proved Napoleon's invasion of the peninsula to have been a rather embarrassing failure, we have ample evidence from the French themselves that it was considerable. In military terms, then, it worked.

In humanitarian terms, however, and by the canons of the publicists, it was a disaster. It at once became notorious for its atrocities, its brutalities, the exceptional degree to which civilians were made to suffer. In brief, it exemplified the problems and

difficulties which guerrilla warfare has notoriously made for the
law of war; a major part of our story, of which much will be heard
in the second half of this book. This dramatic and sudden spot-
lighting of the phenomenon offers a useful opportunity for examining why this kind of war should *always* be so difficult to limit in the
ways prescribed by the publicists for 'ordinary' international war
and more or less practised, within the bounds of circumstances, by
'ordinary' armies. But an important preliminary observation demands to be made. To a considerable extent, the French asked for
what they got. Indeed, in Spain they were asking for it more than
in most other places, because so much of Spain was relatively poor
and infertile, and 'living off the land' became a much tougher and
rougher business than in, for example, the lusher valleys and plains
of northern Italy. That Napoleon should in his St Helena days
have embroidered what he actually said to his troops as they des-
cended into the plains of Lombardy in 1796 is not surprising, since
it realistically represented his troops' expectations and hopes.[57]
But no French general in his senses would have said the same on
passing through or over the Pyrenees. Living off the country was
difficult enough, and brought disagreeable consequences in its
train, anywhere; politically sensitive French officers knew how it
tended to 'nationalize' the war against them. In Spain, this constant feature of France's foreign expeditions was operative in its
most aggravated and aggravating form. In attempting by armed
might to subdue the Spaniards and Portuguese and to chase their
British allies into the sea, Napoleon (with as much ignorance, apparently, as arrogance) was opening the door to many of the horrors
which followed, as surely as night follows day. But not, one may
suppose, to all of them. The nature and quality of the Spanish
resistance must be judged to have added horrors of their own.

The Spanish resistance was popular, passionate, and primitive.
Goya's 'Disasters of War' etchings do not all represent what he
himself witnessed but none of them shows anything that did not
happen. Soldiers who have found comrades castrated, maimed,
impaled, crucified, are likely to do similar things to the men – and
the comrades and womenfolk of the men – whom they believe to
be responsible. Peasants who have been tortured by marauding
soldiers to tell where their grain and sausage are hidden or who
have had their cottages and sheds burned are likely to take it out of
the next soldiers they meet – who may be the brigade cooks and

drummer boys. The spiralling of atrocities and (not the same thing) atrocity stories is classic and regular in all such situations.

Such excesses of cruelty and vengefulness were doubtless deplored and to the best of their ability prevented by most French officers. But counter-insurgency warfare was cruel enough without the atrocities gratuitously added to it. In Spain, as wherever else they encountered the same phenomenon (the Vendée, southern Italy, the Austrian Tirol, a few patches of northern Germany, Russia) the French military leadership responded as such leadership always will. It resorted, when it seemed profitable, to terror. It took hostages to secure peaceful submission, and perhaps shot them if French and allied soldiers continued to disappear at night. It tried to protect 'friendly' villages while burning villages and messing up agricultural properties suspected of sheltering guerrillas and/or providing them with sustenance. As time went by and the guerrilla bands, besides becoming more familiar to the French, also, to some extent, took on regular attributes and recognizable appearance, the French began to deal with them more as equals; in particular, by not killing them when captured, by expecting the guerrilla chieftains to reciprocate, and even by practising that humane courtesy of 'civilized' warfare, the exchange of prisoners.[58] By the end of the peninsular war, Spanish guerrilla warfare against the French, while still clearly 'irregular' and dangerous by the standards of Sandhurst and St Cyr, was in practice 'regular' enough to be counted as an intermittent auxiliary of Wellington's thoroughly 'regular', though intermittently ill-behaved, army. Spain's protean guerrilla war was very different by 1813 from what it had been in 1809–10–11, and its various phases and forms deserve more differentiation than they usually get; but guerrilla remains the best, indeed the only, appropriate word to describe the whole of it, since its essence and strength lay in small-scale, country-camouflaged, peasantry-protected, cat-and-mouse operations; not in visible marches, manoeuvres, and battles. To call it 'amateur-ish' as distinct from the 'professionalism' of the manoeuvring men would be to give a wrong impression; guerrillas were often more skilled and experienced at what they were doing than the green conscripts and newly-commissioned lieutenants in the regiments they were harrying. But they were less professional in one important sense; whereas the 'regulars' fought to some extent 'by the book' – a book including our law of war – the guerrillas fought as nature, nurture, and nationality taught them.

For the law-minded 'regular' soldiers faced with a 'guerrilla' enemy (we will use the word loosely, as regulars usually use it, to mean anything but an enemy just like themselves), the main question then was, as it has been ever since: whom are we fighting? The definition of belligerent status becomes all-important. Conventional soldiers in the eighteenth century recognized each other easily. Neither their code of manly conduct nor their fighting style made disguise imaginable. Their uniforms showed what they were – the king's men, commanded by his officers, fighting for his ends and by his rules. But who were these nondescript, anomalous, raggedy armed men who began to appear on the battlefield or near it from the early nineties? If no shred of apparent uniform hung upon them, they could only be (to the regular soldier's mind) revolting peasants or bands of brigands. If some kind of uniform or common badge did appear, then it was very important to know what it meant in terms of discipline and command; to whom were they responsible, and were they effectively subordinate to his authority? These classic questions were already being put in 1793. The Spanish general Ricardos Carillo for example put them to his French opponent when, gingerly crossing the border, he encountered French resistance dressed like nothing recognizable.

> The rules of war not permitting peasants or bourgeois to have, use, or carry arms, – something neither you nor I would approve, since it would bring about the devastation and the ruin of the land – I declare, and I hope that your excellency's humanity will lead you to declare with me, that any peasant or bourgeois who is found to have arms upon his person or hidden on his premises, and above all, if he uses the same against my troops or any villages which I have occupied, whether he calls himself a 'miquelet' or anything else, and if he is not serving in some company of which he is wearing the uniform, badges and equipment (or if, being an officer, he is wearing anything other than his officer's uniform and decorations) I shall immediately hang him, and shall be justified in doing so. On the other hand, my troops, far from engaging in murder and rapine, will respect the property, goods, liberty and personal safety of all peaceful peasants, no matter what their politics recently have been, pro-

vided they remain at home in their villages and houses, carrying on in their normal way.[59]

The French general's answer, partly cited on page 59 above, missed the point. General Ricardos was not objecting to the whole of the French nation trying to fight him. He merely wanted to make sure, as 'regular'-minded commanders were to continue to wish to make sure through the next hundred and fifty years, that they knew what they were doing and what he would be compelled to do if they did not. Two years later, among the mountains on their newly extended Italian border, it was the French who commendably sought clarification of the status of the 'barbets' (exact counterparts of the Catalonian 'miquelets'), then giving them trouble: 'There are two sorts of Barbets: the first, a kind of light troops . . . paid by the enemy and fighting as they have been trained to do. . . .' They could be recognized as lawful belligerents but recognition emphatically could not be given to the 'brigands' who sometimes claimed to be 'barbets' and who 'infest the neighbourhood of our army'.[60] Again, it was a question not of completely denying legitimacy to 'guerrillas' but of demanding that they should be distinguishable from 'brigands', for their own sake, and from civilians, for the sake of the civilians. So it went on throughout the war.

At some point across the spectrum of less-than-'regular' armed operations, possibly legitimate guerrilla fighters become very difficult to distinguish from 'brigands' or civilians; and that is when the nastiness starts. In Spain, this difficulty was often acute, because the categories were universally confused. The guerrilla bands sometimes really were difficult to distinguish from bands of brigands; they looked like brigands, their ideas of fighting resembled those of brigands, and they exploited the villagers like brigands, raising in rational French officers' minds the question that has been raised in every socio-military situation ever since: do these villagers really support the guerrillas, or are they just terrorized into doing so? Civilians suffered dreadfully, partly because they were caught between the guerrillas and the invader-occupiers and were exploited or suspected by both; partly because their indomitable and perhaps reckless spirit of national resistance led them often to undertake armed resistance of their own initiative, which might kill a French soldier or two and agreeably release feelings in the short run but was bound to invite irresistible retribution in the longer term. A whole community might pay dearly for a defiant gesture by just one of its members. Was he a patriotic hero or a self-indulgent irresponsible criminal? The question was to haunt, and still haunts, the whole debate.

When these wars were over, and humanitarian stock-taking began, the majority of juridical commentators came to the same conclusion, that what had happened in Spain (*a miniori,* what had happened in guerrilla wars elsewhere) was best forgotten about except as a lesson in frightfulness and a warning for the future. I dare not say this of more than a majority of commentators, because I have not been able to find out whether any different views were taken in Russia, where, as we shall see later, partisan warfare was probably thought more admirable and proper than anywhere else. Since we shall recur to this subject later on, we may leave it for the moment with two contrasting mid-nineteenth century appraisals of it. They nicely express the ambivalence with which it demanded to be viewed. The English liberal historian and educationist Thomas Arnold wrote, in 1842 :

> The truth is, that if war, carried on by regular armies under the strictest discipline, is yet a great evil, an irregular partisan warfare is an evil ten times more intolerable; it is in fact to give a license to a whole population to commit all sorts of treachery, rapine and cruelty, without any restraint; letting loose a multitude of armed men, with none of the obedience and none of the honourable feelings of the soldier . . .[61]

A very different appraisal was offered by Tolstoy twenty-five years or so later. At the beginning of the part of *War and Peace* covering Napoleon's retreat from Moscow and the Russians' mainly partisan warfare against the French all the way to the Polish borderlands, he celebrated and magnified the Russian people's intervention in these terms, which seem equally calculated (Tolstoy went all out for whatever he believed at the moment) to glorify them, the people, and to denigrate the law of war. The law of war he likened to the rules of duelling : known to, and respected by, gentlemen of honour. But what would happen, he asked, if 'one of the combatants, feeling himself wounded and understanding that the matter is no joke but concerns his life, throws down his rapier, and seizing the first cudgel that comes to hand begins to brandish it?' The French army, he said, was like the duellist who wanted to stick to the rapier; the Russian people were the opponent who picked up the cudgel regardless of the rules and enemy's protests – 'the cudgel of the people's war was lifted with all its menacing and majestic strength, and without consulting anyone's tastes or rules and regardless of anything else, it rose and fell with stupid simplicity, but consistently, and belaboured the French till the whole invasion had perished.'[62] Within a few years Tolstoy had dropped the knee-jerk patriotism which partly underpinned this risky image and was recommending general pacifism to duellists and cudgel-wielders alike. But this powerful passage in *War and Peace* surely enough represents an opinion or prejudice commonly met with in nationalist literature, where it is of course part and parcel with patriotic historiography and mythology and folk-lore. The difficulties it makes for the law of war are incalculable.

8 Conventional armed forces in conventional operations

Little remains to be said about the main branches of our subject before we quit the great wars of the revolutionary and Napoleonic periods. We have proceeded by elimination of the large and striking topics. We have given as much space as can be given within the confines of this book to the giant subject of civilians' experience under the 'new system of making war' introduced, and in this period practised principally, by France.[63] We have considered in some detail the ways in which Blockade and Devastation were used deliberately to frighten and hurt enemy civilians, and to disadvantage neutrals. And we have marked the peculiar awkwardness of the problems made for the law of war by guerrilla warfare. The relatively little that remains to be said about conventional troops' observance of the law of war in more or less conventional situations may even be diminished in proportion as this is by far the best known part of our story; the marches and battles, the sieges and assaults which are the standard red-blooded stuff of much 'military history' and almost all popular historical writing.

Soldiers, conventional soldiers, kept to the rules and codes of conduct inherited from the eighteenth century, and developed them in the same spirit; adding new battle honours to their regimental roll, new glories to the national record, and so on. The influx of men from broader cross-sections of the national community than had been normal under the *ancien régime* seems to me to have made no significant difference; indeed I reckon that the chances of the law of war's observance were heightened by the intermittent presence within the French armies of representatives of all classes of French society, naturally including some of great moral sensibility and refinement. But I do not wish to seem to be saying that 'ordinary soldiers' would lack such qualities. Military memoirs, journals and folklore (in which the wars of this period are particularly rich) must convince any candid reader that common human kindness and decency were not less to be met with among the professional soldiery than common human brutality and egoism. When soldiers could afford to be indulgent and decent with civilian populations, they perhaps usually were so; the trouble was, that circumstances so rarely allowed them to be so, unless they were to show a quite unreasonable degree of self-mortification. Almost enough has been said about this already. But a bit more must be said about Booty and Pillage, closely-related terms often loosely used to cover more than one thing. Beyond the normal booty which might lawfully, of course, be taken from the persons, baggage, camps and buildings of defeated enemy armies and governments (and which generals and governments were becoming better at preserving from dissipation and turning to their own public advantage), the inherited law of war allowed soldiers a traditional right to look forward to enriching themselves from the spoils of a successfully assaulted city. The booty to be gained therein was successively inducement and reward for undertaking the risks of the assault; it might occasionally come as the fruit of pillage deliberately permitted for a fixed number of hours, as a place's punishment for 'unreasonably prolonged' resistance. Securing booty, amidst the confusions, hazards, and high-wrought excitements usual on such occasions, was almost impossible to distinguish from, and to prevent turning into, inhumane assaults, robberies and rapes, excesses of drunkenness and squabbling. Officers and governments increasingly through the eighteenth and early nineteenth centuries sought to check, and worked towards the ultimate abolition of, this appalling traditional incident of war, which was bad for discipline, wasteful of resources, and provocative of international recriminations. Our later Enlightenment publicists noted that opinion was turning against it. But the ideas of booty (legitimate) and loot (illegitimate) were so twinned and embedded in soldiers' minds and in assault practices alike, that there could as yet be no question of moving towards denying the soldiers' right to booty, on those particular occasions. In the event, the problem more or less evaporated, with the disappearance from war of the formal siege-and-assault which had, time out of mind, been so famous a part of it, with the radical improvement of army supply services, and as soldiers became better paid. This little humanization of warfare through the mid- and later nineteenth century depended more on the cook-house, the paymaster and the railways than on any positive change in military minds.

The 'etiquette' of war remained through these wars very much as it had been for at least a hundred years; governed and enforced quite effectively by those codes of honour and 'manliness' which none could transgress without forfeiting their reputation and standing among their own kind. Such sanctions were stronger, I suppose, at sea than on land. It was less easy to desert, simply to disappear, at sea. Individual seamen could of course desert, as desert they did in droves from some British warships whenever they got the chance; but for the officers charged with the safety of their ships such inconspicuous fading away was no more easy a proposition than making their ships disappear as well. Naval officers formed a very tight-knit fraternity, and, so far as the law of war was concerned, seem to have led, by comparison with their landlubber counterparts, a relatively uncomplicated existence. Knotty questions about searches and seizures of neutral and enemy shipping they could leave over – indeed they *had* to leave over – for decision by Prize Courts; civilians got in their way hardly at all; it was accepted unquestioningly in all navies that proper battle conduct was to fight like blazes until someone surrendered – 'struck his colours' – or went down, after which you turned at once to even self-endangering efforts to rescue survivors. I am driven to conclude that the most complicated and mind-wracking law of war questions that normally came the way of commanders at sea were those to do with *ruses de guerre*. Without doubt, sea fighters went in for these much more than land fighters did, or in the nature of things could. Camouflage and deception played a bigger part in sea war than in land war, and it was proportionately more difficult to distinguish between what were 'fair' and what were dishonourable tricks and dodges. But the captain of the *Sybille*, for example, went classically too far when he flew flags of distress to lure the *Hussar* within range of his broadside. He lost the battle which

ensued and the *Hussar*'s captain stigmatized his conduct as perfidious and dishonourable by publicly breaking his sword.[64] Such
severity was justified. By the complicated conventions of law at
sea, pretence of neutrality was permitted (up to the moment before
action) but pretence of distress was not, on the ground that
humanitarian action absolutely depended on confidence that the
signal of it was genuine.

Another kind of action which, according to the law of war,
doubts and suspicions must never be allowed to prevent, was that
connected with or leading towards humanitarian actions or peace
negotiations. The publicists and their international lawyer successors have insisted that, however intense the temptation to hate
your enemy to the point of non-communication with him, and
despite the delicacy of distinguishing between *ruses de guerre* and
perfidy, some fundamental minimum of mutual confidence must
be retained. Most often in modern war experience this shows itself
in relation to the symbols of the white flag and the Red Cross; if
they cannot be trusted, nothing can. Two 1939–45 instances
illustrate the point: Quaker ambulance men very properly refusing to go on Red-Cross-marked ambulances carrying anything but
wounded men or medical personnel; a German officer not unreasonably ordering the summary execution of FFI men who had
covered their approach to his men with a Red Cross.[65] In the wars
of 1792–1815 the white flag and other conventional indications of
desire to parley were much used and not more complained about,
one might think, than such devices are bound to be when their
normal field of employment tends to be full of smoke, noise, confusion, etc. It was the word of the officer that mattered most.[66]
Allegations about officers breaking their parole were common
enough; but they don't seem nearly as common as cases of paroled
officers who honourably kept their word. The white flag might be
only a preliminary to something that mattered more; an important
statement by an officer upon his honour. The most often mentioned incidents involving such officers' statements seem to be the
occasions when, on 12 November 1805, Lannes or Murat or
General Bertrand assured the Austrians defending the bridge
across the Danube at Vienna that an armistice had been signed and
that they could therefore be allowed to cross it; and when Blücher
and his cavalry escaped from French pursuit in 1806 only in consequence of his affirmation to General Klein that his king had

agreed to Napoleon's armistice terms.[67] In each case there is, naturally, dispute as to what exactly happened and who exactly said what. We need not go into all that. The principle is what matters. If no channel of trustworthy communication remains between combatants and belligerents, no barrier remains between them and (what is proclaimed so much more often than it is really intended) war to the death!

Not much need be said about the law as it related then to those categories of combatants which within the next hundred years came – perhaps rather oddly – to dominate public awareness of it: prisoners, and wounded. They occupy little space in the relevant literature before 1815. Quarter was given in what had become by this date a standard conventional way, and prisoners were marched or transported to safe places of detention. Some might be got rid of *en route*, as a burden and/or an actual danger, as many Russian prisoners were got rid of by the retreating French in 1812.[68] Whether they were decently looked after or not when they got to the place of detention depended on a variety of factors which seems not significantly different from those operating one hundred or even one hundred and forty years later: the adequacy of government preparedness, the qualities of camp commandants (some being sadists, some saints), the behaviour of the prisoners, the extent to which charitable and friendly local civilians were allowed to show an interest, the character of the place itself. Britain's 'hulks' (disused, dismasted, and permanently moored old battleships) had an infamous reputation and were arraigned by the usually judicious Morvan as examples of the oblique nastiness which many French obviously thought typical of the British; 'afraid to tackle the soldiers of the Empire face to face, Britain revenged itself on those French soldiers who fell into its hands, by giving them consumption.'[69] But a little earlier he had said of both sides that, so far as prisoners were concerned, each behaved badly: 'claiming to be models of humanity, they proved to be rivals only in lying and cruelty.' This impartial conclusion finds support in Francis Abell's invaluable book. Both Britain and France (I know not about others) had a good deal to be ashamed of. Exchanges took place, but irregularly and unpredictably. A principal cause of the foundering of some attempts to exchange prisoners certainly appears to have been each side's suspicion that the other would cheat; but another cause was calculation of military advantage. The French, for ex-

ample, insisted that the British ought to count their allies the
Spaniards and Hanoverians as equal with their own men in the
calculation; the British (who had none but Frenchmen in custody)
declined to consider that a released foreign ally would be as valuable to them in what remained of the war, as would be a French-
man returned to Napoleon's service. This insistence on strict reciprocity obviously had much equity on its side but at the same
time – given the disproportion between numbers of prisoners
which alone would cause concern about equity – it was unlikely to
promote humane treatment of the mass thus grudgingly held.
Arguments on this matter continued through the nineteenth century and hardly ceased until the 1907 Hague Regulations assured
minimally humane treatment, about the same time as exchanges
of prisoners had become confined to crippled ones anyway.

Now having entered upon what was to become the basic Red
Cross territory, it is natural to conclude with a glance at the treatment of the wounded. Pierre Boissier concluded that there was in
the revolutionary and Napoleonic wars and their aftermath a
lamentable falling off from the generous humanitarian conventions
observed by the military of the *ancien régime* and smiled on by the
publicists.[70] By the later Enlightenment it was normal, in European continental wars, for 'cartels' or conventions to be signed by
the opposed commanders before battles, establishing the sites of
field hospitals and guaranteeing their security from attack or molestation; in effect, 'neutralizing' them. Moreover it had become conventional to except not merely wounded soldiers but also 'medical
personnel' from liability to capture as prisoners of war. They were
non-combatants, their role was humanitarian; not only was there
no military point in making prisoners of them, there was positively
a point in not doing so. Much of this civility ceased after the
Revolution. Since other of the civilities of the later Enlightenment survived and continued, I cannot offer any other explanation
for this falling off than a combination perhaps of these factors: the
greater rapidity of movement of post-revolutionary armies, the
arousal of national animosities, the rise in the costs of failure, and
some reluctance to trust the other side (which certainly played a
large part in the failure of many prisoner exchange proposals). In
these three aspects, then, the lot of the wounded deteriorated:
medical personnel were at least usually (there may have been particular exceptions) made prisoners of war, so usually were the

wounded, and field hospitals apparently (I have no first-hand knowledge about this, but Boissier was rarely wrong) lost the immunity from gunfire which had conventionally been accorded them. The spirit of the later Enlightenment survived, nevertheless; the falling-off of standards was noticed and deplored by some good medical officers; and a movement for the recovery of the former standards showed itself in most countries after the wars were over. But they had to wait until the middle of the century before they got anywhere.

Chapter III

The Legislative Foundations, 1815–1914: Conscience, Codes and Compromise

I do not love my Empire's foes,
Nor call 'em angels; still,
What is the sense of 'atin' those
'Oom you are paid to kill?
So, barrin' all that foreign lot,
Which only joined for spite,
Myself, I'd just as soon as not
Respect the man I fight.

Rudyard Kipling, 'Piet' (1901)

Instead of calming their conscience with the thought that War is God's judgement and that its origins are divine, nations ought increasingly to realise that War is really the outcome of their own ambitions, passions, and mistakes, their virtues and their crimes.

Feodor de Martens, *La Paix et la Guerre* (1901)

This made th'way clear f'r th'discussion iv th'larger question iv how future wars shud be conducted in th'best inthrests iv peace.

Mr Dooley, on the Hague Peace Conference, cited by McDougal and Feliciano, (1961)

Pale Ebenezer thought it wrong to fight;
But Roaring Bill (who killed him) thought it right.

Hilaire Belloc, 'Epitaph on a Pacifist'

1 The cultural context

Most of this chapter will be an analysis and explanation of the series of legislative landmarks between 1856 and 1909 which have proved so satisfactory or so irremovable as to dominate and condition the development of our subject ever since. Within the second half of the nineteenth century, the conventional (i.e. formally embodied in conventions and treaties) foundations of all subsequent law of war were laid, and the case law in the books at last became predominantly modern. No more was heard of Alexander, Scipio, Cicero and Caesar, and not much of such as the Chevalier Bayard and Gustavus Adolphus either. This decisive transposition into the modern and contemporary mode was part and parcel of international law's 'positive' swing and to some extent indicated a rejection of the idea that anything helpful and 'relevant' might be learnt from the past. The accompanying neglect of classical and medieval natural law may well be reckoned rather tragic. On the other hand, the present was taken very seriously. The law of war now entered its epoch of highest repute. Between 1870 and 1914, one may safely say, it was more enthusiastically studied and widely talked about than ever before or – except perhaps for the past ten years – since. It appeared as part of the mosaic of modern civilization, even as, for many people, war did. Not surprising, therefore, that its intensive development during these years impressed upon it something of that civilization's motley appearance and psychological confusion.

The European law of war, it may once again be remarked, had its origins in a religious-based philosophy which exalted peace as the highest and most 'natural' condition of humankind and reluctantly accepted war as no more than an occasional, unwelcome and discreditable incident of mortal frailty and wickedness. This weighting of the preference in favour of peace remained firmly characteristic of it through the eighteenth century, by when the theorists about the natures and inter-relations of States and nations had made the phenomenon of war more officially welcome among themselves than it had been earlier on. But still it was of temporary, transient and limited wars that they were thinking: wars to ease the passage from one state of peace to another, wars intervening only intermittently and partially in the real business of mankind, its mainly peaceful progress and improvement. The law of war was conceived therefore as an instrument of peace, and its principal claim on the attention of men was supposed to rest in their preference for that state of public affairs, that image of their preferred state of mind.

Matters came to seem less simple through the nineteenth century, and the purpose of the law of war became liable to less unambiguous presentation. In this transformation it followed the war phenomenon itself. Peace obviously remained the ideal state of affairs for many, but war became attractive for many too, and by the second half of the century there were schools of thought a-plenty to present war not only as the more natural but also (which need not have been exactly the same thing) the more healthy condition for mankind. The war-mania – for such it seems to me to have been – of the later nineteenth and early twentieth centuries clamours for much more study than it has yet received. Perhaps it has not yet received it because the fact of the mania can be no more than imperfectly visible to those who still, at least partly, suffer from it, just as it may be semi-concealed from the clearer-headed by the absence, in fact, of many great wars on the European continent between 1871 and 1914. The lack of actual war-experience through those years may have contributed to the vogue for vicarious war thought and war play. Anxious analysis of this had begun well before the 1914–18 war – indeed, external criticism of it had been available since the early nineteenth-century beginnings of 'the peace movement' – and the experiences of the war itself thickened them a thousand-fold. Good books about the attractions and compulsions of war in the modern world, and specifically through the history of its last hundred years, are not now difficult to come by. Yet one might expect them to be more plentiful. After all, their object of study is the formation of that part of the mind of modern (European) man which has enabled the international wars of the twentieth century to occur. In another book, I may attempt to remedy part of this lack. Here, I dare do no more than is minimally necessary to fill in the cultural context of the legislative foundations of our modern law of war, and thus to make it intelligible.

To say that nineteenth century thought about Peace and War splits nicely into two branches, is only too simple to the extent that there was a great deal of overlap and confusion between them. This characterized the minds of individuals as well as the inclinations of groups; giving to each on occasion the appearance, at least of inconsistency and perhaps even of schizophrenia or dementia, if those be apt words to describe the conditions of people who want now one thing, now another, or do not know what they really want at all. This overlapping and confusion are of great significance to our story, and we shall recur to them later. Meanwhile, it will be helpful to distinguish the two strong tendencies and movements of thought which can be seen marching through the nineteenth century towards the twentieth, and competing, so to speak, for the minds of men; the one of them advancing as best it could the cause of Peace, and the other – exactly parallel and equivalent, though constituted completely differently – advancing not less perceptibly the cause of War. We will call them the Peace Movement and the War Movement respectively.

The Peace Movement called and recognized itself as such. It was very natural that it should be the more concentrated and recognizable of the two, since for most of the time – in its formative years before the eighteen-thirties, and again from about the eighteen-seventies onwards–it was swimming against the tide, and membership in it required particular conviction. Quakers, Mennonites and other radical Protestant denominations especially typified it for most contemporaries; indeed, those who were concerned to combat the conventional cult and acceptance of war on religious grounds were all the time at its heart. But it was not only thorough pacifists, or religious persons merely, who belonged to the many varieties of 'peace societies' from the eighteen-thirties, thronged their meetings, read the 'peace classics', and sent delegates to the Peace Congresses which were among the most spectacular international events of the mid-century. The inclination towards peace rather than war which wholly or partly possessed so many nineteenth-century minds had a much broader base in the economic development which was, for so many countries, the most exhilarating experience or prospect of the age. The ideology of free enterprise capitalism exalted commercial and industrial progress as *ipso facto* making for Peace rather than War. The more material achievements men stood to sacrifice in the destructiveness and waste of war, the closer their international ties to one another became through trade, investment, and the division of labour, the more must they perceive the superior desirability of peaceful relations and non-violent resolution of disputes. Commercial competition even became for some theorists of this cult a non-violent surrogate for armed conflict: 'The Moral Equivalent of War', was how the most famous of them, William James, expressed it (– only three years after his compatriot Brooks Adams had maintained precisely the opposite: 'War as the ultimate form of economic competition'!).[1] Within countries, the excitements and challenges of competitiveness could be presented as diverting what we would now frankly call 'aggression' into socially beneficial channels, at the same time as they enriched not only that particular country but also the general riches of mankind. Those general riches were of course seen to be most directly diffused by the increase of commercial intercourse between countries, which was believed sooner or later to benefit *all* participants and persuasively to spread the news from pole to pole. At the end of this road of thought lay the total Free Trade position. Great Britain, the only complete subscriber to this, remained faithful to it from mid-century onwards; not least because it suited her commercial interests to do so. For some British Free Traders, Peace and Free Trade seemed mutually necessary conditions, the one promoting the other and the two together offering mankind at last the age of gold. Protectionists, in a minority in Britain (indeed, almost extinct for a few decades), were generally in the ascendant in other countries; but wherever international trade was happening on anything like equal terms, voices were heard to commend it as making for Peace rather than War, and as indicating the better shape of things to come. The United States was quite aggressively protectionist at the turn of the twentieth century, but it was the senior United States delegate to the 1907 Hague Peace Conference, Mr Choate, who proclaimed commerce to be 'the nurse of peace and international amity', and, describing 'the growth and development of international trade and commerce during the last fifty years' as 'one of the marvels of history', asserted that 'It tends more than anything else to bind the nations together in the bonds of peace, and creates a community of interest which is immediately disturbed by any violent interference with it in any part of the globe.'[2] For those who thought and felt like this, belief in the pacific virtues of international trade had a quasi-religious quality, and provided a common ground on which met many Britons, a good many Americans, and substantial sprinklings from countries with more or less advanced economies. The patronage and leadership of great captains of industry brought the movement both dignity and dollars, its sublime apogee coming around the time of the establishment of Nobel's Peace Prize in 1897 and Carnegie's Endowment for International Peace in 1910, its rather ridiculous swan-song in Henry Ford's 'peace ship' venture in the winter of 1915–16.[3]

Embracing basically the same belief in the pacific virtues of commerce but ranging far beyond it in political thought and innovation was that non-identical twin of the Peace Movement which is best described simply as 'Internationalism'. With intellectual and moral roots going back almost time out of mind, the internationalist way of looking at things and trying to do them perceptibly strengthened through the nineteenth century, and in its achievements offered proof that the nations and peoples of the world were becoming more cooperative with one another. This movement included every kind of informal organization and arrangement, formal institution, agreement and treaty which could promise to bring different nations, and people within different nations, together more easily, and to promote whatever interests they might have in common; peace, not least, and the peaceful resolution of international disputes. The Carnegie Endowment from the start was peculiarly devoted to such good works. It published most handsomely the proceedings of the 1899 Hague Conference 'to seek the most effective means of ensuring to the peoples a lasting peace, and of limiting the progressive development of military armaments';[4] the bigger 1907 one 'for the purpose of giving a fresh development to the humanitarian principles' which underlay its precursor's work; and the related conferences which established the Permanent Court of Arbitration in 1899, and laid groundwork for the Permanent Court of International Justice twenty-one years later. These achievements of the early twentieth century (which many believed to lack their keystone until 1919 brought a League of Nations as well) came after a hundred years of internationalist endeavours of all kinds and at all levels: for example, the opening and (so far at least as riparians were concerned) internationalization of the Rhine and Danube rivers; dozens of international arbitrations, in consenting early to which the United States set a noble example, and whose most famous one before 1900, the 'Alabama' arbitration between the United States and Britain, took place in the same great room where only a few years before the first Geneva Convention had been framed; 'multipartite conventions' for the better administration of the common business and concerns of nations – mail, telegraphs, telephones, public health, railway freights . . . ; religious denominational gatherings, at the head of which stood the first Vatican Council of 1870 and the Pan-Anglican Congresses; the politically liberal Inter-Parliamentary Union, the socialist and perhaps revolutionary Workingmen's Internationals; professional and academic bodies like the Institute of International Law, founded in 1873[5] and conferences of the members of such; voluntarist philanthropic associations like the YMCA and the Red Cross; and most prominent of all, those great international expositions which every proud and ambitious country felt it necessary to mount after 1851.

Internationalists hold it as a matter of faith that contacts between people of different countries and cultures increase their mutual liking and understanding. Whether all these new-style international occasions really made peace and collaboration more likely than not is a question which may be debated to the end of time. They could equally serve as demonstrations of incompatibilities; as did – many commented upon it – the juxtaposition, at the 1867 Paris Exposition, of the displays of the 'Sociétés de Secours', forerunners of the National Red Cross Societies, and the latest products of the firm of Krupp. The minds of many avowed internationalists were pulled in contrary directions as well. Those who were not pacifists had to be ready for the worst. But for all that, the inclination or even yearning towards international harmony and co-operation was remarkably strong and resourceful.

Such, then, was what may fairly be called 'the peace movement' through the nineteenth century: a dedicated, organized, explicit Peace Movement at its core, proclaiming the excellence of peace and actively promoting its achievement; an inter-locking Internationalist movement, inventive and optimistic, busy in knitting nations together in all kinds of ways which promised to advance their common interests and welfare peacefully; supporting both, more unquestioningly in some countries than in others, the liberal ideology of economic development and social improvement; and wrapping round the whole, to some extent everywhere, a pervasive sentiment of or disposition towards 'humanitarianism', as if the more economically advanced and politically self-confident countries were more morally advanced as well, and could now afford what was in any case their duty, a gentler approach to social relations. So substantial was the sum of all this, that the completeness of its collapse before the challenge of its opposite in the early twentieth century gives one a startling measure of the greater power of the latter; to which we must now turn.

Arrayed against the peace-promoting tendencies just sketched were others equally clear and pronounced which may fairly be called 'the War Movement'. It was not thus explicitly known and talked about by contemporaries, to the best of my knowledge, and my use of the term no doubt requires a few words of justification. I am simply applying to the period 1815–1914 the same method of analysis that might be applied to any other historical patch of human society. A modest acquaintance with the social sciences relevant to 'conflict' and 'violence' confirms my belief that, just as the mind of man may be understood for practical purposes as being subject to pushes and pulls in opposite directions at once – e.g. towards social harmony and comradeliness and 'peace' on the one side, and towards competitiveness, quarrelsomeness, and in the end, 'war' on the other – so also, though in more complicated and usually more roundabout ways, may political societies in their relations with one another be understood as experiencing simultaneous contrary inclinations, some towards peaceful relations with their neighbours, and others towards unpeaceful ones. Even more than in the case of individuals, circumstances (economic, political, etc.) bear powerfully upon the nature of decisions made on particular occasions for the one or the other, and no sound historical analysis could dare to leave them out. Nevertheless, the texture and content of mind remains all-important. Those circumstances impinge upon decision-making only through the perceptions made of them. 'War' or 'peace', harmony or conflict, are cultural choices as well as material ones. Even after allowing for all the complications obviously involved in unravelling webs of causation in particular cases, it may still be expected that the relative strengths of inclinations towards 'peace' or 'war' will be found to vary from time to time, from country to country. Returning abruptly to our matter at hand, I venture the suggestion that in pre-1914 European and North American society there flowed strong inclinations and pressures in *both* directions; perhaps to an historically unusual degree.

The most salient fact about this war movement, from our point of view, is that it blossomed and burgeoned in historically unprecedented ways from the eighteen-fifties on. Not that it was weak or unresourceful before then! To the armoury of justifications and motivations for war inherited from earlier times, the Revolutionary epoch had added at least three: nationalism, a protean doctrine but in any of its varieties capable of turning warlike; the Hegelian theory of world-history and the role in it of successfully aggressive

States (caviar for the general, but intoxicating for many of the more philosophically-minded); and, purely and simply, Napoleon, whose multiform cult no doubt had much to do with the nineteenth century's relish for thoughts and things of war. There were already available then, through the first half of the century, stronger inclinations towards war than there had been in the Enlightenment, and, in the combined contexts of nationalism and Napoleonism, a belligerent popular literature and national folklore of, apparently, a totally new kind.

But these early nineteenth-century years were years also of that peace movement, making counter-calls on the interest of thinking men and flourishing exceedingly in the forties and fifties. Its very success in those mid-century years appears to have been one reason why the men of the war movement, gravely threatened, mounted an increasingly irresistible counter-attack through the following decades. But they did so also because a number of new weapons came into their hands. The second half of the nineteenth century and the early years of the twentieth produced a number of new ideas and institutions capable of raising to hitherto unexperienced heights the apparent desire for war. I use the word 'capable' advisedly, because it may be that these ideas did not lead in the war direction only. Darwinism, for a start, is a case in point. It had a 'peaceful' potential, as Kropotkin for one clearly apprehended. But the Kropotkins were the minority. It was the imperialists, the nationalists, the militarists, who appropriated (and in so doing adulterated) Darwinism, turning it to their competitive and aggressive purposes as if those alone were proper to it. Hegelian doctrine of the State, often keeping Darwinism company, through the same congenial years developed into simpler, vulgarized versions of political thought exalting the sovereignty of the State, freeing its nature and will from appraisal by all normal moral criteria, and positing an international society much more like the jungle of heated quasi-darwinist imagination ('nature red in tooth and claw', and all that) than the polite club of mutually respectful gentlemen desiderated by our publicists. To this might be added, from the seventies onwards, a torrential new movement of thought designed precisely to reject and destroy the rational bases and heart of the publicist's philosophy: 'antirationalism', the cult and exaltation of feeling, instincts and passions expressed in one form supremely by Nietzsche, in others by Barrès, the later Tolstoy, Georges Sorel,

D'Annunzio. . . . Men moving down that stream might pick up neo-darwinism, they might not; their influence would be the same in either case, and whether they expressly intended it or not – tending towards War, rather than Peace, and towards Death, excitingly, rather than calm and (to their minds) dull longevity in Life.

Common to many who clearly belonged to the war movement during the two generations preceding 1914 was the critique or rejection of 'materialism'. This was a ground on which many usually disparate interests could meet; aesthetes, intellectuals, the military, the religious. . . . The 'bourgeoisie', which was both producer of the relative prosperity and social security of the later nineteenth century, and product of it, was not objectively as peace-promoting a class as most men of the peace movement liked to make it seem. Radical and socialist (*a fortiori*, marxist) critics had never been taken in by this, and even if there seemed to be much superficial evidence for it in the immediate experience of Europe and (*a fortiori*) North America, the continuing tale of the richer countries' imperial and colonial acquisitions and rivalries told another tale. But, one must acknowledge, 'bourgeois civilization' undoubtedly cultivated a public air of placidity, legality, predictability (of necessity!) and an all-embracing respect for the possessions and satisfactions of this world which sensitive and eager spirits found irritating and challenging. Not surprising, therefore, that outspoken criticism of this 'materialism' was a common feature of the war movement wherever it appeared. The need to get people generally into a fighting mood was crucially important to it. ('What if we were to have a war and nobody came?') Recalling a 'humorous incident' from the 1907 Hague Peace Conference, the American jurist James Brown Scott says the Chinese military delegate elicited 'a hearty laugh' from the others when he asked, 'what should happen when one nation declared war against another if the latter did not wish to fight?'[6] More congenial to their minds were the values of the recent vanquishers of China, Japan. The sudden 'arrival', so to speak, of Japan among the States that really mattered, placed useful new cards about this time in the men of war's hands, for here appeared to be a country of pristine virtues, not yet corrupted by 'materialism', where the grand old aristocratic-military codes of patriotism, sacrifice, and 'Death Rather than Dishonour' were revered and, as Japan's two short sharp wars of imperial expansion conveniently showed, religiously practised. New World and Old World alike were given stimulating shots in the arm by this resurrection of a world still older.

To these cultural innovations between about 1860 and 1914 must be added, among the explanations of the swelling strength of the war movement at the expense of its opposite, mention of a technical innovation, the effect of which was to spread and strengthen the dominant beliefs of society with historically unprecedented vigour : the cheap and popular daily press. There had not been much of the kind, except in the United States, before the mid-century. Popular journalism, in whatever modes it operated, was rarely of the daily newspaper sort, primarily because the means did not exist to print and circulate it at a price that could be popularly afforded. From about the sixties on, however, newspapers of this cheap variety became increasingly practical, at the same time as (from the same causes) higher-class newspapers grew fatter and juicier. The existence of so powerful a new means of influencing and/or voicing (there was and there continues to be much argument as to how exactly it worked) the views of the populace ensured that the stronger currents of popular belief and desire, whatever they were, would be magnified and their political representation enhanced. The character of much of this journalism, at every social level, was notoriously sensational, xenophobic, inflammatory and nationalistic. The wise Westlake perceived what consequences this would have upon the humanitarianism which was also part of the popular mind of the period. 'The pity which is effectual to work great changes', he wrote, 'is that which, in running at once through millions of men, is intensified by the enthusiasm which masses engender. But pity for suffering in war is liable in democratic times to encounter other feelings of equal extent and opposite tendency, the consciousness that the war in which the nation is engaged has been willed by it, and the national determination to triumph at any cost.'[7] 'Equal and opposite' is a more optimistic estimate than historians generally have made, the new medium of mass communication being considered to have worked more to encourage thoughts of war than of peace.

We may now sum up this sketch of the cultural context in which the historic movement to humanize warfare achieved its greatest single steps forward : the foundation of the international Red Cross, and the codification of the international law of war.

Ideas of Peace and War were both strongly present in many people's minds; often simultaneously. It is as if people then thought they could have both, or the best of both, at once. Perhaps this is a common condition of mankind. If so, the situation in the period 1870–1914 would be singular only insofar as enthusiasms for 'peace' or 'war' were peculiarly passionate then, or because such enthusiasms then took peculiar forms. My own impression (it can be no more) is that those enthusiasms were more keenly alive then in western and central Europe than ever before or there-after, except for the inter-war period, during which they took similar forms (war enthusiasms continuing in much the same vein, peace ones clustering round the culmination of the previous period's efforts, the League of Nations). The endeavour to human-ize warfare was both helped and hampered by this climate of ex-citement and confusion. The peace movement was far too strong not to make its mark in national politics and international affairs. Three instances from British diplomatic correspondence will illus-trate how statesmen and politicians came to weigh the con-sequences of their expressed attitudes to it. As far back as 1856, during the run-up to the first 'statutory' measure, the Declaration of Paris, Lord Clarendon was pointing out that Britain might reap moral advantages as well as (what interested him more) strategic ones: 'It is far better to do the thing *grandement* and to pay hom-mage [sic] to the civilization of the age.'[8] Thirty years later the British Foreign Secretary received similar advice about the forth-coming Berlin Conference on West Africa: 'This country is not likely to gain or lose anything by the Conference [but] it has oc-curred to me that Great Britain might carry off all the honours of the meeting by being the State to propose (on so fitting an oc-casion) an International Declaration in relation to the traffic in slaves . . .'[9] Fifteen years later, the war minister was writing to the British military delegate to the Hague Conference: 'You have a very difficult hand to play. It is clear that the conference has availed itself with avidity of the opportunity of at once achieving something in the interests of humanity and gibbeting us as *the* inhuman power of the age . . .'[10]

Everything that I have read of French and German diplomatic correspondence about the Hague conferences, and all that I gather therefrom about Russian attitudes, persuades me that the states-men of those countries were conscious of the same need to appear to satisfy the expectations and longings of the peace movement, while sacrificing none of the essential demands of the movement for war. Even if the great powers were not able or willing to do anything concretely to reduce the chances of armed conflict, their rulers felt it desirable to pretend otherwise. Heights of theatricality are scaled in the correspondence between the American managers at the 1899 conference and their German counterparts, apropos of the arbitration proposals, about which the Kaiser proved peculiarly sticky. 'The greatest thing', wrote Andrew D. White to von Bülow, 'is that there be a provision made for easily calling together a Court of Arbitration which shall be seen by all nations, indicate a sincere desire to promote peace, and, in some measure, relieve the various peoples of the fear which so heavily oppresses all, the dread of a sudden outburst of war at any moment.'[11] This need not *mean* anything, explained his German-born colleague Holls a few days later. He explained that the American delegation felt obliged to secure 'the establishment of an institution the very existence of which shall count as a most solemn declaration and demonstration in the right direction. At the same time the purely voluntary character of the jurisdiction proposed [the international court of arbitration] should be so clearly emphasized that the very last trace of any compulsion, moral or otherwise, upon any nation, be it great or small, should disappear.'[12]

That Hague Conference, and the second one in 1907, were viewed by the faithful of the peace movement very much as the statesmen managing it hoped it would be viewed; as marking certain steps, small perhaps but concrete, in the institutionalization of internationalism and the propaganda of peace. The conferences attracted an enormous amount of attention, and their full history has still to be written. Exactly how the peace people appraised it, I should very much like to know. Perhaps for many of them these Conferences cast a glow of glory, not dispelled until 1914. Perhaps others were more quickly disillusioned. Observers who had never experienced any marked hopes or illusions about the Conferences' prospects of bringing the Peace and (to begin with) Disarmament they promised commented on their curiously mixed and ambivalent character; conferences supposedly about peace, but much more obviously concerned with war. Mr Dooley's refreshing scepticism has already been cited among the epigraphs to this chapter. A historian of the law of war may allow that there is much truth in what he says, adding however a rider to the effect that on this occasion Mr Dooley is not quite as smart as usual; 'to conduct war in the best interest of peace' being precisely, however paradoxically, what the law of war seeks to do. The most profound evaluation of the Hague Conferences known to me was written by one who was a complete outsider to them, Josef Conrad. Acutely describing 'The Hague Tribunal' as a 'solemnly official recognition of the Earth as a House of Strife', he went on to glance at the psychological roots of the preoccupation with war and came to this ironic conclusion:

> Never before has war received so much homage at the lips of men, and reigned with less disputed sway in their minds. . . . It has perverted the intelligence of men, women and children, and has made the speeches of Emperors, Kings, Presidents and Ministers monotonous with ardent protestations of fidelity to peace. Indeed, war has made peace altogether in its own image: a martial, over-bearing, war-lord sort of peace, . . . eloquent with allusions to glorious feats of arms. . . .[13]

Let a Japanese diplomat, about 1898–9, sum up from a different standpoint this same startling paradox: 'We show ourselves at least your equals in scientific butchery, and at once we are admitted to your council tables as civilized men.'[14]

The impression that our theme in this period experienced a rather remarkable confusion of goals and values is confirmed by two of its other developments which may conveniently if clumsily be described as the militarization of humanitarianism, and the dehumanization of the military. By the former, I mean the way in which the national Red Cross societies (which by the end of the seventies were to be found all over Europe, and by the end of the century all over the *soi-disant* civilized world) acquired much more the tone of the war movement than the peace one. They became, what they had not been absolutely predestined to become, wedded to their countries' war machines and highly valued parts of them. That is not to say that they did not maintain faithfully the founding principles of the movement. They doubtless intended to deal with enemy sick and wounded as carefully as their own. The ideal which led some of them to dedicated service and heroic deeds was at least partly transnational, transcendent. Yet it is difficult to believe that their efficient and in many cases total integration within their respective countries' war machines was quite what Henry Dunant and his co-founders of the movement had expected or desired.

For sure, Dunant in 1863-4, the critical foundation years, took it for granted (as everyone else seems to have done) that this new form of charity had best begin at home, and that the most obvious and direct supply of sufferers needing humanitarian help would come from one's own army. All this was perfectly clear in the resolutions of the inaugural conference of October 1863. Dunant and his fellow-philanthropists, moreover, can never have doubted that so bold a project could only be 'sold' to the governments of Europe if their military advisers pronounced it safe and worthwhile. But if attachment to armies was necessarily part of the Red Cross programme, the Red Cross idea was not thus tied. In any case, military thought and action in the eighteen-sixties weighed less in the esteem and experience of society than they were to do by the nineties. The war movement, as we have defined it, was only just beginning; the peace movement still felt full of power. The Red Cross movement initially aimed straight between them. Its philosophy in its early years was expressed in its ingenious principle of 'neutralizing' all who looked after the wounded; removing that category entirely from the risks of war (see below, page 150). But the 1906 Geneva Convention, as we shall see, abandoned that notion at the behest of the military, who found it unsettling and difficult; and the Red Cross movement conformed to their specifications. That extraordinary 'neutral' status disappeared in the 1906 revised version of the Convention, and the whole military and ambulance business was brought under strict military control. While remaining a great means by which self-sacrificing and humane persons (especially, of course, females) could devote their services to the relief of a conspicuous class of sufferers from war, the Red Cross movement through its national societies became also, very soon after 1870 where it was not so already, a means by which those unable, through age, station or sex, to serve their countries directly by fighting for them, could serve almost as directly by caring for their fighters.[15] Their organization and equipment paralleled and complemented that of their armed forces; in the top tiers of their quasi-military hierarchies regularly stood representatives of the royal families and related aristocracies (or equivalent republican top people). The equipment of which they were most proud, if their magazines and publicity material are anything to go by, were field hospitals and ambulance trains. No wonder, then, that when the Japanese, eager to gain acceptance among the world's greater powers and almost over-anxious to do everything right, set up their national Red Cross society in the late eighties, it quickly grew (in the encouraging atmosphere of the 1894–5 war with China) to an astounding nominal membership of 900,000 (clearly bespeaking moral if not legal compulsion), and advanced from being merely 'a private undertaking of associated philanthropists' to become 'a public organ, recognized by law and holding a definite position within the military organization of the realm', with the wives and daughters of military governors and generals regularly at the head of its ladies' division.[16] Yet this ingenuous literalness in emulating the best Western examples seems not to have damaged the quality of the service. Humanitarianism may thus have been to some extent militarized, but as humanitarianism it was tough enough to survive. The super-patriotic Japanese Red Cross, from whatever motives, did its impartial duties scrupulously; in its war with Russia in 1904–5, Japan more thoroughly observed the law of war than did its semi-Western enemy.[17]

Parallel with that militarization of the humanitarians (such as it was), appeared also in these late nineteenth-century years something it is not inappropriate to call a dehumanization of the military; an unpleasant expression, which must at once be explained. I do not mean, and in any case am in no position to make a judgement, that soldiers and sailors became nastier than they had been before or that nastier people than before became soldiers and sailors. I mean that the language used by military men explaining and justifying their avocation acquired a new toughness, a novel relish for what they liked to present as the realities of war that went well beyond what was usual for their predecessors. Why this tough and bloody tone should have come into war talk and literature is not difficult to understand. In large part, it was the natural consequence of all those new war-encouraging mental and moral influences I have already mentioned. When politicians, preachers and pedagogues were likely to be absorbing into their thoughts a newly conflictual, pain-accepting, death-daring vision of the world, how should the minds of the military not be similarly affected?

But in part this new toughness was simply a reaction to the humanitarianism of the peace movement. The military seem to have felt themselves part-threatened by it, part-affronted: threatened, inasmuch as the peace movement had much explicit anti-militarism in it and increasingly brought into ridicule, contempt and criticism, values and practices which to the military had the inviolability of the sacred; affronted, in so far as the peace movement included enthusiasts and utopians whose vision of the possibilities of human nature and social relations could be criticized for being as innocent and naive in its own extreme way as its opposite, war-lover's view, was open to criticism for being unnecessarily savage and cynical.

It was not unreasonable to believe – as even the most pious and personally kindly military men might in those years believe – that neither the world nor war were as some of the peace people conceived them. Pure pacifists might be ignored, unless they meddled with conscription; international socialists needed to be watched by the police; but prestigious international lawyers, who tended to bring the humanitarian matter most closely home to the military, were a different matter. This new profession, self-confident and well-organized by the end of the seventies, presumed not only to offer advice to the military but also to advise government on how to control the military. It evidently gave the generals much cause for concern.[18] Not all international lawyers, one must hasten to add; plenty of them were as nationalistic and military-minded as any general could wish. But there were differences of opinion among them, even more than there had been among the publicists, and some of them presumed more than others. Of these, in the crucial decade of the seventies, the Swiss-born, Heidelberg-based Bluntschli was the foremost. It is therefore fitting that he should have been the object of the later nineteenth-century military's two most heavy-weight rebukes. One of these is quite well known. It was politely administered by the most famous soldier of the age, Field-Marshal von Moltke, in an open letter dated 11 December 1880.[19] The occasion was Bluntschli's sending him, for his comments, the model code of war law produced that year by the Institute of International Law.[20] Moltke did not think much of it. He was far too cultivated and sensitive a man to meet Bluntschli's well-meant efforts with vulgar or brutal war-talk, but all the same he thought Bluntschli and his friends misguided (though not as misguided as were pacifists). 'Before all else,' he wrote, 'I entirely appreciate the philanthropic efforts being made to alleviate the evils of war. [But] perpetual peace is a dream, and not even a beautiful dream. War is an element of the divine order of the world. In it are developed the noblest virtues of man : courage and self-denial, fidelity to duty and the spirit of sacrifice; soldiers give their lives. Without war, the world would stagnate and lose itself in materialism.' The ability of codes of law to control what happened in war was very limited; there was no sovereign to enforce it, and war itself was such an unpredictable and imperative phenomenon, the object of which could by no means be restricted (as maintained the model manual) to the reduction of the armed forces of the enemy. 'No, beyond that one must attack all the resources of the enemy government, his finances, his railroads, his supplies, and even his prestige.' The more detailed a code of war law might become, the more often would force of particular circumstances be likely to compel its violation. Only statements of general principle were of much use, and those only to commanders. In the longer run, nothing except the rise of the moral sensibilities of societies at large could much change men's approach to war and their conduct of it; and even that would have to accept the limitations imposed by 'the abnormal circumstances of war'.

The other grand rebuke I have in mind is that addressed, only less directly than Moltke's, to Bluntschli by the Hanover-born Prussian general Julius von Hartmann.[21] In the autumn and winter of 1877–8 he published three solid articles on 'Military Necessity and Humanity/Humanitarianism (*Humanität*) : a Critical Inquiry' which went over the whole ground as it appeared to an avowed disciple of Clausewitz (later nineteenth-century German style), and showed to general military satisfaction that what we may call the Bluntschli school of international law was asking for the moon. This monograph, at once separately published, quickly became celebrated, and was repeatedly referred to by participants in the law of war debate through the next thirty years, as if it were a statement of official military doctrine – which it may well literally have been, if, as is credibly alleged, Hartmann had been asked by some higher authority to write it.[22] It seems to me to be a peculiarly revealing text, the exegesis of which by a Clausewitzian scholar could be particular rewarding, as revealing the points at which its pompous mysticism about war and human nature in war, and its no doubt unconscious departures from Clausewitz's clearest dicta about the priority of political purpose, had led Hartmann and his whole tribe into heresy. But throughout the whole of it ran, in elaborate variations, this single and not un-Clausewitzian leitmotif; that war was a phenomenon which, far from being within the power of well-meaning men and publicists to set limits and controls upon it, must burst all moral and legal boundaries and impose upon its devotees its own rules and necessities. And among these, insisted Hartmann, not without professional relish, was the necessity of forgetting about humanitarianism when it was a question of winning or losing a battle or a war. Short wars, he said – it was a common refrain in those years – were the most humane; whatever apparent severity finished a war quickly might in the long run appear to be the superior humanity.[23] So, again conforming to a contemporary pattern which he, I believe, did much to refine, he turned the tables on the humanitarians by arraigning them as perhaps the less humane in the long run.

It was a dangerous argument, and one may think that it had dreadful consequences; but its vogue in these years was significant of the way the thought of the orthodox military was going.[24] If my examples are all German ones, that is not to be taken to mean that only German military thought went this way. It was an international movement. But it is to my mind hardly contestable that Germans led it. Scarcely less celebrated than Hartmann's book was the semi-official handbook produced for the German officer corps by the historical section of its 'Great General Staff' in 1902 : *'Kriegsbrauch im Landkriege / The Usages of Land Warfare'*.[25] Its avowed purpose was to counteract the effects of what the author (one might think, mistakenly) took to be the major intellectual tendency of the age : concern 'for human considerations which not infrequently degenerates into sentimentality and flabby emotion'. 'In war', wrote one of Germany's most respected international lawyers in the early nineteen-twenties, 'everyone is a sacrificial lamb. The humane thing is, in a higher sense, often the most inhumane.'[26] 'In war', the Belgians were advised by their new German masters in 1914, 'the innocent suffer for the guilty.'[27] I believe one may see neatly concentrated instances of the results of this deliberate cult of harshness in the legally disputable and politically counter-productive executions of Nurse Edith Cavell and Captain Edward Fryatt in 1915 and 1916 and in the arguments used to justify them.[28] Such argumentation attained rare heights of cloudy confusion when the Leipzig 'war crimes court', on 30 May 1921, gave its judgement as to whether Reserve Captain Emil Müller had been cruel to the prisoners in the camp of which he had been the commandant.

> His excesses [such were not disputed, even by that court] were only due to that military enthusiasm which worked him up to an exaggerated conception of military necessity and discipline. ... He showed himself severe and lacking in consideration but not deliberately cruel. His acts originated, not in any pleasure in persecution, or even in any want of feeling for the sufferings of the prisoners; but in a conscious disregard of the general laws of humanity [sic].[29]

2 The protection of combatants

This was the area of the law of war in which developments most obviously happened during the fifty great formative years 1860–1910. Humanitarians who worried more about civilians – and there were some who did – found that there was a larger sympathetic response to the wartime sufferings of combatants; which was not surprising, in a Europe where universal conscription for military service became the rule for all European great powers but one, and national resistance to hostile invasion the realistic expectation of all the lesser ones. In promoting and applauding developments of that part of the law which protected combatants, the manhood of the 'civilized countries' was in a strikingly real sense attending to its own interests, and the womanhood was looking after its menfolk's. But there was another reason for the predominance of the interests of the military. The law of war could not be developed at all without the assent of the generals and the admirals, and these were years (as I have already sought to state) when their power and influence were very great. Civil-military relations are a fascinating and complicated study. Not only must they vary from time to time and country to country. Also variable are the effective contents of the terms 'civil' and 'military' themselves; the apparently 'civil' (in the sense that the people composing it are not professional military men) being sometimes capable of most ferocious and belligerent sentiments, the undoubted 'military' sometimes being barely distinguishable from the ranks of professional men in general.[30] Within this general relationship will come the particular branch of civil-military relations about which I should like to know most, the extent to which governments (in which 'civilian' opinion may or may not have dominated) took, or did not take, the advice of the military about entering upon international legal undertakings respecting the planning and conduct of war. It is at least clear that governments never lightly reject the advice of their chosen military leaders (or the military leaders whom they have no choice but to accept). It is therefore understandable enough that, during these years of super-heated nationalism and militarist enthusiasm, those parts of the law of war which were most congenial to the military mind should have been the ones to flourish in the public arena, while those parts most troubling to it (the parts dealing with civilians) should have figured less prominently; and it is not unintelligible that 'civilian' enthusiasm should have given itself so largely to the soldiers' cause.

What is perhaps more curious is the vastness of the military field that invited philanthropic and humanitarian attention. Soldiers – the rank and file of them – appeared to be a category of the poor much neglected and often disregarded by their employers. They therefore became regular objects of philanthropic concern. Societies were founded in, to the best of my knowledge, all countries where voluntary charitable associations had any place in public life, to assist in one way or another the religious, educational and welfare interests of the rank and file. Already begun in a small way in the eighteenth century, this had been given a fillip by the patriotic enthusiasm of the French wars, and had gone on during the relatively peaceful years which followed. Who made the first humanitarian steps towards the battlefield, I do not know. Florence Nightingale, I suspect, was not quite the first. But that well-publicized lady, and all the other French and British women who were with her on the skirts of the Crimean campaign, undoubtedly had something to do with making the eighteen-fifties a pivotal decade in the history of international humanitarian law. They called the attention of the philanthropic public at large to a topic which seems thitherto not to have been much known or cared about outside an intra-professional circle of unusually humane army and navy medical officers and a few unusual civilian doctors : the scandalously inadequate arrangements made by armies for looking after their wounded and sick. The ladies with their lamps in the hospitals well behind the Crimean battle-front showed one way forward; the Genevan businessman philanthropist Henri Dunant only a few years later was led to point out another, by his experiences directly behind the north Italian battle-front; to be precise, just after the battle of Solferino, 24 June 1859.

The idea embodied in Miss Nightingale's work was that medical and nursing volunteers should improve the conditions and prospects of recovery of sick and wounded soldiers once they had got back to the hospital. The peculiar idea elaborated by Dunant and his Swiss associates (who, for the rest, were enthusiastic admirers of the kind of work which the Crimean nurses had done) was to improve sick and wounded soldiers' chances of getting back to the hospital in the first place. Most of the obstacles typically diminishing those chances became revealed to Dunant as he worked over his Solferino experiences.[31] Ambulance workers on and around the battlefield, apart from being far too few, had no conventional protection from fire (as they had had – though actually he did not yet know this – in the period of the Enlightenment); field hospitals and ambulance wagon trains were liable to be fired on, obstructed, captured; local inhabitants who tried to succour vanquished sufferers were victimized by suspicious victors. With other members of his city's Société d'Utilité Publique, Dunant – a persuasive enthusiast who however was no mere visionary; most of his schemes, this 'Red Cross' one included, actually achieving fulfilment – rallied enough support among 'top people' of Europe for a conference to meet in Geneva in the autumn of 1863, to inaugurate an International Committee for Succouring the Wounded. In its general design appeared, among the obvious other things, a proposal for reviving, in effect, and institutionalizing the protective conventions of the eighteenth century. Both branches of this programme blossomed, though somewhat more separately from each other than its promoters can have intended. National societies for succouring the wounded were founded everywhere, and in course of time adopted the common name and creed of the Red Cross movement; the Geneva group (alas! minus its magnetic main protagonist, whose philanthropic zeal had led him into a disastrous neglect of his business affairs) continuing to take a constructive interest in the humanizing of warfare, and with the first Geneva Convention of 1864 as its, so to speak, title deed, gradually turning into the International Committee of the Red Cross; while between it and the national societies steadily developed a symbiosis binding the whole together in a palpable prospering international Red Cross movement dedicated to promoting, in more or less co-ordinated ways, humanity in warfare.[32]

I now leave that great movement and its many forms and aspects, to focus on its hard legal centre, the Geneva Convention. Fifteen States sent representatives in August 1864 to an International Conference for the Neutralization of Army Medical Services in the Field, which concluded two weeks of intermittent deliberations when most of them signed the epoch-making Convention for Bettering the Condition of Wounded Soldiers. A brief and businesslike document; no more than ten articles. Only one of them was concerned directly with the sick and wounded themselves. It specified that they should be humanely treated and cared for, whatever their nationality; the principle behind this being that a soldier once wounded was no longer an effective enemy but just an unfortunate human being.[33] The immense significance and importance of this declaration was not that it was particularly original (for it had been implicit in the Enlightenment publicists' consensus) as that it now became accepted as a general rule (or even as a general truth, for those who liked to look at it that way) among the signatory nations. The other great principle in the first Geneva Convention was perhaps even more interesting but more controversial and, as things turned out, less permanent: the 'neutralization' of all involved in helping the wounded. This was a radically new approach to the good old end. It proclaimed the supremacy of the humanitarian ideal and purpose above immediate military considerations and intruded boldly into the military's normal territory. Busy with their work of mercy and relief, ambulances and military hospitals and all who worked therein or therefor, including transport personnel, were to be accounted 'neutral' and were to be recognized by distinctive flags and brassards: 'a red cross on a white ground'. Two remarkable gestures of confidence in the moral power of what we may henceforth call the Red Cross idea accompanied this striking assertion of it. 'Neutrality will cease to be recognized if these ambulances or hospitals should be under military guard'; and a positive invitation to the local civilian populations to join the good work by making them too 'neutrals' to the extent that they did so, and preserving their houses from requisitioning and billeting, so long as Red Cross work was being done there.

Such was the first Geneva Convention, signed on the spot by twelve States' representatives,[34] and (another of its originalities) open to accession by others as and when they wished. From the Red Cross point of view, it was only the beginning of a programme set out at the movement's inaugurating conference of 1863, and in 1868 certain Additional Articles were agreed on which extended 1864's protections to maritime warfare, and clarified or amplified its land war uses. But these 1868 Articles did not achieve the same legal status and reputation as those of 1864,[35] and among the many reasons for that was the wariness and even resentment of the professional military interest at the humanitarians' intrusions into their affairs; a momentous matter already mentioned, which must now be studied more closely.

Not until 1906 was the first, small Geneva Convention brought up to date. By then, the Red Cross movement was flourishing mightily, and the meaning of the Red Cross was well understood throughout the European-American dominated world. The National Societies in distinctively different yet not unco-ordinated ways, the entirely Swiss-run International Committee in its own steadily expansive style, had become natural features of the landscape of modern civilization. The 1864 Convention had been signed and ratified by forty-eight States, including China, Japan, Siam and the Ottoman Empire.[36] In principle it commanded universal respect. Everyone agreed that the principle should be extended to war at sea. But it had not worked out in practice as smoothly as it might have done, and from the soldiers' point of view it badly needed reconstitution. Their complaints about it, which of course tended to go beyond humanitarian reason but which also were reasonable enough to persuade all but perfervid anti-militarists that something needed to be done, were founded largely on the experience of the Franco-Prussian war; and what gave those complaints so much weight, was that they came from the soldiers whom that war had made military masters of the continent, the Germans.

This was a change from the sixties. Then, enough rays from the Napoleonic sunset remained to put upon the French a continuing appearance of military mastery, and while the Prussian and other German armies had commendably adopted the Geneva Convention and taken it very seriously, the French had in fact taken it very lightly and made difficulties about its enlargement. The French got their come-uppance in 1870. Roles suddenly reversed. The French, who on the whole had known little about the Convention, and whose practice had considerably misused or abused it and its emblem, now became prominent in recommending its strengthening, while the Prussians and Germans, who had suffered (or at any rate felt that they had suffered) a great deal both from French slackness and from outsiders' casual misunderstandings, became loud in demanding that it be put on a better footing before it was next needed.[37] The current vogue for humanitarian good works, they complained, coupled with the lax language of the Convention (i.e. its repeated invocation of that risky word 'neutrality') had fathered all kinds of bothersome problems for the high command: principally, the cool assumption by cosmopolitan do-gooders that they only needed a Red Cross label to get them the freedom of the battle-zone; the prevalence of the notion that neutral 'Red Cross' organizations were invited to relieve the wounded more or less where and when they chose; and the idea which the French took to enthusiastically, once they heard of it, that a minimal show of looking after some wounded and a Red Cross flag on the front of the house were guaranteed to protect house-owners from invaders' importunities. French and Germans alike had observed, with equal nausea, that advantage had been taken of the Genevan emblem by those who still pursued the immemorial occupation of robbing the wounded and dead after battle. It was understandable that the Germans should feel especially affronted by all this slackness and nastiness. The Convention needed to be tightened up, and the authority of the military unmistakably restored. When at last a new improved model of the Convention was developed, therefore, the place of the national societies was precisely defined. Volunteers from belligerent countries would of course be taking their proper place within the national military organization; like soldiers, 'subject to military law and regulations'. As for would-be volunteers from neutral countries, there were to be no further misunderstandings as to what they could do; they could 'only afford the assistance of [their] medical personnel and units with the previous consent of [their] own government *and the authorization of the government concerned*.[38] (My italics.) No more unwanted guests at the military feast!

Another respect in which the text of the 1906 Convention marked a big and significant change from the way things had been forty years before, was in its repeated use, in one form of words or another, of the phrase, 'so far as military exigencies permit'. The men who composed the 1864 Convention had not found it necessary to bring that into it, although the matter had been sensibly aired in the debates. What, indeed, if strict observance of the Convention should threaten gravely to impede decisive military operations? The argument of 'necessity' demanded an answer. The president of the conference, General Dufour, an elder statesman among soldiers with many years of distinguished French and Swiss service behind him, gave the answer. If such a situation should arise, he said, he would feel obliged to make exceptions, while, of course, accepting full personal responsibility for doing so. The law, he argued, must face facts. Supreme commanders were free to do what seemed necessary to be done, but they were responsible for what they did. 'No rules whatever can absolutely bind generals; what binds them are the directions they are given.'[39] What Dufour had thought it sufficient to leave implicit, now was made aggressively explicit; in no way was practical humanitarianism to be allowed to jeopardize or, some might interpret it, inconvenience the smooth conduct of military operations. So much had the pendulum swung in the meantime.

But although the pendulum swung between the humanitarian ideal and the soldiers' idea of war necessity, it stayed securely on its hinge between them, and in other respects this 'improved' Convention of 1906 faithfully adhered to the founders' principles and incorporated various of the Red Cross movement's suggestions. Article 3 laid upon victorious commanders responsibility for seeking out the wounded and 'insuring protection against pillage and maltreatment both for the wounded and for the dead', as also for making sure that the dead really were dead before causing them to be buried or cremated. Article 4 took into consideration the feelings of soldiers' relations, requiring belligerents to furnish lists of dead and wounded and to put personal belongings on their way back towards the next of kin. It was no detraction from the virtue of the 1864 invitation to local inhabitants, that Article 5 in 1906 required their 'charitable zeal' to find an outlet under 'the competent military authority's direction', since only incompetent military authorities would have failed to direct it anyway. And, perhaps most significant of all intimations that the Red Cross idea was not less highly valued than before, Article 26 said that 'The Signatory Governments will take the necessary measures to instruct their troops, especially the personnel protected, in the provisions of the present Convention, and to bring them to the notice of the civil population.' That the civil populations of States as well as the armed forces should know about the Geneva Conventions and be stimulated, perhaps, to thought about their implications, has always been among the aims of the International Red Cross, and it is interesting to find the general failure of most governments to honour their obligations in this respect goes so far back as the sixth year of our century.

In 1864 and again in 1906 'Geneva law' – i.e. that part of the general law of war thus far distinguished by special treaty treatment – was still confined to the joint category of sick and wounded military personnel (naval, after 1899–1907, as well as land-based) and all involved in looking after them.[40] But Red Cross practice had for thirty years or so been involving itself with the overlapping category of prisoners of war. This further involvement was in the nature of things as well as according to the International Committee's inclinations. Wounded soldiers and medical personnel who fell into enemy hands (e.g., after their fighting companions had withdrawn without them) in effect became 'prisoners', even though the 1864 Convention did its best to obscure the fact by refraining from calling any of them so, by providing for their repatriation as soon as possible (on condition, if they were cured, of no further service), and by casting that cloak of 'neutrality' over ambulances, hospitals, and their staffs. This vagueness of status and easy assumption about repatriation had seemed altogether too sloppy and trusting to military critics of the Convention after 1870–1. Article 2 of the 1906 version accordingly made it clear that 'the wounded and sick of an army who fall into the hands of the enemy are prisoners of war', and no repatriation was required except what might seem 'expedient' to the captor. But apart from this functional involvement with disabled prisoners, the Red Cross movement's dedication to relieving the sufferings of at any rate the military victims of war had increasingly involved it, so far as circumstances permitted, with prisoners in general. The International Committee's willing services as a philanthropic and mediating go-between had proved so useful in the war of 1870–1 and subsequently that it achieved extraordinary and unique status as the first non-governmental organization customarily accepted by States within the international community as the proper principal agent for a particular part of their common business. But none of this actual status and activity was noticed by name – nor were prisoners of war made the subject of a Geneva Convention – until 1929. What the International Committee did, it did behind the formal scenes. Prisoners remained subject to customary international law and its 'Hague law' hardenings, in which not even national Red Cross bodies were specifically mentioned as such, although their activities were discernible in the Hague Regulations, Articles 14, 15 and 16.[41]

That degree of humanitarian intervention apart, the law-makers found little to concern them in respect of prisoners of war other than the relatively uncontroversial business of settling agreed minimum standards for their detention and treatment. Some residue of earlier prejudices evidently remained in the sixties and seventies. The key document of each decade displayed consciousness that it was necessary to protect prisoners from misunderstandings and underestimates of their protected status. In the sixties, it was the great document known as 'Lieber's Code' which magisterially declared the law regarding prisoners. The full title of this document was 'Instruction for the Government of Armies of the United States in the Field'. It was US Army General Order No. 100, issued from the Adjutant-General's Office at Washington on 24 April 1863, and although its final version emerged from a board of officers, it was above all the work of the German-American jurist Francis Lieber, by whose name it is therefore appropriately known.[42] Lieber was already well-known before the war in such military and administrative circles as cared about such things as the law of war, and a series of controversial unpleasantnesses in the early months of the war produced within President Lincoln's administration an urgent desire to have as neatly as possible a definitive statement of the current state of the law of war drawn up for the Union army's guidance. It was so good and comprehensive that it became the prototype and model for Europe's emulation in the succeeding decades, and we shall have many occasions to refer to it again.

So far as prisoners of war were concerned, its language indicates both a keen awareness that among the law's classical purposes was the prevention of things being done in war which might hinder the return to peace, and an awareness that popular passions were actually pressing for the execution of such drastic and severe war measures as were sure to do that. Hence the elaborate definition: 'A prisoner of war is a public enemy armed or attached to the hostile army for active aid, who has fallen into the hands of the captor, either fighting or wounded, on the field or in hospital, by individual surrender or by capitulation' (Article 49). And, in Article 56: 'A prisoner of war is subject to no punishment for being a public enemy, nor is any revenge wreaked upon him by the intentional infliction of any suffering, or disgrace, by cruel imprisonment, want of food, by mutilation, death or any barbarity.' He is to be 'fed upon plain and wholesome food whenever practicable, and treated with humanity' (Article 76). (But in one significant respect there was a limit to this humane generosity: 'All prisoners of war are liable to the infliction of retaliatory measures', in Articles 59.)

There is no need to list the other provisions of the Lieber Code with regard to prisoners. They became, as did so many other sections of that remarkable document, the basis from which subsequent codifiers went to work. But it is significant, no doubt, of the well-nigh universal extent to which prisoners of war had become accepted as a distinct category of war's sufferers or victims, meriting protection in much the same way as did the wounded, that Lieber's elaborately defining language about the prisoner – explaining, as it were, to those who doubted it, his innocence – almost at once disappeared from the basic documents. The next one was produced in 1874, at the Brussels Conference on the Proposed Rules for Military Warfare: a famous occasion to which, as to Lieber's Code, we must often again refer.[43] The idea of the conference came from Russia (now, as already in 1868 and again in 1899, taking the lead in these matters), and the debates were based on a Lieber-like Russian draft code.[44] Of prisoners it found it necessary to state: 'Prisoners of war are not criminals but lawful enemies. They are in the power of the enemy's government, but not of the individuals or of the corps who made them prisoners, and should not be subjected to any violence or ill-usage.' At some point in the debates (I regret I have been unable to find out exactly when or why) the reference to the very bad old idea that prisoners were any sort of criminals was removed, and their protection increased by re-defining them as 'lawful and disarmed enemies' who 'should be treated with humanity'.[45] The remainder of this prisoners' section of the Brussels Code (which, although it never became 'official' in the sense of a signed and ratified convention, in fact was accepted by armies as an agreed statement of the law) devoted itself to determining the kind of treatment which prisoners should receive; its general tendency being to protect them from neglect, maltreatment, and exploitation. Nobody seems to have objected much to any of this; the only small indications of argument I can see are the German delegate's reminder to the arch-humanitarians, that in the last resort even prisoners might have to be made to do things and go places by force, and the worried Austrian emperor's reported observation, 'that to secure to prisoners of war great comforts and indulgences would be to hold out an inducement to cowardly or effeminate soldiers to escape the dangers and hardships of war by surrendering themselves to the enemy'.[46] Nothing worth mentioning happened at The Hague in 1899, when the definition shrank to this (Article 4): 'Prisoners of war are in the power of the hostile government, but not of the individuals or corps who capture them. They must be humanely treated.'

3 The principle of limitation and restraint

Limitation and restraint of course are, of all principles pervading the law of war, the most central and crucial. It is nothing without them. The publicists of the Enlightenment repeatedly invoked them, expositors and critics of the law of war have never been able (even should they have so wished) to avoid arguing mainly in terms of them, they come into the debate about the law and its observance as much today as ever they have done. They alone mediate between what is demanded in the name of 'necessity' on the one side, what in the name of 'humanity' on the other; they somehow or other relativize those absolutes. If now, in telling the part of the story that runs from about 1860 to 1914, I shine my spotlight peculiarly upon the principles of limitation and restraint, it is not because they did not matter much before or since, but because during these years – years, significantly, of special and formative importance in other respects – the argument about them became unusually tense and the decisions that were made or not made relative to them were fraught with unusual importance for the future.

What was happening in these years to bring these principles thus far to the forefront of debate? Above all, it seems, a sense that pressures and temperatures were rising, and that observance of customary limitations and restraints, being made yearly more difficult, needed whatever new strength might be given to it by formal definition. In the first section of this chapter I noted some of the cultural developments which contributed to raise tempers and polarize opinions. Their general effect on the debate about particular limitations and restraints needs no further emphasis. The will towards total war had been present in Europe since the French Revolution but the means and the money for it at the disposal of Carnot, Bonaparte, and Gneisenau was as nothing compared with what was going to be at the disposal of Lincoln, Schlieffen and Lloyd George three or four generations later. Clausewitz in the eighteen-twenties had wondered whether all wars in the future would be national, popular and 'elemental' ones like those of the past two decades, or whether governments would in fact sometimes recover enough freedom of action to be able to wage limited wars for limited objects. 'Such questions are difficult to answer', he wrote, and he would not launch into prophecy. 'But the reader will agree with us when we say that once barriers – which in a sense consist only in man's ignorance of what is possible – are torn down, they are not so easily set up again. At least when major interests are at stake, mutual hostility will express itself in the same manner as it has in our own day.'[47] Indeed it did, with all the added force and fury that later nineteenth-century imperialism, nationalism, industrialization and enrichment could give it. At the same time, as Clausewitz anticipated, men's awareness of what was or might be possible radically changed. Limitations and restraints were accordingly brought into debate in a newly specific manner by the scientific and technical progress of the age, and military men, with such gigantic popular pressures behind them and such awful new weapons in their hands, understandably felt obliged, as never before, to demand that their critics and would-be restrainers recognize some necessary elasticity in the interpretation of 'necessity'.

Scientific and technical matters, so far of little relevance, now become important to our story. Between 1750 and 1850 the machinery of war, as one might broadly describe it, had changed remarkably little, and where there had been big change (as for example in the mechanical applications of steam-power and the use for signalling of electricity) it had not yet got far beyond the experimental stage. About the eighteen-sixties, however, new inventions, techniques and materials began to make a decisive mark. The metal-hulled, screw-propelled warship was a revolutionary phenomenon which came into its own in the sixties : national railroad systems revolutionized strategy by so greatly enhancing the size and mobility of armies; the needle-gun, the *chassepot*, and then above all the machine gun demanded (though they did not fully get) revolution in infantry tactics. So it went on, remorselessly, on land, at sea, and, very soon after the turn of the new century, in the air; quick-firers, smokeless powder, melinite, mines, torpedoes, submarines, gas, aerial bombs, etc., etc. Both the means and the measure of destruction and killing became far greater than they had ever been before. For this reason, if for no other, the need for more precise ideas about restraint and limitation became, for some, acute; and it is no accident that the first specific 'treaty' mention of either, in the St Petersburg Declaration of 1868, was apropos of a newly-invented missile of unprecedented wounding power.

If this branch of our subject – lawfulness or otherwise of weaponry – were concerned only with what combatants did to each other, it would matter less than it actually does. Through most of history, indeed, its concern was thus confined. But the principle at stake in it is of wider application, and its recent practical application has in fact correspondingly widened. Weaponry developments in the twentieth century have made available types of weapons which cannot be used discriminately or which irresistibly invite indiscriminate use. This side of 1900, though admittedly hardly before, the question of what weapons are permitted and what ought to be banned in warfare between law-abiding States became of intimate interest to non-combatants too.

Their involvement, perhaps surprisingly, did not appear to

modify the terms of the debate as much as might have been expected. Those terms have traditionally been peculiar. T. J. Lawrence, whose 1895 *Principles of International Law* includes some of the best pages on its history ever written, remarks of the polemics accompanying weapons development, that most of them 'were due to a confusion of ideas. Men could not make up their minds whether means of destruction were to be deemed unlawful because of their newness, or their unfairness, or their secrecy, or their cruelty, and they generally solved the difficulty by objecting to what they disliked, and regarding as unobjectionable what suited their tastes or worked to their advantage.'[48] It seemed to him that a new era of rationality had dawned since all the European powers (except Spain), meeting at St Petersburg in 1868 to consider the use of certain newly-invented explosive or inflammable bullets, agreed to ban them and justified their decision in these terms:

> Considering the progress of civilization should have the effect of alleviating, as much as possible, the calamities of war; that the only legitimate object which States should endeavour to accomplish during war is to weaken the military force of the enemy; that for this purpose, it is sufficient to disable the greatest number of men; that this object would be exceeded by the employment of arms which uselessly aggravate the sufferings of disabled men, or render their death inevitable; that the employment of such arms would therefore be contrary to the laws of humanity. . . .[49]

About this branch of the law of war at any rate there was no serious disagreement during these contructive years when so much else was disputed. Military experts and enthusiasts were only too anxious to believe (what then was so much talked about by almost everyone) that 'the progress of civilization' brought with it not only efficient weaponry but also ('short wars are the most humane', etc.) less inhumanity in warfare. From St Petersburg to The Hague it was downhill all the way. The Brussels Code concentrated the matter into its Article 12: 'The laws of war do not allow to belligerents an unlimited power as to the choice of injuring the enemy', and by adding to the traditional list of forbidden means in Article 13 (poisons) a general category of 'arms, projectiles, or substances which may cause unnecessary suffering'.[50] The Oxford Manual in 1880 repeated the Brussels Articles 12 and 13 in slightly different words and added that belligerents 'must abstain from all useless severity'.[51] The Hague Regulations went back to the Brussels formulations: 'Belligerents have not got an unlimited right as to the choice of means of injuring the enemy' (Article 22) and, in Article 23's conventional list of forbidden means, 'arms, projectiles, or material calculated to cause unnecessary suffering'.

Here were limitation and restraint indeed! – the crucial principle accepted almost without discussion by the great military powers of the world and embodied in a treaty (annexed to it, strictly speaking) governing how they would in future conduct their wars! But even at the moment of triumph the sceptic might rest unconvinced. 'Suffering' could not be objectively measured as could be the weight of missiles or even – this was a matter into which some military surgeons made curious experiments – the physical effects of bullets entering human flesh. Implementation of these restraints, after all, depended on decisions made according to two sets of more or less subjective judgements: how the military themselves perceived and evaluated new weapons, and, second, how the military and everybody else involved in war decision-making decided what was 'necessity'?

Of the first, little need be said here, except that some of the same confusion and irrationality which always marked the historical debate about weapons innovations has continued; and that only a study of military psychology could explain (this seems to be the crucial instance) why injury or death by means of relatively, perhaps entirely, painless, gas has never apparently been thought preferable to the many forms of mutilation and life-long pain following injuries from exploding shells and shrapnel, incendiary weapons like flame-throwers and napalm.

The second judgement, about relative 'necessity', is much more important. By its very nature it goes beyond the particular question of lawfulness of weaponry to the general question of conducting wars by means of whatever kind. What, after all, *is* 'necessary'? The question was repeatedly put by the publicists, for whom the particular matter of 'military necessity' represented but one branch of a larger, embracing question. The more the law of war became a specialized study, separated for purposes of convenience from the general bodies of international law and international relations, the more the concept of 'necessity' was appropriated by the military, who made more and more of it in their struggle to prevent the

Bluntschli-ites from boxing them in. Their insistence got it written into the texts many times, as we have seen and shall see further, in the debates and writings of these later nineteenth-century years. But the St Petersburg Declaration and the Hague Regulations brought back, even if half-disguised, the concept in its old broad application, relevant to the whole of the war-making business. In principle it embraced every issue in war, from the greatest to the smallest; from ultimate questions such as whether it was worth going to war in the first place and whether winning a war in the short term is worth the certain recurrence of war and possible reversal of its fortunes in the longer term (e.g., 1871, and probably 1919 too), to the smallest literal questions like that practical weapons application actually talked about at The Hague in 1899, the use of 'dum-dum' bullets.[52] Dum-dums, named after the small Calcutta factory where they were first made for the British Indian army, had the capability of spreading out on entering the target body and of inflicting a much bigger wound than did the normal hard-nosed high-velocity rifle bullet. The British argument in their justification was that nothing less would stop 'savages' like the tribesmen of the Indian North-West Frontier and the followers of the Mahdi in the Sudan. This was not an edifying argument, inasmuch as it placed these alleged 'savages' on the same level as big-game, for the execution of which such fearful missiles had originally been invented; it was not intelligently deployed, inasmuch as the embarrassed Britons at The Hague found themselves defending dum-dums with the argument that, after all, they didn't work very well; and in any case it had within it deadly germs of self-defeat, it being always the case with new weapons, whether open to the charge of causing unnecessary suffering or not, that one nation's introduction of them will be followed by others. The matter is one with which the Strategic Arms Limitation Treaties have made us of the nineteen-seventies and -eighties unusually familiar. In the age of relative innocence one hundred and twenty years or so ago, when submarine mines were accounted 'infernal machines', Montague Bernard wrote of weaponry inventions : 'It is possible to go too fast and too far in this direction. The quickest road to victory is not always the best, and even a certain saving in the sum-total of bloodshed and suffering may be too dearly bought, by the use of means which shock the instincts of humanity.'[53]

Part of the case against recourse to new and nastier or more awful weapons is, precisely, that humanity's threshold of shock, in that sense, can be lowered just like an individual's. When we get to the vexed question of area bombing in the second world war, we shall face the high probability that, for example, the idea of dropping the first atomic bomb right in the middle of a city could only have occurred to statesmen and soldiers whom three years of steadily more intensive area bombing had, so to speak, morally desensitized.[54] Perhaps that 'saving in the sum-total of bloodshed and suffering' *was* 'too dearly bought by the use of means which shock the instincts of humanity'. Whatever the answer to that intensely interesting and arguable question may be, we observe that the Hague conferences of 1899 and 1907 marked a high point of overt concern in this respect. To the traditional inventory of atrocious weapons (poisoned ones, principally) and the kind of bullets specifically banned in 1868 were now added, as candidates for similar treatment, dum-dums, asphyxiating and noxious gases, projectiles and explosives launched from balloons or analogous inventions, and submarine contact mines.[55] What precisely was done with regard to each of these is of less immediate interest than the fact that thus much effort was made to deduce appropriate legislation from the principles of limitation and restraint so much talked of. In fact not much was done with regard to any of them. But those principles were felt by enough participants to matter enough, apparently, for their existing strength in treaty law to receive its greatest ever increment of strength, to which we must now turn: the Martens Declaration.

Fedor Fedorovitch Martens was a jurist in the service of the Tsar, who served as Russia's principal active expert in international law from the seventies until his death in 1908.[56] Besides technical works on international law and jurisprudence, showing a special interest in the related topics of the law of war and arbitration, he wrote about Russia's contemporary international relations and also, in the book published in France in 1901 as *La Paix et la Guerre*, about the phenomenon of war in its larger philosophical and historical context.[57] His being engaged so heartily in the public service distinguished him, I presume, from most of his Russian juridical colleagues (with at least one of whom controversy is apparent),[58] and it might be a nice topic for an adequately equipped researcher to ascertain the extent to which Martens was his own man or the Tsar's. This wide range of his intellectual, moral and practical interests in fact made Albert de Lapradelle think of Vattel: 'the clear-minded but slightly superficial jurist-diplomat of St Petersburg and The Hague, a man better qualified than any other to understand the diplomat of Berne and jurist of Neuchâtel', was how he referred, I think rather patronizingly, to Martens in his introduction to the 1916 edition. A most unflattering picture of him as a mere gas-bag, and not even an impressive one, was given by the main German delegate, Marschall von Bieberstein, in 1907. The Germans specialized in scepticism about peace conferences in general, Russian motives in particular, and Marschall's hostility need not be taken too seriously. Yet Martens is a bit of an oddity. His career and writings present in microcosm the same intriguing problem as does Russian international policy in general: the voice being so often the voice of justice and peace, the Realpolitik being forever suspect as that of unregenerate imperial and militarist bear.[59] The fact however is – whatever may be made of it – that it was initiatives from the Tsars which convened the 1868, 1874, 1899 and, almost as directly, the 1907 conferences, and that Russia figured in the public eye (well sanded, thought resentful diplomats of other powers, by hired press propaganda) as, of all the great powers, the one which cared most about peace, disarmament, and the law of war. Martens's role in all this was conspicuous, from his slightly late arrival at Brussels in 1874 until his last appearance as one of his country's three delegates plenipotentiary (the others were the Russian ambassadors to Paris and The Hague) in 1907; and in 1899 he made upon the law of war a bigger mark than any other individual jurist, by acting as the promoter of the singularly important amendment clause known by his name.[60]

The Martens Declaration is about limitation and restraint, and its singular importance as a declaration of principle and a point of constant reference lies as much in its generality as in its uniqueness. The actual occasion of its production was an argument about the law respecting resistance to invasion (see below, Section 6), and it had its valuable part to play in settling that local difficulty; but its relevance is universal. A proper preface to it may be found in his speech on the occasion when that difficulty became acute. He looked back to 1874, when it had been said by some that the law of war was better left vague and general, 'in the exclusive domain of the law of nations.' 'But', he asked:

... is this opinion quite just? Is this uncertainty advantageous to the weak? Do the weak become stronger because the *duties* of the stronger are not determined? Do the strong become weaker because their *rights* are specifically defined and consequently limited? I do not think so. I am fully convinced that it is particularly in the interest of the weak that these rights and duties be defined. It is impossible to compel the stronger to respect the rights of the weaker if the *duties* of the latter are not recognized.

He himself, he repeated, was all in favour of explicitness about these matters. It was not enough to leave them

... to the generally recognized principles of the law of nations, and ... to the hearts of the captains, commanders in chiefs, and military authorities. But, gentlemen, the heart has purposes which the mind does not understand and in time of war only one purpose is recognized, and that is the purpose of the war. I bow with respect before the great deeds which the human heart has performed during war and on the field of battle. The Red Cross is the best proof of this. But ... the noble sentiments of the human heart unfortunately very often remain a closed book in the midst of combats.

Our present task is to remind peoples of their duties, not only in time of peace but also in war. .... We wish to elaborate, in a spirit of concord, humanity, and justice, the uniform bases for the instructions which the Governments will pledge themselves to give to their armed land forces. We have always recognized the imperious law of the inexorable necessities of war. [But] permit me to believe that we are unanimous in the desire to mitigate, as far as possible, the cruelties and disasters in international conflicts which are not in any wise rendered inevitable by the necessities of war. It is our unanimous desire that the armies of the civilized nations be not simply provided with the most murderous and perfected weapons, but that they shall also be imbued with a notion of right, justice and humanity, binding even in invaded territory and even in regard to the enemy.[61]

The degree of preciseness which Martens preferred being, for political reasons, unobtainable, and to leave the matter wholly vague and general being, to his mind, a confession of failure, his Declaration cannot have been, for him, other than a second best.

For the subsequent development of the law of war, however, it is more likely to have been a godsend. Too much specificity at that date, when the technical and ideological context of the law was beginning to change so rapidly, might have made the Hague achievements look dated more quickly than they could do so long as Martens's Declaration (only slightly modified) remained firmly built into the preamble of the Convention to which the Regulations concerning the Laws and Customs of War on Land were annexed. I give the Declaration in his original wording:

> ... It is extremely desirable that the usages of war should be defined and regulated. In this spirit [the Conference] has adopted a great number of provisions which have for their object the determination of the rights and duties of belligerents and populations and for their end a softening of the evils of war so far as military necessities permit. It has not, however, been possible to agree forthwith on provisions embracing all the cases which occur in practice. On the other hand, it could not be intended by the Conference that the cases not provided for should, for want of a written provision, be left to the arbitrary judgement of the military commanders. Until a perfectly complete code of the laws of war is issued, the Conference thinks it right to declare that in cases not included in the present arrangement, populations and belligerents remain under the protection and empire of the principles of international law, as they result from the usages established between civilized nations, from the laws of humanity, and the requirements of the public conscience.[62]

Some vagueness about detailed application remained; but nothing more emphatic about the subjection of 'military necessity' to the principles of limitation and restraint could have been said. The remainder of this chapter studies four fields in which it was of peculiar significance, marking in each case the extent to which it received embodiment in pre-1914 legislation. The record, as we shall see, is mixed.

4 Reprisals and military necessity

'Reprisals' has always been a particularly tricky and controversial topic throughout the history of the law of war, because in practice it is difficult to distinguish between the motives for pursuing 'reprisals', 'retaliation', 'retribution', and 'revenge' (and even 'retorsion'). But 'reprisals' has become the morally more elevated and juridically acceptable concept. Its respectability derives from the lawful and indeed law-enforcing purpose to which acts of reprisal/retaliation may be put, and the word is therefore likely to be preferred by parties conscious of a just grievance. 'Revenge' rings meanly in many civilized ears, and 'retaliation' lacks moral overtones. But 'reprisals' has acquired a character of active virtue: in contemporary international law parlance, it is an act, perhaps unlawful in itself, justifiably undertaken with the specific object of paining a law-neglecting enemy back into conformity with the law.

Such became, sometime in the recent past, the proper and technical international law of war meaning of 'reprisal'; a meaning supposed to be distinct from that of 'retaliation', for which practice and concept also justification can be made. Beneath both titles, indifferently, the topic was very often under discussion during the years we are currently concerned with. It is safe to say that every jurist and military spokesman whose pen or tongue joined in those discussions concurred that an agreed definition and measure of justifiable reprisals/retaliation would be a good thing. But they could not come to such an agreement; above all, it would appear, because of the weight and momentum of military reluctance to be tied down by any such definition, and because there were, as a matter of fact, enough sympathetic jurists – we might call them, after their most striking exponent, the Lueder-ites – to make the military feel that they had enough law on their side.

Agreement however that reprisals/retaliation ideally needed definition was real enough, and for these reasons: because they stirred up exceptional amounts of unpleasantness and recrimination; because they could not be exercised without making the relatively, perhaps the absolutely, 'innocent' suffer instead of the 'guilty'; because whatever name they went under, the psychological reality prompting them was often merely thirst for revenge, lust to hurt and punish, or simply self-indulgent desire to save trouble; and because, unless very carefully regulated, they tended to escalate into horrid spirals of cruelty and counter-cruelty. Yet they could not be dispensed with. At the higher, governmental level, a respectable and justifiable meaning rested beneath the confusing mixture of motives and the self-righteous rhetoric. In the last resort – which, in the case of international law, is also normally the first resort – reprisals are the law of war's only regular sanction; necessary, because only they can do what may be necessary to be done. At the lower level of actual military operations reprisals/ retaliation were claimed to be occasionally necessary by the fighting man doing the job which governments had committed to him. I give a few random examples of reprisals as armies in the field actually knew them: (1) *American Revolutionary HQ, Spring 1782* – Washington, getting no satisfaction from the British in response to his complaints about what he alleged to be the murder of a captured New Jersey militia captain, driven to order 'the designation of an English officer, to serve as a reprisal. The time and the place are fixed' – he hoped however that it would yet be possible to avoid 'this terrible alternative'. (It was.)[63] (2) *Spain, 1808* – partisans snipe at French column as it slowly advances up the valley of the Sil – non-combatant camp-followers injured as well as troops – so, as soon as it can be done, 'the French Almanazor, General Loison' leads a punitive column into the snipers' hinterland – villages on fire everywhere – 'Never before can so terrible a storm have hit this previously peaceful valley. Its people got out and watched its destruction from afar; those we were able to find, we killed.'[64] (3) *France, 1870* – The French have interned the officers of a number of German merchantmen taken in their waters; Bismarck, alleging that this detention is unlawful, orders the imprisonment by way of reprisal of forty prominent citizens of Dijon, Gray and Vesoul; and, (4) *early in 1871*, French guerrillas having blown up the railway viaduct at Fontenay, and the German 'prefect's demand for French labour to repair it having gone unanswered, he declares a total shut-down of all factories and workshops in the department of La Meurthe, and prohibits the paying of unemployed workmen.[65] These were the kinds of situations with which the great debate from 1860 to 1914 was particularly concerned, and whether they were called reprisals or retaliations made no difference, for all such had some sort of necessity to justify them: either the superior, governmental, sort, or that which the experienced warrior deduced from the realities of warfare. But to men with a mind for the desirability of setting limits to the violence and cruelty of war, the two levels of necessity merged in their shared characteristic, that without formal regulation they gave a blank check to superior force, and encouraged escalation through counter-reprisals.

It is important to note also, that governments and generals were not the only parties to the promotion of these acts. Behind both stood more and more obviously, as the later nineteenth and early twentieth century years went by, the populations of belligerent States, involved in many different ways by the political theories and practices of all States. Whether formally 'democratic', representative, or not, no State from now on could manage war without eliciting and maintaining at least an adequacy of popular enthusiasm for it; and since this was usually welcomed, it could hardly be ignored when it became a nuisance. The history of every modern war has to take into very careful account the shuttle of relationship between government and public opinion, the extent to which each can drive, or has to submit to be driven by, the other. The historian of the law of war especially notes that public opinion has often taken with relish to policies of revenge and retribution, which governments driven to implement them of course tend to dignify with the title of reprisals, if they feel obliged to offer *legal* justifications at all.

It is no wonder that Lieber and his professional peer and collaborator Henry Wager Halleck (Chief of Staff from March 1864) should have had to deal with 'reprisals' in this as well as its other common forms, their country being one in which the forces of public opinion were particularly unrestrained and urgent. In the later months of the war between the States there was a clamour in the North that the South's maltreatment of prisoners (which indeed was a fact, though of course and as usual its extent was exaggerated in the popular telling) should be answered by retaliation upon their men held captive in the North. Halleck expressed himself passionately against this. Such measures, he maintained, achieved nothing but the relief of violent feelings, and hurt only 'innocent' parties. Let justice be done after the war (he was all for post-war trials), when the guilty men could be accurately got at! He cited with approval a letter Lieber had just written to the Washington *Daily Globe*, saying that retaliation if it works (*if*) is all right, but that mere revenge is demeaning. In any case, Lieber had argued, the people of the Union were too decent to bring themselves to do what they frothed about. 'God be thanked you could not do it, and if you could, how it would brutalize our own people! . . . And as to starve those who have starved our sons, and by the thousand, why everyone knows the thing cannot be done, and heaven be praised it is so.'[66]

Political pressure for retaliation/reprisals must be considered a normal component of modern national wars, and is always likely to be an element in the making of decisions at governmental level. But closer by far to the law of war in process of codification in the later nineteenth century were the reprisals habitually used by soldiers in the field and justified simply as being, within whatever meanings of the word, 'necessary' if wars were to be regularly fought at all. How could this mercurial and explosive part of customary warfare be brought under the dampening influence of the principle of limitation and restraint?

The attempt so to bring it failed, but not ignobly. Lieber, who liked to spell out the reasons for everything, dealt with the matter in the first section of his Code, where he also gnawed at the equally sensitive matter of 'military necessity'. Himself with memories of Prussia's war of national liberation and, it is hardly too much to say, heartily accepting war as a natural and proper incident in the progress of mankind and its leading nations (like the United States and Germany), he made more room for military necessity than most of his jurist successors found comfortable. But at the same time he balanced against it principles by which even it must submit to be limited if war were not to become pure beastliness : 'Men who take up arms against one another in public war do not cease on this account to be moral beings, responsible to one another, and to God.'[67] So, when he came to treat of retaliation (he used that word only), he at once accompanied his recognition of its necessity and inevitability with conditions for its lawful use :

27.   The law of war can no more wholly dispense with retaliation than can the law of nations, of which it is a branch. Yet civilized nations acknowledge retaliation as the sternest feature of war. . . .

28.   Retaliation will therefore never be resorted to as a measure of mere revenge, but only as a means of protective retribution, and, moreover, cautiously and unavoidably; that is to say, retaliation shall only be resorted to after careful inquiry into the real occurrence, and the character of the misdeeds that may demand retaliation.

Unjust or inconsiderate retaliation removes the belligerents farther and farther from the mitigating rules of a regular war, and by rapid steps leads them nearer to the internecine wars of savages.

Lieber's Code, I have already remarked, served as the quarry from which all the subsequent codes were cut. They were all shorter; usually by a great deal. They eschewed explanations and arguments, and very soon they abandoned his bold attempt to define and limit reprisals. Something like Lieber's definition indeed appeared in the Russian original draft for the Brussels Conference:

69. Reprisals are admissible in extreme cases only, due regard being paid, as far as shall be possible, to the laws of humanity, when it shall have been unquestionably proved that the laws and customs of war have been violated by the enemy . . .

70. The selection of the means and extent of reprisals should be proportionate to the degree of the infraction of the law committed by the enemy. Reprisals that are disproportionately severe are contrary to the rules of international law.

71. Reprisals shall be allowed only on the authority of the Commander-in-Chief . . .[68]

The Russian delegation fought hard for this, or for something like it; but it proved far too hot and sensitive a subject for the conference to handle. Memories of the war of 1870–1 were still fresh, unjust severity of reprisals was the principal charge which French and most other writers had made against the Germans, and, reported the British delegate, another factor demanded consideration as it tends to do on such occasions: 'The labours of the Conference also were drawing to a conclusion. So far perfect harmony had prevailed among the delegates. . . . It seemed, therefore, undesirable to open at the last moment a discussion which would probably go far to undo the progress already made. . . .'[69]

So reprisals disappeared from the agenda of international conferences on the law of war for over fifty years.[70] This must be accounted a tragedy.[71] They did not sink without a swan-song. One of the Russian delegates, presumably Martens, remarking that they had intended to 'limit' reprisals, not 'sanction' them, made these pregnant observations over the grave:

I regret that the uncertainty of silence is to prevail with respect to one of the most bitter necessities of war. If the practice could be suppressed by this reticence, I could but approve of this course. But if it is still to exist, this reticence may, it is to be feared, remove any limits to its exercise. Nevertheless, I believe that the mere mention in the protocol that the committee, after having endeavoured to regulate, to soften, and to restrain reprisals, has shrunk from the task before the general repugnance felt with regard to the subject, will have a most serious moral bearing. It will, perhaps, be the best limitation we have been able to affix to the practice, and especially to the use which may be made of it in future.[72]

What, at bottom, had killed the endeavour to get reprisals-limiting clauses into the codes, was the insistence of the military of the great land powers that no limits should be set to the freedom given them, they felt, by the principle of 'military necessity' in dealing with the populations of invaded and occupied territories. Before coming directly onto that next branch of our subject, it will be helpful to note the extent and nature of the claims being made for military necessity, which seems at this time to have become among the military a preoccupation as it had never been before. Lieber had said a great deal about it, but he had also said a good deal about the limitations to which even it must submit. The most prominent German writer of the next generation, Lueder, was like Lieber without the limitations.

Lueder's statements about military necessity are peculiarly interesting. Appearing as the law of land war section of Holtzendorff's four-volume *Handbuch*, the most elaborate and comprehensive account of international law yet published, Lueder's two-hundred pages naturally were taken as an expression of a significant part of the mind of the world's greatest military power, and attracted much attention.[73] Recalling what I said earlier about the 'militarization of humanitarianism', I note that this Würzburg professor had first come to public attention as winner of the international Red Cross award established by the Empress of Germany, the Augusta Prize, with his book on the history of the Geneva Convention.[74] It was a fine book, and also a patriotic one. Lueder scored so many points off the French that the International Committee, approaching its publication, asked him if he would allow them to tone the French edition down a bit. 'But Mr Lueder objected to that, and the International Committee did not press the matter.'[75] What Mr Lueder had written, he had written. Toughness remained his characteristic, and never showed more prominently than in the part of his *Handbuch* chapter which dealt with 'military necessity'.[76] To what the military in these years were increasingly saying, Lueder now offered juridical authorization. Basing himself on a considerable quantity of mainly German literature that had tackled or touched on the topic, he set the powers of military necessity, *Kriegsraison*, higher than any respectable jurist had set them before. Taking up the old German distinction between *Kriegsmanier* and *Kriegsraison* (roughly, 'customs/usages of war' and 'military necessity'), he now argued that the former included all the normal restraints and limitations of the basic law of war, and that the latter offered, in extreme circumstances, exemption from the obligation to observe them. His definition of such circumstances was:

> 1. In case of extreme necessity, when the object of the war can only be achieved by non-observance and would by observance be frustrated; 2. as retaliation, in case of unlawful non-observance of *Kriegsmanier* by the enemy. Any departure from *Kriegsmanier* is justified when circumstances are such that the accomplishment of the war-aim, or the escape from extreme danger, is hindered by sticking to it.[77]

It was not just what he said that attracted criticism, it was also how he said it. Lieber, for example, had gone out of his way to provide for military necessity a large measure of freedom and discretion; but he had accompanied it nevertheless by moral and humane qualifications, and had expressly brought reprisals under their governance. What Lieber and the rest treated as exceptional and potentially dangerous, Lueder harped on with militarist relish. He treated retaliation as a military procedure to which *Kriegsraison* gave particular cover. He was peculiarly insistent that nothing in international law (or the moral philosophy which some found to be attached to it) obliged you to stick to the rules if your opponent gave you any excuse or pretext for breaking them. Assuming (as I believe it is safe to do) that Lueder shared his country's generals' conviction that the conduct of a war once started was entirely their affair and that their proper and exclusive object was the absolute ascendancy of their arms, Lueder's doctrine egged on the military to whatever forceful measures *they* (as theoretically distinct from their political masters) saw fit, and sustained their natural proclivity to think that whatever secured their exclusive military idea of mastery was legitimate.

Whether morality and human nature recommend *Kriegsraison* in [such] circumstances, and whether man will exercise it by way of retaliation or forego doing so, is a special question. The law on retorsion however is clear enough. The side that departs from *Kriegsmanier* cannot expect the other side to keep it. And in war it can happen, that omission to retaliate against the offences of the enemy can place you at a disadvantage in respect of the supreme object of the war : breaking the enemy will and winning the war.

It is time to turn to Lueder's critics. Edouard Odier of the International Committee, reviewing his prize-winning book on the Geneva Convention, expressed surprise that Lueder stuck up for it as much as he did, even maintaining that what the Convention expressly protected, *Kriegsraison* must not touch. Apart from that, though, he was pained by Lueder's insistent affirmation of the 'need to subordinate the Convention's humanitarian purpose to the material ends of the war', he could not make out why the 'neutralization' principle annoyed Lueder and other Germans so much, and he thought the book needlessly nasty about the French.[78] Later on, Nys, de Louter, Garner, Hall and Oppenheim all in turn expressed alarm about his extreme positions.[79] But the most powerful of his critics, who is worth a few lines on his own, was Westlake of Cambridge.

He came upon Lueder several times in his writings and clearly believed him to represent an attitude and a theory that must at all costs be opposed. He rejected Lueder's extreme doctrine of 'war treason' (*Kriegsverrat*), which we shall come to in the next section.[80] He was unconvinced and somewhat appalled by what Lueder said in justification of his extreme doctrine about retorsion/retaliation/reprisals. There were, he agreed, limits to the degree to which meticulous fulfilment of moral obligations by one party to an agreement could be expected in the event of persistent non-fulfilment by another : '. . . but we must record our dissent from the generality of the assertion that a mutual obligation is dissolved by the failure of one party to perform it.' As for reprisals specifically, Westlake could not swallow the sweep of Lueder's justifications of them: '. . . no analogy that can be drawn either from ethics or from national law will warrant anyone's being deliberately made to suffer for the fault of another from whom he is regarded as distinct.' So far as he understood Lueder's arguments by analogy from German law, he wasn't impressed by them; one might commit homicide in self-defence, of course, but not kill someone other than the attacker 'in order to throw on him, rather than bear yourself, the consequences of a fatality in which neither was at fault'. Lueder's argument that 'anything' was justified in dealing with states of emergency and their alleged like merely encouraged military men to feel relieved from normal moral obligations and in consequence to behave immoderately.[81]

All this was strong enough, but it was nothing compared with what Westlake said about Lueder's *Kriegsraison*. Implicitly recalling the publicists' principle that all the other 'necessities' of war derived from and were, so to speak, contained within the original grand necessity of war itself, he reproved Lueder for introducing novel false distinctions between measures of war that were 'normal' and measures that were 'extraordinary'.

Little or nothing therefore seems to be gained by making two classes of measures, distinguished not really by necessity but by so vague a test as the degree of necessity, while much may be lost by the opposition in which such a system inevitably stands to any extension of the list of absolute prohibitions beyond those already existing. The two sources from which it seems possible to hope for an amelioration of the practice of war are such an extension, and a better recognition by public opinion of the duty of weighing scrupulously the degree of necessity or the amount of advantage under or for the sake of which recourse is had even to permitted measures.

The positive law of war had developed out of the old *Kriegsmanier* and was by now:

. . . a code in which humanity to the enemy on the one side, and the essential needs of war on the other, have been considered. And the question raised under the term of Kriegsraison is not whether that code is defective or misconceived in any of its clauses, but whether a necessity, not of war but of success, is to be allowed to break it down. It is contended in effect, however innocent may be the intentions of authors, that the true instructions to be given by a State to its generals are: 'Succeed – by war according to its laws, if you can – but at all events and in any way, succeed.'[82]

Again we are driven to note, that the law of war had come to a critical juncture. The tension between its two poles 'military necessity' and 'humanity' was becoming unbearable. Perceptive people were more and more doubting whether any satisfactory accommodation between them was possible, and the effort to maintain some middle position was proving more than some could stand. Were those giant strides in civilization and moral sensibility, which it was so common to think of as affecting all social institutions, after all going to miss out on war? The peace movement's excitement over the Hague Peace Conferences had something of the hysterical in it. Josef Conrad's assessment of their extraordinary ambivalence has been cited above (p. 141). The two most famous figures of the internationalist-philanthropic world had withdrawn from the middle way to extreme positions: Tolstoy and Dunant had both become pacifists. To less sensitive or tormented characters, such a drastic resolution of the dilemma offered more loss than gain, and the way ahead still seemed to lie through such reaffirmations and further developments of the law of war and its Red Cross superstructure as were, in fact, taking place about the turn of this century. But to this process, the military for their part were becoming increasingly resistant. At any rate, they were clearly determined that, if there was to be any such further development, it would be on their terms.

The increasing frequency of references to 'military necessity' betrayed their uneasiness. The military interest was being driven, not least by the assaults of its peace-preferring and humanitarian critics, to declare frankly that there were points beyond which it would not go. One such point, for example, came into focus with unusual clarity when Colonel Gross von Schwarzhoff, the German army's 'technical delegate' at The Hague in 1899, put a stopper on an otherwise interminable wrangle by firmly saying: 'At this point ... my concessions cease; it is absolutely impossible for me to go one step further. ...'[83] Military leaders in those years must often have felt like that. Their stubbornness, the sense that they were being pushed to the limits of their patience and resources increased, but not necessarily because their kind was becoming more bloody-minded and ruthless than before. What went on in the military mind was one thing; the military situation as it could be objectively appraised by law of war experts was another; and such experts could see that nothing was to be gained, and much perhaps lost, by pushing the military, on paper, further than on the battlefield they could possibly go. What the distinguished Dutch jurist and humanitarian Bert Röling said about the 1949 Geneva Conventions was applicable in principle to 1899, though there was not yet nearly as much cause for saying it: 'The question even presents itself, whether there is any reality in provisions that go beyond the field of military indifference.' He went on to quote a distinguished Red Cross writer, J. P. Maunoir: 'Nothing is to be gained by ignoring military necessities, so long as they really are expressions of reality and not just pretexts. . . .'[84]

Over the law of war, to the extent that it became codified between 1899 and 1907, there hung therefore the novel and disturbing question: how much latitude would 'necessity' seize, now that it was so specifically on the military mind and being specifically mentioned in the codes? We have already noted how the 1906 Geneva Convention made much mention of it. The Hague Regulations did the same. The preamble of their Convention described them as having 'been inspired by the desire to diminish the evils of war, so far as military requirements permit. . . .' The shadow of 'necessity' hung over the Regulations themselves in three ways: once by specific mention ('unless such destruction or seizure be imperatively demanded by the necessities of war'); several times in such expressions as 'so far as possible'; and by way of the generally understood gloss put upon it by the military delegates in the debates, that this or that provision must be understood as conditional on military capacity. Thus, when it came to Article 46 protecting persons and private property in occupied territory, the German delegate's bid to add 'so far as military necessity permits' was only rejected on the understanding that everyone knew that that was implied.[85] His country still believed this twenty years later. The Reichstag's committee of inquiry into alleged war-crimes said that 'it had been made clear during the formulation [of Articles 46 and 52] that military necessity can override the rights of the occupied. . . .'[86]

The effect of the Hague Regulations on the minds and conducts of armies in the early twentieth century invites study along two different lines. First, how seriously did the military high commands take those Regulations? Paper reproduction, paraphrase or explication of them in national military manuals would only have been the beginning of the matter; what was thought and said about them in club, mess, barracks and class-room is what we really need to know about. Second, as far as the Regulations and their Convention were taken seriously, what construction actually was put upon the references to 'military necessity'? Was it to be allowed to undo any of the Regulations, as and when such 'necessity' might be thought to have arisen? – or, strictly construing the wording of that preamble, were the armies of signatory States to be instructed that as much allowance had been made for it as could be made, and that no further discretion was permitted?

It is impossible within the proportions of this project to do more than catch some straws which the wind has blown in my direction. Most of them are about Germany, which is not surprising, given the general impression among experts in other countries that the Germans wrote more about military necessity than anyone else,[87] and the fact that, during and after the first world war, the Germans were particularly anxious to meet the charge that their conduct of warfare was less lawful than others'. There was even for a short while after the armistice the possibility of the allies' instituting war crimes trials.[88] The Reichstag therefore set up a committee of inquiry into alleged war crimes, whose long-drawn-out labours issued in the four-volume report published in 1927: *Völkerrecht im Weltkrieg*.[89] Its very first section was on the introduction of the Hague Regulations to the German army.[90] Its special concern was to lay the ghost of the *Kriegsbrauch im Landkrieg* (see above, p. 146). Its defence of its author rested largely on his sworn testimony that he knew nothing of the Hague Regulations when in the autumn of 1901 he wrote his little book and that he did not notice their publication in the *Reichsgesetzblatt* in the middle of his labours. But what is more astounding, is that, apparently, this high-powered general staff major had heard nothing about the Hague Regulations thitherto; which surely suggests that the conference which finished its labours at The Hague on 29 July 1899 and at which Colonel Gross von Schwarzhoff had played so prominent a part had not, to say the least, become a topic of conversation in officers' messes. The Reichstag's committee showed to its own satisfaction that the *Kriegsbrauch* was not in fact so 'official' a publication as foreign critics had liked to assume, but admitted that its provenance gave it an appearance official enough to make the juridical insensitivity of its author rather regrettable.[91] Going beyond that unfortunate incident to the more general question of how the German army was familiarized with its new obligations, the Committee's findings were insufficient to enable it to affirm that as much had been done as should have been, and one army order, a *Kriegs-Etappenordnung* dated 12 March 1914, had to be recognized as directly contrary to Hague Regulations, Article 50.[92]

Beyond this again comes the field of inquiry – probably the most important of all – into which I shall no more venture than did the committee: what actually was thought and said about military necessity by the German ruling class, especially those writers, speech-makers and preachers who expressed its mind for it? Similar inquiries could be made about the military in every country just before 1914. Their proper interpretation would require much tact and skill. With how much seriousness, for instance, should Admiral Fisher's remarks to his German *confrères* at The Hague be taken? Captain Siegel reported to the Auswärtiges Amt that Fisher had told him that, even if the British government did fall in with the Americans' wish for a convention on the inviolability of private property at sea, such a convention would doubtless be 'ditched' in the event of war; Count Munster reported that Fisher had privately called the whole Hague business 'nonsense'.[93] One cannot help wondering whether British admirals and German generals did not have some attitudes in common. As for British generals, their standard source of guidance on the laws and customs of war was carefully brought up to date on each necessary occasion but – another straw in the wind? – the eminent civilian jurist, Holland, who had done the earlier versions for the War Office, was dethroned in 1906–7 and the revision was placed instead in the hands of a committee of 'officers having knowledge of war', by whom was brought in as their legal technical expert, in place of the veteran Holland, the younger Oppenheim.[94]

5 Invasion, occupation and 'the peaceful population'

This and the last two sections are concerned mainly with questions of conduct towards enemy civilians, and (in respect of land war anyway) conduct of enemy civilians. What conduct was it right and proper for a belligerent to observe towards the 'peaceful population' of a country he had invaded (and otherwise attacked) and occupied, and how peaceful was it right and proper for that population to remain, and what could lawfully be done about it if it turned from passive acceptance of its fate (the invaders' dream) to active resistance?[95]

These questions together provoked many heated arguments. The wars of 1861–71 brought them abruptly to the fore, and the shock of recognizing them was enhanced perhaps, for the historically informed, by realizing that everything that had been most unpleasant and discreditable between 1792 and 1814 had happened again. Was the progress of civilization, men might well wonder, as defective as that?

In the conferences of 1874 and 1899 and throughout the often passionate literature enveloping those debates, it was often assumed, and sometimes frankly admitted, that the solution to those questions was to be found in a sort of bargain struck between the two interests, the invader/occupier and the invaded/occupied. Let the latter only be still and obey orders, argued the spokesmen of the former party, and nastiness and suffering would be minimized. The very language about 'peaceful persons' and 'peaceful population', which crept into official usage at and following Brussels and The Hague, betrayed this overbearing implication. Customary usage until then had found it sufficient to classify the populations of belligerent countries simply into 'combatants' and 'non-combatants': the former, everyone directly active in military operations of some kind or other; the latter, everyone else. Now the military appropriated both 'combatant' and 'non-combatant' to its own swelling uses, thus severing the remainder of the population the more decisively from connexion with hostilities, in order (in effect) to ensure its taking no part in them. Another way of describing civilian populations which achieved symptomatic popularity in these years was as 'prisoners of war on parole'; i.e., liable to very drastic treatment if they did not do exactly as they were told.[96] Let us now examine the main branches of the idea of occupier's rights held by those who took them most seriously. We might for analytical convenience call it the arch-occupier's argument; found close to perfection in Lieber's Code, in almost all German and most Russian opinions, and in some others, especially the eminent Belgian Rolin-Jaequemyns, who shared with Bluntschli pride of place in the seventies as the most eminent of their kind.

The arch-occupier argued that the ends of humanity in warfare were met as best they could be when an invaded or occupied populace stayed in its homes and went to its normal work-places, and kept itself assiduously and conspicuously apart from whatever hostilities might still be going on. The point of their staying at home was not just to make the invader's requisitioning easier, though it certainly did that too. How silly it was of the French to flee from the villages through which the Germans passed on their way to Paris!, noted a distinguished and (to judge from what he put in his diary) humane officer. 'Our soldiers, after all, cannot be left on the road when there are houses beside it.' So the soldiers had to break in. 'In order to get from the road to the top rooms, chairs and tables are piled one above the other, and are left there afterwards.' If there was no proper fire-wood, furniture would be broken up to provide it. 'All this kind of destruction would be avoided, and the necessary requisitions be carried out in a more orderly manner, if the inhabitants remained at home.'[97]

The arch-occupier preferred government officials to stay on the job because they could be so useful in

> ... re-establishing and securing, so far as possible, public safety and social order. The functionaries and officials of every class who, at the instance of the occupier, consent to continue to perform their duties, shall be under his protection. They shall not be dismissed or be liable to punishment unless they fail in fulfilling the obligations they have undertaken, and shall be handed over to justice only if they violate those obligations by unfaithfulness, ...[98]

We are reminded how easily 'collaborators', as mid-twentieth-century usage would call them, could be made sacrificial victims on behalf of the very principles in whose name they might subsequently be judged: patriotism and humanity. Their presence might restrain the invader from roughness and rudeness and increase the likelihood that his demands would be spread fairly over all who ought to help bear their burden. But what a cost might not this delicate work exact! What did the people of Rheims in 1870 think of their mayor when, left by the army and the prefecture to face the Germans on his own, he broke the horrid news to his townsfolk and ended thus?

> We are henceforth defenceless, and it would be insane to attempt an impossible resistance, which would expose the entire population to the greatest dangers.
>
> We are driven then, with death in our hearts, to beg you to remain calm, to restrain the feelings which struggle within all of us and to accept with tragic resignation the sufferings we can no longer avoid.[99]

Mayors in other cities addressed their people in similar terms. But the extent to which they might be understood and trusted by them was something over which they might have little control. It would depend mainly on the nature and the scale of the demands made by the occupier. Here is an unusually moderate and conciliatory proclamation by a German commander at Beauvais:

1. The French local authorities now take orders from us.
2. The troops under my command come not as enemies of peaceful citizens; they mean to have good relations with the people of the department of the Oise.
3. The prime necessity towards that end is our security from surprise attacks. Such attacks will be met by the instant burning of the places they seem to be launched from.
4. All arms must be handed in instantly – or else!
5. The municipality will be held collectively responsible for hostile acts committed on their territory.
6. House owners on whom soldiers are quartered are responsible for providing ample and good food. If any really can't manage to do so, the Municipality must help them.
7. All streets and passages must stay open.
8. No curfew or ban on movement but *no demonstrations or threatening gatherings.*[100]

Many such proclamations were couched in much more forbidding terms, beyond which it must be remembered that the real severities of occupation only began when – what even the most adeptly tight-rope-walking mayors could often not prevent – local acts of resistance or resentment or merely failure to produce the goods gave the occupier an excuse for taking hostages, imposing vast fines, and so on.

The very definition of 'occupation' was argued about. Arch-occupiers pressed for a large, loose definition; representatives of peoples likely to be occupied wanted the definition kept close and clear. The argument was strikingly parallel to that about blockade in war at sea. 'Blockades, in order to be binding, must be effective', declared the 1856 Declaration of Paris; meaning that there must be no more 'paper blockades' and windy assertions of dominance where it did not actually exist. Similarly, with respect to occupation, the arch-occupier's argument was that a country was 'effectively occupied' when the occupier had the means to impose his power at will, as for instance by being able to make arrests and impose punishments by means of *ad hoc* expeditions; his idea of it was not that his forces had to be physically present everywhere he claimed to be occupying, all the time. This definition mattered very much, because upon it turned the lawfulness of popular armed resistance; a *levée en masse* against an invader being one thing, an insurgency against a legally warranted occupier being another, much more serious in its consequences (as we shall see in the next section). The arch-occupier, far from being ready to consider insurgents and guerrillas on their law-fulfilling merits, expected absolute docility and subservience from his temporary subjects, offering them such modest benefits as he did offer (martial law and order, principally) on condition that they inconvenienced him not at all.

Extreme doctrines of the obligations of the occupied were put forward in the debates and discussions of these years, the like of which never again appeared in the texts; the Lieber and Brussels Codes reflected them as the Hague one, a quarter of a century later, did not. Many of the proclamations of invading and occupying generals in these wars of the sixties reflect this extreme inclination. I choose as an example, less known in Europe than the German batch from 1870–1, the Union's General Pope, a protégé of the fire-eating radical republicans, who crowned his series of orders to the inhabitants of the area of Confederate Virginia in which he was operating with his at once notorious order of 23 July 1862, warning all males that if they refused to take an oath of allegiance to the United States they would be 'conducted South beyond the extreme pickets of this army, and be notified that if found again anywhere within our lines . . . they will be considered spies. . . .'[101] It was not difficult to consider that he was going too far. Lincoln and MacClellan, the nominal commander-in-chief, were embarrassed by him, and Lee, on the other side, seems not to have known quite what to make of it; MacClellan, they admitted, was ostentatiously waging war 'in strict conformity to the usages of civilized nations, but here is Pope, right under the eye of Mr Lincoln, violating all the so-called principles of modern warfare. . . .'[102]

The Pope problem solved itself when Jackson thrashed him at the second battle of Manassas; and by the spring of the following year, Lieber's Code had imposed some uniformity on Union generals' practices. But in point of fact the dislikeable Pope was only carrying to an impolitic and perhaps inhumane point the arch-occupier's persuasion that absolute docility could be expected from the occupied, as if already conquest had been followed by formal incorporation into their former enemy's territory. This expectation often revealed itself, in the years we have here in view, in the use of the term 'war treason', *Kriegsverrat*, to stigmatize the most unacceptable forms of occupied behaviour and to justify their drastic punishment.[103] In Lieber's Code it was almost any transaction between occupied people and 'their own' government which came under that term. 'War rebellion' for Lieber was something else;[104] but in practice the two were, for a while, often confused. That confusion is another indication of the lengths and refinements to which the arch-occupiers went in seeking to cement their security. Westlake, as usual, steers a reasonable middle course :

> There is no [good] foundation for the epithet of 'war treason' which German writers apply to every act of [a] population directed against the occupying army, for the duty owed in return for the maintenance of order will not extend so far. No act of that kind can be regarded as treasonable without violating the modern view of the nature of military occupation, and to introduce the notion of moral fault into an invader's view of what is detrimental to him only serves to inflame his passions, and to make it less likely that he will observe the true limit of necessity in his repression of what is detrimental to him.[105]

Many of the bitterest arguments at Brussels and The Hague turned on the extent of an invader's and occupier's rights to demand, not only docile acquiescence, but also positive assistance, from the enemy population over whom he had power. The Hague Regulations marked several victories for the Westlake view of this matter, specifically prohibiting occupiers from compelling the occupied to swear allegiance to them, from treating them as spies, from making them 'take part in the operations of war directed against their own country', and from 'compelling them to furnish information about the army of the other belligerent, or about its means of defence'.[106] To this last clause a number of States, Germany and Russia at their head, entered reservations, maintaining to the last that, whatever services from occupied peoples they could, perhaps, dispense with, they absolutely could not agree to give up the liberty to compel them to serve as guides through difficult and unknown country.[107]

We may conclude this sketch of the arch-occupier's view of things with his expectations specifically concerning Requisitions.

Requisitions between the 1860s and 1914 were just as much of a problem as they had been between 1776 and 1816, mainly for the same reason – that armies of any size could not manage without them – but with this distinguishing difference, that by now the juridical and political communities were acutely aware of them as a problem and were under pressure from the peace-and-progress side of civilian opinion to do something about it. In no branch of the law of war was the clamour for limitation and restraint more urgent than in this one, and in no branch of the discussion did the military find the civilians more troublesome. This was largely because of the persistence of the Rousseau-an idea, that 'private property' was normally inviolate in war, and because it might still confusingly be the custom for a belligerent to proclaim, as King William I did so emphatically on 11/12 August 1870, 'I am making war against the soldiers and not the citizens of France.' We have already seen how war practice both on sea and land contradicted this idea, and how the only difference was between those who knew that they were contradicting it and those who pretended that they didn't.

The deliberate, precise, and much publicized seizure of enemy private property in maritime wars indeed attracted attention as the more inevitable, incidental and unadmitted seizure and destruction of it in land wars did not; and it may even have been the case, in some eighteenth-century wars, that damage and loss to private property could plausibly have been reckoned a larger problem, by financial calculations, in sea than land war. But one's impression of the extent of damage to property during the land wars of 1792–1815 is that it was vast; and by the time the wars of 1861–71 had provided their store of up-to-date examples, voices (and not only British ones!) were increasingly heard to say that, whatever the principle of the thing, in practice private property suffered *more* from involvement in the land variety. A French diplomat, for instance, thus apparently put a stop to a German attempt to exploit this old line in 1871 :

> When the plenipotentiaries of the parties to the treaty of peace met at Brussels, Count Arnim proposed an additional article, to the effect that private property on the high seas should be respected in time of war; to this Baron Baude replied that, if such a proposition were entertained, he should insist on equal respect being paid to private property on land, and claim the restoration of sums levied on private property and private property confiscated during the late war. . . .[108]

The Russian Katchenowsky, addressing the (British) National Association for Promoting Social Science in 1872, made the same point :

> Up to 1870 private property seemed to be more exposed to depredations in maritime than in continental war; now we find quite the reverse of it ... in the last war [1870–1] the pacific population of the invaded country was utterly helpless and unprotected against the enemy, and no change for the better can be expected in future wars before human rights are secured by international law.[109]

He agreed with Colonel Hamley, one of Britain's top military authorities, that what was really needed was (to jump to the language of 1949) a Civilians' Convention. I have come across only one other affirmation as bold and early as that. But from then on, the parallel between sea and land war so far as private property was concerned was quite often drawn, at least by sea warriors, as a legitimate tactic of self-defence, and the arch-occupiers' demand for adequately spacious requisitioning rights was thereby the more critically scrutinized.

Since the Prusso-German requisitioning system was recognized to be the most efficient and elaborate in the civilized world, we may as well use it as a model for discussion. A French military reformer, who thought that the French might learn a lot from it, analysed it thus for their benefit soon after their disaster. The heart of the Prussian system, he wrote, was the regular use of 'cantonment', the billeting of troops (and their voracious horses) upon private householders, with an obligation to feed as well as shelter them. All this was planned well in advance. 'Feeding areas' (*zones d'alimentation*) would have been designated for each brigade, and officers knew exactly what to do when they arrived; they didn't have to wait for the administration to do it for them.

> Generals, statistical tables in hand, assign *this* group to *that* brigade. Cantonment goes ahead as planned; sentinels are placed at the liquor shops, the grocery stores, the butchers and the bakers, so that the inhabitants will have no trouble in provisioning themselves; and that's all there is to it – each family has its contingent of soldiers and has to feed them ... perhaps there is a bit of unfairness, following the hazards of the game, but the great end is attained – the troops are sheltered against bad weather and are well and quickly fed.[110]

Such was the system for troops on the march; those steadily-advancing, ever victorious, short-war-winning troops dearest to the German imagination. But of course wars could not always go precisely according to plan, and other modes of raising requisitions (in kind or money, the latter much confused with, and sometimes described as, 'contributions') had to be employed. There is no need to go into the rather intricate discussions which took place about these. Behind them all, in the period we are dealing with, lay the facts that the two biggest armies of the European continent, the German and the Russian, were going to live off the lands they invaded by one means or another, that they were going to live as well as they could, and that their readiness to respect the susceptibilities and convenience of the populations of invaded and occupied territory had to be matched with their conviction that, war being what it was and the powers of the victor being what they were, the invader and occupier was not going to have to pay for what he consumed.[111] To the argument that it would be more humane to pay for provisions beyond some peremptory minimum, the arch-occupiers replied that indeed they would pay where it suited them but that where it didn't, they would only give receipts for what they took, leaving it to the victims to get their money back from their government after the war was over. Levies of money were declared to be necessary, sometimes as cash equivalents to gross requisitions (and a means, often, of spreading the net burden more fairly), sometimes simply by virtue of age-old *Kriegsmanier* (old-fashioned soldiers could still think of them as ransoms in lieu of pillage), and sometimes in the forms of fines, as punishments. 1870–1 practice showed much fudging between money raised punitively or minatorily, and money raised from alleged necessity. An embattled German controversialist, like General von Voigts-Rhetz, who was to lead his country's team at Brussels, could maintain that this exhaustive system (exhausting, also, to its civilian victims, in proportion as hostilities continued) did not mean that the Germans were inhumane or practically lacking in that respect for enemy private property to which his country stood committed. 'Military requisitions and other necessities which are the sad law and one of the most regrettable scourges of war are not inconsistent with soldiers' respect for private property. ...'[112] It was simply a matter of Necessity.

Necessity repeatedly entered into his arguments at Brussels, as he tried as patiently as he could to explain to the small-country critics just why this or that limiting idea of theirs was unacceptable. On one occasion he expressly refused to agree that the question could be 'reduced to knowing whether the occupying army must be *allowed to take* or whether it is to be given the *right to take*'. 'No,' he replied, in an exchange wonderfully revealing of his state of mind; 'the *right* is not given, it is only declared that the *fact* exists [and] is one which no one can prevent occurring in practice, and that it is desirable that it should be limited to cases of inevitable necessity.'[113] Thus he brought the others up sharp against a concept of necessity which not all of them shared. But he and at least the Russians at that conference were inexorable, and got more or less the result they wanted. General Horsford summed up the key debate thus:

Three principles for regulating the levy of requisitions found advocates: (1) They shall be levied to the same extent as the national defending army has the right to demand from its own country. (2) They shall be levied to the same extent as the invading army has the right to demand from its own country.

(3) The extent to which they shall be levied shall be determined solely by the necessities of war.

. . . .

The third was that which received the support of the first German delegate, and was in fact the only one to which he would assent. [He] pointed out that on the subject of requisitions it is impossible to go into details. Abuses must always occur, but by the adoption of general principles their number may be diminished. . . .[114]

The definition upon which they managed ultimately to agree was:

only such payments and services as are connected with the necessities of war generally acknowledged in proportion to the resources of the country. . . .

and the undertakings that

for every contribution a receipt shall be given [and] for every requisition an indemnity shall be granted, or a receipt given.[115]

The Hague Regulations said much the same.

Necessity, however, was not the only savage spirit stirring behind these rules and Regulations. Of course it was the one most often mentioned; it was the most presentable and producible of them. But analytically distinguishable from it, however often cloaked by it, was (what indeed we have already slightly noticed) the intention to punish or to oppress. The whole heavy business of living at enemy expense spanned a wide range of intentions as well as situations, and between what might be demanded in high harvest time by a cheerful, confident column, here today, gone tomorrow, and what might be demanded in mid-winter by a sullen, irritable army of occupation waiting for a war to end that ought to have ended long ago, there was an enormous gulf. Because the same words were often used for them, the difference of their realities is often obscured. The fact is, that requisitions and contributions became one of the several means by which pressure could be put upon a hostile people. Other sharper means had to be used when that hostility took to arms or sheltered behind them; and with those means the remaining two sections of this chapter will be concerned. But it must be noted, in concluding this section, that whatever their protestations to the contrary, the Germans were using requisitions (as well as the other, sharper, means, the 'war of terror', as Rüstow put it)[116] to turn the screw on the French during the later stages of the war of 1870–1, as they had done to the Danes in 1864.[117] 'However one may argue round the matter, there is no doubt that in past wars [Germany] employed the system (as Mr Sutherland Edwards, no enemy of Germany, states) "to crush the occupied portion of the country and make its inhabitants long for peace".'[118]

6 Resistance: the limits of lawfulness

We have been enumerating the essentials of the occupier's dream: a docile, accepting population, behaving as if conquest and transfer to the victor's sovereignty had already happened.. I have made much of it because it was extraordinarily prominent in the great debate from the sixties to the early twentieth century, and it only didn't succeed in wholly conforming the law of war at its highest, treaty, level to its demands because of the passionate opposition it aroused; an opposition which, not very successful in 1874, did somewhat better at The Hague, and sensibly moderated what got into the agreed texts there. (What continued to be thought of as customary law was, of course, another matter.)

Invasion and occupation, in reality, never went as smoothly as the dream desiderated. Accidents would happen. Patience was not inexhaustible. Even German soldiers were not so perfectly disciplined that they would not sometimes do a bit of unauthorized damage and looting; even the German army, of whose nationally representative character its spokesmen were so proud, necessarily contained some criminal elements.[119] But beyond such occasions of roughness, either adventitious like the weather or unavoidable like weak links in a chain, there was the likelihood that the occupied population would not take it lying down; might indeed be provoked to resist it, standing up. The arch-occupier had his instant answer to such affronts: 'War Rebellion!', 'War Treason!', 'Banditry!', etc. But there was another and more sympathetic and, arguably, more just way of looking at it, in considering which we move abruptly into a familiar, contemporary, atmosphere. Requisitions (though not their next of kin, economic exploitation) are, from a later twentieth-century point of view, rather a dead duck. Guerrillas are very much alive.

The argument about 'guerrillas' (using the word loosely), which became very bitter during these years, was bitter and confused not least because several logically separable issues became practically intertwined: above all, drawing a distinction – as some though it very necessary to do – between invasion and occupation; and ascertaining the credentials of the lawful fighting man.

As to the first, almost enough has already been said in the preceding section. There was a strong disposition among the military of the big land powers – whose combined weight at conferences was all but irresistible – and the juridical community to agree that the continuation of hostilities in an occupied zone was bound to make life so unpleasant for its inhabitants that a *prima facie* case therefore existed, on humanitarian grounds if no other, for declaring such continuation unlawful. Yet it was difficult to deny that such hostilities could be carried on by indisputably lawful soldiers; by, for example, the Confederate Colonel Mosby, whose operations behind Grant's lines caused much military nuisance, or the French group which early in 1871 made the Fontenay raid already mentioned (above p. 168).[120] If these men had not been in uniform, they could, when caught, have been shot as spies and/or as civilian saboteurs; but they were neither; besides possessing proper credentials they wore uniforms and carried arms openly; they were guerrillas by a modern loose use of the word but their adventurous operations were very like those which the *ancien régime* had known as the 'small war',[121] the lawfulness of which had never been doubted. If the perpetrators of such daring attacks could not be caught, what could an enraged occupier do except vent his frustration and rage on the local populace whose complicity, even if by simply keeping quiet, could be suspected? They might be terrorized into making occupied seas too hot, or cold, for partisan fish to swim in; or the occupier could do as the Spanish and British did in the later stages of their suppressions of, respectively, the Cuban insurrection and the second Boer war, and 'concentrate' the peaceful population within guarded camps, leaving the continuing combatants outside on their own. These were drastic measures, but they appeared to have some justification as long as the occupier could plausibly argue that he could not maintain any kind of humane governance unless all hostile activities absolutely ceased. To that however could be replied, from the other side, that the demands he made on the occupied were saving him from 'inconvenience' rather than disaster, and that the very fact that partisan operations continued to take place at all could be taken to prove that the occupier's power was not so great as he claimed. Occupiers may long to be loved, but it is not, after all, a reasonable expectation.

But what if such deeds, so annoying to occupiers seeking the peace and refreshment which regular soldiers expect when away from the battle zone, were made doubly annoying by being perpetrated by less regular types, or by types who had nothing regular about them at all? No case for such could have been argued during the *ancien régime*, when, whatever room the publicists left in principle for popular self-help against enemy invasion, their preference for relatively regular operations under decidedly regular troops was so strong as to support the normal practice of the period, which was to put all but regularly levied and commanded troops under the ban.[122] But things had changed since the revolution. First the *levée en masse* in France, then its equivalents in several other countries (most of all, Prussia), and thirdly, in some indefinite and worrying way, the various national inheritances of partisan warfare, had fomented the idea (at least in the more democratic, purely defensive countries like Belgium, Switzerland, Holland, Norway, Sweden, supported by Britain and to a considerable extent also France) that 'the people' at large should not be inhibited from taking up arms in the countries' defence (as patriot writers always assumed they were anxious to do), even if that meant – an extreme and desperate recourse – insurgency against an odious occupier.

So a bitter argument developed between these two poles : on the one side, the invader/occupier, professing respect for humanity and a willingness to abide by reasonable limitations and restraints, but alleging that none was reasonable which increased the difficulties of his invading/occupying task; on the other, the invaded/occupied, demanding that up to some reasonable point the invader/occupier ought to accept such limitations and restraints in his encounters with irregular and guerrilla forces as he did willingly enough when he encountered regular ones. At bottom, it was an argument, again, over the meaning of 'necessity', which often sounded as if it really meant 'convenience'. Must the invader's convenience – if it was no more than that – require of the invaded such self-abasing humility as the arch-occupier's demands, at their highest, required?

One of Britain's leading military writers, Edward Hamley, at the time commander of the Staff College, wrote powerfully about this in *The Times* on 22 February 1871.[123] He began by placing himself squarely in the great tradition of the publicists and the international Red Cross movement, by urging the British public to exchange its normal insular and sentimental preoccupations for a grappling with international matters of larger import.

A people easily excited to indignation by the insufficient nutriment of a pauper, or the undue suffering of a convict, seems to regard with equanimity the calamities endured by a neighbouring nation at the hands of its invaders. . . . As I persist in believing that the question, whether an invader is entitled to devastate a country and oppress a people at his pleasure, is one which concerns the whole world, I will . . . state . . . my reasons for thinking that the system of warfare pursued by the Germans should no longer be tolerated.

He declined to accept arguments from precedent, and thought the Germans should know better than even partly to rely on them; but,

. . . though precedent be no warrant, though to tell us that Napoleon did thus and thus is no better justification than if Attila were quoted, let us by all means hear whatever can be said in extenuation of the horrible warfare of the Germans. If it can be shown to be politic, it may be so far excused; if it can be proved necessary, it may be condoned; but if it be neither politic nor necessary, can it be too loudly condemned?

The extent of German requisitions and so on, he described as 'nothing but a system of organized plunder', far beyond what could legitimately be claimed on any ground of real necessity. Its motivation, he perceived, was largely punitive, terroristic, and vindictive; 'the gratification of rapacity on the one side, and the aggravation of impoverishment and despair on the other'.

His contention that it was impolitic rested mainly on its having aroused popular resistance where such would perhaps not otherwise have bothered them. (Was he in turn unrealistic here?)

The non-combatant populations, even of the most war-like countries, are very tolerant of the defeat of their armies; such disasters leave no rancour behind; it is the oppression and humiliation of the inhabitants which stir up lasting hatreds.

Magnanimity was so obvious, so easy, so politic, that the difficulty was to avoid it.

This oppression and humiliation, he thought the Germans had indecently overdone.

This system of terrorism . . . has been adopted by the Germans, and justified by their apologists, as a means of giving security to their troops and communications, by compelling the inhabitants, through fear of instant and tremendous penalties, not only to refrain from acts of hostility, but to aid in protecting their oppressors by betraying the enterprises of their own countrymen . . . compelling them to treat their friends as enemies, their enemies as friends; a kind of tyranny which will appear to many more horrible than the arbitrary infliction of death . . . an outrage on humanity. . . . The grand mistake of the Germans is that, while ascribing great influence to fear, they ignore the counter-influence of desperation.

The conclusion of his observations and emotions was that it had become necessary to 'substitute recognized rules for the savage will of an irresistible invader'. 'The fact is – and it is a fact which has encouraged the Germans to push licence to an extreme – that the world has hitherto been too indulgent to invaders.' And for officers and gentlemen 'the question for decision seems to be – is war brigandage? Is it to continue to be an occupation which honourable men can follow?'

Hamley's indictment of the victors of the Franco-Prussian war makes a suitable introduction to our study of how those who were concerned with the law of war fashioned this part of it during the decades preceding 1914, because the war of 1870–1 was the war showing most sharply on their screens. Had they been much interested in it, the Europeans would have found at least as much to think about in the American civil war of 1861–5; and this side of the Franco-Prussian war might not have become as nasty as it did, if more attention had been paid on both sides to Lieber's careful distinction between the variously unlawful categories of 'war-rebels', 'armed prowlers', and spies on the one side, and the lawful category of 'partisans' on the other: 'soldiers armed and wearing the uniform of their army, but belonging to a corps which acts detached from the main body for the purposes of making inroads into the territory occupied by the enemy. If captured, they are entitled to all the privileges of the prisoner of war.'[124] But not much interest was, as a matter of fact, shown by Europeans in that great war; least of all in its many guerrilla facets, which most military orthodoxy in the old world was content to lump in with all the other aspects of it which made it seem messy, mob-like, amateurish, and anarchistic.

Was German conduct of the war of 1870–1 as 'horrible' as Hamley said? Upon this awkward question, which the Germans emphatically would not allow to be mentioned at Brussels in seventy-four, experts differed. The Germans had some non-German defenders, were not without critics within their own country, and were at first thought to be leaning insufficiently hard on the French by that experienced leaner, General Philip Sheridan, who told Bismarck's entourage that: 'Nothing should be left to the people but eyes, to lament the war!'[125] I offer a short-cut summary of the rights and wrongs of their case. They marched into France expecting (whether reasonably or not, is open to debate) a short, sharp, clean war, which would be decided by indomitable courage and morale on conventional battlefields and superior staff work in getting them there; requisitions and so on being made mainly on behalf of a mostly moving army, the French 'peaceful population' would hardly feel them. They soon found themselves enmeshed in a spread-out national or people's war, partly a guerrilla one, with no hope that conventional battle decisions would precipitate an end. The general cast of their thought about war, besides being prickly with dislike of the French and an obsessive desire to 'get even with them' for damages and slights all too well recalled by popular literature and history, included at least three tendencies which were sure to make it all nastier once the war began to go 'badly' (a relative and subjective term): (1) their doctrine of military necessity and occupation propriety, which we have already noticed; (2) their determination not only to keep hostilities off their own territory but also to conduct them at enemy expense; and (3) their particular detestation of irregularities and improvisations (such as came more normally to the French). Faced with something like a people's war both in front of them and behind them, their reactions were uniformly unsympathetic, suspicious and severe; sometimes inhumane, unreasonable, and unfair. Because some peasants no doubt took pot-shots at them and evaded notice by mingling with the rest of the blue blouses, subsequently Germans rushed to the conclusion that every shot taken at them behind the front came from a blue-blouse-camouflaged peasant; because some trains were sabotaged, they said it was sabotage every time something went wrong with a train.[126] Because some French public persons and journalists spouted wicked nonsense, they assumed that all Frenchmen believed it.[127] Not having made any plans for dealing with guerrilla warfare, and believing the worst of their enemy, they reacted to it and anything that looked like it with much pedantry, a good deal of savagery, and sometimes great unfairness; what Lieber's Code prescribed for the Union army would have been more reasonable. On the whole, Hamley seems to have been right in saying that wherever the Germans had a choice between a more severe and a milder course, they chose the former, out of principle, habit or preference: a proclivity perhaps neatly displayed in their impromptu reaction to the saucy French use of balloons to carry important travellers above the German lines and occupied territories. They showed, writes Hall, 'a strong inclination' to treat all such as spies. 'Neither secrecy, nor disguise, nor pretence being possible to persons travelling in balloons, the view taken by the Germans is inexplicable.'[128] An historian must be pardoned for thinking otherwise.

To German minds, much at least of that indictment would have been thought unfair, on the ground that the way the French conducted their national resistance, and more particularly the guerrilla part of it, was itself so lawless and law-defying that the Germans were driven to drastic responses. We turn therefore to the French side of this story. The French, although relying like the Germans primarily on a conventional 'regular' army and expecting to win or lose the war by battles, expected to make some use of less conventional and regular forces, and expanded them as the war went on. There were Gardes Nationales, Gardes Nationales Mobilisés, the Gardes Mobiles, and from the very beginning of the war some small amount of volunteer companies of '*francs-tireurs*' founded on the 'civil defence associations' of 1868.[129] Once the imperial armies had disappeared, and Gambetta's government of national defence had called for an all-out effort of resistance and recovery, those 'irregular' force-forms naturally multiplied greatly. German response to them varied from commander to commander and from time to time, and it seems impossible to lay down any easy generalizations. But this, I think, can be said: some of these irregulars and semi-regulars were behaving like thoroughly lawful combatants and ought to have been accepted by the Germans as such; while others behaved in ways which thoroughly justified the Germans' complaints about, and unrelenting loathing of, them.

The former kind, clearly aware of the requirements of the customary law and seeking to meet them, wore uniforms of one sort or another, carried arms openly, knew at any rate as much about the law of war as the ordinary infantryman would have done, were under the command of men themselves responsible to higher military or political command. But that was the best of them. It is difficult to say which were the worst and what they were like, except that they were like nothing a German officer could ever have dreamt of.[130] There is no need to believe everything that Germans said about them. What French and other writers said about them was disturbing enough. The picturesque Garibaldians were internationally the most trumpeted; Brenet says they were almost completely useless and absurd, though they knew enough about war to abide by its customs and, as a matter of fact, were treated as lawful combatants by General von Werder.[131] But what could he have done with the 'Garibaldiennes' whose appearance at Dijon 'stupefied' the inhabitants? – 'These women are wearing fantastic costumes, of military cut. Some of them are got up as *officers*, ... Others bear the badge of the International, and the red cross on a white ground. ...'[132] Monod's summary (which he believed to represent the views of 'serious men' in France after the war) was that on the whole they had done more harm than good; bad characters were attracted to them, like the 'train and bank robbers' said to have joined their equivalents in Kansas eight years earlier; their operations were usually unwelcome to the local populace, not just because of the reprisals that were likely to follow; some were simply bandits.[133]

There was a zone of uncertainty, then, between the partisan proper (whom all parties agreed to recognize) and the bandit improper, and it did the former no good that the problem of recognizing his credentials should be thus aggravated. But that was not the only aggravation of this most difficult and tragic of all of these years' arguments. With it was mixed also (and much confused in the mixing) the separate questions of the *levée en masse*, the citizen's right spontaneously to join in the defence of his country, and the nature of the encouragement or instruction he was given to do so. A large part always of the case against popular private military enterprise is that those undertaking it cannot normally be aware of the obligations resting on lawful combatants. Properly officered and disciplined soldiers at any rate are supposed to do what they are told; and if they are told to restrain their passions and forget about their prejudices, they may do so. But what were civilians likely to do when encouraged in such styles as were employed by some Frenchmen with access to paper and ink? The Préfet of Côte d'Or was at least tactless in causing this bill to be posted all round his department:

> Your fatherland does not ask you to gather in large numbers and oppose the enemy openly; it only expects that each morning three or four resolute men will leave their village and go to where nature has prepared a place suitable for hiding and for firing without danger on the Prussians. . . .[134]

Much more offensive was the language and more awful were the encouragements given to lawlessness and savagery in many of the radical newspapers, which the Germans not unreasonably took to represent French popular feeling. I do not know how seriously to take a proclamation reported in the *Journal de Genève* in September 1870, informing the Vendéens that the Germans would soon be there:

> Disembowelling women, slitting children's throats, imprisoning able-bodied males, robbing houses, burning villages and churches, breaking statues of the Virgin Mary, murdering prisoners of war – that is how Prussians make war![135]

This sort of thing, of which Bismarck's government and press made great and effective play, emphasized, for all who paused to think about it, the impossibility of sanctioning the most enthusiastic demands, that the citizen's right to fight should extend to a right to insurgency against an established occupier. The lawmakers could never say more to that than they could to the spy – that he might be heroic and what he did might be useful, but it was incapable of legitimization. Unorganized, 'spontaneous' insurgency – as distinct from organized partisan warfare – against an occupier was ruled out by all sides. Spontaneous resistance against an invader however was different. What was the legal status of peasants or other civilians who should help their national armed forces defend their village against an invader, or even defend it on their own? This happened sometimes during the German invasion of France in 1870. It led to enormous outcries of indignation from both sides. The Germans were of course justified in shooting at civilians who shot at them, but they quickly overreacted, shot at civilians who were not so clearly doing so, subsequently shot or otherwise beat up civilians who could not be proved to have done so, and burnt houses and villages from which such shooting had come. Untangling the horror stories of what happened, for example, at Bazeilles on 1 September and Châteaudun on 18 October 1870, is extremely difficult;[136] my conclusion after studying a good deal of the relevant literature is that French complaints about these and similar incidents unreasonably neglected the fact that when miscellaneously uniformed and completely non-uniformed persons were sharing in the armed defence of a place not fully evacuated of unarmed civilians, many of the latter were likely to get hurt; on the other hand, the common German belief was at least as unreasonable, that no non-uniformed non-officered persons at all should lift a gun against an invader.[137]

I have given the arguments about 'guerrillas' in enough detail by now, I hope, for it to be unnecessary to go through the Brussels and Hague debates about them. They are intensely interesting, and, along with the debates on requisitions and the rest, should be required reading for all who wish to understand the military history of pre-1914 Europe. But although they were passionate and long, they made little mark on the 'status of belligerent' part of the texts originally before those conferences. Other parts of the drafts came out of the conference much more altered; a few never came out at all; some additions were proposed in the course of the debates which no one could previously have foreseen – the most important of such by far being Martens's 1899 Declaration, a gloss on those definitions of the status of lawful belligerent which the great land army powers could not bear to be stretched. So, between the Brussels Code and the Hague Regulations in their final, 1907, form, that crucial definition of the lawful belligerent, given doubled emphasis by being moved up from ninth to first place, remained adamantly almost the same; and we had better give it in its brief entirety, since it was to stay the same through both world wars. After what has gone before, its terms may be left to speak for themselves.

The Status of Belligerent: Article 1.

The laws, rights, and duties of war apply not only to the army, but also to militia and volunteer corps fulfilling all the following conditions:

1. They must be commanded by a person responsible for his subordinates;
2. They must have a fixed distinctive sign recognizable at a distance;
3. They must carry arms openly; and
4. They must conduct their operations in accordance with the laws and customs of war.

In countries where militia or volunteer corps constitute the army, or form part of it, they are included under the denomination 'army'.

Article 2.

The inhabitants of a territory not under occupation, who, on the approach of the enemy, spontaneously take up arms to resist the invading troops without having had time to organize themselves in accordance with Article 1, shall be regarded as belligerents if they carry arms openly, and if they respect the laws and customs of war.[138]

7 The civilian as enemy: bombardment and destruction

Throughout the previous sections it has been clear how much and how often was the pretence broken down, that the bulk of the enemy country's population, being 'peaceful', could stand so external to a conflict as to be spared its disagreeable consequences while the combatants alone shouldered them. It did not work out thus in practice, and impatient or irritable invaders/occupiers gave up trying to make it work so, if they had ever tried much in the first place. We come now at last to the devices of war typically adopted by those who never pretended that civil populations could or should be wholly passed by, and we find that the practice of parties most likely to talk in Rousseau-an terms turned out to be little different from that of those who normally eschewed it.

Our first and main concern must be with bombardment and similar destructive procedures. In principle there is little to add to what was said about the same in the last section of Chapter II. Bombardment continued to be controversial through the nineteenth century for the same reasons that it had been so in the eighteenth; but the range of examples and styles available for comment was interestingly enlarged during the wars of 1861–71, which made it clear that Americans and Germans, sufficiently pressed, yielded to none in their readiness to undertake it.

Most of the arguments about bombardment in the generation before 1914 turned on the German instances of the Franco-Prussian war, which far eclipsed the small precedents of 1864.[139] Bombardment of fortified cities was not something the German high command had much expected to have to do. But in availing themselves of the unexpected opportunities offered by the collapse of the French imperial armies, the rapidly advancing German armies bypassed a number of fortresses which sooner or later had to be dealt with. Most of these fortresses were as ill-prepared for their job as were, at first, the Germans, and there was a good deal of improvisation on both sides, which no doubt partly explains some of the more unfortunate incidents which occurred and much of the subsequent slanging-match about them. The means adopted for the reduction of these places were starvation and bombardment, and in only one case – the biggest of them, Paris – did the starving-out process go on long enough to play a big part in the result.

In trying to sort out the charges and counter-charges made about these bombardments, as usual one has to separate emotional, ignorant and even mendacious chaff from substantial juridical wheat. It was, for example, almost regularly alleged that hospitals, churches, artistic treasure-houses etc., were being *deliberately* hit. This may sometimes have been the case, inasmuch as commanders of artillery units can no more always ensure that each gun-crew really is aiming where it is told to aim than infantry officers can make sure that none of their men is not actually nicking the noses of his bullets to 'dum-dum' them, as evil-minded infantrymen have been credibly said to do.[140] But there is no serious evidence that German commanders ordered the deliberate aiming at such targets except when they suspected, as they were certainly sometimes right to do, that towers and spires of churches, being usually by far the highest buildings in a place, were being used as look-out posts.[141]

On the other hand, there is no doubt that German bombardments were sometimes – not always – indiscriminately of the civilian parts of the cities with the old object of terrorizing the civilian population or to make the government behind them feel unbearable guilt about the pain they were, by the bombarder's process of reasoning, causing that populace to undergo. (Allegations from each side that the other was responsible for causing the harshness and inhumanity were normal.) Of course there were arguments among the bombarders themselves. Soldiers were sometimes less enthusiastic about bombardments than their domestic publics, some types of soldier (not least artillery men), would be keener on them than others, and so on. The officer commanding the first German army in 1870, von Manteuffel, for example, told his subordinate waiting to go to work on Mezières not to rush it; until the proper siege-train was there, he wrote: 'I forbid any half measures, such as bombarding the town and the like, which only cause loss of life and destruction of property, without obtaining any military result.'[142] Obviously, he did not set much store on mere terror effects. Others however did. Terror must have been among the somewhat confused purposes of the general who had Strasbourg to deal with, von Werder, whom we know from the subsequent episode of his operations against the Garibaldians and General Bourbaki in the south-east (also from the fact that he was affectionately regarded by the very humane Crown Prince) not to have been a hard man.[143] It was under his authority that this most questionable of all the bombardments was undertaken.[144] The usual mutual accusations of provocative and/or unlawful conduct took place – some of them unusually trivial, reflecting perhaps the confusion of counsels within the invader's camp – and Rüstow rightly reminded his readers that French attitudes had not been consistently admirable: 'In France, the bombardment of the city was regarded as an act of barbarity; but when General Uhrich [the French commander: an Alsacien] said that if the Germans succeeded in entering the town he would himself retire into the citadel and thence destroy the town, the speech was praised in all the French newspapers as heroic.'[145] Yet, after all, that bombardment seems to have been a foolish thing to do. There was no great garrison in Strasbourg waiting to pounce out. Its citizens obviously were not as preponderantly pro-German as German propaganda claimed, because if they had been, they would have clamoured for surrender, or otherwise made the defence impossible; and it was, to say the least of it, odd, for the Germans to inaugurate their expected Anschluss with Alsace (which by the time of this affair was universally expected to be among the peace-terms) by damaging some of the finest buildings of its world-famous capital. The bombardment achieved nothing positive except to make the bombarders disliked; Uhrich held out until the last of his ammunition was gone and he faced an imminent *assault* which he knew he could not withstand. Nor is there any evidence that the biggest terror bombardment of all, that of Paris during the winter, did anything but relieve many Germans' feelings; it had no decisive effect on either the city's surrender or the end of the war.

While the Germans established themselves as the leaders in bombardment on land, the British retained their pre-eminence in bombardment from the sea. British admirals believed in it as a sovereign remedy for all ills. Richard Cobden commented, apropos of a far eastern naval bombardment of more than usually disproportionate intensity, that the admiral in charge was 'exceeding, as usual, his instructions from home'.[146] The interesting possibility presents itself, that British admirals, indulging a Palmerstonian variant on the Nelson touch, were no more immune from that tendency than have been certain chiefs of land and air forces. Pending a systematic study of the British navy at its familiar work of bombardment between 1815 and 1914, I can only point out certain episodes in which the essential spirit of this activity is to be seen. There was a good deal of it during the Crimean War; some up the Baltic, the rest in the Black Sea and the Sea of Azov. Sailing in the opposite direction from contemporary juridical opinion, Admiral Deans Dundas thought it had not gone far enough. Having carried out a proper bombardment of the more military parts of the port area of Odessa, and finding himself, when he returned home, accused in some part of the press of 'mawkish sentimentality', he 'sought to clear his character . . . by persuading a "friend" in the House of Commons to move for papers to show that his desire to revisit Odessa in the coming autumn, to bombard it effectually, had been frustrated by the reluctance of the allied generals to part with a division of the fleet.'[147] So Odessa was spared (except by such of Dundas's shells as went beyond their

marks): '. . . even Odessa, fair and opulent, basking on her sunny
slope, has flaunted unhurt before a great fleet, baffled and panting
for action, her almost defenceless charms.'[148] Naval counsels seem
to have been divided when working out how best to fight a war
with the United States. Just before the *Trent* incident, 'Newcastle
had talked of the regrettable necessity of having to burn New York
and Boston'; but Admiral Milne, commanding the North
American station, sensed that respectable opinion was changing:
he didn't think it would be proper to attack anything but the forts
defending the great American ports, '. . . as modern views dep-
recate any damage to a town'.[149] During the last two decades of the
century, when Alexandria received a classic dose, the rage for naval
bombardments was possessing other countries as well.[150] Admiral
Aube led a dashing school of thought in France which looked forward to bombarding and destroying as much of British coastal
property as they could get their guns on,[151] and in 1899 Admiral
Mahan said that as a last resort the American squadron was ready
to bombard the Spanish coast, if the Spaniards did not recognize
that they were beaten.[152]

Near the end of the eighties, T. E. Holland sought to stem this
passionate flood. Surveying from the shelter of the Athenaeum the
progress of the current British naval manoeuvres, he inquired of
the editor of *The Times*,

> whether or no the enemies of this country are conducting naval
> hostilities in accordance with the rules of civilized warfare. I
> read with indignation that the *Spider* has destroyed Greenock;
> that she has announced her intention of 'blowing down'
> Ardrossan; that she has been 'shelling the fine marine residences
> and watering-places in the Vale of Clyde'. Can this be true, and
> was there really any ground for expecting that 'a bombardment
> of the outside coast of the Isle of Wight' would take place last
> night?[153]

The navy and its admirers rose to the bait. Holland's innocent inquiry provoked a lot of correspondence and articles which clearly
displayed not only how far the idea of bombardment continued to
grip the naval mind but also 'the existence of a considerable
amount of naval opinion which [Holland] ventured to think in
contravention of international law'.[154] So far as the Hague conferences were concerned to establish in treaty form exactly what

was international law, they fully vindicated Holland's view of it. British objections prevented the discussion of anything to do with international law of sea war in 1899 but by 1907 a different government in changed international circumstances was instructing its delegates 'that the objection, on humanitarian grounds, to the bombardment of unfortified towns is too strong to justify a resort to that measure';[155] so that, among the several Conventions there drawn up relative to war at sea, one prohibited naval bombardment 'of ports, towns, villages or buildings which are not defended', permitting it only of places which (whether defended or not) were in fact naval or military bases.[156] Nor was this the whole of the attention given at The Hague to the question of bombardment, upon which the development of ever more long-range artillery and the invention of practical-looking airships had been causing many to concentrate their minds as never before. With an eye to what might soon become possible in the air, the Article prohibiting bombardment of undefended places in the Hague Land War Regulations had the phrase inserted in it, *'by whatsoever means'*;[157] to which naval warriors had their attention drawn by the conference's closing *vœu* that 'the Powers should, in all cases, apply, as far as possible, to war at sea the principles of the Convention concerning the laws and customs of war on land';[158] which of course included the Martens Declaration.

Close kin to bombardment, but from force of circumstances, until the invention of bombing aircraft, much less common, was the destruction of enemy public, and if necessary also private, property believed to be useful for its war effort. For the major variety of this, the publicists had the technical word 'Devastation': the deliberate wasting of lands in order to prevent enemy forces passing through, or subsisting in, them. As a lawful species of deliberate destruction, it was related to the undoubted right of belligerents to destroy property which interferred with their military operations; e.g. cutting down trees, knocking down buildings which obstructed the defence of a place or the development of an attack upon it; and it was subject like that other to the general rule of proportionality, to which we have already amply referred. But devastation could mean bigger things than such routine tactical activities, and it had always invited critical attention because the human cost exacted by it – rendering of thousands homeless and

foodless, not to mention blighting the prospects of their progeny
– could be so large. Classic reference point for discussion of devastation in the eighteenth and early nineteenth centuries was
Louvois' devastation of the Palatinate in 1689; claimed by French
writers to have been justified by military necessity, condemned by
others (Germans above all) as having been either disproportionate,
or vindictive, or both. No devastations of this directly military kind
during the wars of 1792–1814 were of anything like that awful
earlier scale, but some of them were big enough; notably the
Russians' devastation in the face of Napoleon's armies, and their
burning of Moscow; and Wellington's devastation of as much of
Portuguese territory in front of his defensive perimeter of Torres
Vedras as the Portuguese would permit. And these were different
from the Louvois devastation not only in scale but in character;
the Russians were devastating their own territory, which they had
every right to do, while the British were devastating that of an ally
– a fact on which French propagandists did not fail to comment!

Between this kind of devastation, directly to prevent enemy use
of particular pieces of territory, and the twentieth century's
peculiar style of destroying, by means chiefly of aerial bombardment, the enemy's transportation system, his food resources, his
munitions manufactories etc. – in short, his means of waging
modern war – there is not in principle much difference. The two
may conveniently be studied together in their convergence during
the American civil war. That war's claims to the title of 'the first
modern war' rest on several characteristics which made that convergence likely: its industrial base, the direct involvement of entire populations, and the total-ness of its war aims on both sides,
after the Secessionists had failed to persuade the Unionists to write
it off as a lost limited war. It was a war which ran to extremes of
juridical permissibility just as (and for the same reasons as) it
prompted many striking technical innovations. It may have looked
messy from Potsdam and St Cyr (Moltke wrote it off in some such
terms as 'an affair of armed mobs') but in many respects there was
to be nothing else resembling it until 1914. Prominent among
these, which include also its maritime dimension, were its strategic
devastations and (to the extent that they should be distinguished)
destructions.

Its masterpiece of devastation in the classical sense was that
wrought by General Philip Sheridan in the Shenandoah valley in

the late summer and autumn of 1864. From that fertile part of Virginia, menacingly close to Washington, had repeatedly come Confederate raids and expeditions; most recently, Jubal Early's nearly successful raid on the Union capital in July of that year. Sheridan's mission was not merely to push Early right back beyond where he came from but also to ensure for once and for all that the valley of the Shenandoah could be of no further military use to the South, neither to its more regular forces like Early's nor to the varieties of guerrillas and 'bush-whackers' who hung around them. 'No houses will be burned, and officers in charge of this delicate but necessary duty must inform the people that the object is to make the Valley untenable for the raiding parties of the rebel army.'[159] Of course in reality it did not work out as smoothly as that. Houses, for example, did get burned, perhaps because of disobedience to orders, or of resistance offered by their inhabitants; perhaps because, published orders notwithstanding, someone on high intended that they should.[160] Yet, write Randall and Donald, 'violence to persons was avoided' and the residents were not left 'utterly without subsistence'. Penetrating the dust-storms of prejudice and passion which all such episodes provoke, and in which this particular war for obvious reasons was particularly rich, one has to conclude that this militarily justifiable operation was probably conducted as decently as circumstances permitted. But it was a grim business. 'The burning of houses and barns, the destruction of food, and the removal of Negroes and animals were done with systematic thoroughness until the smiling valley presented a scene of grim waste and ruin.'[161] Sheridan, who saw nothing so drastic in France in 1870, did not live long enough to witness something far more scientifically drastic on the German side of the Somme in 1917.

But it was not Sheridan's operations on the northern frontier of the Confederacy that invited the most intense controversy, it was his colleague William Sherman's operations within the heart of the Confederacy itself. Sherman's 1864–5 march from Chattanooga to Atlanta, from Atlanta to the sea, and then up through the Carolinas to Raleigh, which he reached just as the war ended in April 1865, was unique. In principle it turned out to be an anticipation of twentieth-century strategic bombing, and is often instanced as such. The expedition had not originally been conceived quite in those terms. Certainly its place in Union grand strategy was to disrupt the communications of the lower South and to do what incidental damage could be done to its war industries; but Sherman was also expecting to have to come to conclusive grips with the large Southern army which withdrew, fighting continuously, from Chattanooga to Atlanta, and let him take Atlanta rather than be hopelessly caught there. That Southern army then got out of his way completely by moving to invade Tennessee, expecting Sherman to be lured north in pursuit of it. It was at that juncture, in mid-autumn of 1864, that the momentous decision was made, not to pursue the other army but to drive on through the enemy territory, living off the land, damaging the economy as much as possible, and in the process lowering enemy morale. Subsequent serious argument about Sherman's march has turned at least as much on the manner of its execution as its planning; and through it may also be followed, for those with a taste for such things, the development of Sherman's own thoughts about war, which are intensely interesting.

Evidence is abundant that neither William Tecumseh Sherman nor his friend the supreme commanding officer of the Union armies Ulysses Simpson Grant – nor for that matter their very sensitive and humane President, by whom their grand strategy was approved – was, in any normal sense of the words, inhumane or ruthless or brutal. Moreover, during the early phases of the war Sherman yielded to none in his explicit regard for the limitations and restraints enjoined by the law of war, which his unusually wise, knowledgeable, and copious correspondence shows to have been often the beacon of his thoughts. But by 1864 he, along with Grant and Lincoln and no doubt many more of similarly natural moderation, had been driven by, so they felt, the inexorable logic of events, to go beyond it. What else could they do, unless they were to admit defeat? They became willing to lose unusually large numbers of their own troops, to conduct the most extensively damaging expedition of modern history, and to risk being vilified as Goths, Vandals, Barbarians and so on, none of which was pleasant for them. But they were driven to this by a common realization that the war had become (in the ordinary sense of the words) a people's war and that it could only be brought to conclusion by fighting it in (to use the Clausewitzian concept) an absolute style.

Sherman had begun by scrupulously distinguishing civilians from soldiers, seeking to preserve the former from any but most inevitable and necessary hurts, and doing these law-abiding things not least for the political reason that a humanely-handled populace was, he thought, more easily managed by an invader/occupier than one which had been ill-used. But his mind gradually changed. Going easy on the people of the South, he concluded, merely encouraged them in their delusions and intolerance. Trying to restrain and limit the war against such people was in effect saving them from the consequences of their own irresponsibility. The essence of his argument, in discussion with people on his own side and in argument with chieftains of the enemy, was : You asked for war, War then you shall have. 'A people who will persevere in war beyond a certain point ought to know the consequences. Many, many people, with less pertinacity than the South has already shown, have been wiped out of existence.'[162]

If any one letter of Sherman's expresses better than any other the essence of his comprehensive thought about war in general and the particular war he was engaged in, it is the one he wrote on 12 September 1864 to the Mayor and councillors of Atlanta, which he had entered on the 2nd. For good military reasons, he had ordered the inhabitants to move out. Mayor Calhoun and two councilmen petitioned him to revoke the order in a letter which described the anticipated hardships of the people in pathetic terms which did their hearts credit but which Sherman must have read as yet further evidence of the remoteness of those people from the war which he believed them to have inaugurated, to be sustaining, and to be able, if they wished, to bring towards an end. After sketching so far as he prudently could the military situation which forced this decision upon him, he turned to the more general issue.

You cannot qualify war in harsher terms than I will. War is cruelty, and you cannot refine it; and those who brought war into our country deserve all the curses and maledictions a people can pour out. . . . But you cannot have peace and a division of our country. . . . Once admit the Union, . . . and instead of devoting your houses and streets to the dread uses of war, I and this army become at once your protectors and supporters. . . .

You might as well appeal against the thunder-storm as against these terrible hardships of war. They are inevitable, and the only way the people of Atlanta can hope once more to live in peace and quiet at home, is to stop the war, which can only be done by admitting that it began in error and is perpetuated in pride.

After a passage telling them not to believe everything they read in the Southern papers, and informing them that their lot was no different from that of thousands who had been de-housed in the war-zones further north, he returned to the heart of his homily:

> Now that war comes home to you, you feel very different. You deprecate its horrors, but did not feel them when you sent car-loads of soldiers and ammunition, and moulded shell and shot, to carry war into Kentucky and Tennessee ... But these comparisons are idle. I want peace, and believe it can only be reached through union and war, and I will ever conduct war with a view to perfect and early success. ...
>
> Now you must go, and take with you the old and feeble, feed and nurse them, and build for them, in more quiet places, proper habitations to shield them against the weather until the mad passions of men cool down, and allow the Union and peace once more to settle over your old homes in Atlanta.[163]

My judgement of that letter is that it could not have been more delicately done. It is indeed, like many of Sherman's letters in these days, an extraordinary letter, not least so in that he was willing to write so patiently and at such length. (Imagine what reception a petition from Frenchmen to their invader would have got six years later!) When he wrote it he was not yet sure what to do after securing the city. By October his plan was formed. There is no need to quote further from his letters and dispatches during the march to Savannah. Its principle was what he had already explained to the mayor. Apart from pursuing such orthodox destructive measures as destroying railways, war-serving factories, stores and food-supplies beyond the immediate needs of the civilians, he was deliberately, and it would seem with increasing impatience and irritation, making war come home to the Southerners. On 19 October, for instance, just ten days before he set out, he wrote thus to the Union Chief of Staff:

> I will turn up somewhere, and believe I can take Macon and Milledgeville, Augusta and Savannah, Ga., and wind up with closing the neck back of Charleston so that they will starve out. This movement is not purely military or strategic, but it will

illustrate the vulnerability of the South. They don't know what war means, but when the rich planters of the Oconee and Savannah see their fences and corn and hogs and sheep vanish before their eyes they will have something more than a mean opinion of the 'Yanks'. . . .[164]

The execution of this march was not as creditable to Sherman as the philosophy inspiring it and the sense of responsibility which drove him so often to explain himself to friend and enemy alike. That in principle the law of war allowed it, he had no doubt – nor could any but old-fashioned Southerners with war ideas derived largely from Sir Walter Scott and King Charles's cavaliers seriously think he was wrong. Sherman was very well-informed about our subject; as he testily remarked to General Hood at the close of an exchange about the propriety of his conduct at Atlanta : 'See the books.'[165] There was certainly more pillage, pilfering and wanton damage than there should have been in a well-disciplined army, whose own good elements were numerous and articulate enough to save one from the necessity of documenting the excesses from more highly-coloured Southern sources. Yet when all is said and done, Sherman's march was nothing like as nasty as it could have been. Randall and Donald, whose summary of it is excellent, point out that 'outrages on persons were rare'.[166] Upon the whole, a proper distinction was preserved between property and persons; which, after all, from the viewpoint of the law of war, was the main thing.[167]

Finally we come to the remaining one of the three major means of conducting war against an enemy population at large : maritime commercial warfare – blockade, seizure of contraband, stoppage of enemy trade, etc.; and we may pass over it swiftly, for it will bulk very large in the next chapter. It excited a larger quantity of writing and argument, I reckon, than the other branches of international law during the nineteenth century, as was only to be expected in an age when so much value, even so much religious respect, was given to the growth of manufactures, trade, and communications. To all who subscribed to this general creed, war at sea, because of its traditional interferences with such necessary things, had a more odious air than war of land. Unremitting therefore was the pressure from what we may for convenience call 'the commercial interest' for such limitations and restraints as would minimize those interferences. That interest's two main concerns were the rights of neutrals in time of war, and the rendering of 'private property' – that is, *enemy* private property – inviolable in wartime. Both of these lines of argument came directly from an eighteenth-century ancestry to which the nineteenth brought little that was new other than its boldness and confidence.

Governments' responses to this pressure, which had little counterpart in questions of war on land, had largely to be conditioned by – another singularity presented only by the maritime dimension – the need to calculate, from time to time, whether a state of law that would suit them when neutral would suit them also when belligerent. Because of these complications, and because admirals' views about the proper ways to conduct war were at least as strong as generals', governments also had to expect more divisions of opinion on sea war issues than they did on land war ones. The story of the development of the law of war at sea is therefore politically more intricate, and embedded in a stickier economic substance, than that of the law of war on land. Although much clearly remains to be discovered, the literature on it is already extensive. I dare leap over this nineteenth-century stretch lightly, because we shall recur to it more attentively when the first world war brings suddenly to boiling point all the issues so long and angrily debated. But my lightness has this further excuse, that this essential part of the law of sea war, for all that it was continually written about, figured on the agenda of no diplomatic conference between 1856 and 1900. A principal cause of this long gap was the refusal of the government most concerned, the British, to join in any open discussion of it. By 1907 however the balance of power had changed enough – and the weight of American insistence had become heavy enough – for it to come into discussion a great deal. What was not settled in The Hague that year was dealt with in London two years later, with the result, apparently happy for the neutrals and at least part of the commercial interest, that some advance at last seemed to be made beyond where their claims had got stuck in 1856.

In 1856 their claims had, in fact, carried them at one stride very far. The Declaration of Paris in that year cleared away several of the long-standing uncertainties which maritime belligerents had exploited at their expense. Privateering, the guerrilla warfare of the seas, was abolished. Blockades, it was declared, 'in order to be binding, must be effective' – i.e. must be maintained by enough ships really to catch any vessel making for or from the port or coast proclaimed to be blockaded; must not be mere paper blockades. And it was declared, not only that 'free ships make free goods' (i.e., enemy goods on neutral ships were free from seizure unless they were contraband) but also that enemy ships did not make forfeit neutral goods carried on them unless, again, they were contraband.

Like all such international conventions, the terms of this 1856 one represented a compromise between the primary participants. After considering not only their own potential roles as neutrals or belligerents but also the relations in which they wished to stand to neutrals and 'the commercial interest', they had to decide what risks it was worth taking for what advantages. The commercial and neutral interest was much gratified by these 1856 accords which promised freedoms from the harassments and hazards of paper blockades and a large guarantee that the normal courses of commerce – neutral to neutral, neutral to enemy (except for contraband) would flow uninterrupted. All that remained to perfect the commercial interest's case in its more extreme form was to extend the last-mentioned clause of the Declaration of Paris to cover enemy non-contraband goods: i.e., (enemy) 'private property at sea'.

The strength of this branch of 'the peace movement' (see above, p. 132) in its demand for radical reforms of the law of the sea may now surprise us, since its scenarios included members of the 'peaceful populations' of countries at war with one another continuing to engage in every kind of commercial intercourse that did not directly assist the operations of war. The idea of Southampton or Dover dock-workers unloading toys, clocks and sausages from German freighters during a war between Britain and Germany did in fact surprise a high-level British Inter-Departmental Committee preparing for the 1907 Conference.[168] Yet this vision of a world where the lion might soon lie down with the lamb really did have many backers right up to the first world war.

That part of the neutral and commercial interest's programme, then, came to a stop. The other parts got further. Sticking to what mattered most in relation to humanity in warfare, we find that the biggest issues under discussion were 'blockade', 'contraband', and 'the doctrine of continuous voyage': 'blockade' because the many technical advances made since 1856 facilitated (for powers big and rich enough to use them) 'effective' blockades at a much greater distance than had hitherto been possible; 'contraband' because maintenance of the vital distinction between combatants and civilians demanded a parallel distinction between goods that were essential for military purposes and goods that were not; and 'continuous voyage' because that was the technical term signifying the practice, begun by the British in the mid-eighteenth century and carried to its furthest lengths yet by the United States in 1861–5, of extending the idea of blockade to cover goods going (if it could so be proved) in neutral bottoms to enemy ('blockaded') destinations.

The Declaration of London which issued from the 1909 Conference, the articles of which were designed to be a sea-war equivalent to the Hague Regulations for land war, did not disappoint the expectations of the neutral and trading parties in its handling of contraband and 'continuous voyage'. Uncertainties about contraband were to be put to rest by its threefold definition: Absolute Contraband, a list of stuff about whose war-supporting nature there was no doubt; a 'Free List' of stuff which was never to be treated as contraband; and, intermediately, the Conditional Contraband, stuff which could be confiscated as contraband if it was clearly going to be used for war purposes. And the long-standing grievance about 'continuous voyage' seemed to be allayed at last by Article 19:

> Whatever may be the ulterior destination of a vessel or of her cargo, she cannot be captured for breach of blockade, if at the moment she is on her way to a non-blockaded port.

The reader will have noticed in how cautious and qualified terms I have sketched the main points of the Declaration of London. That is because, within only five years, it fell to pieces. The proximate cause of its collapse early in the first world war was that Great Britain, host to the conference and signatory of the declaration, had never gone on to ratify it; and until the major naval power ratified it, no lesser ones would. But beneath that was the deeper cause, that the several provisions of the Declaration, however sensible and just individually, together were too much to be workable in a total war between irreconcilable enemies. What happened to undo those provisions, the next chapter shall show.

Chapter IV

The Trials of Total War

The first to go are the niceties,
The little minor conformities
That suddenly seem absurdities.

Soon kindling animosities
Surmount the old civilities
And start the first brutalities.

Then come the bold extremities,
The justified enormities,
The unrestrained ferocities.

> F. R. Scott, 'Degeneration', *Selected Poems*
> (1966)

'The irresistible', Mr Justice Brandeis is said to have remarked,
'is often only that which is not resisted.'

> Isaiah Berlin, *Historical Inevitability* (1953)

In strategy, the moral element is that which chooses right, before
war reduces choice to acts which may produce untoward or untold
reactions.

> Anthony Verrier, *The Bomber Offensive* (1968)

... the most agonizing of all the doubts of the soul, the doubt
whether true salvation must not come from the most abhorrent
passions, from murder, envy, greed, stubborness, rage and
terrorism, rather than from public spirit, reasonableness,
humanity, generosity, delicacy, tenderness, pity and kindness. The
confirmation of that doubt, at which our newspapers have been
working so hard for years past, is the morality of militarism; and
the justification of militarism is that circumstances may at any
time make it the true morality of the moment.

> George Bernard Shaw, Preface to *Major Barbara*
> (1905)

1 Soldiers and civilians

The development and closer definition of the law of war, which had gone so far between the middle of the nineteenth century and the first decade of the twentieth, would presumably have continued along its already established lines, had not 1914 intervened. A third Hague Conference was scheduled soon to follow the second, 1907, conference; the Declaration of London, providing regulation for maritime warfare analogous to the Hague ones for war on land, was awaiting its ratifications; the 1912 Red Cross Conference in Washington had shown great eagerness to formalize and extend its advances into the field of prisoners of war. But none of these and other such expected advances were quickly to be achieved. Hardly anything further of comparable stature was in fact to be achieved until two world wars had revealed with cruel clarity how much there was in twentieth-century total war that could militate against the law's working, what alone were the circumstances and conditions in which it could work well, and how large were the gaps and defects in it which needed to be remedied.

Those gaps were found to be great and painful, and with their exploration this chapter is mainly concerned. Yet the story is not all one of gaps and failures. No more than in 1793–1814 were the obligations and advantages of the law of war wholly neglected or forgotten in the war-storms which burst upon the law's new edifice. They sometimes showed remarkable powers of survival. This book not intending to be a systematic and comprehensive history of the law of war, item by item, I can only remark rather summarily that the circumstances most advantageous to observance of the law were when armies of not dissimilar race, religion and general ethical notions (i.e. armies able to recognize in their foes 'people of our own kind'), their minds unclouded by the grosser sorts of nationalistic prejudice, folk-lore and propaganda, and under the command ultimately of officers trained in the classic European or Europe-originated tradition, faced and fought each other in ways old-established enough to have accumulated a solid wrapping of law and custom.[1] Much of the fighting on the European western front(s) in both world wars and much of the fighting at sea was of this kind. Deeds of chivalry and simple humanity continued to be met with, even when they might seem inconsistent with the political or other principles of the men evincing them. The Red Cross sign was generally respected in the ways due to it; quarter was usually given to soldiers who sought it in circumstances that did not make it impossible; prisoner of war camps varied in quality (some commandants in world war one seem to have enjoyed unusual latitude to run things the way they thought fit within their own constructions of the relevant Hague Regulations) but on the whole did not disgrace the governments responsible for them; the ICRC, rapidly building up a huge voluntary staff from scratch in its central neutral redoubt, orchestrated the performance of prodigies of humanitarian usefulness through its agencies in the other neutral countries (it seems to be axiomatic that the level of humanity maintained in a conflict rises in proportion with the amount of active neutral interest) and the belligerents' national societies, with all of which, from 1914 to 1918 (with only a few Russian confusions at the end) it retained close touch.[2] The 1914–18 war was no doubt better in almost all these respects than the 1939–45 one, yet some phases even of the latter displayed much that the founding fathers of 1864 and 1874 could have applauded; the German military (one must distinguish them, so far as facts permit, from the more direct agencies of Nazi rule) seem to have conducted their *Blitzkrieg*s of 1940 with much professional propriety, and the desert wars of 1941–3, like the battle of Britain in 1940, are looked back upon by some as fine late flowerings of old-fashioned gentlemanly warfare, each side taking pride in its respect for the rules and the opponent, thankful that there were no wretched civilians or amateurs to get in the way. Right to the end of the second great war, proprieties continued, however unpredictably, to receive some respect in the fighting between Germans and their foes on the European western side.

I have phrased that sketch as carefully as I can, to do the amount of justice I believe to be due to the facts without implying that things were better than they actually were. My sketch should be read, perhaps, as people read the descriptions in house-agents' hand-outs, with an eye to what has *not* been said. The conditions I have mentioned as being necessary for any regular recognition of the limitations and restraints of the law of war were the exception, not the rule. In horrid contrast was what happened when the law of war was defective or inapplicable, and/or when the opposed forces either had their heads already naturally filled with hatreds and contempts for their enemies, or had been suitably indoctrinated for producing the same result: absence of feeling of human kinship with the enemy, and insensitivity to the claims of the law (supposing that the law had been known about in the first place). This darker side of our picture is dominated, of course, by the contempt for Slavs and other non-German/Teutonic peoples enjoined by Nazi-ism upon all Germans and upon such of their allies as did not already possess it, and the consequent mass slaughter in Russia and eastern Europe. The spectacular centrepiece of that slaughter, the 'final solution of the Jewish question', fell right outside the categories of the law of war. It was not something in which the German military were generally directly implicated, and was tried under a separate head at the 'war crimes' trials after the war. But for the not less terrible inhumanity practised, with the necessary participation of much of the German army, towards Polish and Soviet prisoners of war and civilians, German race-obsessed policy also was the substantial explanation, the Soviet Union's failure to have become a party to the 1929 Geneva Convention for prisoners of war being only the excuse.[3] In the case of Japan, the same diplomatic omission may have worked the other way; the Japanese military administration being wholly unprepared to look after as large numbers of prisoners (and civilian internees) as quickly came into its hands. The atrocities and inhumanity which notoriously marked so much of the Japanese handling of their prisoners seem to have been as much the result of administrative inadequacy and excessive devolution of authority as of race-based policy or cultural inclination.[4]

It is natural to look at race-related ideologies and racist prejudices in seeking explanations for the peculiar horrors that marked the second world war, Nazi-ism having called so much attention to them; but distinct, or supposedly distinct, racial differences were not *sine qua non* to the creation of war circumstances highly unfavourable to humanity in warfare. Ethnic differences and smaller differences still might produce the same effect, within one's own territory as well as within the enemy's. What the Russian army did to the Tsar's Jewish and German-speaking subjects behind its own lines in 1914–15 seems to have been no less barbarous (and politically stupid) than what it was willing to do to any of the Kaiser's subjects, when and if it got to them;[5] it has to be remembered, however, that Russian governments' ways of handling their own subjects have always been *sui generis*. Classic ethnic antipathies, at their worst amalgamating every notion, feeling, habit and circumstance that can make one social group hate the very idea of another, alone explain, for example, why so much of the warfare in the Balkans and eastern Europe generally in both world wars was so savage and lawless; and wherever such antipathies exist, the prospects for limitation, restraint, and humanity in warfare have always been, as they remain, poor indeed.

There is no doubt that the law of war as developed up to 1914 (substantially enlarged by 1939 only to the extent of the 1929 Prisoners of War Convention, a straight continuation of pre-1914 trends) was at its most protective and successful in respect of the military in areas of war where the law was, so to speak, 'fully operative'. In areas where it was not, much would depend on local circumstances to determine whether the military were any better protected than civilians or not. Soviet soldiers who fell into German hands were infamously maltreated, but German soldiers who fell into Soviet hands were much more likely to live to see home again, the Soviet government having at the outset been willing to approximate to the Geneva standards and never having fallen anywhere near German depths in this respect. Formal inapplicability of a Convention did not mean that either it or the obligations of customary law would be wholly forgotten. But such softening recollections were not likely to spread their effect far beyond the military, with whom, after all, the Conventions to date were most concerned. Civilians took second place or worse in them. We have seen how the sources of both Geneva and Hague law lay in military self-interest and self-respect at least as much as in civilian humanitarian zeal on behalf of suffering soldiers, and how, when the civilian's interests were expressly noticed, it was much more usually in the form of protection of his property than his person. It was as if the civilian interest had been lulled by a mixture of its own sentimental nature, its vicarious love of war, and its attachment to its property and prosperity, into neglecting for far too long its need for personal protection against the consequences of the wars it liked to read, sing and talk about, and the military licence that happened in them. Consequently, when the cycle of the two world wars began in 1914, the number of sentences in the Conventions devoted to civilians was small and relatively negligible compared with the number concerning soldiers, sailors and the medical personnel looking after them (them *alone*, so far as the literal wording of the Conventions was any guide); which partly explains why civilians emerged from these thirty bad years as the category of human beings most in need of protection in war. The other part of the explanation why this turned out to be so is however to be found in the larger historical context of ideas and material circumstances within which these world wars were fought; to which for a few paragraphs we must turn.

The matter can be most expeditiously dealt with by examining the commonplace, which is certainly true enough so far as it goes, that war in our century has become 'total' in ways not often, nor all at once, and in some ways not at all, realized before. Tendencies towards this can be divided into three groups.

First, means have appeared by which war can be made more 'total' than before in terms of killing and destructive ability. All kinds of means of making war which can only have been strategists' and military technicians' dreams before the last hundred years have turned out to be realizable. Blockades, which could never be entirely effective except in respect of particular ports and estuaries, have in this century been applied with great effect to whole nations. Artillery has become much more powerful and accurate than ever before, and to it, as a means of bombarding enemy places, has been added first the aircraft and then the missile. More important by far, the aircraft and the missile have proved able to bombard places hitherto normally unattainable; not just armed forces behind and away from the battlefront, but government offices, military headquarters, munitions factories, transportation centres and so on. Weapons have become bigger and better (in range and power, if not always commensurately in size) and after developing through stages characterized by relative inaccuracy (I am thinking especially of area-bombing 1941–5 and the first two decades of nuclear weapons) have achieved great accuracy as well. We need not extend the list, which surely is familiar enough, including as it does the whole historic arsenal with which both world wars were fought, and most of what it talked about whenever the limitation and reduction of contemporary arms, whether strategic or tactical, was being discussed. The material means of injuring enemies have multiplied exceedingly, not so say exponentially, during the past eighty years or so; and the possibility of taking war towards its theoretically total (or, as I suppose Clausewitz would have put it, absolute), form, has to that extent increased.

To these material means have also become added arguments for fighting 'civilized' wars in 'total' ways which were not so perfectly or persuasively present in earlier times. The publicists of the eighteenth century and the international lawyers of the nineteenth congratulated themselves that wars between civilized countries were not as they thought the wars of 'savage societies' to be, total and absolute and cruel. Their anthropological information was selective and they too readily forgot how total and cruel often had been the wars of their favourite exemplars in civilized virtues, the Greeks and Romans of the ancient world, let alone some very recent episodes in their own national histories. But of course there was some truth in what they were saying and what they were proud of.

Progress in 'civilization', which they measured by Eurocentric, commercial criteria, brought with it arguments for reducing the incidence of war to the minimum and minimizing its destructiveness, to be done mainly by observing the restraining law of war and restricting the effects of hostilities to the official armed forces alone. But we have already had cause to notice that that language was to some extent unrealistic, and in contradiction with much that was common political and military talk. The distinction between the combatants of the armed forces and the 'peaceful' rest of the population, conceptually indispensable for a law of war that is to mean anything, has always found itself jostling for living-room with the more aggressive sorts of democratic, patriotic and nationalist rhetoric, which imply if they do not actually affirm that there really is no significant split between the combatant at the front and his family and neighbours at home, and that all are 'fighting' together for the same great common goal. The coming into use of the phrase, 'the home front', to describe ordinary life back home, epitomises this confusing modern usage. So does extension of the concept of the 'fight' beyond the soldier's proper field of activity to cover the whole of national life. To the already enormous range of inducement and inclinations in that direction, fascism and communism added new ones peculiar to themselves: the fascist by his presentation of the world as a jungle in which nations are bound to have to fight, and in which only those welded into organic unity and disciplined for the effort may survive and become their true selves; communism, by its presentation of the world as an arena of class struggle unceasing, turning now and then, inevitably, into wars either international or civil or both at once, wars in which whole classes are necessarily involved whether they know or like it or not. Even devils may quote scripture. Hitler, Mussolini, and Stalin, to judge from appeals they now and then made to the principles of the law of war, were well aware of its principles of limitation and restraint, especially as concerning civilians. But it needed a cool head and a solid grounding in the principles of the law of war to sort out the wheat from the chaff when such talk came from mouths more accustomed to speak of the belligerent unity of their people in the war effort, their indomitable will to win, and the totality of the struggle in which they were all engaged; not to mention the totality of the defeat they looked forward to inflicting upon their enemies. Such hyperbolical language and sustained passion incidentally helped to promote, in some countries on both sides, in both world wars, that other notable feature of total war, the not knowing when to stop.

To such super-heating of belligerent collectivism, which has not equally affected all countries (though all major powers at war, non-fascist and non-communist ones as well, have been obliged to work up some equivalent sense of indissoluble national unity and common cause), has been added, in all 'advanced' countries according to the measure of their industrial sophistication, the fact that modern wars, fought with the products of modern industry, involve much larger numbers of people in the making of war possibly than has ever been the case before. Behind the front-line combatant lies the home front and its army of indispensable civilian supporters. All those workers in the factories, airports, railway yards and so on, have become indispensable to the conduct of a twentieth-century war in ways to which history further back than the eighteen-eighties offers only diminishing counterparts. This fact may or may not add strength to arguments for the carrying of war straight to such people (see below, p. 268) but it has given such arguments a plausibility which it never had before, and has in turn contributed to erode the barriers and distinctions between combatants and others which used to seem so obvious in the pages of the law of war books and which still have to be taken account of unless the law of war is wholly to dissolve.

To sum up this short review of the circumstances increasing the risks of civilians being damaged in the twentieth century's wars, we may then crudely say that the technical means of damaging them had been perfected, plausible economic reasons for damaging them had multiplied, and their own apparently willing participation in the decisions to make or to continue war seductively suggested that they deserved to be damaged. I leave aside the question, to what extent that appearance may have been produced by manipulation or deception. To the extent that it was 'genuine', however, it could provoke observations such as this, written in 1936 by a reviewer of the official history of the 1914–18 war in the air. Acknowledging the very disagreeable aspects of aerial bombardment, Major Oliver Stewart wrote:

> If it involves certain things which have hitherto been regarded as outside the rules of warfare between civilized nations, two comments are possible: either that civilized nations ought not to make war on each other, or, alternatively, if they do, they must put up with the kind of war they themselves invent.[6]

The Major's words contain much grim truth. He who seeks to maintain respect for the law of war in these historical circumstances is bound to feel that not the least part of his problem is to save mankind from itself.

2 The civilian and land war: occupation and resistance

Occupation of enemy territory was nothing like as widespread a phenomenon in the first world war as in the second, but it included a four-year stretch which for one reason or another proved to be of exceptional interest: the German invasion and occupation of Belgium, north-east France, and Luxemburg. The fact that I know much less about occupations in eastern, south-eastern and southern Europe, let alone the Ottoman Empire (and for completeness one should add German Africa), is no doubt partly a reflection of my western European orientation and linguistic limitations. But it must also be said that Belgian and French experience dominate our inter-wars textbooks, including the German ones; for the obvious reason that, as the source of so much of the wartime propaganda and post-war reparations claims against Germany, the cases of occupied Belgium and north-east France were the most familiar. From the point of view of the general historiography of the war, it is much to be desired that more of what went on in the other occupied zones should be brought to light. From our point of view, however, nothing is lost by sticking to Belgium and occupied France, for their experience offers examples of everything the historian of occupation could desire.

The potentialities of an occupying power under the law as it then stood were not less completely revealed than the proclivities of the power which actually did the occupying. Germany's treatment of Belgium in world war one constitutes an unlovely chapter in modern German history. Belgium after all was a small neutral State which wanted to remain neutral and which Germany, France and Britain had agreed by treaty to leave neutral. The German invasion of Belgium as part of Schlieffen's plan for a *Blitzkrieg* against France (such a *Blitzkrieg*, anyway, as was possible before armies became motorized) was an extraordinary breach of international law, a rejection of treaty obligations justifiable only by the argument of necessity. That the cover-story at first used by Germany was mendacious – the story that French troops had entered Belgium from the other side, and that the simple right of self-defence entitled Germany to enter too – need not lead one to forget that Belgium indeed offered strategic seductions to both antagonists, and that the French general staff in earlier years also had yielded to them. The likelihood of Belgian neutrality being violated was in fact frankly discussed by pre-1914 military writers in all countries, and in a sense it was no great surprise when Germany did it. What was not so readily to be expected was, first, that close inspection of this idea of using Belgium as an invasion route would conclude it to be technically a good idea, or, second, that any such plans would be approved by their respective governments – the moral and political disadvantage predictably attaching to such a violation being calculated, perhaps, ultimately to outweigh whatever military advantage might accrue. As things turned out, the French government became firmly persuaded that it would be politically unsafe to think of going into Belgium until and unless asked to do so by the Belgians themselves. Accordingly it instructed its generals to relegate Belgium to a secondary and contingent place in its strategic planning. The German government, by contrast, besides being itself more militaristic, had no such control over what its generals planned to do when the war started, and, lacking opportunity to pit its view of the political consequences of the invasion against the claimed military ones, could do no more than try to patch up the political damage after it was done. The German Chancellor's remarkable admission on 4 August 1914 to the Reichstag that the invasion of Belgium, though (as he loyally argued) necessary, was illegal, was a first step in this direction, and the terms used by Germany's first governor-general when he introduced himself to the Belgians contained language calculated to do the same. 'Citizens of Belgium,' he said at the end, 'I do not ask anyone to renounce his patriotic sentiments, but I expect from you all reasonable submission and absolute obedience to the orders of [my] government. I invite you to give it your confidence and cooperation.'⁷

The manner in which the invasion and occupation proceeded, however, reduced the likelihood that the Belgians would respond cordially to von der Goltz's invitation. Belgium, having declined to abase itself by giving the German armies free passage and accepting German promises that its complete independence would be restored inviolate by a victorious Germany after the war, found itself in effect punished for its refusal and its patchy military resistance by being treated as a thorough enemy. Occupied Belgium received treatment at least as harsh and unpleasant as did the eight French *départements* which Germany occupied next door.

The more I read about this German occupation of the inoffensive Belgians (inoffensive, that is, except inasmuch as they existed at all), and the bulk of the German public's readiness to believe the worst of them, the more do I feel the need to go beyond the German military ethos to find its explanation in such profounder cultural sources as Prussian protestantism's contempt for Belgium's famous devotion to roman catholicism, darwinist Geopolitik's special contempt for little countries (*'Kleinstaaterei'*),⁸ and some psychological compulsion, perhaps, to reverse the actual roles and to find that the Belgians, far from being as innocent and offended-against as the rest of the world thought, were actually a scruffy and contemptible lot who *deserved* to be given what the Germans in fact were giving them.

Whatever may have been the cultural and psychological explanation of the manner of the German occupation, the only explanation given to the Belgians (not to mention their French fellow-sufferers) was 'necessity'; the immediate, day-to-day military sort, executing the commands of the ultimate, political, State sort. Not pausing to distinguish between measures decided on before the invasion and measures only conceived after it, I note that this alleged necessity required: requisitioning and so on until the point when the Belgian population was starving; raising huge contributions of money from Belgian cities and districts; imposing colossal collective fines as punishments for even slight individual offences against the invader's pretensions and pride; imprisoning hostages to compel obedience; punitive taxation of the property of Belgian refugees who declined the invitation to return; economic exploitation of the country for German war purposes; absolute prohibition of correspondence and even, for most of the war, of the transmission of basic family news between civilians in the occupied territories and friends or relatives elsewhere (thus making the civilian's lot much more anguishing than that of military prisoners); and, when Belgians were discovered to be reluctant either to work willingly for German purposes in their own country, or to go voluntarily to work in Germany, their forced deportation to do the latter in a manner unprecedented in modern times.[9]

It seems difficult to maintain that this catalogue of oppressions (in many respects a sinister pre-run for the occupations of world war two) was justified even by the most liberal stretching of the few relevant Hague Regulations and a sympathetic interpretation of the 'necessities' in which the Germans found themselves, not least because the Belgians kept up as much passive disobedience as they dared. The Hague Regulations indeed quickly showed themselves to be inadequate, and at least two German dignitaries, no doubt conscientiously seeking in their own fashion to obey the law as they found it, are known to have remarked that while they knew exactly how they were expected to treat military victims of war (prisoners of war, etc.), the Hague Regulations said little to guide them regarding civilians. All that those Regulations said about who should feed whom was that the occupied people should feed the occupying army![10] Article 47 'formally prohibited' pillage. Old-fashioned loot and thievery was what the legislators had in mind – but at what point did the systematic exhaustion of the resources of an occupied country amount to the same? Articles 49 and 52, governing levies and requisitions in money and kind, referred to 'the needs of the army (or the administration) in question', and the latter article further limited them to what was 'in proportion to the resources of the country'. The rapporteur at the 1899 Conference, summing up the gist of a great deal of passionate argument, commented that the Regulations did not mean that 'the country might be systematically exhausted'.[11] The Martens Declaration must certainly have seemed to confirm that, for anyone who took it seriously. But exhaustion of that degree was precisely what happened. Only the spirited intervention of American humanitarianism and generosity, brilliantly engineered by Herbert Hoover, brought Belgium enough food in the winter of 1914–15 to save it from starvation, then and thereafter.[12]

What had in fact happened in Belgium during the first fraction of the war was a perfect epitome of the plight in which the modern unprotected civilian could find himself. The war, professed by continental international jurists to be 'between states and not between peoples', was actually being fought at the (would-be neutral) Belgian people's expense and over their dying bodies. Their plight, in itself, was not particularly a twentieth-century one. The poor people of Genoa, for example, had found themselves in a very similar situation in 1800, when their French master Masséna and their British and Austrian blockader-besiegers Keith, Ott and Melas found no way to release them from their lethal situation between the upper and the nether mill-stones.[13] All that was different in the case of the Belgians from 1914 onwards was that the size and severity of the problem was the larger in proportion as the 1914–18 war was more 'total' than the 1793–1814 one, and, second, that a most powerful neutral was at hand, to come to their rescue. Had Hoover been a Swiss, Swede or Spaniard, his chances of success could not have been anything like so great.

In London, on 30 January 1915, he issued a statement to the press, outlining the nature and extent of the problem, and explaining to the American public, to whom it was primarily addressed, the form of the inhumanitarian deadlock into which the belligerents had got themselves. 'If we denude the statements of both belligerents of arguments based on initial responsibility,' he said, 'the following are the views generally expressed to us as the *de facto* situation:

> We are informed from the German side that there is not only no provision in the Hague Convention obliging an occupying army to feed the civil population, but that, on the contrary, there is a provision that the civil population can be called upon to support the occupying army. More broadly than this, how-

ever, the Germans state that the people of Belgium have always imported their food supplies and that this population still possesses resources; and that could a gate be opened through their double wall of steel by which they could import foodstuffs and raw materials and export their industrial products and thus restart credit, they could provision themselves. That in taking the harbor of Antwerp and in throwing it open to neutral trade the Germans have acquitted themselves of the responsibility, because nothing prevents the normal flow of trade except the Allied Navy. The Germans state, furthermore, that the Belgians by their continued hostility require a considerable force in occupation and, by refusal to operate public services, necessitate more soldiers to carry on these services, and that the Allies benefit therefrom and are therefore morally obligated to at least open the gate of trade to this population. They state further that while the German food supplies, with great economy, are sufficient to carry this war to successful fruition, if they have to take upon their backs an additional ten million people their stores would be seriously jeopardized, and that it is the duty of the Germans to feed their own people first; that as this war is a war to maintain German national integrity they do not propose to jeopardize the issues in such a manner.

The English and French affirm that they cannot allow free trade with Antwerp, for there can be no assurance that the enemy will not be supplied thereby; moreover, in the traditions of international law it is the duty of the occupying army to provision the civil population, and the importation of foodstuffs into Belgium and Northern France would relieve the Germans of their moral and legal responsibilities. Broader than this, however, although the civil population alone be supplied with foodstuffs, the Germans are relieved of the drain which would otherwise have fallen upon their own stores. That in general the situation is akin to that of a siege where the succor of the population relieves the moral and physical strain on the garrison; that the ending of this war will be by economic pressure and any relaxation of this pressure assists the enemy.

We were convinced at the beginning that the fixity of opinion on both sides as to the righteousness of their respective attitudes was such that the Belgians would starve before responsibility could be settled, for the logical consummation of these views could only mean the decimation of these ten million people.

Hoover went on to describe the work that his Relief Commission had done during the past three months, and how with increasing *and equal* co-operation from each side (it is significant that everything depended on reciprocity) a way was appearing by which 'the world's greatest tragedy' might be avoided. Having given in more than sufficient detail the arguments used by the belligerents to explain why they had to ignore the dictates of humanity, he reported that muted indications of their better selves could also be heard:

> On the English and French side there are many who say that their people should be prepared to abandon the military advantages and give way on contentions of moral and legal issues and come to the support of these people through this Commission; but they add with vigor that they cannot be expected to go so far, so long as the Germans continue draining the resources of these wretched people by way of monetary levies and the continued requisition of foodstuff outside the list agreed with this Commission.
>
> On the German side we are told that the German people have not themselves food supplies to spare, and we believe it is true. We are told that they cannot take food from their already short supplies to feed an additional ten millions of people belonging to their antagonists. They say, however, that these people must be fed and that no action of the Germans should stand in the way of the work of this Commission; and that, although it may mean the giving up of the undoubted right of the occupying army to secure supplies either in money or in kind, the German people are great enough and humane enough to forego all these military advantages rather than that even the shadow of the responsibility for such a debacle should be cast at their door.[14]

How much weight this appeal from the belligerents drunk to the belligerents sober could have had if he had not been appealing equally to the feelings of the American public and relying on the belligerents having some regard for them, one can only guess. Hoover talked softly but carried quite a big stick. Difficulties in administering this relief programme remained to the end (Spain took over its management after the United States' entry into the war) and one sees it dogged all the time by mutual suspicions, nagging insistence on reciprocity, conflicts between the army and the foreign office outlooks, and, perhaps most abrasive of all, casual, careless or malicious departures at lower levels of command from the rules painfully agreed higher up.[15] Yet it worked, and its history offers a remarkable example of humanitarian intervention to remedy the incompletenesses of the formal law: the kind of intervention often made and managed by the ICRC.

The ICRC, not directly concerned in Hoover's great American enterprise, did as much as it could to relieve civilian victims during the first world war, and an enormous amount to relieve them the moment it was over (especially in Russia, when the war there became revolutionary and internecine). Its intermediary work was not made easier by the mutual repugnance the belligerent governments affected towards each other – French and German representatives refusing until the last year of the war, for example, to be in the same room together – and the much lower value they placed on civilian than on military interests. With one new class of civilian victim the ICRC was especially concerned: the internee. One of the many retrograde novelties of the war was the internment of 'enemy aliens' resident in the country, or too late transient through it, when the war broke out. Napoleon's internment of Britons in France when war resumed in 1803 was little to the purpose, it having been justified largely as a reprisal for British premature seizure of French shipping, and although purporting to affect men of potential military value, being in fact indiscriminate. 1803 in any case was a long way back. The French national government's *expulsion* from France of 80,000 or so Germans in 1870 was a sort of precedent but a bad one; its source was the government's desperate readiness to exploit popular xenophobia and to work up a national rage against the enemy; among its consequences, of course, was the stiffening of German indignation against the French. Popular feelings seem to have been the principal explanation of each belligerent's internment, sooner or later, of its resident enemy aliens, forty years later. Legitimate military considerations were present too. It was not wholly unreasonable to intern men of ages suitable for military service, at least until exchanges could be arranged, and some of the aliens may have been spies.[16] But the

rest of it was mere popular hysteria and hatred, to which governments willy-nilly felt obliged to yield. Such 'prisoners' never having been envisaged by the developers of the Geneva and Hague
Conventions to date, and customary international law offering no
guidance beyond its general injunction to humane and civilized
usage, the ICRC – for if the ICRC did not attempt to do something,
who would? – having failed to persuade the German and French
national Red Cross societies to take civilian internees under their
wing along with military prisoners, urged belligerents to confer
on the former benefits of equal treatment with the latter, and set
about promoting schemes of repatriation. But not much came of
these before 1917, and the treatment of civilian internees remained
irregular, unpredictable, and internationally ungoverned.[17] The
suffering and loss caused to individuals was incalculable; the military advantage accruing to belligerents, negligible where it was not
non-existent.

Development of the law to protect civilians became a major concern of the ICRC and the Red Cross movement directly after the war
and remained so until the outbreak of the next one. Already at the
first post-war international red cross conference, in the spring of
1921, there was unanimous support from all present for resolutions
which, turned by due ICRC process into the clauses of a draft Convention, ready for the final stage of a diplomatic conference, would
have met most of the needs so strikingly demonstrated.[18] But
nothing was achieved until 1949, after another and far worse war.
Why?

The necessary close research has not yet been done to answer
that question. M. Durand chronicles the major phases of the failure
in his admirable history of the ICRC but offers few clues as to its
explanation.[19] What representatives of national Red Cross societies
wanted and what the ICRC considered to be practicable, and what
foreign offices believed to be bearable, could of course seem undesirable, impractical and unbearable to the generals and admirals
who had to be consulted and squared before conclusive diplomatic
action could be taken. My suspicion is that a large part of the explanation lies in the difficulty of persuading armies, navies and air
forces to be collectively enthusiastic about proposals for improving
any parts of the law of war other than those most directly serving
their own professional interests.[20] Beyond that, certain other facts
are likely to be relevant. France and Belgium stayed away from

the 1921 conference because the Germans would be there. The nineteen-twenties, full though they were of red cross good works, witnessed also a good deal of argument and dissension within the upper echelons of the movement about its constitution, and the United States, with I know not how many others in its pan-American train, stayed away from the 1923 and 1925 conferences. The apparent success of the League of Nations through that decade and the still not undimmed prospects of genuine disarmament had a lulling effect, once immediate post-war reforming zeal had dissipated. The general question of civilian protection (whether it concerned residence in a foreign country or occupation of one's own) became somewhat tangled up with the particular question of protecting civilians against the effects of aerial bombardment, of which there was continual talk. And when, the other entangling matter of military prisoners had been got out of the way in 1929, the ICRC sought to press on with the civilians matter after the 1934 conference, it received discouragement from several significant governments, especially, it seems, that of France. Consequently, nothing had been achieved by the time of the London Conference in 1938. Great speed was there enjoined. By the beginning of 1939, the ICRC was sending round to governments, as standard preliminary to a diplomatic conference planned for the following year, a comprehensive 'Project for an international convention concerning the condition and the protection of civilians of enemy nationality who find themselves in a belligerent's territory occupied by him'.[22]

But 1939 was not a good year for projects like that.

It is impossible to be sure that such a Convention for the Protection of Civilians, had it been signed and ratified by belligerents before the second world war, would have brought them great benefit; but it certainly cannot be assumed that it would not. Civilians stood in much greater need of protection in the second world war than the first. Much more territory was under enemy occupation or hegemony than earlier, and the occupier was not only more ruthless but his policies included selective extermination and systematic maltreatment. The mixture of miseries and privations which Belgium had suffered became familiar all round Germany's perimeter. Not, indeed, equally in all places, or all at once, for Hitler's policy included relatively gentle handling of peoples he approved of so long as he thought them potentially sympathetic or helpfully submissive; and some regions could better feed themselves than others, despite their occupier's demands. That scatter of saving points apart, and setting aside for separate accounting the effects of the German government's racial policies, the sufferings of civilians under occupation in 1939–45 were the same in kind as they had been in 1914–18, though often attaining more ghastly proportions. The ICRC did what it could, where it was allowed to operate (which generally was much more in southern and western Europe than eastwards), and overcame manifold difficulties made by both sides to save the greater part of the population of Greece from starvation from 1941 onwards (with the notable help of the Swiss and Swedish Red Cross societies), the Dutch from a disastrous onset of the same in the winter of 1944–5.[23]

How the protection of civilians was taken in hand again after 1945, and to what effect, we shall see in the last section of this chapter. It is time to turn now to the other and probably more difficult aspect of civilian protection against excess or abuse of occupying power; the aspect implied by the word *guerrilla*. So far, we have been considering the civilian in his most peaceful aspect and situation; the civilian who accepts the invader and occupier docilely and unresistingly. But what if he should resist, or others should undertake to resist on his behalf?

This was much more of a problem in the second world war than the first. The second proved to be richer in guerrilla warfare (using the term for the moment loosely) than any European war since Napoleon's, and raised it abruptly to share pride of place with civilian protection at the head of the agenda for post-war legal reconstruction. Once again I have to confess that I don't know as much as I could wish about what went on in eastern and southeastern Europe during and after world war one. The western European bias of the British, French, American and, to not much smaller an extent, German law books leaves in obscurity what lay behind those longer, ill-defined battle-fronts. Perhaps it was left so with relief by authors uneasily aware that the norms so widely recognized and observed in 'the west' were little known, respected or observed by the more traditional, tribal, pain-full, pogrom- and massacre-accustomed societies of eastern Europe and the Balkans (let alone Asia Minor, North Africa, etc.).

If world war one's manifestations of guerrilla warfare and so on were neglected for such causes, they shared that fate with the guerrilla and national resistance episodes of the French wars which, however undying their fame in popular song and story, were viewed by the jurists of the ensuing century with a mixture of distaste and embarrassment; distaste, for a style of warfare intrinsically inimical to a capital city's idea of law and order, and demonstrably barbarous as well; embarrassment, because after all some of those episodes had done their own countries good, and invited from the criticized a *tu quoque* response. The *francs-tireurs* of 1870-1 had not significantly improved the respectability of the guerrilla image in governing circles. Undoubtedly the idea of guerrillas received a new lease on life in the popular fiction and war literature which rattled on until 1914 and had its share in explaining some curious things that then occurred, but we have seen how the balance of official and juridical opinion viewed it with an unfriendly eye, at the same time as the plans of the general staffs made no place for it. What national defence could not be organized in terms of Articles 1 and 2 of the Hague Regulations – open, identifiable, officially led, instructed in the law, and all of it, emphatically, prior to the establishment of occupation – was not to be undertaken at all.

In fact hardly any guerrilla warfare or national resistance of a related kind was undertaken in 'the west' in world war one, and the only bit of it with which we need concern ourselves is not something that happened, but something the Germans thought had happened: guerrilla resistance in Belgium.

The French for obvious reasons revelled in guerrilla stories more than most, but such did not occur in their literature alone. Its mirror-image was to be found in German books about the next war, wherein dastardly *francs-tireurs*, egged on by stereotype representations of the kinds of foreigners good Germans most distrusted, waged unlawful and dirty war against their own upright soldiery. Such next-war fantasies, compounded by the stock German version of the *francs-tireurs* in 1870-1, undoubtedly taught the Germans to expect to meet that sort of resistance when they next invaded France, and provided them with a ready explanation for sights, sounds and sensations not otherwise easily accountable. This is precisely what happened during their invasion of Belgium. Having this bee already in their bonnets, the merest buzz in Belgium made them think they had come across a hive. The

Belgian people had been expressly instructed by its government (therein doing the correct thing, as the Germans did when the Russians marched into East Prussia) *not* to engage in private resistance.[24] It was not to be expected that not one Belgian would refrain from 'having a go' in misguided zeal for king and country, let alone refrain from acts of self-defence against drunken or insolent invaders. Inevitably there were incidents, which the law and custom of war entitled the invader to punish. But nowhere, ever, was there anything like the *Volkskrieg* or *Franktireurkrieg* which German imagination, expecting it and naturally at first excited and edgy with the drama, tension and fatigue of the long march, conjured up. It was in reaction against this imaginary menace that the occupying troops – necessarily of inferior quality, for only such were given communications and occupation duties – reacted so memorably. The most memorable occasion of the many which marred those first bad weeks in Belgium was the near-sacking of Louvain, the shooting of many of its citizens, and the burning of its internationally-famous university library.

The German troops on the spot who did this maintained that they were defending themselves against guerrilla attacks, and appropriately punishing the people and the place responsible; a case which all the resources of German government publicity and propaganda at once espoused and magnified. Some Belgian and allied comment on the other side, working under the disadvantages of distance and imperfect information (and incidentally undermined by the allies' own propaganda ventures into exaggeration and mendacity), was at first not much less incredible. It was also unhelpful to the Belgian case that intemperate irresponsible patriot pamphleteers had published inflammatory calls to arms. But already by 1917 the essentials of the true explanation of what had happened were all there, in one of the most valuable and admirable books that can ever have been published by an exiled historian in wartime; F. van Langenhove's *Comment naît un cycle de légendes: francs-tireurs et atrocités en Belgique.*[25] This cut no ice in Germany. Too much patriotic and emotional capital had been invested in the German version of the Louvain story for such books as Langenhove's to make any impact on it. Finding it still intact and infectious after the second world war, a mixed group of distinguished historians, three Belgian and three German, undertook in the nineteen-fifties the interesting experiment of entrusting what they believed could be a definitive historical inquiry to a young historian, Peter Schöller, and vetting his findings.[26] All six of them agreed that the Belgian story had from the start been the more correct, and that the German one was mainly propaganda: e.g.,

'(2) It is beyond doubt that, inspired by their fears of *francs-tireurs*, German troops fired on each other. (3) It is beyond doubt that neither the populace of Louvain nor the civic guard made any attack either systematic and planned or improvised.'[27]

The Louvain incident, like dozens of others in Belgium that summer and autumn, revealed how profound remained the German army's fear and hatred of anything resembling 'irregular', guerrilla warfare, and how reckless and ruthless it still was in dealing with it when it encountered, or believed it had encountered it. *Franc-tireur* had become in German usage, in fact, a generic term for all that was judged improper, hasty, and unexpected in war, by sea as well as on land: 'Q-boats' and Captain Fryatt both, for instance being thus denominated.

The German army stands in the limelight of this discussion simply because it had so much more to do with guerrillas than any other. It must not be thought that the Germans' handling of (what, no doubt culpably, it allowed itself to believe to be) guerrilla resistance was more savage than would have been that of any other major military power. Certain aspects of German military theory and outlook perhaps made this likely, and we have already had occasion to glance at them; but the ways in which the British army had responded to the real thing in South Africa, and the United States to it in the Philippines, only twenty years earlier, should have made Britons and Americans at least cautious about judging the German performance in Belgium too severely.[28] Bad though it was, it was not anything like as atrocious as Anglo-American-French propaganda fabrications made out. History however determined that it should be the German army which alone of those in conflict on the western front in the first world war was to meet anything like guerrilla resistance and to reveal its feelings so nakedly. It was put much more conspicuously into the same position twenty years later, when it ran into guerrilla warfare and national resistance on a scale which made the imagined Belgian *Volkskrieg* of 1914–18 seem a mirage of a drop in a bucket.

It is not easy to pick out what is relevant to our theme from a scene of oppression, conflict and murder so murky and confusing. Murder, for example, is an 'ordinary' crime, not a 'war crime'. Soldiers in war have a licence to kill as no' subjects or citizens of functioning States can have except in time of war. In lawful war – it is either one of its outrageous wickednesses or one of its mysterious paradoxes, according to how you view it – lawful killing is not murder, though unlawful killing may be, and during the years of Axis hegemony certainly was. Beyond common murder lay the uncommon array of oppressions, tortures and exterminations decreed and carried out, usually, by the special agents of the fascist dictators (especially Himmler's SD) and their puppets and hangers-on. They are not directly our concern either. Outside the fascist homelands, these deeds were variously odious, evil and criminal, and the German army and its associated armies lost reputation and 'honour' by assisting in their doing, but such deeds were not themselves inherently connected with what alone we here are studying; the German army's handling of armed resistance inside its 'occupied' territories. ('Occupied', incidentally, needs qualification, because there was sometimes room for argument whether a territory was really occupied or not.) But before we get to that, there is another tangled shroud of violence to clear away. Hitler's authority ran through many and diverse channels, including above all the puppets and satellite-rulers already mentioned. Direct German rule over his German empire was, in its central and western parts anyway, the exception rather than the rule. Where he thought it possible and desirable, Hitler sought to rule through local national figures, whose own armed forces (mainly 'militias' and police) normally had prime responsibility for the suppression of disorder and rebellion. The infamous *milice* of Vichy France is the best known though not the most typical of this kind. The armed conflict that ensued in such circumstances had the character at least as much of civil war as of national resistance against an outsider; and the law on civil war was very different from that on international. But in the eyes of non-Vichy Frenchmen, for whom France had never surrendered, it remained an international conflict, as it did also, of course, for the differently-situated Soviet partisan, operating under Moscow's orders in an occupied zone sometimes over one thousand miles deep.

That 'law' should be much observed by such parties fighting in such a Europe (for simplicity's sake I am concentrating on Europe) was not to be expected. Strictly speaking, 'law' was often inapplicable. While anti-Axis resistance was 'underground', engaging its enemy by sabotage, spying, and secret killing, it had to run all the risks of the spy and the felon combined. But not all of it was like that. In the USSR and Yugoslavia, more or less from the start, resistance fighters were in effective enough control of enough territory to be able to meet, if they wished, most, perhaps all, of the current conditions of lawful belligerency, and in France, Poland and north Italy, to name but three obvious countries, the same became possible once the liberation of those countries had well begun; partisans were able to 'come out' and conduct themselves as legitimate opponents. The Germans were very, very reluctant to recognize them as such. The ostensible reasons varied, though under and through them all no doubt ran the German army's ingrained detestation of guerrillas and its inability to believe that guerrilla operations were 'in accordance with the laws and customs of war'. So far as Soviet partisans were concerned, there was the additional and overmastering factor that the Führer had decreed that the war against the Soviet forces (doubly odious to the Nazis, as being both Slav or Asian *and communist*) was not to be subject to Hague-style regulation. Still less, therefore, was the need to consider Soviet partisans as anything but 'bandits', which is how such disturbers of behind-the-front tranquillity appeared anyway to the German military mind. Confronted with the 'Free French' partisans in France, the *Forces françaises de l'intérieur* who came out in the summer of 1944, the Germans professed it to be an insuperable difficulty that those forces belonged to no proper party to the conflict! The provisional government of which they spoke was, alleged the Germans, no more than camouflage for an attempt to overthrow the true French government, that of Marshal Pétain, the government which had surrendered in proper form in June 1940 and was still there. As the war neared its end, German rigidity relaxed enough for them verbally to notify the indispensably intermediating ICRC that they would regard as lawful combatants all but Soviet partisans who fulfilled the conditions of Article 1 of the 1907 Regulations; but the ICRC could not persuade them to declare it publicly.[29] About the same time Field-Marshal von Weichs, the German commander in the western Balkans, turned more positively in the same direction, ordering Tito's partisans henceforth to be known as such, no longer (disparagingly) as bands of bandits, on the ground that 'the size, armament, organization and operations of the partisan units justified . . . considering them as an enemy on the same plane with the regular forces of the other nations with which the Reich was at war'.[30] But these *de facto* recognitions (the practical value of which I cannot estimate) were reluctant and late. The clearly approaching defeat of Germany must have had something to do with them, as must also, as usual, the pressure of reciprocity – partisans by this time being active and numerous enough to be taking Germans and their allies prisoner, and therefore having their hands on a lever of reprisals which their opponent ignored at his peril.

Giving quarter to prisoners and treating them humanely was only one of the laws and customs of civilized warfare, observance of which was a condition of belligerent recognition. It was not the most difficult to observe. But the will to observe could be lacking as well as the ability. The anxiously watchful ICRC in fact found it to be another of the virtually insoluble problems, that partisans with the ideals, dispositions and experience likely to be found in Hitler's Europe, for whom observance of these laws and customs could in any case be difficult enough, might perhaps not care much about them anyway. But observance of the law is a two-way business. The legal dice no doubt were loaded to favour the invader-occupier, and it was naturally hard for a partisan force emerging from the almost inevitably lawless ways of the underground (where of necessity, in most cases, it would have begun) to adjust law-abidingly to the style of the Hague Regulations, devised as they were for conflicts of quite a different kind and for armies with an appropriate administrative back-up. But this was what was expected in the nineteen-forties of the partisan who sought belligerent recognition. It was a lot to expect, not least when it could prove suicidal. A US general who had commanded guerrillas against the Japanese in the Philippines recalled, for the benefit of the American Society of International Lawyers thirty years later, that:

> American forces that tried to comply with the spirit of the standards of the law of land warfare found that they could not physically survive. For example, one officer who could not feed

captured Japanese prisoners returned them to the Japanese through a priest. The Japanese promptly returned and executed him. To avoid extinction and to survive, the American-led guerrilla forces decided to take stringent measures. Through official orders it was announced that spies and informers, considered to be the main problem, would be controlled or eliminated. ... Giving these individuals legal or precedural rights that they might have been entitled to was conditioned primarily by reality and was deemed secondary to the primary goal of simply staying alive. The action of the guerrilla forces was consistently conditioned by the fact that compliance with certain legal rules that might have been considered applicable would have resulted, from their point of view, in imminent death. The price of success for guerrilla operations was, simply stated, to destroy spies and informers.[31]

Soviet and Yugoslav partisans in the same war knew that too, and were not burdened with an Anglo-Saxon legal tradition or a bourgeois liberal ideology to make them regret it. The people in the middle – the civilians or would-be civilians – suffered enormously in such situations, with terror impending from both sides and no way of escape except to stake all on the prospects of one side or the other. Of course that might as easily be to lose all as to win it. But such a total commitment may be precisely what the antagonists in an all-out guerrilla war demanded: the occupier's demand for absolute obedience (recall how the Germans in 1870-1 went so far as to demand that the French civilians take their, the German, side against the *francs-tireurs*!) being met from the other side by the claim that the civilians *were* on the side of the guerrillas, *ought to be so*, and were ready to take their share of suffering for the common cause – i.e. to bear the reprisals which were the occupier's standard, even if rather ineffectual, anti-resistance tactic. Guerrillas interested in observing as best they could 'the laws and customs of war' would recall that would-be lawful fighters were not absolutely unlimited in their means of injuring the enemy, and that some means would invite reprisals more surely than others. Pierre Boissier pointed out in his commentary on the affair at Ascq in Belgium, 1 April 1944, that the partisans who sabotaged the main line from Antwerp to Paris for the third time running in the same inhabited place could perhaps have considered moving the site of their intrepid operations to the forests south of Lille, where no easy pretext for reprisals would have offered itself.[32] We read of partisans who kept away from villages whenever they could, to save their inhabitants from victimization.[33] But we read also that it was not an uncommon tactic for Soviet partisans, for example, 'deliberately to provoke reprisals in order to get new recruits'.

Several German or other Axis soldiers would be captured, mutilated, and killed. Their bodies would then be left in a place where the Germans would surely find them, often next to villages sympathetic to the invaders or neutral in their political sympathies. When the bodies were found, German [or other] security troops would take revenge on all the villages in the area by killing everyone they saw, by confiscating all cattle and crops, and by devastating entire sections of land. The survivors fled to the forests where they would be met by the partisans who would sympathize with them and offer help.[34]

Bringing reprisals down upon 'neutral' or unsympathetic villages could be as easy as taking cake from a baby. Preventing reprisals from coming down upon friendly or neutral villages might be impossible. The theory of reprisals in this kind of war, and the only possible road towards justifying them, was that *they worked*, and that subject to the principle of proportionality they could therefore be justified under the title of military necessity.[35] To the best of my knowledge, there is much more evidence that in fact they usually did not work and that they became a mindless routine of the occupying forces (working often to prescribed scales of so many locals to be executed in reprisal for each Axis death), more likely to damage the Axis cause than advance it (except by approaching the extermination of potential resistance, to which some Axis thought was not averse). Reprisals of this order had become so conventionally normal, that much indulgence towards them was shown in the war-crimes trials after 1945, with little inquiry made into their effectiveness or morality.[36]

There is for example all the difference in the world between the burning of a village *known* to be a guerrilla refuge, after removing all civilians incapable of serious guerrilla activity, and the slaughter of the inhabitants of a village *believed* to be such; between the detention of hostages intimately connected with guerrillas, and the killing of hostages connected with them only by accident of time or place; between a humanely and efficiently organized removal of civilians from a combat zone, and a brutal, maladministered one. Conventional forces have often in such ways gone further than humanity, legality and political prudence would have dictated in reaction against the guerrilla menace; excesses which cooler heads on their own side may have deplored. 'It is utter insanity', wrote one such in 1943, to the responsible military chief, 'to murder babies, children, women and old men because heavily armed Red bandits [i.e. guerrillas] billeted themselves overnight, by force, in their house, and because they killed two German soldiers near the village. The political effect of this senseless bloodbath', he went on, 'is disastrous for us; while – to compound the folly of the event – the military effect is negligible; the partisans continue to live and they will again find quarters by use of submachine guns in completely defenceless villages. . . .'[37]

Populations could be made completely irreconcilable by the absolute injustice and savagery of most civilian reprisals, the 'guilty' were rarely punished, and there are in any case limits (no doubt varying from culture to culture) to the degree to which men who have espoused the guerrilla life will pause through sympathy for the folk they have left behind them. Writing of the Yugoslav partisans, who brought to the fighting the implacability of dedicated revolutionary communism as well as Balkan patriotism and, in many cases, mountaineers' *mores*, Basil Davidson (who fought with them) sympathetically wrote :

... they were ready to fight to the limit of the super-humanly possible, and they would accept among themselves no palliation or excuse for failure. ... The conditions upon which they accepted to fight the occupying armies were so frightful in the scale of reprisal on the civil population that weaknesses would have quickly undone their voluntary system and put paid to their movement. And it was clear that they accepted these conditions of reprisal by the enemy as the only alternative to compromise and eventual surrender, and as a necessary moral contribution to the winning of the war.

The notion that they might be open to reproof for entailing their families and the families of their friends in reprisals by an infuriated enemy they emphatically rejected, and on the whole it did not occur to them; they suffered only in their self-respect in not being able to prevent reprisals by the strength of their own arms. . . .

Those from outside who might counsel caution and moderation and the avoidance of action that would 'lead to enemy reprisals' they regarded as soft-hearted fools or partly-interested knaves.[38]

Mr Davidson goes on to admit that some of the explanation of their implacability lay in 'their old traditions of violence and feud'. His very interesting pages offer no clue as to whether any operations in that partisan war he observed at such close quarters could perhaps occasionally have been conducted *more effectively* by more subtle and sophisticated, though no doubt less 'manly' methods.[39] His picture of a population generally behind the partisans and willing to carry the can for them is persuasive and may be true; knowing what one does, however, about guerrillas' normal use of terror in disposing of the hostile and persuading the unenthusiastic, it seems prudent to suppose that the Yugoslav people through whose villages was fought that most bitter of wars could have benefited, along with all other populations similarly circumstanced, from the existence of a Convention defining at least a minimal civilian interest in terms making sense to both 'regular' and 'irregular' belligerents, and binding both belligerent parties to respect it.

3 Sea war and the civilian

From the generals we turn now to the admirals and to two huge linked illustrations of the limitations of the concept of legality during the two world wars : the blockade (using the word largely and loosely) of Germany and its allies by the British and allied navies, and the submarine warfare waged by Germany against Britain and her allies. They are linked, first, because the latter was presented to neutral and other law-conscious opinion, partly as a justified response to the former, partly as justified by military necessity irrespective of other considerations; second, because each did violence to two of the laws of war's most essential principles, by hitting directly (though in very different ways) at neutrals and at enemy civilians. Their history during the 1914–18 war (to go no further back) is extremely complicated. Neither presents a simple picture of steady development. Their pressures were in varying degrees raised and lowered from time to time in proportion with their controllers' calculations of profit and loss. The arguments employed to justify them, so far as their apparent departure from supposedly current legal norms demanded justification, were salted with propaganda for external, and self-righteousness for internal, consumption. The facts alleged in those arguments were often open to dispute, introducing an extra element of obscurity and confusion which the patriotic bias of subsequent historians and international law writers has contributed to preserve. What follows here is not the properly proportioned history of them in their necessary relations with one another which alone might claim to be a full historical explanation of them, but simply an estimate of the lengths this side of the war was taken, and how those who took it there related it to the laws of war.

Blockade was still one of the British navy's principal means of conducting war. Coupled during the later nineteenth century with the seizure, anywhere at sea, of enemy shipping and of contraband carried by neutral shipping, it gave the world's strongest naval power a slow-working but in the end totally effective weapon against any enemy dependent on maritime traffic. Of course it was no more than half of the whole means by which the British navy was used to conduct hostilities. Inseparable from it were the destruction of the enemy's warships (if there were any) and the protection of British shipping from enemy cruisers seeking to seize British merchant ships and cargoes by the same right as British cruisers sought to seize enemy ones; the prevention of invasion of any part of the British Isles (Ireland being the most vulnerable); and the safe carriage of British expeditionary forces to wherever in the world they were needed. It added up to a heavy burden, but it was a burden the British admiralty was well accustomed to carry.

We have already seen how such constant and profitable success of course aroused envious and censorious thoughts in the minds of Britain's enemies and competitors. The mixture of dislikes accumulated for the use of critical continentals during the later nineteenth century included many elements more of emotional than rational force: envy of the good fortune which had saved Britain from every other European State's costly experience of having to defend land frontiers or suffer the penalties of not doing so; envy of the wealth and overseas empire which were to some extent (easily exaggerated, no doubt) due to that initial crowning mercy; distaste for alleged British (or more often, specifically English) perfidiousness and arrogance. With these latter charges we begin to enter a more rational region. To the charge of arrogance we shall come in due course. The longstanding complaint about '*perfide Albion*' had understandable foundations in Britain's continental allies' recurrent experience of a divergence between their interests and Britain's, in wars from which Britain could at will withdraw as they could not. The notion that Britain was in some peculiar respect perfidious or devious in its international dealings – a notion which Britons, observing the perfidiousness, ruthlessness, etcetera, practised from time to time by critic States, have never been able to take too seriously – matters to us only for its supplying emotional steam to the otherwise reasonable belief, pandemic on the European continent, that the laws of war at sea, a British construction for the most part, worked unfairly to Britain's advantage and to neutrals' disadvantage. You did not have to be a continental to know this. I quote from the 1908 report of a high-powered British Inter-Departmental Committee:

> In the past the interests of Great Britain have led her to take a strict view as to the obligations of a neutral State. This suited her convenience, because she was to a very small extent dependent on the right to use neutral ports, and her strength at sea has enabled her, generally speaking, to insist on her own rules.[40]

Neutrals objected to being made to pay the price of British maritime ascendancy and commercial expansion. With the law of contraband, they could have no quarrel – so long as the contraband list confined itself to traditional materials of war. Nor was there much room for quarrel with the law of blockade, it being universally accepted that a neutral ship was liable to seizure if caught 'running a blockade'; though there was always room for argument about what constituted a 'blockade' in any particular circumstances, and there had never been any doubt before about 1900 that blockade must be 'close' (because otherwise it could not be effective). But neutrals did strongly object to having their goods seized along with the rest of the goods on enemy ships, and to being kept from carrying non-contraband goods to or from an enemy's non-blockaded ports. Such goods, from the British point of view, could of course include whatever goods the enemy in time of peace was wont to carry in his own ships; which was good for the neutrals (who could make a profit) and good for the enemy, whose normal imports and exports might thus continue (at some extra cost) to flow; but bad for Britain. Such trade by neutrals, the British between 1756 and 1856 attempted absolutely to stop, and in 1856 only gave up because of the British Admiralty's calculation that its navy was strong enough to safeguard from French or American attack the carriage to Britain of war-essential contraband and to enforce blockade broad and strict enough to stop enemy trade altogether.

From this time onward, neutrals' complaints about the laws of war at sea, or complaints made on their behalf by interested belligerent parties, were restricted to the definitions of blockade and contraband while prospective belligerents made the further claim that the laws of sea-war should be further 'civilized' by exempting enemy (non-contraband) private property from capture. That campaign met its death in 1907 (see above, p. 213) and the law regarding property at sea was therefore unchanged when war broke out. In many other respects, however, the old law of war at sea underwent change. Eight of thirteen Hague Conventions of 1907 were to do with war at sea; and other aspects of it, still to be settled when the Hague Conference closed, figured in the Declaration proceeding from the naval conference in London in 1909. Always the dominant concern of the potential belligerents was their prospective relations with neutrals; of whom it was taken for granted there would be many in the war thought to be inevitable. Some States (France, for example) could manage better than others without neutral shipping's aid, but none wished pointlessly to forfeit neutral good opinion; which meant above all, so far as the great European powers were concerned, opinion in the United States.

The Declaration of London was the over-ripe product of many disparate parties' calculations of moral advantage and material self-interest, prospective neutrals being far more firmly involved than they ever had been – than they ever *could* have been – in the classic debates on the law of land war. To sum up in a sentence a prolix document, it may be said that the law of blockade (which, with that on contraband, mattered most to the British) remained substantially unchanged; while the law on contraband was so refined and extended as to offer neutrals a better prospect of continuing to do business with belligerents in not absolutely contraband goods than they had ever had before; which mattered supremely to Germany, prospectively dependent upon so much that would have to travel via Scandinavia and the Netherlands. British opinion was noisily divided about it. The Admiralty is said by the amplest historian of the first world war blockade to have been in its favour, to have positively desired its ratification, and despite the lack of that to have gone ahead to found the new naval instructions – the ones that were actually in force when the war began – upon it.[41] But a club-land army ('fleet' sounds not quite right) of no fewer than 122 retired admirals lent its presumed authority to the parliamentary campaign against government weakness led by the navalist MP, Thomas Gibson Bowles;[42] we may presume that senior officers on the active list were not unanimous about it; and we know that the master-plotter of the military establishment, Hankey, was against it too.[43] The foreign office however thought it a desirable improvement of Britain's international image, and the Admiralty seems to have believed that, in the fairly short war which was generally anticipated, its blockade of all the approaches to Germany, together with some slight tightening of the Declaration's contraband rules, would exert all the economic pressure that was needed to 'strangle Germany at sea' and cause grass to grow in the streets of Hamburg.[44]

But acceptance *de facto* of the Declaration of London, however it is to be explained, did not mean any softening of the essential attitude within Britain's senior service. Its war-making traditions, as we have several times noticed, were tough ones; every bit as tough, *mutatis mutandis*, as those of the Prusso-German general staff. Germany, instructed by Tirpitz, was not mistaken in taking Churchill's friend, Sir John Fisher, as their representative. Fisher took pride especially in 'the Nelson tradition'. Besides its aggressive battle tactics and intra-service camaraderie, this also included the turning of Nelson's blind eye to his commander's withdrawal signals at the first battle of Copenhagen in 1801, and (by an imaginative extension) the pre-emptive strike at neutral Denmark's navy at the second battle of Copenhagen in 1807. The second incident of course had no more to do with Nelson than anyone liked to imagine. But, in the minds of Fisher and his kind, it stood for

Britain's right to do anything, in the last resort, to ensure national sovereignty.[45] Just as the German general staff felt that, in the last resort, no law could prevent them from doing what was necessary to save Germany on land, so the British Admiralty felt it was entitled to recommend to the government (a big difference there!)[46] any course of action necessary to save Britain at sea. Fisher's jests about 'Copenhagen-ing' Tirpitz's infant fleet sprang partly from the elements of buffoonery in his complicated character but represented also his professional belief that neither neutrals' rights nor enemy civilians' safety should be allowed to stand in the way of 'necessary' naval operations. (In fact, he professed to think it likely that Tirpitz would 'Port Arthur' him!)[47]

So long as bombardment of enemy coastal towns remained an operational option, as it did until the development of mines and submarines in the early twentieth century made it generally too risky, the admirals were ready to do it. We have already seen how, before the close of the nineteenth, Oxford's professor of international law felt obliged to bombard them with admonitory letters to *The Times* about it.[48] How successful his admonitions were, we may judge from this SECRET Admiralty note printed for the Committee of Imperial Defence in mid-1906, during the preparations for the following year's Hague Conference:

> ... The object of the bombardment of [commercial] towns might be the destruction of life and property, the enforcing of ransom, the creation of panic, and the hope of embarrassing the government of the enemy's country and exciting the population to bring pressure to bear upon their rulers to bring the war to a close ... it must not be forgotten that the object of war is to obtain peace as speedily as possible on one's own terms, and not the least efficacious means of producing this result is the infliction of loss and injury upon 'enemy' non-combatants of so crushing a character as to compel them ...[49]

As for submarines, a topic which, unlike bombardment, invited forward- rather than backward-looking reflection, Fisher seems to have anticipated their use against merchant shipping as early as anybody and earlier than almost anyone else. Less intelligent and/ or less single-minded naval colleagues were slower or more reluctant to read the signs of the times. Fisher cannot be unquestioningly taken as embodying the British naval mind even in this limited context of international law. Yet it seems likely that in this respect he differed from them simply in coming more rapidly to conclusions veiled from them by self-conscious humane-ness, by 'honour', and by mental rigidity. Fisher may have been indulging his *penchant* for shocking when he told the German naval representative at the 1899 Hague Conference that, even if the British government 'for political reasons' were to agree to a convention safeguarding enemy private property at sea, they would scrap it, should it become seriously inconvenient.[50] But there is in fact no good reason to doubt that he really was expressing his service's essential orthodoxy. International law was (subject of course to government approval) not to be observed beyond the point of serious strategic disadvantage. 'I doubt the necessity as yet of infringing Norway's neutrality though of course I have often considered it', for instance wrote Fisher's successor Jellicoe to his dashing colleague Admiral Beatty at the end of 1916.[51] 'Military necessity' was just as well lodged in Portsmouth as in Potsdam.

It should have surprised nobody, therefore, when from the very outset of the 1914–18 war, Britain embarked on a course of interpretations of the Declaration of London and the Hague Conventions which aroused Germany and the maritime neutrals to various degrees of surprise and indignation, either genuine or diplomatically feigned. It is impossible in a short space (and might indeed be impossible even in a very long space) to unravel the tangle of angry arguments which at once developed. Britain and Germany sought strenuously to lay responsibility for law-breaking at each other's door. But what exactly was the law? Missing in some particulars, there was room for contrasting its letter with its spirit in others.[52] And what were the facts which each alleged in justification of its law-stretchings or breakings? The road to truth was befogged by statements made for propaganda and forensic purposes before they had been scientifically verified (not that such a thing is readily possible during a war). We shall therefore rise above, or stand aside from, this spiral of confused and confusing arguments about the immediate rights and wrongs of the British conduct of the 1914–18 war at sea, and fasten simply on its distinctive characteristics in the light of the general principles of the law of war.

Once shorn of its attachments to historical detail, the shape of Britain's maritime war is seen to be clear and simple. As an engine for forcing Germany towards surrender, it consisted of a blockade as nearly absolute and total – i.e. as prohibitive of the import of anything whatsoever by whatever route – as political considerations could permit. In fact political considerations never permitted the ideal total blockade, and for a long while even made sure that the blockade could be no more than moderately effective. Neutral interests were far too important to be imprudently disregarded. The neutrals' protests against the British navy's interference with their due freedom of non-contraband trade and interruption of their familiar trade-routes had to be heeded, and compromises struck; the admirals indisputably were ready to recommend very extensive infringement of neutral rights (e.g. controlling traffic through Norwegian territorial waters) the moment the balance of military necessity demanded it. Such a moment never came. But the British navy's control of neutrals' use of what they had liked to call 'the freedom of the high seas' remained extensive enough: the heavy hint that neutral merchantmen might find it pleasanter to avoid British-laid minefields by sailing along prescribed mine-free sea-lanes, and to submit voluntarily to British search for contraband (as currently defined in the British-made lists) rather than run the risks of evasion.

Blockade of this unprecedented character not only kept neutrals from doing the business with Germany which the state of international law in 1914 led them to expect, but also obstructed their trade among themselves and for their own exclusive benefit. The British government was from time to time hard put to it to appease neutrals' wrath; and would have been unable to do so – would indeed probably have had to relax the blockade in many important particulars – had German policy not repeatedly played into British hands by revealing Germany as no more careful of neutral rights and interests than Britain was, and in actual fact more violent in its style of damaging them. The initial invasion of Belgium was necessarily the root of Germany's ill-repute in this respect, but the submarine warfare by which Germany sought to out-match the unexpected severity of the British blockade also of its nature encouraged – perhaps, necessitated – infringements of neutrals' rights and, much worse, losses of neutrals' lives, which put a somewhat incredible and perhaps hypocritical appearance on Germany's pose as the neutrals' friend.[53] Only neutrals sharing the German sense of what was permissible for a great power by virtue of military necessity could fail to resent the German style of disregarding their rights at sea at least as much as the British style. A brief scrutiny of the nature of submarine commercial warfare will soon show why.

The German admiralty had not much, if at all, contemplated before the autumn of 1914 the use of submarines for commercial (or to use the classic term) 'cruiser' warfare.[54] The sea-going submarine had in any case not been in existence for long enough for all its potentialities to be judiciously assessed. The only expectation confidently held was of its adding greatly to the hazards facing warships within submarine sailing distance (not in those days, very great) of enemy bases. But the submarine had hardly yet seemed suited for commerce-raiding which, under the prevailing laws of war at sea, required the stopping and search of vessels according to regular legal forms, the placing of a 'prize crew' on board of arrested vessels, and adjudication upon their fate in a 'prize court' on national territory. Germany was as anxious as Britain to disturb enemy commerce but her only prospects of doing so, at the beginning of the war, lay in the few German cruisers that were already on the high seas, and whatever others could subsequently reach them. The former, which seem to have held honourably to the laws of war so far as they could, were soon hunted down, and, of the latter, hardly any ever penetrated the British navy's screens of mines and warships.[55] Meanwhile the British blockade bit hard. Submarine warfare in its characteristic 1914–18 form was Germany's naval counter-stroke; like the blockade, unjustifiable by the laws of sea-war as they had been understood up to 1914, and therefore to be justified – if justified at all – only on grounds of military necessity, reprisals or retaliation.

The legal and, insofar as 'humanity' was concerned, moral problems of submarine warfare against non-naval shipping became clear as the war went on. The submarine, it was discovered, could not without excessive risk to itself attack enemy merchant and passenger ships by the time-honoured rules of cruiser warfare. It carried too few men for prize crews to be thinkable. Its prizes could not be taken for adjudication in prize courts. It therefore had no alternative but to send its prizes to the bottom. This in itself was not quite as novel or surprising at it may sound. Russian cruisers operating immensely far from base in the war of 1904–5 sank neutral prizes when, by their judgement, they could do nothing else, and Article 49 of the Declaration of London had more or less sanctioned such practice.[56] So far no lives were endangered; and submarines, if they operated by cruiser rules (so far as possible), might be able to give the crews and passengers of doomed ships warning and time enough to get clear in lifeboats, more or less hopeful of survival. But did the nature of the submarine permit even that small measure of traditional regard for non-combatant life and property? A submarine could dare to operate on the surface only if its prize really was an unarmed non-military vessel, passively defenceless. What if it carried a small gun for self-defence – and were instructed to use it, even in anticipation of attack?[57] Or if it were to turn to ram the submarine – and were instructed to do so?[58] Fisher, reviewing all the possibilities in a memorandum of May 1914, asked in conclusion: 'What can be the answer to all the fore-going but that (barbarous and inhuman as, we again repeat, it may appear), if the submarine is used at all against commerce, she must sink her captures?'[59] What if – this was something which Fisher did not apparently think of – the merchant-ship pretended to be defenceless but actually carried a concealed gun, as did the famous or, according to the point of view, infamous British 'Q-Ships'?[60]

The Germans, once having turned to this novel variant of cruiser warfare, were soon complaining that the British, by arming their merchant ships, were driving submarine commanders to attack without warning, submerged. The British reply was that any measure of self-defence and counter-attack was legitimate against such an unwontedly lawless method of warfare, and that although some U-boat commanders might be keeping as close as they could to the old prize rules, other less humane ones were not. The controversy that quickly developed could by its very nature never come to a satisfactory conclusion, because each party with some justice (how much, was scarcely measurable) excused its own unlawful doings by reason of its enemies'; a fruitless game of mutual recriminations in which the German ace – the claim that, to begin with, they had done nothing at sea (except by way of reprisals) that was expressly forbidden by the Hague Conventions and Declaration of London – could always be trumped with the 'Belgium' card. It might not make good law, but it made fine politics! As far as law went, the conclusion of the best legal authority is that German submarine warfare in principle was justified both as legitimate reprisals and 'as a lawful claim of right'.[61]

The German submarine war, like the British blockade, was conducted at different levels of intensity from time to time, tightening or slackening in proportion with the German government's assessments of the international political situation and its current ability to control its military chieftains. The German admirals never achieved the same degree of independence of their country's political leadership as the German generals, though they tried hard enough to do so. No doubt largely because of the unfortunate political consequences of the most striking exercise of that independence, the German Chancellor insisted on keeping close watch on the development of submarine warfare from early 1915 onwards. Neutral interests and neutral opinions, just as for Britain in respect of the blockade, were the decisive factors. I cannot see that either State was in principle markedly more reluctant than the other to offend neutral susceptibilities. In practice however, there were differences which made Germany look the less reluctant and of which a more politic direction of German affairs would have taken prudent account. Time mattered less to the British admirals than the German generals. To the latter, lost days seemed to mean lost battles. Their Schlieffen plan was bred out of anxiety by impatience. But blockade was by definition a slow process. It could not avoid annoying neutrals. It could avoid shocking them. That difference worked to Britain's psychological advantage. So did another difference – perhaps the crucial difference – between the blockade and submarine war as Germany waged it. The blockade of Germany directly killed no neutrals, though the threat that they might get killed if they didn't obey the Anglo-French (and, later, American) rules was certainly there in the background. Ultimately, no doubt, the Allied blockade tended towards the killing of German civilians, if German soldiers were given first claim on food; but this was a very long-delayed conclusion, which could be easily avoided by any government desirous to avoid it. Submarine warfare, by contrast, could not only not avoid killing British civilians; at its most intensive, it killed neutrals too.

Germany took it to that most intensive pitch of 'unrestricted submarine warfare' as an endeavour to stop the traffic of ships in and out of British ports; in other words, to do to Britain what Britain had done to Germany. But Britain's trade could not be stopped as bloodlessly. The virtually complete physical stoppage made possible for the British by a combination of minefields and cruiser patrols was out of the question. Germany could never keep enough submarines in Britain's western approaches to sink every ship in them. But alarm and terror might make up the physical deficiency. British mariners might not yield to terror but, thought the German admirals, neutral mariners would. Unrestricted submarine warfare was therefore twice waged in certain specified operational areas (the first phase in the spring of 1915, the second from early 1917 onwards). Germany gave notice, notice comparable to the formal notification required for a blockade, that *any* ship within those areas was liable to be sunk without warning; and that if neutral shipowners knew what was good for them, they would keep well away. To neutral objections that this was intolerable, Germany replied that neutrals ought to have found the British blockade's restrictions on their freedom intolerable too; to which the neutral response in effect was, that the British blockade was indeed intolerable but that at least it did not cast them suddenly to death. Rightly or wrongly, reasonably or unreasonably, President Wilson's comment was: 'It is interesting and significant how often the German foreign office goes over the same ground in different words and always misses the essential point involved, that England's violation of neutral rights is different from Germany's violation of the rights of humanity.'[62] Corbett in 1911 had supposed that 'No power will incur the odium of sinking a prize with all hands.'[63] He was mistaken.

We may now attempt to sum up the meaning of the 1914–18 war at sea in the modern history of the law of war. Did the Allied blockade etc. and German submarine warfare constitute an example of the wilful conduct of war by means more inhumane than they had to be, and the slackening of the limitations place by 'civilized' belligerents upon it? First, as to its harsh effects on enemy non-combatants, which must have reference chiefly to the effects of the Allied blockade on the Central Powers during the latter part of the first world war, there can be no denying that many German and Austrian civilians were suffering severely from malnutrition by the time the war ended; nor has it ever been persuasively denied that the collective German will to go on fighting was thereby to some extent reduced. Since the German government by the middle of the war assumed complete control of the German economy, indissolubly involving its 'civilian' sectors with its 'military' ones, the direction of scarcening resources of food and clothing to the armed forces at the expense of the civil population might seem to make the latter's privations a matter primarily of German, not British, responsibility. Food and clothing for the German armed forces and the non-combatant supporters of their military efforts could therefore with some legitimacy be stopped. German government policy made it impossible to stop them without stopping also the food and clothing going (perhaps) to those non-combatants who really had nothing to do with keeping the German armed forces in the field.

To have allowed the unfortunate existence of these, so to speak, ultra-non-combatants to inhibit action against the combatants would have been as unreasonable as, for instance, to allow the un-fortunate presence of civilians in defended buildings to inhibit the direction of militarily necessary shellfire against them – a disad-vantageous self-limitation never expected of land armies. The action of blockade, however, could fairly be considered much more humane than that of artillery, bullets or bombs. Blockade gave generous advance notice of its ultimate effects. It did not suddenly, unavoidably, maim or slaughter. British and other apolo-gists of blockade were not being hypocritical when they argued that, given the facts of the case, blockade was a relatively humane device of warfare.[64] German complaints about it during the first world war (leaving aside the question of its continuation after the armistice, which is not relevant to a discussion of the law of war) seem to me to lack substance, and to be dismissable even without inquiring, as one might legitimately do, whether the Allies were doing to Germany anything worse than the Germans had done to Paris in 1870–1, or whether the Germans would not willingly have initiated no less strict a blockade on the British, had they been in a better position to do so.[65] To sum up about the so-called 'hunger-blockade', then, as affecting non-combatants in the enemy land: the concept and the very phrase lent themselves to emotive propaganda purposes, and their popularity with Britain's conti-nental enemies seems more explicable on those than on solid juridical grounds.

In their effects on neutrals, however, Britain's methods and measures seem more questionable. The law of war, after all, never more intimately relies upon restraint than when neutral interests are concerned. It 'works' in proportion to belligerents' willing-ness to exercise self-restraint: not to do this or that, emotionally

or militarily tempting though it might be, because to do it would
be to damage the objects for which the law exists (which is only
one step from saying, the objects for which war itself is undertaken). Westlake took the existence of the law of war for granted
when he defined war as 'an effort by each of two nations to bend
the other to its will, by all the means in its power *which do not
violate neutral rights, and are not ruled out as inhuman*'.[66] Restraint for the sake of neutrals has always been a cardinal principle
of the law of war; particularly of the law of war at sea, which has
necessarily involved neutrals much more than war on land. Reviewing the modern histories of war and the law of war, one can
hardly fail to conclude that the room provided for neutrals and the
safe protection and pursuit of their interests has progressively
shrunk. The will to be neutral may be as strong as ever. It is the
power to sustain neutrality that has, in our century, diminished.
This is largely to be explained by the spread, or revival, of ideological wars. Who is not for a totalitarian ideology must be against
it. But who was not for the League of Nations could be presumed
to be against it also.[67] Further explanations of the decline of
neutrality may be found in the 'shrinkage' of the globe brought
about by modern commerce and communications, and the discovery of weapons and delivery systems which tend towards the
erosion or disregard of neutral rights or character; as was in fact
conspicuously the case with the two methods of warfare we are
here considering. But another element must be taken account of
too: belligerent's choice; whether or not to exercise restraint for
neutrals' benefit.

I have already dealt with the eighteenth- and nineteenth-century
phases of British naval policy. So long-established a policy and
attitude could not be expected suddenly to change in the twentieth,
and did not do so. The extent of British interference with neutral
trade continued to exceed what might have been considered
absolutely necessary. One might argue that it was more discreet
and defensive than it had been between 1793 and 1814, but the
nation of shop-keepers was still under suspicion of being the nation
of trade-grabbers too. This image of Britain, which attained its
most perfect form under the influence of Napoleonic propaganda,
and had currency at the epoch among Britain's allies as well as her
enemies,[68] cast some continuing shadow over the British reputation during the 1914–18 war, when neutrals were quick to sense

in British blockade policy and management an *arrière-pensée* that British trade might sometimes be substituted for neutral; even when it was trade with the enemy.[69]

By the twentieth century, however, war had not the relatively simple commercial *raison d'être* of the pre-revolutionary age. If Britain's practice of blockade continued to bear harder on neutrals than it absolutely had to, mercantile greed could no longer be the main reason. How far in fact the blockades of 1914–18 and 1939–45 did so bear on neutrals, may be endlessly debated. Neutrals of course complained about it, and Germany of course supported them. The controversy that ensued ranged for the most part far beyond the tidy terms of juridical science. Extracting as best we can the more closely legal issues from all the others which have naturally adhered to them in political and historical debate, we discover that the British and Allied blockade of the Central Powers during the first world war was so conducted as to stretch the law in Britain's interests and against those of neutrals. The contraband lists were repeatedly extended. Neutral ships were compelled to enter allied ports for search, a practice for which, the General Board of the United States navy advised Secretary of State Lansing, there was certainly 'no necessity'.[70]

The European neutrals were chivvied into accepting an ever more intense scrutiny and control of their imports and exports; in effect, considered suspect until proved innocent. By early 1916, wrote the French historian of the blockade, it was 'only distantly connected with the monument [sic] of law erected by the Powers in 1909, and was in certain respects entirely out of keeping with it. . .'.[71] According to its best British historian, it would have been even more out of keeping, had some of the suggestions made at the Contraband Committee been adopted![72] Some measure of erosion of neutral rights, some departure from the Declaration of London (which had ramshackle aspects), were only to be expected, as law and usage accommodated to technical innovation and political atmosphere. The question is, whether the belligerents, when they made those accommodations, gave the neutral representatives of humanity as much consideration as they gave their own.

After all that about the first world war, the second may be very quickly dealt with, for it produced no problem or principle which had not appeared in the first. And in Europe, moreover, it was very much of a 'repeat story' : blockade and so on by Britain and, relatively soon, the United States, met by the Axis (which boiled down to Germany) principally by U-boat warfare. Nor did the war in the Pacific and south-east Asia spring any significant novelties. The US navy practised unrestricted submarine warfare there in exactly the same way as the German navy practised it in the Atlantic; Japan became more and more blockaded; there were more surface battles and combined sea-land operations than Europe invited, but nothing that demands special notice here.

The sense of *déja vu* is enhanced by the fact that the law of sea warfare had hardly changed either. That was not for lack of trying. U-boats shared with aerial bombardment and gas the top place on the list of weapons and methods of clamouring for juridical and diplomatic attention, and were on several occasions the whole or partial subject of international conferences. Some countries, Britain urgently at their head, professed themselves ready to abolish them; the French in particular said they would never do so. Some stuck by them on the ground that they were of more value in defence than attack, and that they were therefore the natural weapons of smaller naval powers, inherently non-aggressive. Nothing in the end came of the attempt to ban them altogether. The attempt legally to regulate their use got further. A tangled skein of legislation running from 1922 to 1936 produced at the close of the latter year 'the London Protocol',[73] binding submarines 'in their action with regard to merchant ships' to 'conform to the rules of international law to which surface vessels are subject', and making 'unrestricted warfare' of the 1914–18 kind illegal 'except in the case of persistent refusal to stop on being duly summoned, or of active resistance to visit or search'.[74] Of this protocol, all the major future belligerents by 1939 were signatories.

Yet when the war came, the London Protocol went with the wind. Its rules for 'soft' submarine warfare pre-supposed in the submariners' enemy a comparably 'soft' style of operations. This was not realistic. Exactly the same happened in 1939–40 as had happened in 1914–15. Neither side was able to rest within the implications of their legal agreement. Retaliation was the motive behind, and 'reprisals' the excuse offered for, the series of developments which very soon undid it, but 'military necessity' was their real explanation. Great Britain had for years been planning a

blockade on a scale as extensive as the Foreign Office would
sanction, and, subject to that proviso alone, the place allowed in
the scenario to neutrals was small indeed – much smaller than it
had been twenty-five years earlier. 'Blockade' indeed was scarcely
an adequate description of what was intended. 'Economic warfare'
was more like it, and a government department precisely so named
and natured was in fact to be in charge of the business. A glance at
the terms of reference given to its embryo in 1936 sufficiently
indicates what was in view :

> 'Economic warfare is a military operation, comparable to the
> operations of the three Services in that its object is the defeat of
> the enemy, and complementary to them in that its function is
> to deprive the enemy of the material means of resistance. But,
> unlike the operations of the Armed Forces, its results are
> secured not only by direct attack upon the enemy but also by
> bringing pressure to bear upon those neutral countries from
> which the enemy draws his supplies. It must be distinguished
> from coercive measures appropriate for adoption in peace to
> settle international differences without recourse to war, e.g.,
> sanctions, pacific blockade, economic reprisals, etc., since un-
> like such measures, it has as its ultimate sanction the use of
> belligerent rights.'[75]

Europe's neutrals, and neutrals of other continents wishing to
continue trade with Europe, were accordingly pressed – within
the politic limits of foreign policy, which of course included economic self-interest – to adopt maritime ways which, remarks Professor Mallison, 'effectively integrated [them] into the British and
Allied war effort'.[76] Existence was made so difficult for them if
they refused, that they had little choice but to submit, whether
they liked it or not. 'Thus', concluded the German naval command
in the summer of 1940,

> 'the neutrals directly supported British warfare, for by sub-
> mitting to the British control system in their own country they
> permitted the British Navy to economize on fighting forces
> which, according to the hitherto existing international law,
> should have exercised trade control at sea and which were now
> available for other war tasks.'[77]

Add to such thorough-going measures of economic warfare the

normal predictable use of mine-fields, 'operations zones', armed merchant ships and so on, and it is not difficult to understand why Germany, which to say the least had no intention of being put at a strategic disadvantage by its enemies' maritime measures, resorted quite soon to unrestricted submarine warfare, just as it had on the previous occasion. The usual escalation of measures announced as reprisals and counter-reprisals quickly took these arch-belligerents to an extra-legal realm of operations where no restraints remained but what humanitarian principle or sentiment might occasionally prompt. The task of penetrating the thicket of allegations and counter-allegations accompanying that escalation is not within my powers. One step enough for me : to note the concurrence of two distinguished contemporary jurists in concluding that British measures in restraint of neutral trade were, as of 1939, unlawful, and that Germany's reprisal recourse to unrestricted U-boat warfare was therefore not so.[78] But 'lawful' and 'unlawful' in such circumstances meant not very much, because the law itself – customary international law plus its conventional accretions at The Hague and London between 1907 and 1936 – was not reasonable in relation to the natures either of the weapons or of the war it was supposed to regulate, and, given that the submarine weapon was allowed at all, it raised expectations of restraint beyond what was militarily bearable.

This sketch of the respective natures and rationales of Britain's and its Allies' blockades and Germany's submarine wars has been attempted because, of all the many aspects of the two world wars which demanded scrutiny in the light of the law of armed conflict, and considering only the aspects which marked it as a war of more 'total' a character than previous wars, they were among the most significant for subsequent development. Poison-gas and aerial bombardments might be more spectacularly disturbing; improvement of the arrangements for the care of prisoners of war, and promotion of a convention for the protection of civilians in wartime, were added to every humanitarian agenda for the post-war reconstruction period. But none of them illustrated as strongly and sternly as the blockade and the unrestricted submarine campaigns the essential tendency of war, in the era of mass politics and industrialization, to become 'total', not only in the sense of requiring co-ordinated effort from every side of a State's structure, but also in the sense of obliterating the classic law of war's distinction between combatants and others. Blockades, as soon as political circumstances permitted, became total ones, including food and everything else which a civil population normally needed. Submarine war inspired to totality too, drowning food-carrying sailors (non-combatants, so far as international law had anything to say about it) as a preliminary to starving their civilian compatriots at home. Of course there were degrees of severity in these new styles of total war against, ultimately, the whole enemy population. Such a blockade of countries situated as were Germany and Austria (with exploitable occupied territories at their mercy) might grind small, but it ground extremely slowly. Its ultimate effects could easily be foreseen and, if so desired, avoided. The submarine war, on the other hand, though more sudden, was more patchy. So far as it dealt immediate death and injury, it dealt them to relatively few. Neither war-style bore much trace of that readiness to consign immediately to oblivion whole cities-full of enemy civilians which was the ultimate tendency of aerial bombardment and became frankly accepted as such during the second world war; to which we next turn.

4 Aerial bombardment[79]

Bombing from aircraft was extraordinarily new in 1914 (the precedent was a few bombs dropped by Italians during their war with Turkey over Libya in 1911–12)[80] but the possibility had been coming into view for several years. Those years, as it happened, included the Hague Conferences of 1899 and 1907, where the matter had attracted attention. The very fluid state of aeronautical science is indicated both by the terms of a Declaration made on both occasions by certain States, that they would 'prohibit [until future notice] the discharge of projectiles and explosives from balloons or by other new methods of a similar nature', and by the differences between the lists of States willing, after due calculation of their chances, so to declare; Great Britain alone having declined to do so in 1899, but leading the list of signatories in 1907, followed by the USA, Norway, the Low Countries, and Switzerland.[81] Since this was moreover only a 'Declaration', not a proper Convention, it quickly became nothing more than a historical curiosity.

The determination of the law so far as it could affect aerial bombing was thus left to a few specific prohibitions and a general principle. The most directly relevant specific statement was Article 25 of the 1907 Hague Land War Regulations, which prohibited 'the attack or bombardment, *by any means whatever*, of towns, villages, habitations, or buildings which are not defended'. That italicized (by me) phrase was put in expressly to cover the possibility of its being done from the air. But the definition of bombardable places in the accompanying, ninth, Convention, governing naval bombardment, included those which, though 'not defended', had within them 'military works, military or naval establishments, depots of arms or war material, [and] workshops or plants' of military utility (Article 2). The general principle, which in such circumstances mattered all the more, was that stated in the 'Martens Declaration' in the preamble to the fourth Convention, the one to which the Land War Regulations were attached. Since the *Acte Final* of the Conference desiderated the application of the land war laws and customs, *mutatis mutandis*, to war at sea, it was only perverse to assume that extension to war in the air, when and as it developed, was not meant as well.

So much for the very novel business of aerial bombardment on the eve of the first world war. More copious supplies of precedents and principles came from the controversial history of bombardment by sea or land forces, at which we have already several times glanced. It had always been controversial, because of the extent to which civilians almost inevitably became involved in it. The question had always been, not 'whether bombardment should be prohibited entirely if it could not help hitting civilians as well as legitimate military targets'; but, 'whether enemy civilians themselves were to any extent legitimate military targets?' Bombardments of the interior parts of cities ('indiscriminate' as compared with the relatively 'precise' cannonading of fortifications and gun-emplacements) had been justified by the argument that the civilians thus put at great risk were, after all, 'enemies', and if made wretched enough would press the military commander to surrender. The psychology behind this regularly reiterated assertion was always questionable and was, in fact, never left unquestioned; not much evidence ever came to hand, either that bombarded populaces behaved that way, or that, if they did, commanding officers were much influenced by it. It was however, a belief dear to many admirals' and generals' hearts, and dear also to a body of people acquiring increasing influence after the mid-nineteenth century: the more bellicose and xenophobic parts of their national publics, uninstructed in the law of war and for the most part inexperienced in actual warfare, to whom this vicarious bashing of their imagined foes tended to be attractive. For whatever reasons, the right indiscriminately to bombard besieged or otherwise attacked places was one which the military before 1914 would not resign, and the most that could be done in the Hague Regulations to modify it, apart from the provision already mentioned, was to require bombarders to avoid 'as far as possible', 'buildings dedicated to public worship, art, science, or charitable purposes, historical monuments, [and] hospitals' (Article 27), and to 'do all in their power' to give the civilian population warning of what was coming (Article 26). Complete protection from it, they could not, apparently, have. With this, the international juridical community, somewhat unhappily, had to be content.

No less equivocal was the state of law concerning blockade. We have seen how in 1793 and intermittently thereafter a dominant naval power sought to put painful pressure on its enemy's populace by total economic warfare, and how that enemy retaliated in kind. The American North did the same to the South in the war of 1861–5. Those attempted blockades of whole countries had never got near the theoretically final point of starving them into submission. That point had of course often been reached in the cases of particular blockaded or besieged cities, like Genoa in 1800 and Paris in 1870–1. Its inhumane-ness had been much deplored, but the sufferings of the civilians caught inside the place had had to be accepted by the jurists as inevitable – given that they had not escaped in time or (as sometimes happened) been allowed to leave. In principle no clear difference appeared between the cases of the blockaded/besieged city and the totally blockaded country: it was a matter about which the jurists had nothing positive to say, except to remind themselves and anyone who was listening of the 'Martens Declaration' and the principle of proportionality.

If we articulate the grounds for the jurists' convictions about these matters, we find they run something like this. No matter how closely a civilian might be engaged in war-supporting, indeed war-enabling, work, so long as he was not actually a fighting man, equipped personally to carry on hostilities against you or to defend himself against you, he must not be counted a combatant any more than should the soldier's fiancée, wife or parents. All such enemy civilians might hate you as much or even more. They would not be friendly or willingly acquiescent if you occupied their territory. But the law of war had nothing to do with states of mind or heart. It was concerned only with states of fact. Whether you could fairly win a war against that country or not depended simply on the measure of your armed strength against its armed strength. The factories making the guns, the railways bringing them to the battlefronts, had to be included within the category of legitimate military targets once means were available of destroying them (as they hardly ever had been before the skies were opened), and civilians in them or riskily close to them might have to be equated with civilians in legitimately attacked places; if they were there when the shells, bullets or bombs came in, they would get hurt. But juridical opinion, at its constant task of rebuilding lines of distinction after technical innovations threatened to blur and erode them, found no necessity to count the civilian war-worker the less a civilian because of his war work, any more than the soldier's family and friends at home were the less civilian because their well-being was of perhaps passionate concern to him. There was no guarantee that killing them would reduce his fighting-power; and even if it were to do so, it was an unthinkably inhumane way to go about it, unless one were willing to be classed with Genghiz Khan. Upon the distinction between civilian and combatant, after all, the whole idea of a law of war absolutely depends; the law's abilities – always limited and shaky – to mitigate the horrors of war diminish in proportion as the category of civilian is diluted.

To sum it up so far; blockade of enemy cities or territories had always been done by belligerents in proportion to their means to do it, and civilians suffered in proportion as governments and military commanders chose to let them do so. Civilians and their belongings had been made to suffer likewise (though not normally to the point of personal injury) in circumstances of invasion and military occupation pending peace settlements *and* on much rarer occasions of deliberately destructive expeditions like those directed by the British against American east-coast places in 1813–14 and by Sherman against the interior of the Confederacy in 1864–5. Only in cases of indiscriminate bombardment of cities (usually but not always besieged ones) was injury and death of civilians deliberately and instantly risked.

From the beginning of the first world war, anyone interested in the possibilities of strategic aerial bombardment (we are not concerned with the tactical sort, in direct support of land army operations) had two quite different theories to choose from.

One was precision bombing: the dropping of bombs as precisely as possible on military targets, broadly defined to include manufactories, communications centres and so on, perhaps well behind the land or sea combat zones, with a fair degree of confidence that they, and not much more than they, could be hit. All air forces to some degree tried this. To do it properly, with the equipment available at that time, was difficult. Although unable to judge how much the various national air forces went in for it, I can see that in none of them did it become a dominant interest or activity. But we have recently learnt that in Great Britain, at least, it became a more intense and promising activity than has so far been recognized. Mr Neville Jones's 1973 book *The Origins of Strategic Bombing* tells us that the Royal Naval Air Service, merged with the (army-connected) Royal Flying Corps to form the Royal Air Force in April 1918, specialized in precision bombing and would have done much more of it if it had been encouraged; i.e., if it had not lost out in the normal inter-service, intra-service, and political dog-fights for resources and political influence. That this unusual book, by a former RAF navigator and education officer who is obviously a good historian too, seems to have made as yet no indentation on the orthodoxy it is designed to correct, is a lamentable matter to which we shall recur. His book is not a polemical one, and its scholarly quietness may have contributed to its neglect; but there is no longer, in 1980, any excuse for not knowing the facts about the RNAS.

There was much more excuse (though it still seems rather odd) for, e.g., M. W. Royse in 1928. In his admired book *Aerial Bombardment and the International Regulation of Warfare* he relied on that already entrenched orthodoxy when he wrote, 'aerial bombs and sighting devices were crude and inaccurate, more or less precluding the effectual destruction of individual objectives.'[82] That was what 'the father of the RAF' and his children inclined to believe. But according to Mr Jones they need not have done so.

The RNAS, before it was pushed so thoroughly out of sight, had developed successful techniques of precision bombing; plans for its strategic application, based on calculations of the economic value of the German war effort of, first, steel and then chemical industries within accessible bombing distances – plans which startlingly anticipate the second world war's 'oil plan' etc.; and progressively improved bomb-aiming equipment and bombing techniques which by 1918 were quite reliably efficient. The moment the war was over, the men who had been working on these lines during the war, and who became a diminishing minority within the RFC-dominated RAF, went to Germany to check-up on the results of what they had been allowed to do (it was, as I have said, a lot less than they would have liked) in a strategic bombing survey, which could, says Mr Jones (another anticipation!), have prepared Bomber Command better for what it was supposed to do twenty years later, if anyone had bothered to look at it. Nobody did. When he sought out and opened these files of 1914–18 operational research, the dust of more than forty years lay thick upon them.

The other strategic theory which bombers could adopt or gravitate towards we will, with necessary explanations, call the 'indiscriminate' one; meaning, not that the hope or intention of hitting designated military targets was entirely abandoned, but that there was reconcilement to the certainty that much besides those targets was going to be hit, or much instead; or, to put it another way, that besides whatever target of military importance might be hit, civilian property would be hit as well.

Indiscriminate bombing is much more difficult to establish the facts about, for it had built into it from the very start protections against the moral and legal criticisms to which it obviously stood open. It has in fact a chameleon quality which has enabled those desirous of obscuring its real character to do so by exploiting its operational ambiguities; veiling its main, perhaps improper, purpose and effect under its not improper subsidiary ones. I will summarize those veiling devices right away, for their importance has not been sufficiently recognized.

The most short and easy method to avert criticism was to admit the illegality of the whole thing at once by announcing it plainly as a reprisal; as was often done by all the bombing powers in both world wars. Reprisals by definition are unlawful acts deliberately done to punish and deter an unlawfully behaving enemy. Wars being what they are, and the business of propaganda being what it is, there was never much difficulty in finding pretexts for reprisals, and much advantage in doing so, no further justifications being called for, and the moral responsibility being thrown back upon the enemy.

But justification without going to that length was facilitated by the very nature of this 'indiscriminate' bombing itself. It was, necessarily, the bombing of inhabited areas; if not sizeable towns and cities, then at any rate 'industrial areas'; areas where 'every bomb would count'. But hardly ever was there nothing within such areas that could not be construed as a military target, and often civilian premises in such urban/industrial areas lay close to very obvious military targets indeed. It could therefore truthfully enough be claimed that 'military targets were hit', without mentioning how much else besides military targets was hit or (as became the case with indiscriminate bombardment *par excellence* in the second world war) that the civilians and their houses – the 'collateral damage', to use one of the standard phrases for it – are what you had really been interested in.[83]

And what was the point of hitting all that civilian 'collateral'? So far as it had any intelligible point (beyond indulging impatience for action, desire to please allies, or expressing hatred and vengefulness, which of course could have been its main actual motivations), during the first world war it was, quite simply, to chill the enemy civilian population's enthusiasm for continuing the war and to compel him to divert resources to defence against air attacks likely to achieve that end. It *assumed* that that 'will' mattered so much, and that it could be 'broken'. By the latter stages of world war two, the quantity of 'collateral' damage combined with the damage simultaneously done to more or less military targets could seem big enough for the justificatory formula to run: to break the enemy will to go on fighting and to impose such strain on his society and economic resources that he actually will find it difficult to do so. (That is a paraphrase of Bomber Command's basic doctrine in 1942–3.) But in world war one there was never a hope, outside the ranks of the 'precision' school, that enough damage could be done to interfere materially with the industrial contribution to the war effort. It was enemy civilian morale that was aimed at (looking at some German and British popular reactions, not without reason), notwithstanding the prominence given in official instructions or explanations to more lawful-looking 'military and industrial objectives', and the diversion of resources incidentally effected.

Some, perhaps most, pilots no doubt had 'military objectives' as their aiming-points, and would have liked to hit them; but hit them or not, *it did not much matter*. The two German lieutenants captured after their Gotha came down on the night of 5–6 December 1917 spoke for most night bombers on both sides when they told their interrogators that 'they were able to pick out their targets [the City, Bank, GPO, Admiralty, War Office, London Docks] and endeavoured to bomb them. But they added that if bombs went astray it was of no consequence, as one of the objects in raiding England was to demoralize the civilian population, particularly in the East End of London.'[84] The only fault I can find with Royse's demonstration of the undoubted fact and steady growth of indiscriminate or (another first world war word for it) 'promiscuous' bombardment through the war is that he gives greater prominence to Allied than to German official cover stories. The truth, however, comes out clearly enough in a careful reading of the text and footnotes of his chapter 6, up to where he writes:

'Demoralization of the enemy by means of aerial bombardment was accepted as part of the functions of the bombardment groups [of all major powers] .... In general one principle seems to have been followed in the war; that military objectives could be bombed wherever found, regardless of their location, and, it seems, regardless of the injury to non-combatants and private property.'[85]

I am not sure whether Italy, Austria, and Russia in 1914–18 went in for indiscriminate bombardment to the same extent as certainly did the French, British and Germans. Between the wars, the Luftwaffe became transformed from whatever had been the previous idea of it into an air force of mainly tactical purpose, devoted to helping the Wehrmacht win *Blitzkriegs*. As for the French and Americans, I need only say that, faced in principle with the same choices as the British, they decided differently: the French at last, in the later thirties, and too late to save themselves from what was in store for them, going in much the same direction as the Germans, while America, after the Billy Mitchell turbulence

of the early twenties, and I know not at what pace, took up precision strategic bombing as the only thing it could do and the only
thing which, on reflection, it seemed right to do. But Britain, alone
of the major air powers, continued at least to flirt with its opposite;
by no means to the exclusion of the idea of precision, which with
part of its war-making mind it earnestly pursued; but cherishing,
nevertheless, the idea of something less discriminate as a first love,
upon whose tried affections it was always possible and safe to rely,
and which the precision ideal could conveniently be used to cloak.

Its roots lay not wholly within the military. When Clio's trumpet salutes the publication of the perfect history of this disagreeable side of twentieth-century warfare, it will tell us how much
responsibility has to be allotted to carry-over from earlier forms
of bombardment and economic destruction, to political pressure,
popular clamour, and the common-ness of the assumption, from
1916 onwards, that indiscriminate bombing of this kind was
bound to be a regular feature of war for all time to come; an
assumption to be given literary celebration soon after the close of
world war one by the military futurist Douhet. In Britain, we
early see this assumption, together with a significant moral
insouciance about it, in the famous report of the 'Smuts Committee', the Committee on Air Organization and Home Defence
against Air Raids, in mid-August 1917.

'As far as can at present be foreseen there is absolutely no limit
to the scale of [air power's] future independent war use. And
the day may not be far off when aerial operations with their
devastation of enemy lands and destruction of industrial and
populous centres on a vast scale may become the principal
operations of war, to which the older forms of military and naval
operations become secondary and subordinate.'[86]

The Smuts Committee is renowned not only because of its expression of these sentiments and the prestige of the chairman (no air-
man, by the way) who gave them his imprimatur, but because it
was the proximate start of the complicated reorganizations which
produced in the end the RAF. *En route* thereto, air policy was
determined by a cabinet committee whose directive memorandum
of January 1918 said no more of war industries than that they were
among the desirable objectives, and weighed civilian morale as an
objective equally important with the rest. Heavy sustained bomb-

ng of large industrial centres was therefore particularly recommended 'as a method of attack by which every bomb dropped could be made to count'.[87] As the chief of the Independent [Strategic Bombing] Force reassured the Air Minister, when the latter told him not to bother about precision overmuch: 'The accuracy is not great at present, and all the pilots drop their eggs well into the middle of the town generally.'[88]

The chief was Hugh Trenchard, first Marshal of the Royal Air Force, and to several generations of RAF officers and fellow-spirits, its 'father'; a powerful, aggressive character who left his mark apparently irremovably on its nature, its style, and – because of the momentum of admiration and loyalty to him and his tradition – its historiography. My use of the single word 'Trenchard' to describe the source of RAF policy-making of course bypasses many possibilities of intricate inquiry into bureaucratic politics and military decision-making which might profitably be made, but for present purposes will not, I believe, be misleading; Trenchard, after all, was famous for being master in his own house.

His main preoccupation for many years was to win the battle being fought by or on behalf of air forces in every country advanced enough to possess them: the battle to become effectively *independent* of the old-established land and naval services, and to secure a worthwhile share of whatever resources were going. In Britain, as generally everywhere else, generals and admirals disliked the challenge presented by the new men of the air to their traditional grandeur, and disliked especially the prospect that the cake of resources, shrunken to Britain's usual niggardly peacetime proportions, now had a third applicant for slices. Trenchard won his battle against the generals and admirals in fine style. 'External' circumstances in some respects favoured him. Aviation was an exciting new thing and many journalists, politicians and businessmen were eager to promote all forms of it. Alarmism about the next war became so fixated on air-raids that it became difficult for politicians not to assume that a bombing capability was desirable, even if only as a deterrent. Reflections upon the last war were bound to make people listen hopefully to the promise of a war to be won without any Sommes or Gallipolis – i.e., by subjecting what was promised, for no good reason, to be a smaller number of civilians, to the same processes of suffering and death as the worse western front battles had brought to a large number of soldiers.

For the special role which Trenchard claimed for the RAF as an independent, third, armed force, was as a bombing force. Bombing would not be its only job. There was also home defence, coastal vigilance, reconnaisance, even perhaps a bit of tactical support of Britain's minuscule army; but bombing, more or less long-distance bombing, was what it offered as its peculiar contribution to the nation's future belligerent activities: whether as a defensive deterrent (which is how Trenchard's bomber force was first conceived) or as an offensive arm. Some of the claims made for strategic bombing in those years were enormously great. Under the name of the Italian air-war pundit Douhet, there gathered a considerable body of theory (most of which had needed no Douhet to get it off the ground) promising that wars in the future would be won or lost in the air, and there alone; partly by achieving 'command of the air', and partly by the massive bombing of enemy cities, assumed to produce psychological collapse and political surrender. Destruction of enemy war industries and communications was included within this scenario, but its promise rested principally on the breaking of enemy morale, which was continually talked about in these inter-war years, though little really thought about or systematically studied.[89] Trenchard and his school sometimes talked as if their air force could win the next war on its own; as often, however – and always, to the best of my knowledge, when in direct confrontation with the generals and admirals – they stuck to the slightly more modest claim that, at any rate, no continental enemy could be beaten on land until he had had the daylights bombed out of him first.

As to how that bombing was proposed to be done by the inter-war planners, there were two schools of thought, which we will continue roughly to characterize as 'precision' and 'indiscriminate'. I am more interested in the latter, which is much the more difficult to discern, but which was certainly there all the time. And, apart from citing Trenchard himself, I can do little more than adduce circumstantial evidence and invite the reader to agree with me that, if an air force is doing the same thing in 1943 as it had been doing in 1918, with some of the same people still there, and if moreover there are intermittent indications that those people had never ceased to think approvingly of that thing between whiles, we have a *prima facie* case of continuity. But besides being, as I cannot help believing, unbroken, it was also under protective covers.

It it not surprising that covers were needed. Recalled to reason after the end of world war one's hostilities, so far as national post-war circumstances permitted, the great powers took up again the pursuit of war limitation which had got stuck in 1907–9. Air warfare was now at the top of the agenda, its horrific potential being by 1918 all too clear. Distinguished jurists and technical advisers met at The Hague through the winter of 1922–3 to produce certain draft rules of air warfare. Those rules never went further than draft but they enjoyed considerable status for all that and until 1940 were respectfully quoted in rather the same way as the Brussels Code had been in regard to land war between 1874 and 1899, and the Declaration of London between 1909 and 1915.

The exact implications and the very practicability of these Hague draft rules were much disputed among the experts, but it was at least clear that they pronounced indiscriminate aerial bombardment unlawful – as most jurists, in fact, had always said it was. At the same time many people, thoroughly confused and frightened by the next-war scenarios of 'gas-clouds covering Paris to a height of six feet'[90] and so on, and by what it heard of the effects of the bombings of Guernica, Barcelona, Nanking and Chungking, sought credulously for assurances that whatever nasty thing might happen to the enemy, it wouldn't happen to them.[91] I have an impression that Douhet-ism died down as the thirties wore on, and it is a matter of record that European politicians, Hitler not least, then became free with promises of air-war law-abidingness. Restraint from strategic civilian bombing met the demands of large parts of their publics as well perhaps as it suited their own strategic books; after all, it might be imprudent to be rushed into a competition of mutual destruction before you were absolutely confident you could win it.[92]

Whatever bombing men thought among themselves about the Hague draft rules, and whatever were their actual intentions or expectations, their public performance therefore had to appear to conform to the Hague-hailed norms; which meant, as between 'civilized nations' anyway, precision bombing of military targets precisely. And how seriously this was taken (quite apart from whatever else was in Bomber Command heads) in the RAF we know from, for example, Air-Vice-Marshal Ludlow-Hewitt's alarm when his critical inquiries discovered in 1937 that Bomber Command had no navigational equipment suitable for getting it at night to where it was supposed to be going, or for then dropping its bombs accurately where they were supposed to go.

The 'precision' pole of bombing operations, in fact, was always there, and became perhaps more cultivated in the later thirties than it had been since the demise of the old RNAS.[93] Yet the other pole never collapsed. Presumably it had a continuous history within the bowels of the RAF; it was clear enough in the planning department in 1938, anyway, to be the subject of express comment by the official historians,[94] and Trenchard's disciples brought Bomber Command rapidly back to it in 1941-2. Here is his classical statement of it, written in 1928 for a Chiefs of Staff subcommittee reviewing, yet again, the relative claims of the land, sea, and air arms. It requires to be read very carefully, and between the lines as well; as his army and navy rivals read it. With an eye on the Hague draft rules (and stretching the construction of them further than anyone else could have done) he denied that an air offensive of his kind was 'contrary to international law or to the dictates of humanity'. Civilians living close to factories, power plants, stores and communications centres would of course get hurt, but so they did when subjected to naval bombardments.

> The fact that air attack may have that result is no reason for regarding the bombing as illegitimate provided all reasonable care is taken to confine the scope of the bombing to the military objective. ... What is illegitimate ... is the indiscriminate bombing of a city for the sole purpose of terrorising the civilian population. It is an entirely different matter to terrorise munition workers (men and women) into absenting themselves from work.

'Moral effect is created by the bombing in such circumstances but it is the inevitable result of a lawful operation of war – the bombing of a military objective.' The RAF, he conceded, would not win the next war on its own, but it would do more to win it than the other services, because (this was perhaps the most central article of the bomber's faith) it attacked the enemy where he was weakest, and where he would break soonest: in his morale. Foch, he said, had summed it up thus:

> 'The potentialities of aircraft attacks on a large scale are almost incalculable, but it is clear that such attack, owing to its crushing

moral effect on a nation, may impress the public opinion to a point of disarming the Government and thus becoming decisive.' ... This form of warfare is inevitable. ... In a vital struggle all available weapons always have been used and always will be used. All sides made a beginning in the last war, and what has been done will be done.[95]

The respondent memoranda from the War Office and the Admiralty were not impressed. Of course they had their own preoccupations of inter-service rivalry,[96] but beyond that they perceived the extent of Trenchard's affront, for all his legal references, to their common law of war. Besides contesting his construction of the draft rules, they put their finger on the heart of the indiscriminate matter in their appeal from theory to practicality:

> though the objective might be a given boot factory, the actual target would be the town in which the factory happened to be located. ... It is ridiculous to contend that the dropping of bombs would hit only the so-called military targets ... the impression produced by the acceptance and publication of such a doctrine will indubitably be that we are advocating what might be termed the indiscriminate bombing of undefended towns and of their unarmed inhabitants.

Beyond such moral and legal objections, the generals and admirals also doubted whether it was to be taken so much for granted, that enemy morale was thus easily crackable; also whether it was to be taken so much for granted, that the bomber would always get through. A mutual bombing match was not inevitable any more than it was desirable. They concluded (or rather, General Milne concluded; but the army and the navy rejoinders ran pretty close together) with a moral knock-out punch; 'it is for His Majesty's Government to accept or to refuse a doctrine which, put into plain English, amounts to one which advocates unrestricted warfare against the civil population of the enemy.'[97] Ten years later, His Majesty's Government's policy, formally expressed in its assurance to President Roosevelt on 2 September 1939, was that it would certainly not bomb civilians.[98] But within Bomber Command the readiness to do so was latent, awaiting only government authority to begin.

World war two began with assurances to the United States that there would be no 'civilian bombing'. These assurances were not only politically profitable *vis-à-vis* the USA, whose potential support was the biggest stake outside Europe for which the belligerents could play, but were profitable also domestically. The German government was expecting to carry war into other lands and to preserve German cities behind their favoured doctrine that bombing with 'collateral' risk was legitimate only in 'combat zones', while the British government (as distinct from foolish elements of the British public) was well aware that any bombing match in which the RAF might engage at that early stage would be one it would probably lose.

This discouraging calculation of the odds only hardened after the Luftwaffe had acquired bases in Scandinavia, the Low Countries and France by the early summer of 1940. Inter-city bombing nevertheless began within a few months. Since Britain, very predictably, for many months suffered much worse than Germany, there is some puzzle as to why Churchill's government began it; which it did by ordering the bombing of 'military' targets in Berlin on a succession of nights following 25 August. The avowed pretext for this was the accidental dropping on the night of the 24th of some bombs on London (which the Luftwaffe had been under strict and irritating instructions to avoid). Since the Luftwaffe's onslaught on Fighter Command's bases was threatening just about then to win the Battle of Britain for Germany, it has been surmised that this retaliatory bombing of Berlin proceeded from the political calculation that Hitler would be lured by it into counter-retaliations on London, and so take the pressure off the fighter airfields.[99] That, at any rate, is what happened. The Battle of Britain, which by some judgements the Germans had once stood fair to win, was won in the end by the British; and the Luftwaffe turned instead to that series of nocturnal bombardments of British cities of more or less great importance to the British war effort, known in Britain (through some characteristic misunderstanding of German semantics) as 'the blitz'.

Strategic bombing thus began in the winter of 1940–1, with the German 'blitz' and with Bomber Command's first series of essays in the same genre. It included indiscriminateness on both sides. Each seriously sought out major industrial and communications targets, but the question is, of course, how much they were interested also in what they would hit on the side. For the Luftwaffe, the job was made delightfully easy by the fact that such targets, in the older British cities, were so familiarly mingled with residential streets as to offer unavoidable and rich collateral on a plate. Coventry was the prime example of this but it was true to not significantly smaller degrees of every other city 'blitzed'. German cities, usually more given to industrial zoning, were not so often like that, and many German cities in any case were still well beyond the RAF's reach. Bomber Command undertook both precision and indiscriminate bombing. The former was gradually revealed to be a failure; hopelessly inaccurate. The fact of such inaccuracy took a long while to come out, in part, it seems, because of the sincerity of those bombers' intentions and endeavours to conduct precision bombing, and their reluctance to believe that they had failed. But while some operations were certainly of that precisely-conceived kind, others were indiscriminate, though their true character may not be perceived without preliminary dispersion of the fogs of disingenuousness and euphemism seemingly habitual within the RAF when it was handling this forbidden fruit as well as when it was protecting itself from outside observation. The pages dealing with bombing policy from 1939 to 1941 in Verrier's *Bombing Offensive* are quite difficult to unravel – not because he is not a perspicuous writer, but because he had so much tangled unravelling to do.[100] Webster and Frankland too note, in their usual discreet way, gaps between explicit instructions to bomb precisely and implicit expectations of something else.[101] But by the last month of 1940, indiscriminateness within a general city area had been explicit in the instructions for the first 'area' night bombing raid, that on Mannheim on the night of 16 December.

The story now begins to move faster, and to become more one-sided. The Luftwaffe had shot its bolt. It had not been designed for long-distance strategic bombing, and from 1941 on in any case it had plenty to do elsewhere. The situation of the RAF was very different. Its bombing equipment at the start of the war had been nothing like as good as it should have been, given the extent to which Trenchard talk had been its bombers' stock-in-trade. But bigger and better equipment was on the way. Unlike the Luftwaffe, the RAF had always meant to do strategic bombing, and was only waiting for the means to do so. From late 1941 onwards those means accumulated at an ever-increasing pace, though never to the vast extent that Trenchard's successors sought. At the same time the grounds for political restraint dissolved. The idea of 'pure' civilian bombing, with a primary terror object and no conventional military purpose at all – the sort of thing Nazi propaganda had sometimes liked to portray the Luftwaffe as doing, presumably to the respectable part of the Luftwaffe's embarrassment – was of course impossible to entertain. But there was no longer any reason for holding back from Trenchard-type indiscriminate bombing around military targets, hoping to hit them but meaning to hurt civilians at least as much.

There was also this reason for embarking on it – that Bomber Command could not do much else. Precision bombing had been found to be far too difficult – for the time being, anyway. The only way in which Bomber Command, and Great Britain through it, in fact, could do anything substantial to hurt Germany in 1942–3 (given that no 'second front' was thought manageable) was by – as it now became called within the service – 'area bombing'. This remained the case until the spring of 1944, after which time the argument about the morality, legality, and mere common sense of British strategic bombing becomes a different one. But up to the spring of 1944 the argument could run thus :

1.   There must be military advantage generally in damaging factories, railway installations, docks, shipyards, and so on; to which the unconvinced replied, that however surprising it might be, Germany evidently remained well supplied with everything it needed to sustain hostilities – which post-war inquiries showed indeed to have been the case.

2.   German morale (not just that of civilians; combatants were supposed to be affected by what was happening to their families) must sooner or later crack; as to which the sceptics answered, that this remained, what it always had been, mere assertion, and that the bulk of historical evidence – not least that from the 1930s – indicated otherwise.

3.   We must do *something* directly aggressive against Germany (still expanding its empire, remember, until the end of 1942, and fighting far outside its own territories until near the end of the war) and this – since we have decided we can't (afford to)

start a 'second front' – is all we can do; which was true enough, until 'Overlord'.

4. We owe it to the Russians (bearing the brunt of the war, once they had been brought into it) and the people of occupied Europe, who may otherwise give up in despair; as some might have done, until liberated.[102]

Before turning to the big change of 1944, we must look briefly at the contribution of the United States Army Air Force in the European theatre. Its governing principle was precision bombing, necessarily by daylight, of scientifically selected industrial and communications targets reckoned to be of special value to the enemy war economy. This is what it had trained to do, and this is what it did (except when pulled from its own course, as sometimes also was Bomber Command, by urgent grand-strategic necessities) from the time of its first arrival, in 1942. To this course it adhered despite many discouragements. Precision bombing in European weather against German defences was found to be difficult, the losses were sometimes awful, and their British brother bombers were unremittingly sceptical. The chief of Bomber Command (from February 1942, Air Vice-Marshal Arthur Harris), a proudly tough disciple of Trenchard, was utterly unpersuadable that there was any merit in the idea of precision bombing of such targets as the USAAF set itself and as the precision-minded minority in the RAF, quite powerfully supported by outside advice, recommended. Harris, for his part, would have had the USAAF change over to Trenchard-type work. General Spaatz and his men however stuck to their guns and bombs, and became the more admired by assessors of the allies' respective air war efforts who were well enough educated to bring the principles of the law of war into their reckonings.[104]

Now we come to 1944, when circumstances radically changed. I confine myself to those circumstances bearing directly on my theme. The heart of the matter is that more precise bombing, by night as well as day, now became possible; that very considerable, perhaps decisive, military advantages could now be quite confidently predicted of it; and that Harris's area bombing, by contrast, had not apparently done enough vital damage to the German war economy to justify the damage and losses incidentally incurred –

whether to British and Commonwealth aircrews and aircraft, or to German civilians and non-military property.

More precise bombing had become possible by the early summer, partly because the Allies had achieved 'command of the air' (though they had to continue to fight hard to keep it and were to get some nasty surprises before the end), partly because radio-directional techniques had been developed to a rare pitch of reliability and accuracy. The case for believing in the probably decisive value of precision bombing of super-vital industrial and communications targets – a case in which so many outside Bomber Command, and some inside it, had always believed – was much strengthened by the experiences of the operations of early and mid-1944, when programmes of precise and intensive bombardment of transportation centres and of oil plants were accounted to have been remarkably successful, so far as such attacks could ever be. In some of these operations some of Harris's bombers had participated, and he knew that they had been successful. But he could not be weaned from the Trenchard track. Gratifyingly aware, one cannot doubt, of the vast amount of destruction being wrought to German cities by his finely-planned and bravely-executed mass raids, Harris evidently found it impossible not to believe, first, that German morale was continually on the point of cracking, and second, that continued area, not precision, bombing was the way to ensure that the German armed forces should be deprived of their essential weapons and fuels of war.

It is at this point – the radical change of circumstances by mid-1944 – that the case against British area bombing solidifies and hardens. Hitherto it was not indefensible. At least there was the argument of desperate necessity to support it – that Britain had to hit Germany somehow, and this way alone offered. But that argument, if accepted, was only valid so long as no better way was available. So far as it included an implied admission that in itself Harris's area bombing was far from an ideal way to fight, so much the more urgent became the responsibility to exchange it for something more respectable at the first opportunity. By the second half of 1944, the opportunity was there for those with eyes to see and minds to understand. Area bombing, always morally repugnant and legally dubious, had not even worked. Costly and painful to the bomber force, it had been seen to be of no exceptional value towards winning the war. The money, some said, might have been better spent, the men and machines better employed. What was past, was past; but even without recriminations, area bombing was no longer the thing to do.

But Harris went on doing it. He 'did as he damn well pleased insofar as objectives were concerned', was how the American Chief of Air Staff, H. H. Arnold, put his British counterpart, Portal's, view of the matter.[105] Against the 'advice' of that nominal superior, who, conveying to him the general instructions of the combined Chiefs of Staff, seems not to have felt able to 'order' him to conform to them,[106] and sheltered by his curious relationship with Churchill, Harris kept the greater part of Bomber Command busy with area raids of ever greater technical accomplishment; in which by the end of 1944 it was more and more often joined by the supposedly pristine puritans of precision bombing, the USAAF. One of those occasions was when Dresden was destroyed, on the 14–15 February 1945: the destruction of a hitherto almost untouched city of exceptional historic and cultural value with very little conventional military justification for it; far from enough to carry weight in the scales of proportionality.[107]

The Dresden raid did not quite finish area bombing,[108] but it did open up the great debate about it which has gone on ever since. Critics of the area system who had till then had to keep quiet, or had chosen to keep quiet, about it, now came into the open. The few British voices which had dared to make themselves heard on the subject, and been branded as fools or semi-traitors for their pains,[109] found themselves joined by a multitude in the United Kingdom as well as the United States (where criticism of at any rate the RAF had never been muted). It was as if the penny had suddenly dropped, and a lot of people – extraordinarily led by Churchill himself – had woken up at last to the bad smell of what had so long been cooking.[110] Trenchard's children found themselves unexpectedly on the defensive, and did not like it. Sir Arthur Harris was among the very first of Britain's great war captains to publish a book of memoirs, because of his thirst to vindicate himself and his not unjustified feeling that Churchill and the others who had first ordered and approved his works, and latterly not actually forbidden them, had left him in the lurch and denied his men the honour due to them. He still believes that what he did was right, and that bombing won the war.[111]

If Trenchard and Company had been correct in claiming that their sort of mass bombardment could 'win the war', would that have mitigated or excused its illegality? Portal and Harris, who chiefly carried Trenchard's torch after his retirement before the war, both felt that they had been denied the resources to do the job properly, and that an even bigger indiscriminate bombardment could have 'knocked Germany out of the war' on its own, as promised, and earlier. Albert Speer's immediate reaction to the destruction of Hamburg was that if the RAF had been able to do the same to six other big cities in succession directly afterwards, his country would have been demoralized and dislocated to the point of collapse.[112] Other evidence in his book suggests that those first thoughts were unrealistically pessimistic; more often his comments on the allied bombings confirm the judgement that precision bombing of vital industrial targets was a greater threat than area bombing could ever be. But if Bomber Command *had* been able to force Germany out of the war by Hamburging half-a-dozen cities, I suppose that the moral and legal arguments for and against it would have corresponded to those for and against 'Hiroshima', and the value of the 'peace' attained would have been lessened by the extent of the deserts and the mainly civilian holocausts caused in the process.

As it was, the British part – the less discriminating part – of the Allied air offensive made no 'decisive' contribution towards winning the war. The word decisive is picked on because it was the bombers' own; often used, and when not used, meant. The brief, intense, and aggressive history of their service drove them to absolutes and excesses in their thinking. They wanted to do the greater part of war-winning on their own, and historians writing within their tradition (an exceptionally loyalist one) regularly couch bombing's claim to distinction in terms of its 'decisiveness'. But the very concept makes no sense in the context of complicated wars. If one element in a complex equation is 'decisive', it can only be so at the expense of all the others. How can one disentangle the contributions made to Germany's defeat in world war two by, for example, 'the Russians', 'Overlord', the European Resistance, the battle of the Atlantic, American bombing, British bombing, . . . ? There is no need for *me* to summarize the consensus of reputable historians since the great historiographical break-through of 1961, the year when Webster and Frankland's magnificent official history was published; Gordon Wright did it at the close of his highly-reputed *Ordeal of Total War*: 'Mass bombing, then, undoubtedly hampered the German war effort in much more than a marginal way. What it failed to do was to destroy civilian morale – to break the German people's will to work and to endure'.[113] And of the two kinds of bombing, 'precision' did the more vital damage, as was discovered soon after the war by the United States Strategic Bombing Survey. The RAF, which could do it very well when it tried, did not go in for it much. That seems to have been a great pity. Bomber Command could have gone along the same track as did for so long the USAAF, but decisions were made which turned it in a different direction. The full story and explanation of those decisions must be taken back to world war one and be freed from the constraints of the Trenchard tradition. How much longer must elapse before the origins and development of strategic area bombing get the fresh appraisal for which they are obviously overdue? Mr Neville Jones, for one, has opened the door a bit, but I am not aware that any have yet gone through. The latest big product of the Trenchard tradition, Mr Montgomery Hyde's 1976 book *British Air Policy Between The Wars*,[114] says nothing to the purpose. He makes no mention of Mr Jones's book and shows no more understanding of the real importance of the RNAS than was shown by Webster and Frankland, and even less appreciation of the central importance which the appropriate humanitarian and legal norms must have in any comprehensive appraisal of the making of strategic decisions and of their operational consequences. Loyalty in time of war may be a duty, but it easily becomes idolatry in time of peace.

Loyalty has not been the only barrier to the discovery of truth in this matter. Duplicity has been another. I have found cause to comment on the apparent disingenuousness or muddle-headedness which tended to mark discussion of indiscriminate bombing from the very start, both within the RAF and around it. Worse must now be said. During the second half of world war two the indiscriminate nature of area bombing was systematically concealed from public criticism by the RAF's political spokesmen.[115] A few in Britain – rather more, I think, in the USA – knew enough of what was going on to try to get the subject openly discussed. They were thwarted and rebuffed, as people usually are who, while their own country is at war, publicly question whether it is fighting the war as cleanly or efficiently as it should (let alone the question, whether the war should be being fought at all). All but the most obstinate and pertinacious of them had their doubts allayed by assurances from above that the bombings, however seemingly nasty, were legally justified (because on 'military targets') or 'necessary'.

But the targets were not military ones in the sense that was disingenuously meant to be conveyed, and the raids were not *'necessary'* in the implied dreadful ultimate sense of the word. Denied opportunities for a proper scrutiny of what was going on, the British public was willy-nilly made participant in what seems in retrospect to have been the only big blot on Britain's war record, and to have sullied the cause for which some fifty thousand gallant airmen died,[116] and some untold much larger number of German civilians were immolated. Some of those airmen, we know, had doubts about the morality of what they were engaged in; doubts which their leaders busied themselves to dampen down. It is no doubt difficult for a society at war to tolerate the questioning of what its government and warlords are doing, but a Briton may surely presume – as may not, I venture to think, Germans or Americans or Russians, who have their own blots to worry about – to wish that his own countryfolk had paid more attention to the law of air war from 1914 to 1945. In conclusion and to sum up, then, I observe with regret the lack, or the failure, of adequate criticism of Trenchardism from its earliest days – its lodging in the central, even arcane, orthodoxy of one of the country's three armed forces – its share in lowering the moral sensibility of Allied war-leaders so that, in 1945, it was not unnatural for them to think of dropping the atomic bomb on cities as it surely would have been even three or four years earlier – its inviting one of the most admirable American prosecutors at one of the most worth-while war crimes trials, that of the mass-murdering *Einsatzgruppen*, to concede that the bombing of 'urban industrial centres' (which by the time and case of Dresden meant civilian bombing) had become 'an accepted part of modern warfare'[117] – and, since then, the coming of Trenchard's chickens home to roost, in the argument regularly advanced by those today who injure and kill civilians in armed conflicts, that they are following, generally in much more modest ways, the precedent and example set by the British bombing offensive, in the end copied enthusiastically by the Americans.

And so the whirligig of time brings in its revenge. There is no neater example of what may be called the nemesis-effect of infringements of the law of war.

A paragraph to summarize a long chapter. It has been mostly about civilians. Objectively and quantitively, they constitute the category of human beings for whom the law of war was most found lacking. Historically, the course of events and developments which produced the state of affairs is tolerably clear, at least in outline. From the juridical and humanitarian points of view it includes two awkward and embarrassing features : first, that the line of material distinction between 'soldier' and 'civilian' became more blurred than it was when the publicists and the earlier international lawyers of the positive school built it into their foundations; second, that civilians themselves – counting as such the greater parts of the political publics in modern States – whether they meant to or not, accentuated that blurring by so behaving, or by allowing their leaders to behave, as to invite a superficial identification of themselves with their country's active combatants. Thus the classic clarity of the textbook categories could seem incredible equally to soldiers enforcing an odious occupation and to the resistance-minded among the occupied, to sailors measuring their capacity to stop an enemy country's supplies, and to airmen with the power to bomb enemy cities and some natural urge to find justification for doing so. In this chapter now concluded we have seen what happened to the classic categories in the fires of the wars of the first half of our century. In the chapter to come, we will see how the international community, during its second half, has sought to put the law together again.

Chapter V

The Law of War in a World of Co-existences

'. . . the people's war. Any nation that uses it intelligently will, as a rule, gain some superiority over those who disdain its use. If this is so, the question only remains whether mankind at large will gain by this further expansion of the element of war; a question to which the answer should be the same as to the question of war itself. We shall leave both to the philosophers.'

Karl von Clausewitz, *On War*, Book 6, Chapter 26 (1832)

'War is a collective concern; to turn one's back upon it, to refuse to consider it as a possibility, is to leave it entirely to those who are least prepared to deal with it in a broad spirit.'

H. G. Wells, *First and Last Things* (1908)

'What is called the "law of war" is, essentially, a barrier against the abuse of force, a brake put on the unleashing of bestial passions aroused by the heat of battle; it is therefore necessary, after proclaiming this law, to take special measures to get it into the mind (esprit) and the conscience of any society willing to pursue its end by war . . . It is an illusion to believe that last-minute preachings of moderation to men already excited by the smell of powder, will bring any worthwhile result.'

Gustave Moynier, in *Anniversaire de L'Institut de Droit International* (1878-9)

'Anything worth living for', said Nately, 'is worth dying for.' 'And anything worth dying for', answered the sacrilegious old man, 'is certainly worth living for.'

Joseph Heller, *Catch-22* (1961)

The texture of this last chapter will have to be different from that of the preceding ones, and I feel obliged at its outset to explain

286

why. It is not because the law of war in this latest period under-
goes any essential change of character. The alterations and new
departures of these years all grow from or are grafted onto the
historic stocks with which we are by now familiar; and the main
landmarks continue to be international treaties – very conspicuously, indeed, the four Geneva Conventions of 1949, and the
Additional Protocols proposed in 1977 to be added to them. Most
of this chapter hangs on the texts produced in those years. But the
context of this development and its accompanying debate change
very much.

Up to the first world war, the number of States involved in the
legislative process was small, the process itself was relatively self-
contained, and its cultural context (predominantly that of the
'christian' world, which increasingly through the nineteenth century was styling itself the 'civilized world') was relatively simple
and unitary.[1] By the outbreak of the second, things had not
changed much.[2] More States, notably the 'succession States'
emerging from the collapse of the European continental empires
(above all the Habsburgs') were attempting to make themselves
heard, and had the League of Nations as a regular rostrum for
doing so, but the newcomers had little influence on what was decided about the law of war, while the roll of really influential
powers was actually shortened by Russia's semi-withdrawal from
the community of States; the League, much more concerned with
preventing war than with qualifying it, in fact took no initiatives
that came to anything; and the cultural context and ambience remained superficially the same, whatever profound changes were
going on beneath the surface of the European and American
empires and, so to speak, round the corner from them. But since
world war two, these centres ceased to hold, and the context
changed utterly. The number of participating States went up by
leaps and bounds. The final act of the 1907 Hague conference had
been signed by forty-four States; that of the 1949 Geneva conference by sixty-two; that of the one which concluded its four
years' labours in 1977, by one hundred and two.[3] This great legion
of newcomers marched almost without exception under the banner
of national liberation from out of the ruins of the old empires,
bringing with it much feeling to the disadvantage of their imperial
former rulers; resentment against racial slights and discrimination;

the pride and boldness acquired, often in armed struggle for independence; and a readiness to ascribe the 'backwardness' or 'underdevelopment' of their economies to imperialist/colonialist exploitation. For the incorporation of these States and micro-States in the world's political order (by the sixties they collectively figured as 'the third world'), the United Nations Organization provided a ready mechanism, and the swing in the balance of power in its general assembly followed the change in the world's political complexion. What had begun as an organization of States nominally united in the specific commitment to defeat the Berlin-Rome-Tokyo Axis and a general commitment to construct thereafter a more just and peaceful world order became an instant arena and sounding-board for the tensions and animosities within a society of States discovered not to be united at all; a contentiously pluralistic society, criss-crossed with divisions of ideologies, religions and interests, in comparison with which the worlds of 1907 and 1929, and even of 1949, could in retrospect seem enviably simple.

Within this complicated and quarrelsome society of States and in a cultural context utterly different from that of its history to date, the law of war had to make its way. What began as a branch of a law of nations subscribing to a common religious faith and sharing a culture formed largely by it, had to be developed and reaffirmed (to quote the ICRC's insistent phrase for it) so as to rouse responsive echoes in the hearts of people of every religious and cultural affiliation, in the heads of whom some variety or derivative of marxism was likely to hold sway.[4] To what extent the law of war can find acceptance and usefulness in such a context remains to be seen.

Not the least of the problems I have encountered in writing this last chapter is that my story has no conventional ending. No doubt that is as much a subjective problem as an objective one. There is, theoretically, no good reason why the unrolling of two hundred years of a still continuing story should not stop with a question-mark. The question-mark as I see it, unfortunately, does not crisply appear all at once, but materializes fuzzily over a course of two or more decades. My discomfort comes partly from the methodological cause that seeing things 'in perspective', a practice in which historians like to think they have some skill, becomes for obvious reasons more difficult in proportion as those things happened within one's own lifetime; partly because those events themselves were, in fact, tumultuous and confused, and will indeed seem so to historians half my age. So another of the difficulties which has hit me in this stretch of the book is that of preventing its thirty years from swelling out of proportion with what has gone before. With some reluctance therefore I find it necessary to advise the reader that the closer we draw to the present, the starker my outline must become. Regrets about that may however be mitigated by the fact that there has been a great deal of writing about the main events of the past generation: the dawning of the inadequacies of the 1949 settlement, and the turbulent run-up to the 1977 attempt to remedy them. Though no good general history of this latest phase is yet available (being probably as yet unwriteable), materials for its writing accumulate annually; especially juridical analyses, of which – such is the importance now accorded to the subject by international lawyers in most countries – there appears even to be a plethora.[5] The keenly contemporary reader will quickly find more to his purpose than he can cope with.

1 The post-war reconstruction, 1945–9

Initiative and leadership towards the reconstruction of the Geneva Conventions after world war two came from the Red Cross movement; political will and pressure to do it came from the fact that it could be presented as – and to some extent actually was – a vindication of the avowed standards of the victors. That the Red Cross movement should press to get something done, and quickly, was of course to be expected. It had sought something of the same sort directly after the first world war; it had intermittently kept trying through the years between the wars; it was apparently near success when the second world war intervened. The rapid summoning of *ad hoc* meetings directly after the war ended, to pave the way for the indispensable brace of conferences of 'government experts' and diplomatic plenipotentiaries, was only the resumption of old unfinished business, revealed by recent terrible events to be even more overdue than anyone could, six years before, have thought.[6]

The speed with which the business was accomplished needs, however, another explanation. Governments had not, historically, been expeditious in reaching international agreements of this kind – and some, the governments of the United States and the United Kingdom among them, were to prove unconscionably slow about the ratification.[7] But on this occasion the stage of signature was reached quite rapidly. This was because two of the three most notable novelties in the reconstruction purported to prevent belligerent excesses of the sort in which the prime losers, Germany and Japan, had specialized (undue oppression of civilians in occupied territory, and refusal to recognize legitimate resistance fighters). The third (extension of the principles of restraint to *civil* wars), beside being sympathetically related to the others – for the armed struggles in most Axis-occupied countries had a civil war aspect – also seemed attractively consistent with the humanitarian nature of the new world order which many believed the United Nations to bring closer, and some believed their own countries especially to embody. The intensity of arguments within the conferences – arguments sometimes in which the 'cold war' line-up of States was clearly to be seen – did not bring with it anyone's positive refusal to co-operate; refusal bearing too much appearance of retrospective softness on Nazi-ism, and disrespect towards its victims.

Within the United Nations Organization and its associated enterprises, meanwhile, the cold war had by 1949 frozen in its tracks a parallel process of development of the law of war. The movement to bring war criminals to justice, which issued directly the war was over in the Nuremberg and Tokyo and related military tribunals, was closely associated with the movement to establish new institutions of international order and justice which issued even before the war ended in the foundation of the UN. The origins of the two movements are closely intertwined, and until at any rate 1947 there seems to have been no important disagreement in the UN – disunited though its member States had already become on many issues – as to the desirability of a 'progressive development of international law and its codification', incorporating what were generally called 'the Nuremberg principles'. Towards the close of that year the General Assembly instructed its International Law Commission to set to work on the project. Enough steam remained in the UN's boilers for the Anti-Genocide Convention and the Universal Declaration of Human Rights (whose relevance to the principles of the law of war was unmistakable)[8] to be unanimously passed before the close of 1948, and there was no reason why, even after the cold war had reached its coldest nadir with the Korean war, the General Assembly should not accept from the International Law Commission its formulation of 'Nuremberg law'. But by now this vein of possible progress was drying up; nothing came of the ILC's 1951 proposals for a 'draft code of offences against the peace and security of the world' and for an international criminal court; nor has anything concrete, as a matter of fact, been done about them since.[9]

The 'Nuremberg trials' attracted at the time and have continued ever since to attract an immense amount of attention and controversy, and it is very understandable that they should remain the focus of attention of much study of the modern law of war. Before trying to give them a proper place within the proportions of my history of it, it may be well to remind the reader that 'the Nuremberg trials', a code-name so common that it seems silly not to use it, actually infers four entirely different proceedings and places. Nuremberg, formerly the sacred city of the Nazi party, was the site of the International Military Tribunal presided over, in the end, by judges from the USA, France, Britain and the USSR, trying a small select group (only twenty-two in the end) of Germans and Austrians alleged to be major war criminals; also certain groups and organizations alleged to have been of peculiarly criminal character, like the SS and the Gestapo. At Tokyo, not long after, a similar international tribunal, presided over by an interestingly wide-based group of eleven judges, conducted similar proceedings against Japanese political and military leaders. But by far the greater number of war crimes trials were conducted by national courts and tribunals, either in the zones of former enemy territory occupied by victorious forces (thus some of the American military tribunals happened also to sit in Nuremberg), or in the victors' own territory, at or near the scene of the alleged crimes. Within so large a spread, procedures and principles naturally varied, contributing to the difficulties and defects discovered by jurists to lie in the path of determining just what effect these judgements had on the law in places where the law had been to any significant extent unclear. In many cases, of course, there was no room for argument either about the law or about the offence; nor could there be any serious argument about the essential criminality of genocide, and the propriety of stigmatizing it with all the force and authority a parliament of mankind could muster.

Nor, as it turned out, was there to be much argument about one of the matters with which those trials was most concerned: the

plea of superior orders. It was only to be expected that persons –
especially military persons – below the highest levels of command,
charged with offences even of gravest character, would plead by
way of excuse that they were only obeying orders; as indeed they
usually were. Morally and politically this plea, in the circumstances
of the mid-forties, and at any rate in its most literal meaning, was
clearly unacceptable. Crimes and cruelties of such gigantic and
excessive character had been committed, with the more or less
willing connivance and co-operation of so many in the middle and
lower links of the chain of command, that it made nonsense of even
military law (which had thitherto generally enjoined unquestioning obedience to orders), to argue that any and every order from a
superior was to be unquestioningly, in effect mindlessly, obeyed.
Yet such argument was made by or on behalf of many defendants.
The prosecutors and, as it turned out, the courts met these arguments in two ways. First, they declined to take seriously the plea
from avowed supporters of avowedly dictatorial regimes that it
could be any sort of a duty unquestioningly to obey orders from
such a tainted source – a source which, moreover, influential defendants had in some cases themselves helped to construct. 'These
men destroyed free government in Germany and now plead to be
excused from responsibility because they became slaves', said the
chief American prosecutor at the IMT. 'They are in the position of
the fictional boy who murdered his father and mother and then
pleaded for leniency because he was an orphan.'[10] In the judgement on General Milch, the United States military court laid it
down thus:

> In an authoritarian state, the head becomes the supreme auth-
> ority for woe as well as weal. Those who subscribe to such a
> state submit to that principle. If they abjectly place all the
> power in the hands of one man, with no right reserved to check
> or limit or repudiate, they must accept the bitter with the sweet.
> By accepting such attractive and lucrative posts under a head
> whose power they knew to be unlimited, they ratify in advance
> his every act, good or bad. They cannot say at the beginning,
> 'the Führer's decisions are final; we will have no voice in them;
> it is not for us to reason why; his will is law', and then, when
> the Führer declares aggressive war or barbarous inhumanities

or broken covenants, to attempt to exculpate themselves by saying, 'Oh, we were never in favour of *those* things . . .'[11]

Such rebukes were in their nature more appropriate to persons at or near the top of the command chain. For war criminals lower down it, these trials tempered justice with mercy and a realistic recognition of the facts of military life, by taking circumstances into account and by being willing to accept the plea of superior orders in mitigation of the offence.[12] A distinction appeared in the judgements between occasions when the immorality or unlawfulness of an order could hardly have been perceptible to the person ordered, and occasions when it *must* have been obvious to anyone who ventured to think as a human being about it; though even in cases as bad as that, the courts, faithful to the commitment to consider the circumstances of individual cases and to keep in mind military realities, did not expect common soldiers to have behaved like heroes and martyrs. The question is still not perfectly settled and indeed cannot be so long as the international or transnational law claiming a higher allegiance than that normally given to national jurisdictions lacks means and power to protect the national citizen who gets into national trouble for obeying it. But 'Nuremberg' at any rate asserted the principle of individual responsibility for the lawfulness of acts done in war, a principle which the military manuals of some at least of the major military powers consequently embodied, if they had not embodied it already.[13]

'Crimes against peace' were in a class by themselves in the Nuremberg and Tokyo indictments. This book, being primarily concerned with the *jus in bello*, not the *jus ad bellum*, is under no obligation to deal with them. Many critics, by no means all from the ranks of the vanquished, have considered this part of the proceedings as the least convincing and judicious Realpolitik such as the Axis powers certainly practised with glee not being unknown or unrespected in lands with less odious ideologies. Besides which, this side of 'Nuremberg' acquired as did no other an independent political life of its own, in the particular context of the communist countries' 'peace offensive' of the later forties and early fifties. Capitalist and bourgeois countries being, by marxist definition, supposed to take naturally to war and to use it aggressively for the attainment of self-interested ends, marxist/leninist countries ever since the Russian Revolution have for obvious reasons diligently

cultivated the incorporation in international law of formal declarations of the criminality of aggressive war; a sort of war which, by
their own definition of themselves, their own countries are supposed to be incapable of waging. In this connection, the 'crimes
against peace' aspect of Nuremberg took on for masses of people
an appearance of singular importance, inseparable from the war-
banning purposes proclaimed in the Charter of the United Nations
and pursued by interested parties since its foundation. From the
later fifties, this view of international law began to make an impact
on the discussion of the law of war which we shall notice in its due
place. In the later forties, however, the Nuremberg-prompted
argument which, together with that about 'superior orders', interests us most was the one about the powers of occupying armies
over the territories and the populations they presumed to control.

The German position on this was that custom and precedent
justified, and nothing in conventional law forbade, the practices to
which German and subsidiary forces had regularly resorted in
order to secure their military position, whether against an approaching 'regular' enemy or against a guerrilla enemy already
present. Typical practices of the former kind which were charged
against defendants at Nuremberg and the other big trials were
devastations of sometimes enormous areas of territory, civilians'
homes and means of subsistence included, in order to hinder
enemy pursuit;[14] of the latter (much more common), the seizure
and shooting of sometimes enormous numbers of 'hostages'
(questionable use of the word, but usual) in order supposedly to
punish civilian populations for encouraging or facilitating guerrilla
operations or to deter them from doing so.

Such killings, it must be noticed, were conceptually distinct
from the systematic and much more extensive killings undertaken
in pursuance of German policies of racial overlordship and from
those more selectively done, as under the *Nacht und Nebel* decree,
simply to intimidate and terrify. For killings under these heads,
no acceptable excuses could be offered, and the conclusions of the
various kinds of war crimes courts rang harmoniously. But it was
not so clear and straightforward when it came to killings and destructions done by armies of occupation and claimed to be justified
under the title either of military necessity or of reprisals; doubly
justified, according to the usual German defence argument, inasmuch as the guerrilla resistance necessitating these severities

lacked legal status, being no more lawful than the banditry or the espionage to which it was often likened. The courts' mixed and wavering response to these arguments revealed the strength of their appeal to at least some legal minds and to all military ones in 'the West' – some national trials being conducted by the defendants' professional peers. Guerrilla resistance fighters generally were not protectively viewed in these cases; the Hague Regulations were conservatively interpreted, and the view was sometimes frankly taken that guerrillas might have been heroes, but, if they fell short of the letter of those Regulations' requirements, had no more cause than spies to complain about being executed when caught. The benefit of the doubt in doubtful cases was normally resolved to the advantage of the occupier. Pleas of military necessity were sympathetically received, the taking of 'hostages' was accepted as a practice to which all armies in occupying postures might need to resort, and the shooting of hostages, though it was not formally approved, was not decisively condemned either.

It was not therefore surprising that when these same issues came under consideration in the different milieu of the Red Cross conferences working through the later forties towards the revision of the Geneva Conventions, a milieu in which the feelings of the recently occupied were ascendant, the conduct of occupying armies towards civilian populations should have been more restrictively viewed. In the unprecedented convention relative to the 'Protection of Civilian Persons in Time of War' which accompanied the more predictable other three and which was in fact mainly concerned with protecting civilians against what invading and occupying powers could do to them, the occupier, besides being bound by an elaborate code for the management of civilians' internment camps and so on, was thus further 'in all circumstances',[15] obligated:

33. No protected person may be punished for an offence he or she has not personally committed. Collective penalties and likewise all measures of intimidation or of terrorism are prohibited. Pillage is prohibited. Reprisals against protected persons and their property are prohibited.

34. The taking of hostages is prohibited.

This was to tip the balance with a vengeance in favour of the civilians, to an extent which aroused concern not merely among practising soldiers but, more significant for our purposes, in the minds even of jurists most sympathetic to the Red Cross idea.[16] Such a one was B. V. A. Röling, who as the Netherlands member on the Tokyo bench had displayed the measure of his humanitarian principles no less than his independence of mind, by following, admittedly at a distance, the Indian member's example of dissenting from the majority. The remainder of his career has been of the same pattern; he has become one of Europe's weightiest protagonists of international humanitarian law, and been head of one of its main centres of 'polemological studies' (at Groningen). Yet in his Hague Academy lectures of 1960 he wrote of these articles of the Civilians Convention thus :

> The new rules certainly favour the resistance and hinder the fight against it. This is a typical expression of the civilian attitude. Is it a sound legal situation in case of occupation? No belligerent will keep the rules if his very existence is threatened. The new rules will contribute to more anger, more accusation, more reprisal, more deviation from valid law. The new occupation law harbours elements whose effect will be to aggravate hostility by stimulating hatred and contempt. . . . As the Pact of Paris did in former times, it gives the misleading feeling of safety, although humanity was never more threatened. The way to international hell seems paved with 'good' conventions.[17]

Another commentator wrote, much sooner after the event : 'It seems too good to be true. I even wonder if [Article 33] can be reconciled with the idea of war at all.'[18]

Experience since then gives no unequivocal indication whether these assessments of the nineteen-fifties were more pessimistic than they need have been; if only for the poor reason, which we shall soon have to bring into sharper focus, that no States have since then admitted being in such an unequivocally international armed conflict that the Civilians Convention was entirely applicable.[19] That legalistic oddity apart, the record of all the other armed conflicts, allegedly non-international, that have torn so many societies, to which at most a curtailed and unspecific version of the Convention may have been applicable, suggests that Röling, Kraft and Boissier were right. Whether the Additional Protocols will have made any difference, remains to be seen.

Röling remarked that the Civilians Convention 'favoured the resistance'. Indeed it substantially did so, but not explicitly, as the remodelled Prisoners of War Convention was meant to. Here came another triumph for the point of view and passionate feelings of those who had suffered under Axis occupation. The war-crimes trials judgements had as little vindicated the guerrilla resister as they had the unresisting civilian. Within the limitation that they were rephrasing 'Geneva', not 'Hague' law – i.e., according to the notion almost religiously held at that time, the law protecting the victims of combat, as if it were entirely separable from the question of methods of combat – they did something for the patriotic resistance fighter when they tackled the problem of defining the lawful combatant, the only sort of combatant for whom Geneva law's protection was meant. Something was done for him, but not as much as his second-world-war admirers sought, and only after extraordinary difficulties. No part of this reconstruction proved more controversial. The politics and diplomacy that went into it will make a marvellous tale, when it gets the writing-up it deserves. I can only summarize the issues as they were booted back and forth through at least three years' meetings.

The larger military powers' dislike of guerrillas continued to stand in the way of their recognition as lawful combatants, as it had done for the past three or four generations. Germany had no representatives at these meetings, but Germany's cause did not lack supporters, Great Britain at their head.[20] Against them stood the more numerous body of representatives of countries proud of their resistance movements and unable to admit the equity of any redefinition of lawful belligerence which did not go some way at least towards legalizing them. For a long while the argument raged around the insistence by the occupation-minded, that the definition should include a territorial element; that a condition for the recognition of guerrillas or partisans should be their organization's control of a sizeable region. To the resistance-minded, this was asking too much; 'one delegation expressed the opinion that the stipulation regulating that partisans should exercise control, even temporarily, of a region, could not be accepted, as it would render the whole system ineffective.'[21] Another occupier preoccupation which the resisters found vexing, was with partisans' organization and leadership; anything less than visible and audible, unmistakable, tight and effective organization seeming inadequate. At last, at the

1949 diplomatic conference itself, the attempt to cast the definition in a new mould was abandoned, and the old but still, *faute de mieux*, operative 1907 Hague definition was slightly adapted towards mid-twentieth-century needs.

The 1949 definition of the lawful land combatant, the combatant entitled to the protection of the Prisoners of War Convention if he 'fell into the power of the enemy', departed from the 1907 one only in these respects. It added to the categories already protected – 'members of the armed forces of a Party to the conflict as well as members of militias or volunteer corps forming part of such armed forces' – two new ones: 'members of regular armed forces who profess allegiance to a government or an authority not recognized by the Detaining Power' (i.e., such as De Gaulle's Free French forces) and 'members of other militias and members of other volunteer corps, including those of organized resistance movements, belonging to a Party to the conflict and operating in or outside their own territory, even if this territory is occupied . . .'. This was the novelty! – the protecting of organized resistance movements (no criteria of organization stated), belonging to a Party (i.e., to an internationally-recognizable government, even if a government in exile), even inside occupied territory (no criteria of occupation stated). The rest of the definition followed exactly that of 1907, requiring the fulfilment of these conditions:

(a)　that of being commanded by a person responsible for his subordinates;
(b)　that of having a fixed distinctive sign recognizable at a distance;
(c)　that of carrying arms openly;
(d)　that of conducting their operations in accordance with the laws and customs of war.

The third big innovation of the 1949 Geneva Conventions, the third Article which was common to all of them, was in its implications the furthest-reaching of them all. This Article extended a simplified outline of the Conventions to 'armed conflict not of an international character' in any signatory's territory. There had long been some desire within the Red Cross movement (not however spread evenly throughout it) to make such an extension, and the ICRC itself had for many years been convinced that humanitarian interests urgently required that such an extension should be made.

Several of the nastiest recent wars had been civil wars – in Russia, for instance, in 1918–20, and in Spain, 1936–9. The ICRC had established footholds in both situations (very tenuous, in the case of Spain) and a wonderful amount of relief work had been done, largely by the American national society, in Russia, where famine's horrors were added to the rest.[22] But all such interventions were extra-legal, unofficial; dependent entirely on the ICRC's tact in persuading the belligerent parties (so far as they could be dealt with) that it was in their interest to observe certain humanitarian norms, or at any rate not against their interest to do so. The American civil war offered a precedent in the genre which had, as a matter of fact, observed such norms to a remarkable extent; but circumstances were unusually favourable thereto, North and South having so much religion and culture in common, and there being a general readiness in America and out of it to pretend that it was international. The Spanish civil war was dreadfully different; a war between parties antagonistic to each other in every profound way that twentieth-century men could be, in a country whose history and traditions unfortunately included implacable pride, touchy honour, feuds, crusades, and familiarity with bloodshed. The ICRC found that its opportunities of usefulness were drastically limited, first, by the parties' relative unconcern about the sort of humanitarianism it stood for, and second, by their fatal distrust of one another, which militated against observance of agreements, and pulverized the foundations of reciprocity.

The ICRC may not have been able to achieve much in Spain, but at least it got there. More painful still to the ardent humanitarian mind was the refusal of governments engaged in non-international armed conflicts to let the ICRC get there at all. The law of war had so far applied only to the regulation of international conflicts, or, at the furthest extension of it that was imaginable before the twentieth century, civil wars or rebellions which the parties exceptionally agreed to treat, in this particular respect, as if they were something else. If a government declined to do that, the ICRC and the Red Cross movement had no legal leg to stand on. The first attempt to find such a leg, at the international conference of 1912, had been blocked by the chief Russian delegate, who said firmly that 'insurgent bands or revolutionaries . . . can only appear in the eye of the law as criminals'.[23] It was by no means a complete answer to those who maintained that Red Cross principles retained their value irrespective of the legal situations of combatants, but it sufficed in the atmosphere of pre-1914 Europe to put a stopper on further discussion of the question for the time being.

Between the wars, however, the project revived and became something of a pet one with certain of the national societies, some of them not hesitating to press for the full application of the Conventions in *all* armed conflicts, international or otherwise. It can well be imagined that so direct an assault on the fortress-walls of State sovereignty was an undertaking, the prospect of which brought cold spasms to political realists within the movement, not to mention the juridical realists within the ICRC. But the case for it only strengthened after the 1939–45 war, to the extent that revolutionary and national liberationist wars and the mitigation of their horrors now found a wider following. The discussion of this matter, not surprisingly, proved even more contentious than that about the legitimization of partisan movements. Two main lines of approach were opened: the first, proposing a full application of the Geneva Conventions to a specified limited number of non-international wars (which it proved impossible to define to general satisfaction); the second, proposing a limited or generalized application of the essence of the Conventions (a disappointing comedown to those who put their trust in the Conventions' specificity and detail) to all non-international wars. Something had to give somewhere. The compromise eventually adopted was of the second rather than the first character, summarizing the humanitarian rules in question and enjoining their applicability to non-international conflicts in general, but respecting the susceptibilities of governments by offering no clue as to what exactly was an 'armed conflict not of an international character', and by carefully restricting the limited protection thus rather vaguely offered to 'persons taking no active part in the hostilities . . .'; i.e., most deliberately not trespassing on Hague law ground. It also unlocked a door through which the ICRC might, with encouragement, pass, by specifying that 'an impartial humanitarian body, such as the ICRC, may offer its services to the parties to the conflict'.

This common article was a remarkable achievement, both as an innovation in the law of war and as a landmark in the law of human rights. The principle involved was of momentous importance. It was being agreed by governments, on behalf of the whole communities they represented, and whom in another common article they undertook to inform about it,[24] that no matter what pitch of armed violence their internal disputes might attain, certain fundamental inhumanities would be banned:

(a)   violence to life and person, in particular murder of all kinds, mutilation, cruel treatment and torture;

(b)   taking of hostages;

(c)   outrages upon personal dignity, in particular, humiliating and degrading treatment;

(d)   the passing of sentences and the carrying out of executions without previous judgement pronounced by a regularly constituted court affording all the judicial guarantees which are recognized as indispensable by all civilized people.

The only difficulty, as time would soon show, was in getting governments to take any notice of it.

2 The world turned upside down

We have now to consider what happened to the 1949 reconstruction of the law of war – for that is what it amounted to, taking the four Geneva Conventions of that year together with the United Nations' early burst of interest in the matter and the residue left by 'Nuremberg' – during the twenty years or so which separated it from the next reconstruction, which began at the end of the sixties. The intervening years present a world-wide scene of turbulence and confusion, and of changes so vast that in many respects the world of 1970 bore little resemblance to the world of even 1950, and required to be understood in radically different terms. The fields of change which most affect the law of war and must be noticed, however summarily, are: the revolutionary new weaponry of the atom and the rocket; second, the global explosion of marxism and leninism; and third, the sort of war most characteristic of the period: the largely guerrilla war of national liberation.

As to the atom and the rocket, it is as difficult to judge which was the more revolutionary, as it is safe to remark that together they were incontrovertibly so. The quantities of persons killed at Hiroshima and Nagasaki were not as large as in some 'ordinary' area-bombings of German and Japanese cities, dreadful though the injuries and unanticipated after-effects of the first two atomic bombs were, including the leper-like reputation of survivors and the progeny of survivors. The German V1 and V2 weapons, the unmanned flying-bombs and rockets, did not kill anything like as many people as the area-bombings just referred to, but they were significant as harbingers of a new era of weaponry: the remotely (if at all) controlled, the automatic, the electronic. Separately considered, the Anglo-American atomic bomb dropped from a big bomber, and the German unmanned missile filled with conventional explosives, were sufficiently disturbing. The prospect of making a sinister marriage between them was by some incalculable measure the more so.

A common characteristic of all those three methods of aerial bombardment was their indiscriminateness. We have already discussed this quite fully, in the context of the first and second world wars. If the style of area-bombing practised, in the end, by both British and American air forces had subsequently been pronounced unlawful (as by some highly improbable alternative version of the 1949 reconstruction it just might have been), the German V weapons[25] and the two atomic bomb raids would have fallen under the same judgement. Indeed, they already did so fall, to the minds of such jurists and military experts who had never believed that indiscriminate area bombing of civilians was lawful anyway. But not all jurists and military experts were so minded. The war ended with area bombing as much established, to some people's way of thinking, as U-boat warfare had been by the end of world war one; and bombing of any sort was conspicuously absent from the indictments and prosecutors' arguments at Nuremberg. It therefore became possible for some to argue, after the main Nuremberg and related trials were over, that when so many belligerent activities, even quite old-established ones, had been singled out for condemnation, any belligerent activity not thus distinguished must be presumed to be lawful, at least – at the very least – by way of reprisal.[26] And unless the scientific peculiarities of the atomic bomb, notably its penumbra of persisting radiation effects, not at first well understood, were held to put it into a class utterly of its own, the case for declaring it *lawful warfare* was obviously already there. It was indiscriminate to a remarkable degree, yes; almost as much so as the German V weapons, than which however the first two bombs – of tiny power compared with what was to come later – were much more powerful; not much more so than the masterpieces of British and American strategic bombing, from all which precedents it historically emerged and by which, if you accepted them, it stood excused.

This was the state of the argument at the end of the war. Of course it quickly became mixed up with the cold war. The United States possessed atom bombs, the USSR did not. The USA, having used them twice, seemed not unlikely to be ready to use them again, and was vocally urged to do so by the more intemperate of its cold warriors. The USSR for the time being at what looked like a painful and embarrassing military disadvantage,[27] either really not doubting that the US was ready to use 'the bomb' (as it then was familiarly known) again, or pretending not to doubt it, brought the argument about it into political service. It became the centre-piece of a world-view held by the USSR, its clients and satellites (in the later forties, simply those in eastern Europe), and left-wing political parties the world over, more or less influenced as they were by marxist and leninist ways of looking at things. They perceived 'the bomb' as the supreme and ultimate symbol of capitalist imperialism's ruthlessness in pursuit of its domineering and exploiting ambitions, a deadly reminder of the cruel disparity of military power between the proud possessors of the good material things of the world and the masses at whose expense they had been acquired, and, inasmuch as the indiscriminate effects seemed certain to spread beyond even the whole of the enemy population, an indication of the essential heartlessness supposed to characterize the capitalist system. So 'the bomb' acquired an enormous symbolic political meaning, which was scarcely diminished after 1949 when the USSR got it too; explaining, inevitably, that it only got it as a measure of self-defence and as a deterrent, and would never make first use of it.

The same language was used by the other powers which in slow succession acquired it too: the United Kingdom in 1952, France in 1960, China in 1964. Each in turn announced that it needed it only for defensive and deterrent purposes, and that it earnestly hoped it would never have to use the thing. At the same time its destructive power had immeasurably increased beyond what 1945 had shown it to be. The law of war was turned on its head. Discrimination of targets, economy of force, minimization of civilian damage flew out of the window. The United States' plan through the first ten years of the cold war, in case of a Soviet invasion of western Europe, was simply to try to destroy the whole Soviet nation as a functioning country; the H-bomb, which succeeded the A-bomb babies, would create a radioactive desert where several cities had been. Those characteristics made it a weapon unique in the history of warfare: a singularly atrocious one, by all moral, legal, and humanitarian criteria; a prospectively self-damaging one, in that some of its effects would boomerang; an extraordinarily expensive one, professedly produced in the hope that it would never be used; and likely, if it succeeded in that aim, to have damaged no one except the peculiarly innocent victims of 'fall-out' from its atmospheric tests.

Such absurd and terrible circumstances provoked a wide variety of responses. Some argued by analogy with, or extrapolation from, existing legislation (e.g., the St Petersburg Declaration and the Geneva Gas Protocol) that the physical properties of an atomic bomb in action were inherently illegal.[28] Some seized on the mixed absurdities and immoralities of the situation and concluded that such a weapon, necessarily indiscriminate as it appeared to be (for the possibility of small and perhaps precisely aim-able 'tactical' weapons did not appear till later), was better not produced at all, as persons morally and legally affronted by its indiscriminateness had argued from the start. But so long as it existed and the society of States had developed no means of controlling it and of exercising credible sanctions against the lawless, what State that could afford to have it would dare to do without? At the same time, the States that did have it felt more anxious than States had ever done before, to stop other States from following their lead; and not only anxious but because of the rarity of the materials and the sophistication of the techniques involved, optimistic. The debate about nuclear weapons thus broadened into a debate about nuclear power, in which virtually every State in the world might have an interest. Did the bomb-possessors mean it, when they said they would never be first to use it, and how could a State make itself safe if it had no 'deterrent' of its own? Could the prospective advantages of the peaceful use of nuclear energy be obtained without acquiring a military capacity too? Were those peaceful uses really safe (or even, the spread of terrorism made men wonder, really peaceful) anyway? In the course of such complicated arguments, calculations and negotiations, 'the bomb' became a subject of international legislation. The prime possessors discovered a common interest in restricting its atmospheric testing, its proliferation, both as among States and among geographical regions, and even, by the era of the SALT treaties, the extent of its demand on their resources. But they resolutely refused to let it be treated on an equal footing with non-nuclear (by now called 'conventional' weapons) in the international forum where the law of war was seriously debated. They insisted that it be treated separately, as a politico-military matter *sui generis*. Sub-nuclear powers might have nuclear weapons in mind along with 'conventional' ones when they talked of the wickedness of indiscriminate weapons and weapons of mass destruction, but their nuclear big brothers, except when they now and then took time off to score propaganda points, normally preferred to pretend they didn't understand what the lesser fry had in mind.

In that sketch of the place of nuclear weapons in or, as would be more accurate to say, on the margin of the debate about the law of war since 1945, ideological conflict briefly appeared in the context of the 'cold war', in the formation and early years of which 'the bomb' had its share. Enough has been said about the bomb's eccentric place in the history of the law of war since 1945; but not nearly enough has yet been said about the cold war and the relevance to our theme of the ideological antithesis and confrontation it embodied. Marxism, which had been at work among the politically conscious of the world for eighty years or so, about 1944–5 suddenly moved to fill a larger and ever-swelling share of the stage of international action. The effects of this transformation of the international scene and of the concepts loosed upon it were of great importance for the law of war, posing for its upholders a variety of problems, practical and philosophical alike, which they had hardly even had to dream of before.

First among these problems was marxism's predilection for struggle; its assumption, indeed, that the world was an arena of implacable struggle and was bound to remain one until the socialist millennium, when class war would stop, because there would be no more exploiters to exploit and oppress anyone else, and international war would correspondingly stop, because States controlled by liberated and triumphant working classes in an international society made up entirely of the same would have neither cause nor desire to conduct themselves aggressively toward their neighbours. Such, vaguely – for Marx was at his most simply prophetic in his visions of the future, which moreover were few and sketchy – was the marxist idea of the golden age to come; an idea not significantly differing from that common to the more utopian kinds of socialism, and capable like them of inspiring a quasi-religious dedication which could become militant.

But all that was for the future, more or less distant. Between socialist achievements within individual States and the achievement of that ultimately peaceful international order of the future lay, for the marxist, an interim period of struggle and conflict. Bourgeois States, acquiring imperialist and colonialist attributes as opportunity offered, would continue to oppress and exploit less developed societies as much as they could. They would continue, when times got bad, to turn on and to rend each other, such being the nature of the bourgeois beast. And just as they made it their business to prevent socialist revolution from transforming their own societies, so would they continue to make things difficult internationally for such socialist States as might break through the impediments placed in their way; as the USSR, not without reason, believed had been its experience while it was the only one of its kind.

War, in this view of the world, which with reference to history since the first world war is properly called marxist-leninist because Lenin filled in and hardened so much that Marx had left open and soft, was inevitable and on the whole to be welcomed. 'Peace', which the founders of our law of war had so clearly distinguished from 'war' and so much preferred to it, seemed to the marxist-leninist a humbug concept, the crying of peace when there was no peace. The class struggle went on all the time, ruling-class interests ruled the roost as long as they could, and the 'peace' which the bourgeois theorists so much preferred was, to the marxist mind, in any case enjoyed at someone else's expense. Revolution and the defeat of the exploiting class had to be the unremitting aim of the politically-conscious worker and his eccentric higher-class friends. It could hardly hope not to be violent. Readiness for violence, therefore – indeed for decisive ruthlessness and terror, when and if the right strategic or tactical moment came – was a virtue to be cultivated; and because the patterns of international conflict followed the fortunes of the class struggle and because revolutions often turned into civil wars and had to defend themselves by international ones, 'war' was nothing for a marxist-leninist necessarily to weep about.

Now, all this was a way of looking at the world very different from that cultivated in Geneva and The Hague. So long as it coloured the outlook of Moscow between the wars and the militarily unknown quantity behind it, this marxist approach to war and peace lacked enough body much to disturb the international law community; and besides, however its true principles or motives might be assessed, and exception made only for its troublesome penchant for patronizing revolutionary movements in other countries, the USSR's performance as a member of the society of States did not conspicuously depart from the average between the wars, even being in some respects – e.g., in concern for collective security against fascism in the later thirties – rather better. Nor, so far as I can make out, did the change of regimes and the Soviet Union's proclamation of its right to ditch the Tsar's international obligations mean any rejection of the international law of war, in whose making the Tsars and their ministers had played so conspicuous a part.[29] The Soviet government perceived that it contained valuable humanitarian substance of universal value as well as matter more helpful to 'bourgeois' than 'socialist' societies, and by no means cut off from it. But the fact remained that the USSR's allegiance to the existing international law and institutions of international society had in it a certain number (what that number might be, no outsider could be sure) of reservations and equivocations proceeding from its radically different ideological point of view; and whereas this had, as I have said, not mattered too much to the rest of the world before 1939, it mattered increasingly after 1945, because the USSR was then joined by a steadily increasing number of States whose ideology was much the same, and whose political behaviour was cast, in many cases, in the Soviet mould.

It is all but impossible to generalize acceptably about so wide a span of international political behaviour, but one may certainly affirm that the great majority of the self-styled socialist States of the world (we shall have cause to examine a few significant exceptions in due course), far from playing less of a part than States not so styled in the post-1945 history of the law of war, have increasingly played a leading one. With the multiplication of their numbers and the growth of their ability to deliver majority votes in the General Assembly of the United Nations and all conferences attended by its members, they have been able to turn it to some extent in directions congenial to themselves. Marxism-leninism, broadly speaking, has provided the intellectual map upon which those directions have been charted, and the marxist-leninist view of war is of course at the back of it. This need not be thought even by a 'bourgeois' historian like myself to have brought unmixed loss. The marxist view of war in its pure leninist form being quite Clausewitzian (Engels and Lenin much admired him), parties holding it have proved themselves well able to calculate that international peace serves their purpose better than war (witness above all the doctrine of 'co-existence'), and that observing treaties with non-socialist States is more advantageous than breaking them.

Yet this marxian flood through the landscape of the law of war has changed its contours in one remarkable way that recalls what it looked like two or three centuries ago; it has brought back, and deposited with a solidarity which looks unlikely to be easily eroded, the concept and terminology of 'The Just War'.

From about Vattel's time until the early twentieth century, there was not much meaningful talk about the just war except by christians; especially roman catholic scholars, in whose academic tradition (which had however become rather remote from the world of affairs) the concept had retained all its ancient centrality to the discussion of international relations, and others religiously and historically inclined who found that it offered a convenient entry into the discussion of the subject of the rights and wrongs of war itself. From the professional language of international law, however, the just war virtually disappeared, and with it the itch to discover which side in any particular war was 'right' or 'wrong'. Vattel and the other publicists who mixed traditional natural law philosophy with proto-positivism firmly concluded that no good practical purpose was served by seeking to apply just war distinctions. From a pragmatically humanitarian standpoint, the just war seemed better forgotten about. It was simpler and in practice better (better, that is, in terms of limitations and restraints and of the likelihood of their being observed) to take war as it came and to set up the *jus in bello* as a law which required to be observed, irrespective of the *jus ad bellum*, about which, in the heyday of the positive school, the would-be legislators of international affairs hardly bothered to think. That did not stop almost everyone else thinking about it, especially when a war was in view or in progress.

It would be difficult, I imagine, to find any war through those years which was not pronounced a just one by the religious pontificators of each belligerent country as well as by its political leadership, and which was not felt to be so by the men enthusiastically fighting it. But the law schools and the foreign offices remained aloof, preserving their principles from the contagions of popular politics and propaganda. Wars *would* happen, and were, from their point of view, no one's fault but the loser's.

The *jus ad bellum* was reintroduced to the highest levels of international thought and action in the nineteen-twenties and thirties, principally by Americans. No country involved in the first world war attained or sustained as high a sense of disinterested moral fervour as the United States; no national leader cared more or talked more about the establishment of justice in international affairs than President Wilson. The subsequent peace-making was in part judicial and moralistic; little came of its attempts to bring the Kaiser and other alleged war-criminals to trial, but Article 231 of the Versailles Treaty famously declared that the Kaiser's Germany and its allies had been responsible for the war, and other Articles (those demanding reparations, above all) exacted the price. The League of Nations, the establishment of which was more Wilson's work than anyone else's, was meant to promote justice between nations as well as to secure peace between them. The League's particular purpose of banning war 'as an instrument of national policy' received its most notable fillip in the General Treaty for the Renunciation of War of 1928, to which President Coolidge's Secretary of State Mr Kellogg succeeded in getting the signatures of all the major powers; Germany's signature being later made part of the ground of indictment of the Nazi leaders for 'Crimes against peace: namely, planning, preparation, initiation or waging of a war of aggression, or a war in violation of international treaties, agreements or assurances . . .', in those middle-forties years when the League's peace-securing and justice-asserting purposes were reborn in the United Nations Organization.

It would therefore be far from true to say that, when the USSR and its flock revealed particular concern for justice in international relations and claimed a special skill in distinguishing just wars from unjust, they were abruptly reversing the movement of two hundred or so years of juridical history. But it is true enough to

say that the twist the marxist-leninists gave to the Wilsonian movement of the past thirty years turned it upside down. The wars
which Wilson, Kellogg and their like expected to bless as just,
were those aiming to maintain the international *status quo* or, in
cases where it absolutely had to be changed, to enforce a change
which the League had by due process pronounced to be just. The
principle of national self-determination, upon which Wilson set
such store, indeed might be thought to admit potentially troublesome incompatibilities, but Wilson's assumptions were such as to
conceal them from him. He seems not to have doubted that self-
determination and democracy would generate States with whom
the United States would have no difficulty in being good friends.

How different was not the marxist view of all this! The international *status quo* after Versailles, for the marxist, was by definition a bourgeois imperialist one, wherein justice was all on the
side of those who sought to overturn it. Oppressed lower classes
within capitalist or still surviving quasi-feudal countries had every
right to rebel if they profitably could; and as for national self-
determination, that was nowhere more just a cause than for the
oppressed and exploited peoples of the capitalists' colonial empires.
So Wilson's language, which of course was not intended to undo
the world power of the advanced capitalist countries, became in
marxist-leninist mouths an aid to doing precisely that; ironically
enough, somewhat assisted by the next great American liberating
peace-maker, President Roosevelt, who presented himself to the
plaintiffs against European imperialism as a benevolent anti-
imperialist, without taking seriously the fact that, from the marxist-
leninist point of view, to be anti-imperialist was to be anti-capitalist
too.

This ideological twist to the law of war which of course had been
simmering in the Soviet view of it from the beginning and had
perceptibly coloured its attitude – still more, that of its allies North
Korea and the People's Republic of China in 1950-1[30] – did not
much affect the public discussion of the law of war until the later
fifties. What brought it to the boil then was, more than anything
else, the Algerian war of independence.[31] This was by far the best
publicized to date, as it was in military terms the most intense, of
the wars of national liberation which have constituted so large a
part of the world's experience of warfare since 1945. Its wide
publicity was in large measure deliberately cultivated by the

Algerian provisional government, as it boldly styled itself, in the course of its campaign to bring out openly on its side a majority in the General Assembly of the United Nations, many expressions in whose Charter appeared to justify its cause. Such extensive backing, the FLN (correctly enough, as it turned out) reckoned, would increase the pressure on the French to yield to their demands.

This skilful and persistent diplomatic-cum-propaganda campaign, which included the adoption of all the usual attributes and attitudes of an established government whenever its audience would let it,[32] achieved at the end of 1960 a diplomatic success which marks a milestone in the most recent history of our theme; the General Assembly's resolution that it recognized 'the right of the Algerian people to self-determination and independence', and – for our purpose, more significant – the 'Declaration against Colonialism', which stigmatized as unlawful the normal activities of colonial powers in meeting, as was their wont, armed insurgency by armed suppression. Now, in this typical colonial situation, we must remind ourselves, the old law of war had no place. Its field of application was strictly and exclusively international. True, since 1949 there existed the possibility that the Geneva Conventions' common article number three might apply. But colonial governments for obvious reasons showed themselves reluctant, both to admit that the armed conflict which developed within their territories was bad enough to be taken seriously, and to tie their hands in dealing with it in their traditional tough ways. The Algerian conflict, followed with painful anxiety by the ICRC, went through the usual stages of the Article 3 argument, as in their turn did other national independence movements. But what if a national independence movement should, so to speak, trump Article 3 with a claim to be engaged in a *bona fide international* conflict? Such a trump card the FLN, with the applause of its many sympathizers in the marxist and third worlds, resourcefully played. The Algerian people, it argued, were engaged in no mere rebellion (however justified) against a conventionally 'lawful' (however awful) government. They were fighting a just war to recover the independent national status of which French imperial aggression had unjustly deprived them. Their government existed, was a lawful belligerent, and ought to be received and heard as such. Theirs was an international war, and they were willing to observe the international law of war accordingly, provided the French would do the same!

The Algerian war of independence, 1954–61, was the catalyst which crystallized this conception of the war of national liberation into the common one shared by the marxist and third worlds from the early sixties onwards. Thus, by a double stroke of paradox, armed conflicts indisputably 'non-international' from one party's standpoint were represented as intrinsically international from the other's, and an armed insurrectionary movement which might seem to an established ruler to be 'aggressive' (and therefore, if one had to use the language at all, 'unjust'), was represented as a merely defensive (and certainly 'just') response to the imperial power's original aggression, understood to have been sustained by his continuing presence ever since.

We shall see in the next section what indelible impression this juridically revolutionary concept would in due course make on the law of war when the next phase of its reconstruction came round. Meanwhile an incident when an extreme version of it failed to make such an impression demands notice. This marxist adaptation of just war thought was revolutionary from the standpoint of international lawyers accustomed to deal solely in terms of States and to keep as clear as they could of rebels, revolutionaries, and complaining subjects; but it did not affront the law of war as such. The claim made by the Algerians and by the many movements following their lead was not that the law of war was rubbish but that it ought to cover them too; in which claim was implicit some readiness to relegate their just war talk to the level merely of propaganda and politics, where it would do no more good or harm than the just war talk of their enemies and their enemies' allies. Roman catholic conservatives, after all, have commonly used similar hyperbolical language about resistance to atheistic communism, but it has not always incapacitated their presumed admirers from understanding the point of the law of war or from being able, in practice, to observe it. Yet just as some extremities of anti-communist conservative thought – European fascism in the thirties and early forties, for example, and Latin-American military political theory in our seventies – have moved so far beyond common morality as to have in fact become unable to observe restraints or limitations of any kind in their use of violence against their foes, so has the same destructive tendency shown itself among some holders of equally extreme but opposite positions. Just war talk has inflammatory potential, whoever indulges in it, and may be used on different levels of seriousness. Holy war talk, unless it is experientially less serious than those not accustomed to use it suppose, sounds more inflammatory still and must be presumed more likely to elicit single-minded passion. We cannot pursue that interesting inquiry here. But the seriousness of the implications demands that we notice *en passant* the conclusion drawn by some from the just/unjust distinction, 'that only victims of aggression should enjoy the protection of humanitarian law'.[33] This line of thought came to a climax in an expression of views so impenetrably monocular as to seem virtually incompatible with any law of war at all.

At the first session of the diplomatic conference which in the end framed the 1977 Additional Protocols, the Chinese and North Vietnamese delegates (who shortly afterwards withdrew from it) strikingly showed how far simple pursuit of the just war concept could be taken by minds so obsessed with struggle as to have lost sight, perhaps, of anything else. For the Chinese delegate, the *jus ad bellum*, wherein justice could be unequivocally displayed, loomed so large as entirely to ingest the *jus in bello*.

> Wars were divided into two kinds, just and unjust. Imperialism was at the root of all wars of aggression. . . . The first step in protecting victims of international armed conflict was therefore to condemn imperialist policy of aggression and to mobilize the people of the world in a resolute struggle against the policies pursued by the imperialist countries. Moreover a distinction between just and unjust wars should be made in the new Protocols. . . . Wars for national liberation were just and should be supported by all countries that upheld justice.[34]

This extreme proposal to translate new-style just war talk into old-style just war practice did not, as it happened, commend itself to the majority of delegates, who were content with a solution to the national liberation wars problem that did less violence to the traditional law, and it was significant of the extent to which the old world had learnt its lesson that the most pointed rejoinder came, on that particular occasion, from the delegate of the Holy See, Mgr Luoni, who said,

War could never be a just solution of problems. Peace must be sought through negotiation. The problem of the just or unjust war was a thing of the past, and it would be extremely dangerous to introduce such a distinction into the Protocols.[35]

How such a distinction might have been introduced, and what effect upon the law of war it would have had, was made plain in a set of draft amendments submitted by North Vietnam. They were preceded by some 'Basic Considerations' which, whatever else they may be, make interesting political reading. Informing and electrifying the whole lengthy document was the North Vietnamese view that wars such as theirs were wholly just, and wars such as that maintained by the United States against them were wholly unjust. 'Humanity and equality based on justice' was cited as the prime requirement.[36] Geneva and Hague law said nothing about justice, therefore it had become obsolete, dangerous, and unfair.

What should be the position of humanitarian law in face of these new war conditions which set unarmed or inadequately armed men and under-developed and ill-equipped peoples against imperialism's modern war machine? In our opinion, humanitarian law should, *First*, effectively protect human beings against the war machine of aggression, ... *Secondly*, take all possible measures to prevent the use of the war machine of aggression by morally condemning it as a war crime. ... In severely condemning the war machine of aggression as criminal, the rules prohibiting means and methods of criminal combat should be as complete and detailed as possible. Similarly, the inadequate and dangerous concepts of 'unnecessary injury', 'unnecessary suffering', 'due proportion' and 'military necessity' should be excluded.[37]

So the law of war was proposed to be turned into a positive aid to parties presumed, by this extreme variant of standard marxist-leninist theory, to be incapable of aggressive or inhumanitarian warfare, at the expense of parties presumed by the same lights to be capable of nothing else.

The time has now come to establish clearly to which side the international community's assistance will be given – to the combatant who respects humanitarian law, or to the combatant who violates humanitarian law. He who violates humanitarian law does not have the right to be well-treated under that law.[38]

What humanitarian good (assessed by the traditional criteria) this would do was hidden from the more traditionally-minded participants at the conference – except that, of course, the North Vietnamese were taking it for granted that the extention of marxist-leninist rule was *ipso facto* humanitarian, no matter what the cost.

3 The Additional Protocols of 1977

It must by now be clear that the debate about the law of war had become thoroughly politicized by the time it underwent its latest reconstruction, the debate between 1968 and 1977.

1968 was the year when it really started. The General Assembly began to take an explicit interest in it. The roots of that interest reached back into the previous decade or so, through which the marxist and third worlds had learnt to share a common interest in the struggle, usually armed, against old imperialism and colonialism. I present the conflict as it was seen by them and their representatives in the General Assembly and inferior assemblies, without inquiring whether their perception of the situation was always reasonable, or whether self-styled marxist States may not practise a sort of imperialism themselves, whatever they may preach about it; or whether States of *any* ideological cast may not practise Realpolitik because, if they wish to survive, it is the only thing for them to do. The records of even the Chinese and North Vietnamese, who in 1974 placed themselves so far in the forefront of the virtuous, seem not to be above suspicion. . . .[39] Be that as it may, a majority of members of the United Nations by the sixties shared the view that wars against imperialist, colonialist and racist regimes were fought in causes just as good as any for which armies of imperialist and colonialist powers had ever fought, and that the law of war ought not to be allowed to make things more difficult for them. Then there was through the sixties a mounting wave of concern about the character of modern warfare, founded largely on what was happening or believed to be happening in the extraordinarily publicized and propagandized war in Vietnam; a concern related to that which had never died concerning nuclear weapons, which had had napalm on its agenda since Korea, and now had good cause to add also a variety of new weapons and techniques, partly on the ground that they were allegedly intrinsically nastier than they need be, partly on the ground (again, allegedly) that they were necessarily indiscriminate or blind. On top of all this was the perception in which any observer of twentieth-century warfare could share, that civilians continued to suffer badly – indeed, worse and worse – in war, and that something firmer needed to be done about this than had been done in the later forties; not because the civilian theoretically or practically was less involved in war than before (indeed, far from it!) but simply because the multiplication of the means of mass killing, the increasing prominence and dominance of the military in many societies (potentially, perhaps, in all) began to sketch a scenario of the future wherein – unless the civilian's separateness was rescued, no matter how casuistically – the military of opposed powers might kill off the whole of each other's civilian populations before settling things between themselves, the sole survivors.

Such was the general context of the feeling growing through the sixties that the 1949 reconstruction of the law of war had been better adapted to the war gone by than to the wars to come. This feeling had blown up strong enough by the later sixties to reflate the sails of the ICRC's endeavours to do something about it, which had run into doldrums. Many groups within the Red Cross movement, led by the ICRC itself, had never believed that 1949 went far enough. Already by 1956 the ICRC had produced draft rules to fill what seemed to be the biggest lacuna: rules for 'the outlawing of means and methods of warfare that unduly hit non-combatants'.[40] In 1957 the nineteenth international Red Cross conference at New Delhi, approving them, referred them to governments for consideration; which, remarks Judge Baxter, 'can be understood as a form of burial'.[41] They stayed virtually buried for several years, emerging in 1965 as a resolution of the twentieth international Red Cross conference at Vienna, declaring that 'all Governments and other authorities responsible for action in armed conflicts should conform at least to the following principles:

- that the right of the parties to a conflict to adopt means of injuring the enemy is not unlimited;
- that it is prohibited to launch attacks against the civilian population as such;

– that distinction must be made at all times between persons taking part in the hostilities and members of the civilian population to the effect that the latter be spared as much as possible;

– that the general principles of the Law of War apply to nuclear and similar weapons,

and pressing the ICRC to take the matter up again, 'with a view to obtaining a rapid and practical solution of this problem'.[42] By 1967 the ICRC, which in weightiest legislative matters has always believed in hastening slowly, was circulating to all Geneva and Hague Conventions' signatory governments copies of those principles, accompanied by an admirable 'note' summarizing the present state of the law on this matter and pointing clearly along the improving path where the ICRC hoped to lead them.[43]

At this point of time, came the boost from the United Nations. Within that milieu also (where, we must remember, some of the same people operated who were active in the Red Cross world) concern had been growing about the law of war's shortcomings. Armed conflicts – i.e., what the world used frankly to call 'wars' but now might fear to do so lest they affront UN proprieties – abounded. That of Vietnam was the most protracted and publicized[44] but, to mention just the two next best known of the sixties, there were also Nigeria's 1967–70 war against the Biafran secessionists,[45] and the Arab-Israeli war of 1967 which though itself short and sharp left behind it an aggravated controversial legacy of guerrilla and terrorist activities and of disputed occupation.[46] In each case the legal issues were tangled, none being anything like a straight old-fashioned war between clear-cut sovereign States, and the difficulties of getting the Geneva Conventions acknowledged in even watered-down versions were very great. Open admission that an international armed conflict (the necessary condition for full application of the Conventions and for automatic intervention by the ICRC) was in progress being usually impossible, if only because such admission would legitimize revolutionary and liberationist movements, the ICRC had to knock at every door and seek permission to enter. In even the most 'international' looking situations it found that it had to plead, cajole, persuade, and to approach as nearly as it dared the making of offers which belligerents careful of their reputations could not entirely refuse. The best for which it could normally hope was to elicit from the belligerent parties some expressions of readiness to observe at any rate common Article 3. But Article 3 did no more for the ICRC than to establish its mendicant position; 'an impartial humanitarian body, such as the ICRC, may offer its services . . .'; it still lacked the official status which circumstances, often from a humanitarian point of view dreadful, clearly demanded.

All things considered, it was not surprising that people outside the Red Cross movement became persuaded by experience from the later fifties onwards that the 1949 Conventions were not enough. Other humanitarian movements also were in the field. I say, 'other movements', because organizationally they were distinct, and of course the Red Cross had a *prima facie* case for considering the Geneva Conventions as its own special preserve. But just as international humanitarian law included the Geneva Conventions with much besides, so did the Red Cross increasingly find that it was not the only movement seriously concerned about the law of war. Some of those other movements and groups were large and internationally ambitious enough to come into the category of so to speak officially recognized NGOs (Non-Governmental Organizations), offering to governments prospects of usefulness or annoyance not much less than those offered by the ICRC. It was from some of these, who defined their cause as above all that of 'human rights', and especially, it seems, from the International Commission of Jurists, that came the immediate stimulus for the *démarche* of 1968. 1968 had been proclaimed by the General Assembly to be an 'international year of human rights', with a great conference in Teheran to mark the fact. At that conference, the law of war was much discussed, and a resolution about 'Human Rights in Armed Conflicts' was passed, the chief practical consequence of which was a General Assembly debate later in the year and a request therefrom to the Secretary-General to make a report on the subject. This report, valuable not less for its historical matter than for the breadth and closeness of its analysis, constitutes one of the great documents in the modern history of the law of war, and proved to be a mine of information and ideas for the participants in the series of purposeful law-shaping conferences which began in 1971.[47]

By the close of the sixties, the two main drives towards updating the law of war were converging: the older, slower, would-be a-political ICRC drive, which quite independently of the UN had been gathering momentum from 1965, and this new, impatient, rather political drive from the United Nations. This unaccustomed onrush of reforming zeal by, as the ICRC's experts must have thought, inexperienced outsiders, cannot have been altogether agreeable to the old firm, and it would have been no betrayal of the more conservative side of the ICRC's traditions if it had declined to engage in an updating operation on so much larger a scale and riskier principles than any it had so far contemplated. Against that inclination ran the experience of the ICRC on its more adventurous side, which had so often accepted challenges and invitations to enter new fields of activity whenever the need seemed great enough. Inspired perhaps partly by fear lest a continued UN-based initiative should in the end do more harm than good and politicize the armed conflicts side of international humanitarian law beyond hope of practical redemption, the ICRC responded to the challenge by enlarging the scope of its preparatory works to include at least some of the matters which now so intensely concerned the ill-assorted legions marching under the banner of human rights. What human rights, strictly understood, had to do with the law of war was a question upon which clever men might disagree.[48] But that the humanitarian heart of the doctrine of human rights had a title to be concerned about what happened in war, and why, was incontestable; which meant that the law of The Hague was up for revision as well as the law of Geneva. What prospective belligerents planned to do to one another in war, and how they proceeded to do it, could not be kept as separate from the treatment proposed for the victims of war as ICRC practice, with the historical structuring of the international law of war on its side, had hitherto presumed. So the ICRC's drafts for 'government experts', whose going over them was the conventional preliminary to eventual diplomatic progress, took in as much Hague law as might be necessary to ensure that the law of Geneva remained alive.

Upon the history of the conferences which produced in the end the Additional Protocols of 1977, I do not propose to dwell. Anyone who wishes to know the outline of what went on may read the official summary reports and the more descriptive of the articles published by participants.[49] Anyone who yearns to write a complete history must wait many years and even then may, unless the USSR and the ICRC (to name but two principal participants) change their policies about opening archives to researchers, lack the greater part of the materials that would normally be considered necessary. Much no doubt would need to be said about the influence of the more impressive personalities, and knowing several of them as I do, I find myself wishing that I had thought in time of systematically interviewing them. But would it, within these limits, have made much difference? The outline of what happened, after all, is clear enough, and the substance of the debates is really much simpler than their superficial size and the complexity of the issues suggests. The number of participants really equipped to say anything original or even well-informed was relatively small, and the debates themselves consisted largely of the making of statements for statements' sake and the regurgitation of politically-inspired formulae; playing out the roles and following the party lines to which I have already alluded. Rather like what goes on for much of the time in the UN and its associated bodies, it was inconceivably unlike any conference the ICRC had ever helped to run before, and must have been pretty tedious as well as vexatious.

And yet – and yet, something was achieved; perhaps something rather great. These men and women, divided as they unashamedly were by ideologies and politics but united in some shared humanitarian concern, wove around the historic core of the law of war two new garments designed to keep it alive and kicking in our own times and in the times to come. The process was not pretty, including as it did the usual compromises, deals, and posturing. But the product must be taken on its merits. I shall conclude by tersely describing its chief characteristics – not as a jurist would (and as numberless jurists, in fact, already have), but in the way that seems appropriate at the close of this short history.

The outcome of the long-drawn process was two Protocols, additional to the 1949 Conventions: complementing and supplementing them. The first and much the fullest Protocol 'relates to the protection of victims of international armed conflicts'; the second, about one sixth of its size, does the same for 'non-international armed conflicts' (thus picking up and somewhat extending the theme of 1949's common article 3). Except insofar as anything in these Protocols explicitly replaces or alters anything in the Conventions, the latter remain (for their signatories) intact; therefore the following extraction of the relevant essence of the Protocols is *not* to be taken as any sort of summary of the present state even of 'Geneva law', let alone the law of war as a whole. It simply indicates the latest of the major changes proposed to be made in it; the present state of play, so to speak.

First, *Scope*. The wording of the 1949 Conventions was such as to suggest that the kind of international war or 'other armed conflict' to which alone they were fully applicable was easily distinguishable from the kinds to which they were not.[50] The first Protocol makes a big change here. Article 1 (4) expressly includes

> armed conflicts in which peoples are fighting against colonial domination and alien occupation and against racist regimes in the exercise of their right of self-determination . . .[51]

This innovation was made, on the whole against the advice of the ICRC and some of the western European and American countries, at the insistence of the marxist and third world countries, with whom it had become an *idée fixe*. Inasmuch as the tally of still 'unliberated' third world countries has shrunk nearly to nil, the unsuspecting reader might suppose that therefore it was put in for the protection of people fighting for independence and self-determination against *prima facie* oppressive governments of existing countries of all sorts, whether 'bourgeois', 'socialist', or 'third world'; as it might be, for example, Corsicans against France, Quebec against Canada, the Ukraine or Uzbekistan against Russia, the Kurds against Iraq and Iran, as well as Palestinians against Israel and everybody against the Afrikaaners in South Africa. That unsuspecting reader's supposition would be wrong. The expression cited from Article 1 (4) is a term of art, which to the ears of those who coined it and continually use it excludes rebellions and civil wars within 'third world' and marxist States already existing. To the marxist-leninist, in any case, no rebellion can be legitimate against an existing socialist people's republic. By his definition, it simply cannot be so. To 'third world' governments, as indeed to most others, secession movements are terribly distasteful and menacing, and *simply cannot be tolerated*. Initially establishing the independence of a formerly colonial territory is one thing; maintaining sovereignty, once gained under no matter how disputable (perhaps) a claim to represent all the people within that territory, is another. All rebellions and civil wars, not coming within the specific meaning of this peculiar definition, are considered as at best 'non-international' and may be covered by Article

1 of the Second Protocol. But this also marks a gain for the advocates of sovereign rights. Just as the 1977 definition of international armed conflict was enlarged to include a special category of what had hitherto been thought of as non-international, so also was the definition of non-international narrowed to exclude several categories of what had hitherto been thought, by some, to merit inclusion. The scope of the Second Protocol is no more than :

(1) . . . all armed conflicts which are not covered by Article 1 of the [First] Protocol . . . and which take place in the territory of a High Contracting Party between its armed forces and dissident armed forces or other organized armed groups which, under responsible command, exercise such control over a part of its territory as to enable them to carry out sustained and concerted military operations and to implement this Protocol.

(2) This Protocol shall not apply to situations of internal disturbances and tensions, such as riots, isolated and sporadic acts of violence and other acts of a similar nature, as not being armed conflicts.

Sovereignty has already had to be mentioned. A strong doctrine of sovereignty stalks through these Protocols like a riot squad. In one sense this is no change from 1949 or earlier; the Geneva Conventions like the rest of the law of war were built on the presupposition that governments lawfully were masters within their own territories and that States' sovereignty, except insofar as they might voluntarily shed portions of it, was inviolable. The promulgation of the Universal Declaration of Human Rights (December 1948) was only one indication of many from the later forties onwards that, in the interests of a more peaceful, just, and humane world order, States might be becoming more willing than they historically had been, voluntarily to accept certain limitations on their sovereignty. Internationalists became full of hope that progress was piecemeal being made towards the establishment ultimately of those supra-national organs of world government by which alone, they believed, the future of mankind might be assured. They have been disappointed. A little progress has been made along those lines – the European Community with its wellfunctioning courts and its budding legislature, offers the firmest instance – but, generally speaking, talks and aspiration have far outweighed achievement. States' insistence on the plenitude of their sovereign rights has been the mightiest obstacle, and international humanitarian law is only one of the many branches of international law, order and welfare kept weak and undeveloped as a result. Sovereignty's most striking positive assertion of itself in the Protocols comes, not surprisingly, in the opening 'Scope' section of Protocol 2 :

1. Nothing in this Protocol shall be invoked for the purpose of affecting the sovereignty of a State or the responsibility of the government, by all legitimate means, to maintain or re-establish law and order in the State or to defend the national unity or territorial integrity of the State.
2. Nothing in this Protocol shall be invoked as a justification for intervening, directly or indirectly, for any reason whatever, in the armed conflict or in the internal or external affairs of the High Contracting Party in the territory of which that conflict occurs.[52]

The triumph of sovereignty is however most to be seen in the weakness of the provisions for *Inspection and Enforcement*. In fact they are so weak and feeble as to be nearly non-existent.[53] The long history of the endeavours to accompany the Conventions by some regular machinery of inspection and appraisal – even, of judgement – has come to very little : an Article providing for the establishment – after at least twenty States have signified their readiness to accept it – of a toothless 'International Fact-Finding Commission', recognition of which shall be optional;[54] a boosting of the 1949 provisions requiring 'the High Contracting Parties and the Parties to the conflict' to repress and to punish 'grave breaches', to give each other mutual assistance in doing so, and 'in situations of serious violations . . . to act, jointly or individually, in co-operation with the United Nations and in conformity with the United Nations Charter'; and a 'Protecting Power' article of little more strength than 1949's. This last-mentioned matter is crucial. Failing a statuatory inter- or supra-national machinery 'to secure the supervision and implementation' of the law, the 1977 proposals have stuck to the device of the Protecting Power, the first appearance of which in Geneva law was in the Prisoners of War Convention of 1929, and which was built into each of the Conventions of 1949. The 1949 form of it worked very poorly. Professor Draper's terse analysis cannot be bettered :

This system rests on a tripartite consensual basis. One of the belligerents must ask another State for its services as a Protecting Power; this State must consent to act; and the opposing belligerent must agree to allow it to carry out its functions as a Protecting Power. Not surprisingly, there is only a remote chance of the system working at all. This is an area where assertion of the sovereignty of States can, and often does, exclude the Protecting Power system.[55]

The history of the Conventions since 1949 shows that it has in fact done so. The 1977 version seems unlikely to work any better. True, its language is a little more demanding – 'it is the duty of the Parties . . . to secure the supervision', etc. – but that promising beginning soon gets lost in a bog of if's and but's, from which only one thing certain emerges – viz., that a party to a conflict which wishes to evade the purpose of the Article may do so. It is all still, though under thicker wrappings, subject to the parties' consent.[56] Some States wanted the ICRC to be named as an automatic substitute for a protecting power on occasions when a protecting power could not quickly be agreed on; but the ICRC, for reasons which can only be guessed at, absolutely resolutely refused to stand.[57]

The protection offered to *Civilians* is hugely extended. The first Protocol returns to them again and again, resourceful and inventive in devising ways to give the genuine civilian the all-round protection he has been discovered to need. Everyone is a civilian who is not obviously something else.[58] When in doubt as to whether an apparent civilian is really a civilian or an apparently 'civilian object' is really a 'civilian object', a belligerent is to give the civilian side of the question the benefit of the doubt.[59] Civilians and civilian objects as such are not to be attacked[60] and are not to be endangered by military operations except in certain carefully defined circumstances and according to no less well-defined rules; they are never themselves to be the objects of attack (including, specifically, by attempt to starve them),[61] are never to be attacked under the pretext of reprisals;[62] civilians are expressly never to be the objects of 'acts or threats of violence the primary purpose of which is to spread terror'[63] or of 'indiscriminate attacks' (again, quite clearly defined).[64] 'Objects indispensable to the survival of the civilian population' and of no direct or likely military value are specifically protected.[65] *Per contra*, military objectives – the only lawful objects of attack – are defined as they have never been at this level before,[66] and another equally progressive article headed 'Precautions in Attack' spells out a code of proportionality to give 'those who plan or decide upon an attack' quite detailed guidance on striking a just and lawful balance between military requirements and civilian protection when the civilian and the military are not clearly to be distinguished.[67] But the attacker is not alone placed under obligations of this kind. 'Precautions against the effect of attacks' are equally – and equitably – insisted on; belligerents are required 'to the maximum extent feasible' to remove civilians 'from the vicinity of military objectives' and to 'avoid locating military objectives within or near densely populated areas'.[68]

Nor is this all. A long Article, number 75, offers 'fundamental guarantees' of minimum humane treatment to all non-combatants who, because of any of the conflict situations for which the first Protocol is intended, 'are in the power of a Party to the conflict'.[69] A long chapter of Articles is concerned with 'Civil Defence';[70] another chapter, picking up and making more of an idea which had been gathering strength in the Red Cross movement since at least the later thirties, enjoins the establishment of 'Localities and Zones under Special Protection' into which an actual or prospective belligerent could, if he were so inclined, arrange to lodge sections of the population whom it was wished to secure against all wartime dangers.[71]

A reader familiar with even only some of the history of war since 1949, faced with this list of restraints and limitations, may exclaim, this is too good to be true! Its substantive merits as a new-model law of war are not to be dealt with here. But it must be remarked that this amplitude of civilian protection can be read as no more than proportionate to the need and demand that historically has developed. It comes as a cloud-burst after a long drought. It is catching up on seventy years of inaction and inadequacy. Our surprise at it – if we are surprised – should be understood not as a comment on its military unrealism but as a measure of the extent to which we have become accustomed to excesses and horrors. Some part of it may seem unusually optimistic, as some parts were of the 1949 settlement; but that appearance could result mainly from the inadequacy of other sections of the Protocols (the inspection and enforcement bits, above all), the weakness of which is undeniable.

It must now be remarked that the Civilians question is, and has been dealt with as, the obverse of that to do with *Guerrillas*. In 1949 a little was done to legitimize law-abiding guerrilla warfare. By the sixties it was becoming widely felt in that assemblage of countries which increasingly made the running in public debate, that guerrillas and their style of warfare were in fact denied the degree of legal protection they merited. Third world and marxist opinion of course coincided in a belief that a redressing of the 'bourgeois' balance was overdue. The law up to 1945, and still to some degree, as we have seen, after the legal reconstruction of the later forties, had been weighted to help 'conventional'/'regular' armies of existing regimes. Wars of national liberation etc. being considered pre-eminently just, and in any case just as worthy as the wars generally considered so by well-developed countries, it was now only fair that the weight should be moved towards their side. How far this has actually happened and whether it has moved as far to the guerrilla side as it was once on the other, are questions about which much debate, at the time of writing, continues. Leaving that debate aside, we have to notice simply the legal changes proposed to give the guerrilla in a lawful cause (and we have seen how that is now additionally defined)[72] full belligerent status and to make possible his style of warfare, while maintaining those essential though often delicate distinctions upon which the law of war depends : between civilian and combatant, and between lawful acts of war and unlawful acts of terror, difficult though their definition may often prove.

Terrorism is emphatically ruled out and the protections given to the civilians against the effects of military operations refer as much to guerrilla operations as to any others. On the other hand it is understood in the first Protocol that the guerrilla and the civilian will sometimes be superficially indistinguishable. Not, it must be emphasized, during guerrilla military operations, if guerrillas wish those to be regarded as lawful. They must be distinguishable from civilians 'while they are engaged in an attack or in a military operation preparatory to an attack',[73] they must not undertake the killing, injury or capture of adversaries by 'feigning civilian, noncombatant status',[74] and they must of course fulfill the other requirements of belonging to 'parties to the conflict', being properly organized and disciplined, etc., and of observing the laws and customs of war.[75] But collectively these requirements amount to a good deal less than those of 1949, and there is nothing in these 1977 Protocols to prevent guerrillas from living as 'civilians' and looking like civilians in purportedly occupied territory and being entitled to the full privileges and protections of the first Protocol so long as they have not continued to look like civilians while deployed for military operations and actually conducting them.[76] This is a far cry from what all occupying forces have so far thought desirable, and some have claimed to be necessary; it may equally be viewed as an equitable correction of the laxities of the law which have helped occupation forces in the past forty years (to go no further back) to oppress the peoples of invaded and occupied lands, and to maintain their hold relatively so easily.

Weapons and Methods of Warfare figure in the first Protocol to an extent, in Geneva terms, unprecedented, and it has not been the ICRC's fault that they have not figured even more.[77] Its 1957 Draft Rules suggested the prohibition of

> weapons whose harmful effects – resulting in particular from the dissemination of incendiary, chemical, bacteriological, radio-active or other agents – could spread to an unforeseen degree or escape, either in space or in time, from the control of those who employ them, thus endangering the civilian population. . . . [Also] delayed-action weapons, the dangerous effects of which are liable to be felt by the civilian population.

Such and other particularly unpleasant-seeming weapons have been on its mind ever since, as they have been on the minds of many others. The first Protocol is perfectly clear about indiscriminate attacks,[78] it reaffirms in an approved form the old 'Basic Rules' that

> the right of the Parties to the conflict to choose methods or means of warfare is not unlimited [and that] it is prohibited to employ weapons, projectiles and material and methods of warfare of a nature to cause superfluous injury or unnecessary suffering;[79]

to which it adds this salutary new rule that

It is prohibited to employ methods or means of warfare which are intended, or may be expected, to cause widespread, long-term, and severe damage to the natural environment.[80]

In respect of this matter, however, the Protocol's achievements are limited and remain to be carried further. Some further progress may be expected at the diplomatic conference convened for September 1979, pursuant to the diplomatic conference's resolution that this work should continue and its recommendations that the 1979 conference

should reach agreements on prohibitions or restrictions on the use of specific conventional weapons including those which may be deemed to be excessively injurious or have indiscriminate effects, taking into account humanitarian and military considerations . . .[81]

The greater measure of progress perhaps depends however on the readiness of nuclear powers to discover a mutually acceptable means to ban necessarily indiscriminate nuclear weapons; nuclear powers having made it clear that a condition of their participation in the Geneva conference was that (citing the United Kingdom's version of their common concern) 'the new rules introduced by the Protocol are not intended to have any effect on and do not regulate or prohibit the use of nuclear weapons'.[82]

I have by now sketched the 1977 Additional Protocols' proposals which bear most upon the main themes of this book. Many other matters are touched on in them. There is a would-be fierce article banning *Mercenaries* – perhaps the most obvious example of an emotionally motivated innovation.[83] In the section dealing with the old central issue of *The Wounded, Sick and Shipwrecked*, the once relatively simple articles about hospital ships and 'medical aircraft' have become, in consequence of the development in size, speed and commonness of the latter, and the accompanying difficulties of identifying and inspecting them, immensely complicated articles and appended regulations about 'Medical Transportation', and the spirit of the original 1864 Convention is evoked in Article 17:

The civilian population shall respect the wounded, sick and shipwrecked, even if they belong to the adverse Party, and shall commit no act of violence against them. The civilian population and aid societies ... shall be permitted, even on their own initiative, to collect and care for the wounded, sick and shipwrecked, even in invaded and occupied areas; no one shall be harmed, prosecuted, convicted or punished for such humanitarian acts.

Journalists' protection is dealt with by Article 79. This has some relevance to the great problem of fact-finding. Given the proven influence of media information upon political attitudes towards wars in the last twenty years, what journalists write may contribute towards ensuring respect for the law; even tiny contributions being useful, when the proper sort of machinery of inspection and enforcement is all to lack. And in conclusion I mention the Article on that other great problem and need, *Dissemination*.

Article 83. The High Contracting Parties undertake, in time of peace as in time of armed conflict, to disseminate the Convention and this Protocol as widely as possible in their respective countries and, in particular, to include the study thereof in their programs of military instruction and to encourage the study thereof by the civilian population, so that those instruments may become known to the armed forces and to the civilian population.

*　　*　　*

'. . . may become known to the armed forces *and the civilian population*'. This has been a hope of the promoters of Geneva law since the foundation of the Red Cross movement, and an explicit commitment of governments signing the Geneva Conventions since 1906. Now that hope and that commitment have embraced Hague law too, inasmuch as the Additional Protocols bring the two streams together. I shall be happy if my book incidentally gives to some citizens of English-speaking countries some means of evaluating and judging the actions of their governments and military departments in relation to the foundations of these obligations in the international law of war and the international humanitarian law which embraces and inspires it.

At the time of writing, it seems likely that the Additional Protocols will be coming into debate, in countries like my own where free public debate on major policy issues is possible, about the time that this book gets published. The attentive reader will not suppose that I am indifferent to the outcome of this debate, or that I do not hope he may be influenced by my story to take part in it. My story has been a historical one and I have kept my historian's cap on while telling it, but now that I have brought it as vertiginously close to the present as 1977, and the last row of asterisks has been safely passed, I dare to look to 1980 and beyond. The Additional Protocols, I confess, seem to me worth backing; not because they are likely to be more effective than previous conventions have been, and certainly not because our world shows any signs of quickly becoming the sort of world in which observance of such conventions is natural or easy, but because they do offer to States and the peoples inhabiting them something humane, civilized, and decent: a manageable code by which their armed conflicts may be limited and restrained. The will and desire to limit them are no less important than the practical likelihood of being able to do so, for they testify to the survival, even through experiences as discouraging as some through which we have recently lived, of the ideas that, after all, internecine strife is not the highest ideal of humanity; that men and women are not citizens of their nations alone; and that although men still find it necessary sometimes to fight each other, they can still understand the importance of discriminating carefully between the different means and styles of doing it.

Chronological Guide

331

1923   The Hague Rules for Aerial Warfare.

1925   The Geneva Gas Warfare Protocol.

1929   Third generation of Geneva Conventions: Wounded and Sick on Land and at Sea; Prisoners.

1944–5   The United Nations Organization established.

1945–6   International Military Tribunal, Nuremberg.

1946–8   International Military Tribunal, Tokyo.

1949   The fourth generation of Geneva Conventions: Wounded and Sick on Land and at Sea; Prisoners; Civilians.

1956   International Committee of the Red Cross's Draft Rules for Protection of Civilians.

1968   'International Year of Human Rights'; United Nations' Secretary-General begins inquiry into 'Human Rights in Armed Conflicts'.

1974–7   Geneva Diplomatic Conference for the Reaffirmation and Development of The Law of Armed Conflict.

1977   Additional Protocols I and II.

1979   Diplomatic Conference at Geneva on Prohibited Weapons.

Notes

Abbreviations

CICR	Committee of the International Red Cross
PRO	Public Record Office
NLS	National Library of Scotland
RDI	Revue de Droit International

Introduction

1 Michael Walzer, *Just and Unjust Wars: A Moral Argument with Historical Illustrations*, New York, 1977. The whole of section 7 is about this.

2 E.g. Paul Ramsey, *War and the Christian Conscience*, Durham, NC, 1961; William V. O'Brien's long articles in *World Polity*, Georgetown Univ., Washington, DC, vol. 1, 1957, pp. 109–76 and vol. 2, 1960, pp. 35–120; James Turner Johnson, *Ideology, Reason and the Limitation of War: Religious and Secular Concepts, 1200–1740*, Princeton, 1975.

3 Robert Jacomet, *'Les lois de la guerre continentale'*. Publié sous la direction de la section historique de l'Etat-Major de l'Armée. Paris, 1913. My translation.

4 Philip Windsor, in *The Listener*, 5 March 1970.

5 Arnold, p. 162. Nothing, of course, makes more difficulty for this juridical doctrine and matter of proven experience than insistent self-justification. For the doctrine, see above all Meyrowitz. Interesting comments on it are offered by McDougal and Feliciano, pp. 134–5, 532–4, 680–2. Mallison, p. 23 gives a good short summary.

6 Arnold, p. 175.

7 *Conférence sur la Convention de Genève*, Geneva, 1897, pp. 29–31.

8 *Elements of Jurisprudence*, p. 263.

9 Cited by Rosas, 1976, p. 20.

10 *War and Peace*, Book X, Chapter 25 (pp. 486–7 in the Oxford World's Classics edition, 1933).

11 *Edinburgh Review*, vol. 72, January 1841, p. 314.

12 Sidney Hook, *The Hero in History*, New York, 1943, p. 256.

13 Falk, *The Vietnam War and International Law*, p. 127.

14 I recur to this split in section 2 of Chapter IV, below.

15 I refer, obviously, to a certain type of German juridical writing, which I trust is not representative of the whole; e.g. Rudolf Laun, *Die Haager Landkriegsordnung*, 5th edn., Hanover, 1950; Eberhard Spetzler, *Luftkrieg und Menschlichkeit . . .*, Göttingen, 1956;

and Maximilian Czesany, *Nie wieder Krieg gegen die Zivilbe-völkerung: eine völkerrechtliche Untersuchung des Luftkrieges, 1939–45*, Graz, 1961.

16 Westlake, *International Law*, p. 147.

Chapter I

1 W. H. Auden, 'Metalogue to The Magic Flute', 1956.

2 Thomas Gray, 'Elegy written in a Country Churchyard', 1751.

3 Wheaton, 1845, p. 89.

4 The Declaration of Independence, 4 July 1776.

5 This is taken from Boissier, 1963, pp. 203–4. Rabaut, a French protestant clergyman of markedly liberal, even modernist character, was one of the *tiers état* in 1789, and, remaining faithful to the ideas of that year, was guillotined in '93. I have not been able to discover when or where he wrote this.

6 Vattel, 1916, p. 290; Book III, ch. 8, sec. 158.

7 Sorel, *Europe and the French Revolution: the Political Traditions of the Old Régime*. Trans. by Cobban and Hunt, 1969, pp. 108–15. (First edn. 1885.)

8 Farrer, p. 21.

9 I follow the assessment of Nussbaum, pp. 160–3; not unsupported by that of Nys, vol. 1, pp. 255–6.

10 Vattel, p. 302.

11 The English translation, by Heinz Norden, is however entitled *The Sword and the Scepter*. I give Ritter's own translation of his title in vol. 1, p. 325.

12 Speech to Congress, 3 December 1793, in *Writings of George Washington* (Bicentennial edn., ed. J. C. Fitzpatrick), Washington, 1931, vol. 33, pp. 163–9.

13 For some specimen appraisals of Vattel, see Waxel, pp. 18–22; Rivier in Holtzendorff, vol. 4, pp. 448–51; Nussbaum, pp. 155–63; Nys, vol. 1, pp. 255–6; Johnson, pp. 240–51; and Midgley, pp. 184–95.

14 Vattel was not the first to tread this road, nor would a 'positivist' international lawyer consider him to have reached the end of it. However, he does seem to have made a bigger break than anyone else.

15 *The Metaphysical Theory of the State*, London, 1918, p. 6. I am indebted for this strong statement to Dr Stuart Wallace.

16 Hobbes, Thomas, *English Works*, London, 1840 (Bohn), vol. 4, pp. 110–11.

17 Interesting scepticism about such universality was however expressed by Robert Ward in 1795; see W. E. Butler in *Current Legal Problems*, 1977, p. 121, n. 37.

18 The above four citations are respectively from Vattel, pp. 120, 17, 118, 290.

19 Professor Jack Pole has reminded me that Jefferson was to a large extent addressing his inspiring remarks to fellow-colonists less decided about the UDI than he was.

20 Declaration of the National Assembly, at Condorcet's instance, 29 December 1791, in *Procès-Verbal de l'Assemblée Nationale*, vol. 3 (14–31 December 1791), pp. 235–9.

21 Vattel, p. 254.

22 The above three citations are respectively from Vattel, pp. 13, 14, 251.

23 Montesquieu's expression of this Enlightenment commonplace is worth citing (from Book X, chapter 2 of *L'Esprit des Lois*): '... *et lorsqu'on se fondera sur des principes arbitraires de gloire, de bienséance, d'utilité, des flots de sang inonderont la terre*'.

24 Kant, pp. 172–3.

25 See below, pp. 165–6.

26 I do not forget the moralistic strains in marxist-leninism and the explicit moralism of much that has issued from the United Nations.

27 Vattel, p. 279.

28 '*Ma grande maxime a toujours été qu'en politique comme en guerre que tout mal, fût-il dans les règles, n'est excusable qu'autant qu'il est absolument necessaire; tout ce qui est en delà, est crime.*' Taken from Burckhardt by Huber, p. 353.

29 Vattel, p. 289.

30 *L'Esprit des Lois*, Book I, ch. 3.

31 Vattel, p. 289.

32 Speech referred to in n. 20, above. Cf. Abraham Lincoln's 'With malice toward none, with charity for all...', in his Second Inaugural Address, and Winston Churchill's 'In War, Resolution; In Defeat, Defiance; In Victory, Magnanimity; In Peace, Good-Will', the epigraph to his *History of the Second World War*.

33 Sitting of 30 May 1792, in *Le Moniteur Universel*, 1 June 1792. Same sitting as mentioned in Ch. II, n. 3.

34 In respect of Cook, see J. C. Beaglehole, *Life of Captain James Cook*, London, 1974, pp. 684–5. Benjamin Franklin took the major part in persuading his compatriots to follow the French lead: see Franklin, 1907, vol. 7, pp. 242–3. Bougainville and La Pérouse are said to have received similar consideration; see Bonfils et Fauchille, 1912, p. 875, para. 1351.

35 *Autobiography*.

36 *Works*, 12 v., London, 1820. Vol. 2, pp. 368–70.

37 Vattel, pp. 257, 259.

38   Kant, p. 168.

39   Vattel, p. 295.

40   The extracts in that paragraph are from Vattel, pp. 259, 283, 321.

41   '*La guerre n'est donc point une relation d'homme à homme, mais une relation d'Etat à Etat, dans laquelle les particuliers ne sont ennemis qu'accidentellement, non point comme hommes, ni même comme citoyens, mais comme soldats; non point comme membres de la patrie, mais comme ses défenseurs. Enfin chaque Etat ne peut avoir comme ennemis que d'autres Etats, et non pas des hommes, attendu qu'entre choses de diverses natures on ne peut fixer aucun vrai rapport.*'

42   Westlake, p. 40. Nys offers a commonsense explanation of this maxim's celebrity in his *Etudes de droit international et de droit politique*, vol. 2, p. 51.

43   Declaration of Independence again.

44   Vattel, p. 318.

45   '*La force générale de la république se compose du peuple entier. ... Tous Français sont soldats ...*', cited by General Deflers, commanding the army of the Pyrenées-Orientales, in his response to the Spanish general Ricardos's orthodox demand that combatants be clearly distinguished from non-combatants. In the *Moniteur*, 21 July 1793. See above, p. 119.

46   From the '*Levée en Masse*' decree, a slightly improved version of the translation in Anderson, pp. 184–5.

47   Capitulations are the object of an exceptionally good study by Wright, 1934.

48   See Ch. II, pp. 115–16, for more about this.

49   '*Qui veut la fin, veut les moyens ...*'

50   Vattel, pp. 291, 292–3.

51   Moser, *Beiträge*, section 14.

52   Vattel, p. 293.

53   De Rayneval, vol. 2, p. 15.

54   E.g., many an Englishman has known, imagined, and cared about nothing but war at sea; many a Prussian has known, imagined and cared about nothing but war on land.

55   These extracts from Vattel, and that at the beginning of the next paragraph, come from p. 271.

56   Satow, Ernest Mason, *The Silesian Loan and Frederick the Great*, Oxford, 1915. It is excellently summarized by Wheaton, pp. 206 ff.

57   Text from Clive Parry (ed.), *Consolidated Treaty Series*, vol. 49 (1783–6), pp. 332–54. For commentary and background, see Gilbert, pp. 44–54, 67–72. This treaty's status was well assessed by the distinguished Russian jurist F. F. Martens at the 1907 Hague Conference: 'it must be remembered that [it] was signed

by a philosopher-king and a prince among philosophers, who for the rest had few illusions concerning the practical effect of their agreement ...'. Scott (ed.), 1920–1, vol. 3, p. 823.

58 I call it 'Rousseau-an' simply because it was so commonly ascribed to him.

Chapter II

1 Anderson, pp. 103–4.

2 4 May 1792. *Procès-verbal de l'Assemblée Nationale*, Paris, 1792, vol. 8, pp. 76–8. My rendering.

3 *Moniteur*, 31 May 1792, reporting debate of 30 May.

4 *Moniteur*, 7 October 1792. My rendering.

5 These instances are taken from the *Moniteur* of, respectively, 4 December 1792 (the 'Ph. A. Gr.' letter, noted below); 9 August 1793; 18 September 1793. Something like Lullier's scheme was however considered again by Carnot and Hoche in 1795–6: see Phipps, vol. 3, pp. 54–5. Other successful proposals of more or less atrocious means of fighting are listed by Basdevant, pp. 53–8.

6 Bricard, p. 123. Phipps, vol. 1, pp. 322–3. 'We never obeyed that barbaric order', in François, 1903, vol. 1, p. 49. The decree was repealed with every appearance of relief at the end of the year: see *Moniteur*, 1 January 1795.

7 The earliest such mention of reprisals I have noticed is in Condorcet's decree of 29 December 1791.

8 *Moniteur*, 23 September 1793, reporting debate of 21 September. Similarly, Foreign Minister Desforgues' reply to anxious American inquiries, 14 October 1793: See *State Papers and Public Documents of the United States*, 12v., Boston, 1819, vol. 1, pp. 457–8.

9 *Moniteur*, 13 August 1794.

10 Cited by Godechot in *Occupants, Occupés*, p. 22. My rendering.

11 *Moniteur*, 18 October 1793.

12 Aulard, vol. 13, pp. 778–9. My rendering.

13 The French phrase is that of one of war's most eminent and influential students: Gaston Bouthoul, whose *Traité de Polémologie*, Paris, 1970 (developed from his path-breaking *Les Guerres*, 1951) is one of the most interesting, if idiosyncratic, books about it. Clausewitz of course was the founder, as his book *On War* remains the primary text, of this level of war study. Among the best more or less recent books are Quincy Wright, *A Study of War*, 2nd edn., Chicago, 1965; W. B. Gallie, *Philosophers of Peace and War*, Cambridge, 1978; Alexis Philonenko, *Essais sur*

la philosophie de la guerre, Paris, 1976; and Raymond Aron, *Clausewitz: Penser la Guerre*, 2v., Paris, 1976.

14 At the same time as it is a major part of the argument for taking the law of war seriously; war once embarked on being of such a nature that controls and limits, intended to be set upon it, *must* prove to be at least partly unattainable.

15 *Moniteur*, 4 December 1792. Since his word for 'liberate' was '*affranchir*', there was a play between that and '*franciser*'.

16 *Moniteur*, 6 December 1792.

17 *Moniteur*, 18 December 1792, reporting debate of 15 December.

18 I wish I had been able to go further into this very interesting matter. The Austrians, at any rate, seem to have been prone to put themselves at military disadvantage (from a less scrupulous point of view) rather than break the law or depart from firmly-established custom: see, e.g., G. Townsend Warner, *How Wars Were Won*, 1915, pp. 143–4; Vagts, 1959, p. 113; Butler and Maccoby, p. 145; and Bernard, 1955, about the Austrians' requisitioning difficulties in Belgium in 1794 and in general, p. 232. The *Kriegsbrauch im Landkriege*, ed. Morgan, p. 133, scores a point off the French when mentioning a Prussian example: 'As late as in the year 1806, Prussian battalions camped close to big stacks of corn and bivouacked on potato fields without daring to appease their hunger with the property of the stranger; the behaviour of the French soon taught them a better way.'

19 Cited in Biro, vol. 1, p. 93.

20 Werner, pp. 186–9.

21 Morvan, vol. 1, p. 474, cites one of Soult's officers in Portugal, describing the uselessness of commisariat staff, given '*notre manière de faire la guerre, et le système dévastateur ou l'on compte sur les ressources du pays pour faire vivre les armées . . .*'

22 The extent of Soult's regrets is crystal clear in the proclamation he issued at Bayonne to his men on 20 July 1813, ordering them to pull themselves together now they were back in their homeland: . . . '*il est urgent de reprimer l'indiscipline, rétablir le bon ordre, abolir le maraudage et le pillage, mettre enfin un terme aux excès auxquels se sont livrés la plupart des troupes. . . .*' General Senarmont is cited in similar terms, 1807, by Thoumas, 1887, vol. 2, p. 45; '*Je suis las, archi-las, de ce métier qui n'a plus rien d'honorable, sous quelque point de vue qu'on veuille l'envisager.*'

23 I regret that I have lost the source of this remark.

24 20 October 1792. Cited and trans. in Biro, vol. 1, p. 114 n.

25 18 September 1793, in Aulard. vol. 6, pp. 553–4. My rendering.

26 It is well summarized in Godechot's paper in *Occupants, Occupés*, q.v.

27 Morvan, vol. 1, pp. 682–3. Prussia's huge bill of damages as presented to the French may be read in Schoell, vol. 2, pp. 223–88: '*Exposé de la conduite du gouvernement français envers la Prusse depuis la paix de Tilsit.*'

28 There is an excellent book on this Portalis: Lydie Schimsewitsch, *Portalis et son Temps*, Paris, 1936. His son, Joseph-Marie, became no less famous a public man, ending up as a peer of France and first president of the Cour de Cassation. The *Moniteur* index attributes this famous speech (which it printed in its issue on primédi, 21 messidor an 8; 1800, p. 1175) to the son, but in Schimsewitsch, p. 50, it is the father's; which is much more credible on general grounds, anyway.

29 Some passages are cited, without historical explication, in Friedman, vol. 1, p. xiv. The original is in the *Moniteur*, 5 December 1806.

30 Morvan, vol. 2, p. 259.

31 See e.g. Kersaint's proposals in the *Moniteur*, 31 May 1792.

32 *Moniteur*, 15 January 1793.

33 *Moniteur*, 3 January 1793.

34 See Harvey Mitchell, *The Underground War against Revolutionary France; the Missions of William Wickham, 1794–1800*, Oxford, 1965, p. 27 n.

35 Lefebvre, *The French Revolution from 1793 to 1799* (trans., London, 1967), p. 21. I have dealt with this matter somewhat more fully in my essay 'Britain and Blockade'.

36 Cited in my 'Britain and Blockade' at p. 151. Compare the language of Vattel, p. 244.

37 Letter of 7 September 1793, in *The Writings of Thomas Jefferson*, ed. Ford, New York, 1895, vol. 6, pp. 412–16.

38 That 1674 definition comes from Hall, p. 184. (Perhaps it varied later?)

39 Admiral Sir Roger Curtis, in Navy Records Society, *Naval Miscellany*, vol. 3, London, 1928, pp. 327–8.

40 Hall, p. 788.

41 See e.g. the evidence in Galpin, p. 200.

42 Tetens, p. 40. My rendering.

43 Wheaton, pp. 408–20, is very good on all this. Marcus, p. 191, makes it sound like another British triumph.

44 Trimble, pp. 95–6, and Galpin, p. 100.

45 Galpin, p. 101. As usual, what was complained of in the British was something the French *did*, or tried to do, when they could.

The most perfect example of a 'paper blockade' was in Napoleon's Berlin Decree of November 1806.

46 After working most of this out for myself, I have been pleased to discover a useful survey of 'Rules of Land Warfare during the War of the American Revolution' by Martin J. Clancy in *World Politics*, vol. 2, 1960, pp. 203–317.

47 See, e.g., Franklin's letter to the British peace negotiator Richard Oswald, written at Passy, 26 November 1782, in *Writings of Benjamin Franklin* (ed. H. A. Smyth), New York, 1905–7, vol. 8, pp. 621–7. Apropos of the topic of British alleged ruthlessness, I must remark that some mystery surrounds the hair-raising summary of British war principles given in a footnote to Book 8, chapter 4, of the second and subsequent editions of Martens' *Précis*. It was not in the first edition, 1789. It first appears in the 'revised and augmented' edition of 1801 (where did it come from? Paris, perhaps? or Copenhagen?), and stayed put through at any rate the 1864 edition. Montague Bernard, 1856, pp. 104–5, accepted it as accurate and/or authentic; and perhaps it is, in some curious way; but two great experts on that war whom I have consulted, Drs John Shy and Don Higginbotham, gravely doubt it.

48 Cited by Ole Feldbaek, 'The Anglo-Danish Convoy Dispute of 1800', in *Scandinavian Journal of History*, vol. 2, 1977, pp. 161–82 at p. 177.

49 See especially C. T. Atkinson (ed.), 'Gleanings from the Cathcart MSS.', in *J. Soc. Army Hist. Research*, vol. 30, 1952, at pp. 84–6. Such were the sentiments of the military commanders on the spot. Whitehall's view of the job was perhaps less *sympathique*. The First Lord of the Admiralty, Mulgrave, wrote to Admiral Gambier, before the bombardment: 'Mr Canning . . . has information of three million pounds' worth of naval stores being at Copenhagen; this will of course not escape your vigilance or your grasp.' After it: 'The next object, and one which seems to be still open to us and within our reach, is to keep Denmark in a state of dependence on this country for all the resources of her trade and for the retention of any colonial possession . . .' The prime minister, telling Gambier that his success had earned him a peerage, rejoiced that it had been so bloodless! It was as if they had entirely forgotten that Denmark was not an enemy but a neutral. See Chatterton, Georgiana, *Memorials . . . of Admiral Lord Gambier*, 2v., London, 1881, vol. 1, pp. 41–62.

50 It is only fair to mention that, in 1812, Britain 'restored to the Academy of Arts at Philadelphia a collection of Italian paintings and prints which a British vessel had captured at sea'. Spaight, 1911, p. 199, following Wheaton.

51 Letter to the Admiralty, 25 March 1814, in National Library of Scotland, MSS. 2345.

52 Orders ('Most Secret') dated March 1813 and 20 May 1814, in NLS MSS. 2326, fos. 3–10, 112–15. I have conflated the two versions. Of course I would not do so if this affected the sense.

53 Letter of 3 September 1814, NLS MSS. 2345, fos. 11r–12v.

54 *Autobiography of Sir Harry Smith*, London, 1902, vol. 1, pp. 200–1.

55 Prussian behaviour is conveniently summarized and largely explained in ch. 4 of Ritter, esp. pp. 82–91. For a strong British resolve to save the French from 'the merciless acts of a licentious army', see Napier, vol. 1, pp. 154–5.

56 I cannot make out how much the Romanovs used formal militia. The Russian partisans seem not to have had that kind of basis. Tarle, p. 346, does say, '... the Russian national war was different from the Spanish. It was waged chiefly by peasants in army or militia uniforms ...' But he also says some put on French uniforms (p. 348).

57 Napoleon's Address to the Army, 27 March 1796. My authority for saying he polished it up at St Helena is Felix Markham, *Napoleon*, London, 1963, p. 27.

58 See, e.g., *Memorias del General don Francisco Espoz y Mina* (ed. Artola), 2v., Madrid, 1962, vol. 1, pp. 10, 40. Further evidence is scattered in the correspondence of General Thouvenot, early 1813, at the Archives de Guerre, Vincennes, C8*, 214*. German partisans in 1813 threatened retaliation in kind if the French treated them, captured, as less than awful combatants: see Fezensac, 1863, p. 363, and article 29 of the Landsturm Ordinance, 21 April 1813.

59 *Moniteur*, 21 July 1793. 'Miquelets' were a species of Catalonian militia, so-called, apparently, on both sides of the border.

60 *Moniteur*, 6 September 1795.

61 Arnold, p. 160. I refer to his book with perplexed admiration, some parts of it being as intellectually adventurous as other parts are anti-intellectually old-fashioned.

62 *War and Peace*, Bk. 14, chapter 1, in the Maude translation.

63 '*Le nouveau genre à faire la guerre*', was how the British Colonel Skerret (who liked to write in French) put it in 1812 to a German officer friend: see Wachholz, 1907, p. 307.

64 Risley, 1897, p. 119, confirmed in William L. Clowes, *The Royal Navy* ..., 6v., London, 1897–, vol. 4, p. 93.

65 See J. Ormerod Greenwood, *Quaker Encounters*, vol. 1, *Friends and Relief*, York, 1975, pp. 284, 288, and Boissier, 1953, p. 32. (A French 'war-crimes' court subsequently sentenced that officer to

life imprisonment, mainly on the ground that the FFI men had been denied a trial.)

66 E.g.–Colonel Walpole of the 13th Light Dragoons in 1785 brought the Jamaican rebels to a truce and then a surrender, 'pledging himself that they should not be sent out of the island'. The Jamaican government transported them. 'Thereupon Walpole not only refused a sword of honour . . . but resigned his commission.' Fortescue's *History of the British Army*, vol. 4, pt. 1, p. 465.

67 Colin, *La Surprise des Ponts de Vienne*, Paris, 1905, seems to say all that can be said about the incident. The Blücher-Klein incident is matched against it in W. P. Alison, *History of Europe 1789–1815*, 7th edn., Edinburgh, 1847, vol. 10, pp. 59–60nn.

68 Tarlé, p. 355.

69 Morvan, vol. 2, pp. 422, 408. My renderings.

70 Boissier, pp. 208–14.

Chapter III

1 Adams in *Proceedings of the US Naval Institute*, vol. 29, 1903, pp. 829–81. James's essay 'was published in leaflet form in 1910 by the Association for International Conciliation' and reprinted 'in several popular magazines', according to p. 4n in R. A. Wasserstrom, 1970.

2 Scott on 1907, vol. 3, pp. 767, 762.

3 See above all Barbara S. Kraft, *The Peace Ship*, New York, 1978.

4 Scott on 1899, p. 9; on 1907, vol. 1, p. 36.

5 A full account of this body, so important in our context, is given by Yakemtchouk in *Rev. gen. de droit international public*, vol. 77, 1973, pp. 373, 423. He might have given more prominence to the part played in its foundation by Gustav Moynier: see *Bulletin international des sociétés de secours aux militaires blessés*, vol. 5, no. 18, January 1874, pp. 99–103.

6 Scott, 1909/1972, vol. 1, pp. 178–9.

7 Westlake, p. 280; from his 'Chapters on International Law', 1894.

8 Cited by Olive Anderson, *A Liberal State at War*, London, 1967, p. 273. She comments: 'In this they succeeded all too well, for they have confused posterity also into crediting them with soft hearts instead of hard heads.'

9 Sir Julian Pauncefote to Lord Granville, November 1884, cited by S. Miers, *Britain and the Ending of the Slave Trade*, London, 1975, p. 86.

10 Lord Lansdowne to Sir John Ardagh, 2 July 1899. 'Secret'. PRO, FO 30/40. 3/36.

11 'Personal', 16 June 1899. PRO, GFM 21, reel 105. 'Bear in mind,' he said, 'that it is only voluntary arbitration that is pro-

posed, and that it will always rest with the German Emperor to decide what questions he will submit to the Tribunal and what he will not.'

12 21 June 1899, same source as above.

13 From his 1905 essay 'Autocracy and War', in *Notes on Life and Letters*, London, 1921, pp. 143–6.

14 Cited by Röling, p. 27; he gets it from H. Roos, p. 33.

15 Not only publications (often lavish and handsome) concerning national Red Cross societies betray this leaning. See e.g. H. G. Kernmayr (ed.), *Die Waffenlose Macht. Werden und Wirken des Roten Kreuzes in aller Welt*, Wien, n.d. but seems 1950-ish.

16 *The Red Cross Society of Japan. Its Organization and Activity in Time of Peace and War*, presented to the Universal Exposition of St Louis, USA, 1904. Probably written by the Japanese international lawyer Nagao Ariga, whose 1907 Report to the 8th International Conference of Red Cross Societies, *The Japanese Red Cross Society and the Russo-Japanese War*, contains very similar material.

17 My judgement, based largely on others' (not just Japanese) in: Ariga, 1908; *Revue générale de droit international public*, 1910, pp. 630–80; Spaight, passim; Philip A. Towle, 'Japanese Treatment of Prisoners in 1904–5 . . .' in *Military Affairs*, vol. 39, 1975, pp. 115–17.

18 And admirals! See for instance how T. E. Holland, Westlake's Oxford peer, aroused British naval wrath, 7, 18 and 27 August 1888, in his 1914 book, pp. 98–106.

19 My translation is of the text(s) published in *Revue de droit international*, vol. 13, 1881, pp. 79–84. T. E. Holland caused his translation to appear in *The Times*, 1 February 1881 and soon thereafter. Bluntschli also had to defend himself against von Rüstow: see *Rev. droit int.*, vol. 8, 1876, pp. 663–72.

20 It may be found in vol. 2, pp. 403–23, of Lorimer, 1884. Oddly enough, it is not included in Friedman, 1971.

21 'Militärische Notwendigkeit und Humanität'. First appearing in *Deutsche Rundschau*, vol. 13, pp. 111–28 and 450–71, and vol. 14, pp. 71–91, it soon reappeared in Hartmann's *Kritische Versuche*, Berlin, 1876–8. Moltke's appreciative letter of 18 February 1878 is printed, I cannot imagine why, in C. Andler, *'Frightfulness' in Theory and Practice*, trans. London, 1916, pp. 90–1.

22 Garner, 1920, vol. 1, p. 278, gets this from Saint-Yves, *Les responsabilités d'Allemagne*, p. 338.

23 This maxim was no doubt popularized by its appearance in Article 29 of Lieber's Code: 'The more vigorously wars are pursued, the better it is for humanity. Sharp wars are brief.' That

this was believed only by the 'less cultured and less educated military men' (as Gustave Moynier had alleged) was rather indignantly denied by Britain's leading military expert on the Geneva Conventions, Colonel W. G. Macpherson, 1910, p. 607: 'It is an opinion held by some of the most humane and thoughtful officers in the armies of all nations'; also by the Kaiser, who apparently thought 'methods of terrorism' ('alone capable of affecting a people as degenerate as the French') would get the war over in two months: see R. H. Minear, *Victors' Justice*, Princeton, 1971, p. 100.

24 See what Montague Bernard wrote in 1856 – p. 162.

25 It was written, according to *Völkerrecht im Weltkrieg*, vol. 1, p. 27, by one Major Friedrich at the request of Freytag-Loringhoven, the historical director. It at once attracted foreign attention (French trans., 1904, and serious appraisal by Merignhac in *Revue générale de droit international Public*, vol. 14, 1907, pp. 197–239; English trans. by J. H. Morgan as *The German War Book*, London, 1915) and rightly or wrongly was taken to represent the mind of the general staff. I myself have no doubt that it did.

26 Christian Meurer in *Völkerrecht im Weltkrieg*, 1927, vol. 2, p. 218.

27 Cited, not in quite that translation, by Garner, vol. 2, p. 59. See also his bit of Müller-Meiningen in vol. 1, p. 488n.

28 The Cavell case needs no references. The less well known and not quite so amazing Fryatt case may conveniently be studied in *American J. of Internat. Law*, vol. 10, 1916, pp. 865–77, and in *Z. für Völkerrecht*, vol. 10, 1917–18, pp. 563–85.

29 Translation by G. Schwarzenberger, in his *International Law and Totalitarian Lawlessness*, London, 1943, p. 126.

30 The great pioneer book on this theme is Alfred Vagts, *A History of Militarism, Civilian and Military*, 1st edn., New York, 1937.

31 His justly celebrated book *Un souvenir de Solférino*, first published in 1862, ought to be read, if possible, in its original fine French. The English translations to date are awful. Very handsome is the 1969 Swiss edition, *Un s. de S. suivi par L'avenir sanglant*, with a preface by Denis de Rougemont (Institut Henry-Dunant et Editions L'Age d'Homme).

32 For everything to do with Red Cross history to 1906, see Boissier. The only shortcoming of this brilliant book is its lack of an index. Knitel, 1967, is good in support.

33 'Les militaires blessés ou malades seront recueillis et soignés, à quelque nation qu'ils appartiendront.'

34 The original twelve: Baden, Belgium, Denmark, France, Hesse, Italy, Netherlands, Portugal, Prussia, Spain, Switzerland, Württemberg.

35 Boissier, p. 485, says that the United States and Spain agreed to observe the Additional Articles in their 1898 war.

36 From Schindler and Toman, pp. 205–6, I have taken all States that had signed, ratified or acceded before 1906. It includes some curiosities – e.g. Congo, 1888; Holy See, 1868; Korea, 1903; Montenegro, 1875; Orange Free State, 1897; South African Republic, 1896; not to mention all the 'banana republics'. Evidently the practice of registering in Bern as a standard early sign of Statehood began a long time ago.

37 The following judgements about the misuse and neglect of the Convention rest mainly on Monod; Rolin-Jaequemyns; *Bulletin de la société française de secours aux blessés militaires*, 1872, pp. 1–60; Boissier, 1963, pp. 317–56; Macpherson; and Gustave Moynier's 1873 pamphlet, *La Convention de Genève pendant la guerre franco-allemande*. The case against the French need not rest on German accusations, copious and convincing though those are; especially in Lueder and Schmidt-Ernsthausen.

38 Macpherson, at p. 621, remarks upon two 'notorious' experiences as recently as the war of 1899–1901, concerning 'the International Red Cross detachment organized and sent out from Antwerp, and an American Red Cross detachment from Chicago. Both were composed of men who had no other intention than that of obtaining admission into the Transvaal under the guise of the Red Cross, with the object of joining the combatant ranks of the Boers'.

39 Boissier, 1963, pp. 158–9.

40 What happened in these years is complicated, and invited legalistic quibblings subsequently. The additional articles of 1868, adapting the principles of 1864 to maritime warfare, were, suitably modified, turned into a Hague Convention in 1899; which, following the 1906 Geneva Convention, was itself reconstructed in 1907. So some States might have ratified the earlier one but not the later.

41 Art. 15 referred to 'relief societies for prisoners of war' and their 'delegates'. Arts. 14 and 16 concerned the national Information Bureaux in whose activities the societies would, of course, be intimately involved.

42 Of the many writings about Lieber, the best for our purposes are those of Frank Freidel: 'General Order 100 and Military Government' in *Mississippi Valley Historical Review*, vol. 32, 1945–6, pp. 541–56, and *Francis Lieber, Nineteenth Century Liberal*, Baton Rouge, 1947; and the excellent study by James F. Childress in *Am. J. of Jurisprudence*, vol. 21, 1976, pp. 34–70, where all the other Lieber literature is listed and appraised.

43 A full-looking account of the Conference, as reported round by

round to the British Foreign Secretary by Her Majesty's delegate, General Sir Alfred Horsford, may be found in the *British Parliamentary Papers*, 1875, Command Paper no. 1128 (= vol. 82 of that year's whole series, pp. 155–488). Horsford's fine summary of it all, filling pp. 157–82 of the original, is incidentally reproduced by Lorimer, 1884, vol. 2, pp. 337–402. British diplomatic correspondence about it is to be seen in the Confidential Prints, F.O. 881/2483, 2485. Every international lawyer, I believe, felt obliged to publish something about it; many extracts from them fill *Revue de droit international*, vol. 7, pp. 438–681. Schmid, p. 35, refers to other contemporary surveys. The best in English known to me is ch. 3 in Holland, 1898. Particularly critical of Britain's obstructive role are the Belgian General Brialmont's *L'Angleterre et les petits états à la Conférence de Bruxelles*, par le general T . . . , Bruxelles, 1875, and the Russian observations in the 1875 Cmd. Papers nos, 1129 and 1136 (= *Parliamentary Papers*, 1875, vol. 82, pp. 489–510).

44   Russia's prominence in the story of the making of the law of war between 1815 and 1914 is extraordinary. I regret that I am in no position to explain it.

45   'Article 23. Prisoners of war are lawful and disarmed enemies. They are in the power of the hostile Government, but not in that of the individuals or corps who captured them. They must be humanely treated. . . .'

46   Lord Lyons to Lord Derby, 13 July 1874, in PRO, FO 881/2485 no. 48.

47   Clausewitz, p. 593.

48   Op. cit., pp. 439–40.

49   Translation taken from Friedman, p. 192.

50   This English translation has never ceased to invite criticism. The original French is '*maux superflus*', which certainly has a larger sense.

51   The 'Oxford Manual', drafted by Gustave Moynier and unanimously adopted by the Institute of International Law at its Oxford meeting in September 1880, was offered as a model to show Governments how the best juridical thought of the time might be presented for the instruction of soldiers. Along with the Brussels code, it illuminated the approach to The Hague in 1899. Its British signatories were Montague Bernard, W. E. Hall, T. E. Holland and John Westlake (Lorimer, 1884, vol. 2, p. 423).

52   An excellent review of this affair is Edward M. Spiers, 'The Use of the Dum-Dum Bullet in Colonial Warfare', in *J. of Imperial and Commonwealth History*, vol. 4, 1975, pp. 3–14.

53   Bernard, p. 117.

54 Well argued, e.g., by Batchelder, at pp. 176–81.

55 Only mines got into a proper Convention (1907, no. 8). The other matters were the subjects merely of Declarations in 1899 (dumdums and gases) or (balloons etc.) 1899 and 1907.

56 The *Great Soviet Encyclopedia*, 1927 edition, gives his dates as 1845–1909 and mentions no relationship to the earlier Martens who made so great a mark in the same field.

57 I can find no evidence of any (earlier) Russian edition. The Preface is dated 'St Petersburg, Decembre 1900'.

58 His compatriot N. Korkunov found fault with his coolness towards patriotic people's warfare: see Trainin, at p. 537n.

59 Other countries' diplomatic correspondence about each Russian-convened conference are full of this suspicion. Russian military conduct, moreover, seemed less law-conscious than might have been expected. 'I'd like to see the Russian Cossack commander who would observe these rules and instruct his men in them!' wrote Münster, German's first Hague delegate in 1899, to the Chancellor (*Grosse Politik*, vol. 15, p. 356). Boissier, pp. 409–10, quotes Martens's claim that Russia earnestly strove to observe the Convention in its 1877 war with Turkey, but Russia's record in the war with Japan was unimpressive, and Russian behaviour in East Prussia in 1914 seems to have justified Münster's scepticism.

60 He has usually been supposed to have shaped the wording himself but I have found evidence that it was actually drafted by someone else, which I will write about as soon as I have time.

61 Scott, ed., (on 1899), pp. 506–7.

62 As he said it (translated) on 20 June 1899, at the eleventh meeting of the second subcommission of the second commission, in ibid., pp. 547–8. It went into the Convention itself with hardly any change.

63 Captain Asgill was the English officer, in the end happily reprieved. See Charles de Martens, *Causes célèbres du droit des gens*, Leipzig, 1827, vol. 2, pp. 169–82.

64 Fantin des Odoards, 1895, pp. 244–5. It was not untypical of decent French officers like him to reflect, when Loison's avengers had returned with a lot of looted victuals, etc.; 'Such a mode of provisioning is odious, but how can we do otherwise when every inhabitant is our enemy and either fights us or flees from us?'

65 Much discussed incidents, mentioned in all the books. The next stage of the reprisals for Fontenay was much more drastic. See e.g. Rolin-Jaequemyns, in *R.D.I.*, vol. 3, pp. 314–15, 339.

66 It seems that Halleck never published this essay, found in his papers after his death and published in the *Am. J. Internat.*

Law, vol. 6, 1912, pp. 107–16. Lieber's letter was dated 25 January 1865.

67 Last sentence of Article 15.

68 British Parl. Papers, 1874, vol. 76, p. 61 (= Cmd. Papers of 1874, no. 1010, p. 17).

69 *Ibid.*, p. 178.

70 At The Hague in 1899, they were in fact taken for granted, however much some delegates regretted it. 'As Colonel Gross von Schwarzhoff remarked without contradiction', the general rules prescribed for an invader/occupier in Regulations 44–7, 'could not be deemed to check the liberty of action of belligerents in extreme circumstances which may be likened to a kind of legitimate defence'; thus the rapporteur, Rolin's, Report, in Scott on 1899, p. 63. They surface again in the 1929 Geneva Convention on Prisoners of War, Article 2.

71 It figures conspicuously in the 1977 Additional Protocols: see Ch. V, Section 3.

72 British Parliamentary Papers, 1875, vol. 82, p. 274 (= Cmd. Paper of 1875, no. 1128, p. 110).

73 The team of contributors included Bulmerincq, Caratheodory, Dambach, Gareis, Geffcken, Gessner, Lammasch, Lueder, Meili, de Melle, Rivier, and Störk. Lueder's section fills vol. 4, pp. 169–367.

74 The adjudicating committee consisted of Moynier, Vlasitz of Wien, and Holleben the head of the German central committee. All six entries were in German! – See *Bulletin international des sociétés de secours* ..., vol. 6, pp. 26–7.

75 CICR Archives, Box 21 (Travaux ..., 1ᵉ serie, 1863–76), in folder 'Papiers Divers'.

76 Paragraphs 65 and 66, in Holtzendorff, 1889, vol. 4. My translations.

77 Holtzendorff, op. cit. at p. 253. Perhaps old German military manuals were permissive or inviting in this respect. Kossoy, 1976, p. 44, cites G. W. C. Cavan, *Das Krieges-oder Militär-recht* (Berlin, 1801), para. 76: 'Reprisals or retorsions consist of responding by the same or even more harsh treatment of the adverse military personnel and civilians.'

78 *Op. cit.* in n. 64, vol. 7, pp. 79–87.

79 Nys, vol. 3, pp. 136, 204. De Louter, vol. 2, p. 218n. Garner, vol. 2, pp. 196–7. Hall, p. 461n. Oppenheim, vol. 2, pp. 231–2.

80 See p. 184.

81 Respectively: Westlake, 1913, p. 125; 1914, pp. 263, 264. (This latter work first saw light in 1894.)

82 Respectively: Westlake, 1914, pp. 244–6, and 1913, p. 128. The paragraph continued thus: 'Of conduct suitable to such instructions it may be expected that human nature will not fail to produce examples, but the business of doctrinal writers should be to check, and not to encourage it. Otherwise the most elementary restraints on war, which have been handed down from antiquity, are not safe.'

83 Scott on 1899, p. 55.

84 Röling, p. 384, quoting Maunoir, *La Repression des Crimes de Guerres devant les Tribunaux français et alliés*, Geneva, 1956, p. 489.

85 Scott on 1899, pp. 63, 488. What became Article 46 in the final version began as Article 38.

86 *Völkerrecht im Weltkrieg*, vol. 1, p. 193.

87 Some relevant references are given in Ernst Stenzel, 'Uber die "Kriegsraison" des kaiserlichen deutschen Militärismus', in *Z. für Militärgeschichte*, vol. 4, 1965, pp. 342–6; the judgement of which however is too biased to be wholly credible. For persuasive expressions of opinion that an unusually large allowance of military necessity was a German specialty, see Oppenheim, p. 232; Draper, at p. 134; Garner, vol. 2, pp. 195–202; O'Brien, 1957, pp. 119–28.

88 Quick guides to the curious history of this business, and its meagre outcome, are C. Mullins, *The Leipzig Trials*, London, 1921 (one of them, the 'Llandovery Castle' case appears in Friedman, 1972, vol. 1, pp. 868–82) and *Am. J.I.L.*, vol. 16, 1922, pp. 195–7. I have not been able to see E. Fisher-Baring, *Des Untersuchungsausschuss für die Schuldfragen des ersten Weltkrieges*, Düsseldorf, 1954.

89 This important book is difficult to locate. Its British Museum Library classification is: Germany. Nationalversammlung, 1919, 20. *Das Werk der Untersuchungsausschusses...*, Reihe 3, *Völkerrecht im Weltkrieg*, 1927.

90 The section fills vol. 1, pp. 20–51. For the Kriegsbrauch argument see esp. pp. 27–8, 46–9.

91 They were able to cite four German experts who had pointed out its points of incompatibility with the Hague Regulations: Zorn, Strupp, Meurer and Cybichowski.

92 It was so in its authorization of collective punishment of places in occupied territory. The Committee said that allied occupation forces themselves had done this after the war: p. 26.

93 *Grosse Politik*, vol. 15, esp. pp. 229–30, 357.

94 PRO, WO 32/8996 passim, and Holland, *A Valedictory Retrospect 1874–1910*, Oxford, 1910, pp. 13–15.

95 For the law on this (and *not*, whatever the authors may have

thought they were doing, the history) see above all Graber, Uhler and Glahn.

96 See e.g. Waxel, pp. 73–4n., citing Halleck, Calvo and Droop. Their view is endorsed by Rolin-Jaequemyns, *RDI*, vol. 3, p. 512.

97 Verdy du Vernois, p. 172. Confirmed in respect of the major comparable campaign, Sherman's march from Atlanta to the sea and then northwards, in Randall and Donald, p. 637.

98 From the Brussels Code, Articles 2 and 4. It is a measure of the strength of the counter-attack made upon the arch-occupiers at The Hague that this Article 4, found intolerable by ardent smaller-country patriotism, was got rid of.

99 Cited in *L'Indépendance Belge*, 14 September 1870.

100 Cited in *Kölnische Zeitung*, 6 October 1870.

101 *The War of the Rebellion: a Compilation of the Official Records . . .*, Washington, 1880–, 1st series, vol. 12, part 2, p. 52. Admirably restrained Confederate reactions partly appear in 2nd series, vol. 4, pp. 830 ff.

102 Jackson's account of the matter to his brother-in-law Rufus Barringer, printed in Mary A. Jackson, *Life and Letters of Jackson*, New York, 1892, pp. 308 ff.

103 Lieber's Code, Articles 90–2 (and 95–6). For general discussion of it see Spaight, pp. 330–6; Edmonds and Oppenheim, pp. 259, 302–3; Rolin, vol. 1, pp. 372–3; the controversy between Morgan in *Grotius Society Transactions*, vol. 2, 1916, pp. 161–73 and Oppenheim in *Law Quarterly Review*, vol. 33, 1917, pp. 266–86; and Oppenheim, 1952, section 255. The concept was often used in German menacing and punitive expressions, 1870–1, and it was still being used in 1914–18: see Whitlock, 1919, vol. 1, p. 305 (on trials of Belgians under this head) and G. C. Bruntz, *Allied Propaganda and the Collapse of the German Empire in 1918*, New York, 1972, pp. 142–3 (conviction of British airmen for dropping leaflets encouraging German soldiers to desert!). The German proclamation to the people of Brussels about the execution of Edith Cavell, etc., used the word 'treason' twice in this loosest of senses.

104 Lieber's Code, Article 85.

105 Westlake, 1913, p. 100.

106 Respectively, Articles 45, 29, 23 (last sentence), and 44b.

107 Naturally, Guides figure largely in Lieber's Code, Arts. 93–7. Crucial debate at The Hague, 1907, will be found in Scott, vol. 3, pp. 117–23, 131.

108 From a gossipy letter from the British ambassador in Brussels to the Foreign Secretary, 21 June 1874; PRO, FO 881/2483 no. 45.

109 *Transactions of the N.A.P.S.S.*, 1872 (published 1873), pp. 527–36

at 534. Hamley's main philippic against the German handling of occupied France was in *The Times* of 22 February 1877. The other person is Rolin-Jaequemyns in *R.D.I.*, vol. 4, p. 522.

110 Baratier, 1871, pp. 9–13. The General Order to German Armies entering France, dated 13 August 1870, stipulated as daily necessities, for each soldier, 750 grammes of bread, 500 of meat, 550 of 'lard', 30 of coffee, 60 of tobacco or 5 cigars, a demilitre of wine or one litre of beer or one-tenth litre of brandy; for each horse, 6 kilos of oats, two of hay, one-and-a-half of straw. See D'Angeberg,1873, vol. 1, pp. 358–9.

111 What Germans and Russians (I am not sure about Austrians) thought normal, others thought excessive. See e.g. Leroy-Beaulieu in *Revue contemporaine*, 1868, at pp. 27–8; Bernard, 1856, p. 109; Crousse, 1866, pp. 76, 80–3; Brenet, 1902, pp. 51–67.

112 From a public letter to Gambetta, reproduced in *Echo du Parlement Belge*, 14 January 1871. (I am assuming that it is the same Voigts-Rhetz as was at Brussels.)

113 Brit. Parl. Papers, 1875, vol. 82, p. 271 (= Cmd. Paper of 1875, no. 1128, p. 107).

114 Ibid., pp. 174–5.

115 Brussels Code, Articles 40–2. Cf. Hague Regulations, Arts. 48–53. The limiting phrase (Art. 51) had become: 'Requisitions in kind and services ... for the needs of the army of occupation ... shall be in proportion to the resources of the country. ...'

116 Rüstow, vol. 2, pp. 331–4.

117 E.g. *Journal des Débats*, 23 July 1864 (citing *Kreuzzeitung*) and Crousse, 1866, pp. 80–3.

118 Spaight's summary, p. 389. He rests partly on Loening in *R.D.I.*, vol. 5, 1873, p. 107. See also Ferrand, 1891, pp. 113–5.

119 Of course the Germans' behaviour in France was not as faultless as self-righteous patriots claimed; e.g., the officer in the letter quoted above, note 112: 'by insulting our army you have insulted the entire nation of which it is the most direct, intimate and complete expression. This army is, in a word, the nation in arms, and that nation is the most honest, the most scrupulous, the most civilized and the most truthful in the whole world'. ... But there is good neutral and even French testimony to the fact that, all things considered, the amount of *officially unintended* damage was creditably small, and that there was unprecedently little personal violence and violation. See especially Rolin-Jaequemyns and Monod.

120 For Mosby see, e.g., Virgil C. Jones, *Ranger Mosby*, Chapel Hill, 1944. For Fontenay I have relied mainly on Brenet, pp. 14–15, Rüstow, vol. 3, p. 220, Chareton, pp. 222–5, and the anonymous

article 'L'exploitation des chemins de fer français par les Allemands en 1870–1' in *Rev. mil. des armées étrangères*, vol. 63, 1904, pp. 431–40.

121 Better known in military history and old international law as La Petite Guerre, Der Kleine Krieg. On this see especially Johannes Kunisch, *Der Kleine Krieg: Studien zum Heerwesen des Absolutismus*, Wiesbaden, 1973.

122 Hall, p. 613.

123 The long piece on Hamley in the *Dictionary of National Biography* (signed 'E.M.L.') does not notice this letter and its shorter precursor of 24 January; see above, n. 109. Hamley's general argument seems to hold water even if he was writing too soon after the event and swallowing a few tall stories, as Rolin-Jaequemyns believed–see *R.D.I.*, vol. 3, pp. 289–96.

124 Article 81.

125 The heavy-weight Rolin-Jaequemyns was the chief of these. His articles refer to selective criticisms of German excesses by e.g. Bluntschli and Dahn. Busch, 1879, vol. 1, p. 130, thought Sheridan 'rather heartless'. But those were early days.

126 This, my own impression, is also that of van Creveld, 1977, p. 96.

127 See for example, p. 198.

128 Hall, pp. 651–2.

129 See, e.g., Brenet, ch. 3, for a run-down on the several categories. For pre-1870 *francs-tireurs* preparations, Hans Meier-Welcker in von Gersdorff and von Groote (eds.), *Entscheidung 1870*, pp. 110–11.

130 Having now read the contemporary description of the Berlin academic and artistic community's Landsturm troop in 1813 (cited by Kitchen, p. 56), I am not so sure of that.

131 Brenet, 1902, p. 18. The whole of his chapter 1 is about the *francs-tireurs*.

132 *Courrier de Lyon*, cited in *Echo du Parlement Belge*, 13 January 1871.

133 Monod, pp. 105–9, and Charles R. Mink in *Military Affairs*, vol. 34, 1970, at p. 135.

134 Cited by Rolin-Jaequemyns, *R.D.I.*, vol. 3, p. 320n.

135 Date uncertain but must be close before the 24th, since it ends with a summons to meet at Thouars on that day. It was signed by M. F.-L. de l'Hébergemont.

136 Bazeilles was a village outside Sedan which was largely destroyed during and after fierce fighting in which 'civilians' took part, and many non-participants succumbed. At once it became legendary. My conclusion is based mainly on Brenet, 1902, pp. 33–6; Rüstow,

1872, vol. 2, p. 53; Rolin-Jaequemyns, *R.D.I.*, vol. 4, p. 504n.; Monod, pp. 55–6; and a cutting from a September 1870 *Journal de Genève* in C.I.C.R. Archives, Carton 33. As so often, the Germans were 'in the right' to begin with, but over-reacted to an extent which bothered some of them – e.g. even Bismarck and Abeken, according to Busch, vol. 1, pp. 168–70.

137 I follow Brenet, pp. 36–7, Chareton, pp. 240–1, and Monod, pp. 56–7. Moltke (who may not have known all the facts?) wrote of it a week later: 'This unavoidable horrible exhibition has had, however, this result, that Chartres has submitted voluntarily'. Moltke, vol. 2, p. 234.

138 English text as given in Edmonds and Oppenheim, 1914.

139 The American instances again, were not well known; nor was mention normally made of the remarkable number of occasions in the century when government forces bombarded rebellious cities.

140 Only a simpleton could doubt that these things happen. Hard evidence is in the nature of things rare; yet see Verdy du Vernois, 1897, p. 239 – entry for 8 January 1871.

141 See e.g. Rüstow, vol. 2, p. 181.

142 Wartensleben, p. 31.

143 Frederick, p. 138 and elsewhere. His sentiments about Strasbourg on pp. 138–9 are instructive.

144 For Strasbourg I have drawn mainly (apart from works cited in other notes) on Gustave Fischbach, *Le Siège et le Bombardement de Strasbourg*, Strasbourg, 1870; the German official account, translated by Clarke, 2v., London, 1876; 'Die Belagerung von Strassburg 1870' in *Jahrbücher für die deutsche Armee und Marine*, vol. 5, 1872, pp. 147–86, 241–70; and Reinhold Wagner, *Geschichte der Belagerung von Strassburg*, Berlin, 1874.

145 Rüstow, vol. 2, p. 181.

146 Cited by J. A. Hobson, *Richard Cobden, the International Man*, London, 1919, p. 311.

147 Slade, p. 217. Rear-Admiral Sir Adolphus Slade had served the Ottoman Empire as Mushaver Pasha. His pages constitute a stunning indictment of British naval habits. He may have been prejudiced; but so much of what he says is in tune with contemporary juridical opinion that it is impossible to disbelieve it all. Incidentally, Spaight, 1911, p. 132, supports him.

148 Bernard, p. 132. This passage is startlingly suggestive.

149 Kenneth Bourne, 'British Preparations for War with the North, 1861–2', in *English Historical Review*, vol. 76, 1961, at pp. 621–5.

150 The uselessness, to say the least, of the Alexandria episode is attested by as undoubted a patriot as Henderson, 1905, p. 17, and

by E. G. P. Fitzmaurice, *Life of . . . the second Earl of Granville*, 2nd edn., 2v., London, 1905, vol. 2, pp. 260–70 at 267.

151 Aube was not original. Forty years earlier, Joinville had threatened to bombard Brighton, not long before he did bombard Algiers. But Aube led the 'jeune école' which made much noise about that time; see e.g. Marder, 1940, pp. 76, 86; Hall, 1924, pp. 515–16; Higgins and Colombos, 1951, pp. 352–3; Nys, 1904, vol. 3, pp. 464–5; and Westlake, who thought Aube provided evidence that there remained in the world 'many relics of a less advanced moral condition'.

152 *The Times*, 1 April 1899, p. 11, col 2.

153 Holland, p. 98. Letter dated 7 August 1888.

154 Ibid., p. 107. The attacks made on him revealed a frightening ignorance of 'the nature and claims of international law'.

155 Cited by ibid., p. 109.

156 The Ninth Convention, respecting Naval Bombardments in Time of War.

157 Article 25. See further, p. 263.

158 Scott, on 1907, vol. 1, p. 689.

159 Badeau, 1882, vol. 3, p. 22.

160 I write that, partly because I suspect it to be true, partly because it seems to be true about Sheridan's immediate precursor up that valley, Hunter. *His* orders read very well in George E. Pond, *The Shenandoah Valley in 1864*, New York, 1885; but on 28 September 1864 we find Halleck writing to Sherman, 'I do not approve of General Hunter's course in burning private houses or uselessly destroying private property. That is barbarous.' – Sherman, 1875, vol. 2, p. 129.

161 Op. cit., p. 437.

162 Letter to Major Sawyer, 31 January 1864, in Rachel S. Thorndike, *The Sherman Letters*, New York, 1894, p. 232.

163 Sherman, 1875, vol. 2, pp. 125–7.

164 *War of the Rebellion*, 1st series, vol. 39, pt. 3, p. 358.

165 Sherman, 1875, vol. 2, p. 128. The whole exchange of letters with Hood repays study; it begins on p. 118.

166 Op. cit., p. 431.

167 It is worth observing that the same was true of the British anti-guerrilla operations (including much devastation) in the second phase of the Boer war: see D. Reitz, *Commando. A Boer Journal of the Boer War*, London, 1929, p. 169.

168 PRO, FO 881/9041*, Report dated 21 March 1907, section 43.

Chapter IV

1 Circumstances and conditions making for and against observance

of the law of war have been excellently analysed by Karsten, ch. 2, which came to my hand just before this book went to press.

2 On everything to do with the Red Cross since 1944, one must turn first to Durand, whose chapters 2 and 3, pp. 22–112, cover the great war and its immediate aftermath.

3 Durand, pp. 434–41, discreetly says enough about the ICRC's endeavours to bring Germany and the USSR to some agreement to make one regret that the full explanation of their failure is unlikely ever to be known; the ICRC's archives being as impenetrable to the outside inquirer as the USSR's. It looks as if the USSR simply did not believe in the ICRC's impartiality.

4 I have learnt much about this side of world war two from fellow-Fellows of the Wilson Center, especially Dr Ikuhiko Hata. Pritchard opens a new vein of incidental information.

5 Graf, *passim*.

6 He was reviewing vol. 5 of H. A. Jones, *The War in the Air*, in *Journal of the RUSI*, vol. 81, 1936, pp. 95–101.

7 Cited by Garner, vol. 2, p. 59.

8 Treitschke for instance waxed wrathful at Belgium's pride in being a centre of international law. 'Belgium is neutral; it is by its nature an emasculated State. It is such a State likely to develop a healthy notion of international law? . . .' cited in H. W. C. Davis, *The Political Thought of Heinrich von Treitschke*, London, 1915, p. 176. His notion, that international law should be made only by the strong (except England), became orthodoxy for the *Zeitschrift für Völkerrecht* during the war (see especially Kohler's essay 'Das neue Völkerrecht' in vol. 9, 1916, pp. 5–10) and in due course lent itself conveniently to National Socialist purposes; for which see M. Messerschmidt, Revision, Neue Ordnung, Krieg. Akzente der Völkerrechtswissenschaft in Deutschland, 1933–1945', in *Militärgeschichtliche Mitteilungen*, vol. 1, 1971, pp. 61–95, esp. pp. 61–2, 68.

9 Unprecedented – but itself a precedent. . . . There is also evidence that at least some German believed that they were deliberately terrorizing the Belgians in order to prevent their doing things they might regret. See especially Gibson, 1917, p. 190, but also *passim*. Liddell Hart confirms this in *Through the Fog of War*, London, 1938, pp. 311–12.

10 Brand Whitlock, *Letters and Journal*, 2 vols., New York, 1936, vol. 1, p. 50.

11 Edouard Rolin, Scott, ed., 1899 Conference, 1920, at p. 64.

12 This remarkable story may be followed in Hoover's *Memoirs*, 2v., London, 1952, vol. 1, and Gay, G. I., and Fisher, H. H., *Public*

Relations of the Committee for Relief in Belgium, 2v., Stanford, 1929.

13 Well over 15,000 civilians succumbed during that long siege-cum-blockade; see Keith's report to the Admiralty, 10 June 1800, in *The Keith Papers* (ed. C. Lloyd for the Navy Records Society), 2v., London, 1950, vol. 2, pp. 112–13. Thomas Arnold picked on this terrible episode for special comment in the fourth of his *Introductory Lectures on Modern History*, at p. 221.

14 Gay and Fisher, op. cit., vol. 1, pp. 237–40.

15 The most startling expression of that conflict known to me came when the military officer who had prosecuted Captain Fryatt in 1916 told a German commission of inquiry in the spring of 1919 that of course he ignored the Foreign Office's telegram requesting postponement: '*Ich kenne keine Auswärtiges Amt!*' – in PRO, WO 32/5008, Lt. Breen's report on the proceedings of 31 March, 1 and 2 April 1919.

16 That was all right according to Treitschke: 'In the national wars of the present day every honest subject is a spy', in his *Politics*, ed. Balfour, 2v., London, 1916, vol. 1, p. 610.

17 See esp. Durand, pp. 67–8.

18 *Dixième conférence internationale de la Croix-Rouge, tenue à Genève, 30 mars–7 avril 1921. Compte rendu*, pp. 166–7.

19 See esp. pp. 164, 196–7, 214–15, 240–2, and 326–8. Much may be learnt about it from articles by R-M. Frick-Cramer in *Revue internationale de la C.-R.*, 1925, pp. 73–84, 1943, pp. 386–402 and 567–80, and 1947, pp. 228–48, and Paul des Gouttes in the same, 1934, pp. 649–62.

20 I do not mean that they were necessarily wrong to do so. After all, it is more the responsibility of the government whom armed forces serve, than of armed forces themselves, to ensure that preparations for war include moral and legal sense as well as military. My judgement here rests principally on published sources but has been fortified by what I have read, in the US National Archives, relative to the Red Cross and the law of war during the nineteen-twenties and thirties, and in the British Public Record Office, relative to air warfare policy in the thirties and early forties.

21 Durand, p. 241. Also private information from the late Pierre Boissier.

22 Preliminary document no. 6, sent to governments from Bern in January 1939; in US National Archives, decimal file 1930–9, 514.2 A 12B/14.

23 On this see, generally, Durand, ch. 9, esp. pp. 423–33 for Greece, and p. 537 for Holland.

24 See Henri Davignon, *La Belgique et l'Allemagne*, Paris, 1915,

p. 25. The German instruction is in Müller-Meiningen, 1915, p. 234. (But the *préfet* who had advised Nancy to do the same in 1870 was recalled by his government: see B. Schnapper, *Remplacement Militaire en France*, Paris, 1968, p. 274.)

25 Paris and Lausanne, 1916.

26 *Der Fall Löwen und der Weissbuch*, Köln-Graz, 1958; *Le Cas de Louvain*, Louvain-Paris, 1958. The whole story is told by the Belgian historian F. Mayence in *Bulletin de la Classe des Lettres et des Sciences Morales et Politiques de l'Académie Royal de Belgique*, 5th series, vol. 44, 1958, pp. 143–7.

27 From Mayence's summary of Schöller's conclusions. Just how persistent is patriotic myth, when tied to military pride and sense of 'honour', may be seen in Hahlweg's section, 'Belgischer Franktireurkrieg', pp. 97–9 and notes.

28 A terse critical appraisal of British methods is given by Schmid, pp. 40–2. The flavour of US anti-guerrilla methods may be gathered from the cases reported in Friedman, vol. 1, pp. 799–841.

29 Durand, pp. 473, 474, whose account of German concessions in this matter goes beyond the very little indicated by W. J. Ford in *Revue Internationale de la C.-R.*, 1967 at pp. 500–4.

30 Department of the [US] Army pamphlet 20–243, *German Anti-guerrilla Operations in the Balkans 1941–4*, Washington, 1957, p. 67.

31 General Donald Blackburn, in *Proceedings of the Am. Soc. of Int. Law*, 70th meeting, Washington, 1976, p. 155.

32 Boissier, p. 116.

33 And Tito's non-communist rival Mihailovic, recalling the frightful suffering caused by reprisals in the First World War, went as cautiously as he did, partly from desire to avoid provoking them: see *German Anti-guerrilla Operations* . . . as cited in n. 30 above, p. 20–1.

34 In citing from pp. 30–1 of it, I wish to pay my respects to the excellence of Dr Gary Gordon's 1972 Iowa University thesis, *Soviet Partisan Warfare, 1941–4: the German Perspective.*

35 Boissier called attention to so disagreeable a possibility in his article 'Oradour' in *Monde-Nouveau*, March 1953, no. 67, pp. 28–35. In August 1942 the head of the Dutch government in exile wrote to the deputy prime minister about German taking (and shooting) of hostages 'in reprisal for acts of sabotage'. He feared 'that if this be allowed to continue with impunity, the spirit of Dutch resistance will rapidly weaken . . .'. – PRO, Air 8/424, fo. 33.

36 See below, p. 368, n. 14.

37 Hermann Neubacher, the German foreign office plenipotentiary

in SE Europe, to Field Marshal von Weichs, apropos of the Klissura massacre; cited by Telford Taylor, pp. 192–3.

38 Davidson, pp. 29–30.

39 A Yugoslav woman doctor remarked, after 9,000 Serbs had been shot in reprisal (300 to each German): 'Your military objectives may, of course, have been worth all this, but . . .'. Maclean, p. 153, citing C. Lawrence, *Irregular Adventure*, 1947.

40 PRO, Adm. 116/1079, dated 28 May 1908.

41 Bell, pp. 20–3, 38–9.

42 Riste, p. 24.

43 Bell, pp. 20–1.

44 Cited from a 1908 memorandum of the Director of Naval Operations by Marder, *D to SF*, vol. 1, p. 379.

45 I have already touched on this matter in my 1976 article.

46 But there are exceptions to every rule. The Admiralty's 3 November 1914 declaration of the closure of the North Sea, very vexing to the neutrals, was done without Foreign Office knowledge and in fact went counter to its policy at that time; see Bell, p. 63, and Riste, pp. 56–8. I can find nothing about this in Marder.

47 Japan had begun its war with Russia by a surprise attack on the Russian warships in Port Arthur.

48 See above, p. 204.

49 Note on 'Naval Bombardment of Coast Towns' [continuation of CID paper 75B], in PRO, FO 881/9328* 11. It went on thus: 'Lastly, we have the case of bombardments intended to cover, or divert attention from, a landing. It is easy to conceive that a bombardment of this nature might involve undefended towns and villages, and it presents perhaps the most difficult case of all from a humanitarian point of view. At the same time, no Power could be expected to abstain from such an act of war, if it fell within their strategical plan. . . . It must come under the category of inevitable acts of war necessitated by overwhelming military considerations. We could not give up the right so to act, and we could not expect other nations to do so.' . . .

50 See above, p. 179. His own gloss on the same incident may be read in a letter of 25 April 1912 in Marder, *F G D N*, vol. 2, pp. 453 ff.

51 Letter of 20 December 1916, in A. Temple Patterson (ed.), *The Jellicoe Papers*, 2v., London, 1966, 1968; vol. 2 at p. 124. For a terse summary of Admiralty views, see Marder, *D to SF*, vol. 2, p. 375.

52 E.g., conspicuously, in the matter of the mines laid in the first hours of the war by the *Königin Luise*; an incident which Britain vigorously exploited, but which was nevertheless legal by the

letter of what Germany had accepted of the Hague Conventions. (Westlake had seen this coming; 1913, pp. 313–6.) I find nothing to contradict my generalizations about mines in the relevant section of the *Second Interim Report from the Committee of Inquiry into Breaches of the Law of War . . .* , 3 June 1919.

53 It is remarkable how often the swing of the pendulum of neutral opinion against Britain was sent swinging back against Germany by submarine incidents: e.g. the sinking of, successively, the *Lusitania,* the *Arabic,* the *Ancona,* and the *Sussex.* Bell, p. 592, makes a nice comment on this apropos of the *Sussex* incident: 'For the third time running, therefore, the one principle on which the Washington authorities stood firm was breached by a young fellow, less than thirty years old, with nothing to guide him but his periscope, and his desire for professional distinction.'

54 Evidence that it was not however wholly unthought of before the outbreak of war is given by P. K. Lundeberg, 'The German Naval Critique of the U-Boat Campaign, 1915–18', in *Military Affairs,* vol. 27, 1963, pp. 105 ff.

55 But the commerce-raider and minelaying *Wolf,* which got through in the winter of 1916–17, sowed its mines indiscriminately. The war had got rougher by then.

56 Chapter 4 of the Declaration is titled 'Destruction of Neutral Prizes'. Article 48 says such prizes must be, not destroyed, but taken into port for appropriate trial. Article 49 however allows destruction in exceptional cases 'if the observance of Article 48 would involve danger to the safety of the warship or to the success of the operations in which she is engaged at the time.'

57 By early 1916 the German government had evidence of such instructions, taken from the *Woodfield*: see Mallison, p. 110.

58 As had been Captain Fryatt.

59 Marder, *D to SF,* vol. 1, p. 363, says that the Prime Minister, presumably shocked at such sentiments, 'refused to circulate' that memorandum to the CID.

60 These of course were branded as the *francs-tireurs* of the sea. The popular German film *Morgenrot,* produced just before Hitler came to power, shows what Germans thought of the Q-ships.

61 Mallison, ch. III.B.1a in general; esp. pp. 68 and 74. (To avoid needlessly upsetting legal precisions I must point out that his use of the cited phrase refers immediately to 'submarine operational areas'.) His judgement is supported by Tucker, pp. 56–68 *passim,* and O'Connell, 1975, p. 47.

62 Cited by Bell at p. 446. Such a distinction is confirmed and supported by Holland, 1913, pp. 88–9, McDougal and Feliciano,

p. 685 n. 483 (citing Colombos), and Bindschedler in the *Annuaire de l'Institut de Droit International*, 1967 meeting, vol. 2, pp. 211–15, esp. 214n. The basic German view of the matter is given by Ritter, vol. 3, esp. at p. 141.

63 Corbett, pp. 272–3.

64 Circumstances alter cases. That Lloyd George's Britain and the Kaiser's Germany should seek to 'starve each other out' was intrinsically much less inhumane than the use of the starvation weapon by relatively rich representative governments against backward peoples under autocratic governments.

65 B. H. Liddell Hart, *Through the Fog of War*, London, 1938, p. 220 cites a self-critical German, R. Binding: 'How can one bear it, this German shriek of sympathy to America? . . . As if we would not starve out all England in cold blood until the thinnest English miss fell through her skirts!' Birnbaum, p. 12, cites Falkenhayn in 1915 to similar effect. Galpin, p. 200, remarks that Napoleon would have starved out Britain if he could.

66 See above, p. 334, n. 16.

67 The British government brought this up in answer to Dutch complaints about the intensification of the blockade in November–December 1939. See Kalshoven, 1971, pp. 152–5, 159–60.

68 See for example, at one end of Europe, the Spanish nationalists' resentment of British commercial penetration of Spain's Latin American empire as one of the prices of alliance; and at the other, Russian anti-westerners' conviction that Alexander I was being lured by the British to adopt policies furthering their commercial interests at Russian expense.

69 Much evidence concerning this is scattered through the pages of Bell; esp. pp. 177, 181.

70 US Naval History Division, Operational Archives, General Board Studies no. 438 (1915–21), report dated 4 March 1915. This practice, much more time-consuming for neutrals than search at sea, had been declared illegal by the Hague Court as recently as 1913: see Guichard, pp. 29–30. Trimble, pp. 97–8, is very strong about this. But not only was it convenient for searchers; it was also, when submarines were around, safer. In a slightly later Memo, 24 March 1915, the US Navy General Board opined that belligerents had to take their chance: 'nor can they with any right or justice require action on the part of – and at the expense of – neutrals to relieve them from the normal hazards of war' (same file).

71 Guichard, p. 75.

72 Bell, pp. 152–5.

73 A clear summary of it is given by Oppenheim, pp. 490–1.

74 It does not use the phrase 'unrestricted warfare' but that is what it means.

75 Medlicott, vol. 1, p. 17. A striking document, often cited; e.g. Mallison, p. 60, and Meyrowitz, p. 387n.

76 Mallison, p. 130.

77 Admiral Dönitz's counsel at Nuremberg, cited by Mallison, p. 78.

78 My summary of Mallison (see note 61 above) and Kalshoven, 1971, pp. 142–59 *passim.*

79 This part of the book has exercised me more than any other. I can mention only the more scholarly published sources upon which I have most relied: above all Webster and Frankland's great official history, and Frankland's two other bombing books; Gotz Bergander, *Dresden im Luftkrieg,* Köln and Wien, 1977. Verrier; Neville Jones; Hyde; J. M. Spaight's many publications, especially the three editions (1924, 1933, 1947) of his *Air Power and War Rights,* which reward close comparison; Andrew Boyle, *Trenchard;* Martin Middlebrook, *The Nuremberg Raid;* and, of the great quantity of good writing by United States scholars, Hilton P. Goss, *Civilian Morale under Aerial Bombardment 1914–1939* (Air University Documentary Research Division, Maxwell Air Force Base, Alabama, 1949); David MacIsaac, *Strategic Bombing in World War Two,* New York, 1976; F. Craven and J. Cate, *The [US] Army Air Force in World War Two,* 1948–58 (vols. 2 and 3 being the relevant ones); George H. Quester, *Deterrence before Hiroshima. The Airpower Background to Modern Strategy,* New York, 1966; and Robert C. Batchelder, *The Irreversible Decision, 1939–1950.* I must also acknowledge a debt to those in the UK and the USA who have talked with me about this and helped me sort it out, and express my admiration for the paper 'Culmination: Dresden, 1945', prepared at the US Air Force Academy by Marc A. Clodfelter, who kindly let me use it.

80 This fluttered the juridical dove-cots; see Coquet in *Rev. Générale de Droit International Public,* vol. 20, 1913, pp. 533–7, and Rapisardi-Mirabelli in *Rev. de Dr. Int. et de Législation Comparée,* 2nd series, vol. 15, 1913, pp. 565ff. The Institut de Droit International reviewed the whole field at its Madrid meeting, 1911: see its *Annuaire,* Edition Abrégée, vol. 5, 1906–11, p. 1037–1167.

81 Lists of signatories in Schindler and Toman, pp. 133, 136–8.

82 Op. cit., p. 182. Again on p. 186.

83 It is fascinating to find Spaight, 1924, pp. 18–19, expressly expecting that this would be done. He was an Air Ministry official (and an 'expert adviser' at The Hague, 1922–3). His life and works,

especially an assessment of the status of his publications, seem likely to reward research.

84 Cited in *Second Interim Report from the Committee of Inquiry into Breaches of the Law of War*, 3 June 1919, p. 337; strikingly confirmed by H. M. Hyde and G. R. F. Nuttall, *Air Defence and the Civil Population*, London, 1937.

85 Royse, op. cit., pp. 192–3.

86 Cited, along with much else from the report (placed before the War Cabinet on 17 August 1917), by H. A. Jones, *The War in the Air*, vol. 6, pp. 11–12.

87 Neville Jones, op. cit., pp. 160–3. He points out that such a theory encouraged exaggerated expectations of the effects of bombing as well as complacency about operational standards; if precision didn't matter, why worry about being imprecise?

88 Hyde, 1976, p. 42.

89 Goss's admirable dissertation in fact shows how almost all the civilian bombing experience of the nineteen-thirties suggested that civilian morale did *not* 'crack', even under unopposed raids; and that even when it did (as ultimately in Barcelona), no positive political consequences could be predicted.

90 I regret that I have lost the reference to that particular prophecy by a supposed French expert. I recall that he was a colonel.

91 Sir John Betjeman's poem 'In Westminster Abbey' must be cited:
   ... Gracious Lord, Oh bomb the Germans.
   Spare their women for Thy sake,
   And if that is not too easy,
   We will pardon Thy mistake.
   But, gracious Lord, whate'er shall be,
   Don't let anyone bomb me.
       (from *Old Light for New Chancels*, 1940)

92 Especially apropos of this is Uri Bialer, ' "Humanization" of Air Warfare in British Foreign Policy on the eve of the second world war', in *Journal of Contemporary History*, vol. 13, 1978, pp. 79–96.

93 See e.g. what was on the Air Targets Sub-Committee's list in Webster and Frankland, vol. 1, pp. 95–6, 97–8.

94 Ibid., p. 118; commented on by Verrier, p. 57.

95 Trenchard's 1928 Memorandum, in Webster and Frankland, vol. 4, pp. 71–6.

96 It is worth remarking that Harris, Trenchard's most celebrated disciple, could express himself quite contemptuous of the chiefs of the other services. Just one of many possible illustrations: from the *first* (un-watered-down) *draft*, dated 28 August 1942, of his vindication of Bomber Command's ability to win the war: 'In the final issue this War will be decided by Air.' He sketches two

'eventual situations', one or other of which he apparently feels sure must happen (incidentally they much under-rate the Russians), and which leave Germany, even a Germany withdrawn to its homeland, unconquered. But – 'we can get them by Air, and *in the end, no matter what happens in the interim, it will be done that way. That way only – and it will suffice.* I remain perpetually astonished at the reasoning of the United Nations' soldier-strategists. . . . There is no thought and no reasoning behind such action. Only a blind and pathetic urge to do that only thing which they know how . . . *When it becomes possible to defeat the German army on land by United Nations forces transported overseas, there will no longer be any need to defeat them. They will already have broken.* . . . The Generals and the Admirals, ours and the United States', have with unvarying consistency and unanimity been proved to be wrong, and utterly wrong, in every prophecy and pronouncement they have made about air during the past quarter of a century. . . . Let us for once believe the Airmen, ours and the United States'. They have never been wrong in twenty-five years. . . . If they have occasionally overstated their case, they have never done so to any serious extent and it has been due to urgency of pleading necessitated by deliberately deafened military and naval ears. . . .' PRO, AIR 8/424, fos. 19–22. Italics in the original.

97 Webster and Frankland, vol. 4, pp. 76–83. The fact that inter-service rivalry made it profitable for admirals and generals to stand on the side of the angels does not alter the fact that objectively, from a juridical point of view, they may really have been so. The same argument took place in the United States in 1947–8; see how Rear-Admiral Gallery commented on the plans of the atom-bombers, in Rosenberg's article (cited below, p. 369) at p. 70, and Admiral Radford in 1949 (Karsten, p. 91). But that was before the US navy acquired Polaris! (ibid.)

98 Printed fully in J. R. M. Butler, *Grand Strategy*, vol. 2, London, 1957, pp. 567–8.

99 I am following Quester, p. 117. This surmise of Quester's has been singled out for questioning by such experts as Kenneth P. Werrell, 'The U.S.A.A.F. over Europe and its Foes: a Selected, Subjective, and Critical Bibliography', in *Aerospace Historian*, vol. 25, 1978, at p. 242, and David MacIsaac in his review of Quester in *Air University Review*, vol. 18, 1967, at p. 84. I confess that Quester's surmise seems to me very plausible. The PRO has not so far yielded any conclusive evidence one way or the other.

100 Verrier, pp. 124–31.

101 Webster and Frankland, vol. 1, p. 225.

102 A Dutch professor at a great American university, where I gave

a talk called 'Flight-Path to Dresden', afterwards wrote to me: 'I used to be in the middle of that flight-path, and I still remember fondly the drone of all those planes at night, on their way to destroy the forces of evil. Life was simple then, you knew where everyone stood. Even after so many years I have rather unambiguous feelings of gratitude towards the RAF. They were the only ones who were there.'

103 An American colleague tells me that my country's best historian of the bombing offensive has somewhere written: 'People have preferred to feel rather than to know about strategic bombing.' I understand what he means and sympathize with him! But the argument works both ways. It seems to me that Trenchard and Harris, to name but two, were among those who '*felt*' about bombing at least as much as they '*thought*'. Of Harris, e.g., opinion in the Ministry of Economic Warfare, which repeatedly sought in vain to concentrate his bombs on demonstrably worthwhile industrial targets, was that 'his approach was visceral rather than intellectual', and that his 'bombers' Baedeker' was 'a rationalisation of the Harris theory of area attacks rather than any inductive process'. (USSBS papers of 29 and 30 June 1945, in US National Archives, Record Group 243, European section, subdivision 31 g.) The USSBS itself, summarizing its conclusions in the paper headed 'RAF Area Attack Program', referred *inter alia* to Harris's 'emotional satisfaction in seeing a sizeable portion of the built-up area of an enemy city destroyed', and even to 'the state of the Commander-in-Chief's digestion' as a factor not to be discounted in his decision-making process. (Same source.)

104 Spaatz was leery of Trenchard-ism. He and General Eaker (for whom also he wrote) told their chief of staff, Arnold, on 27 August 1944 that they were resisting the British Air Ministry's attempts to lure them into 'morale bombing. . . . I personally believe', wrote Spaatz, 'that any deviation from our present policy, even for an exceptional case, will be unfortunate. There is no doubt in my mind that the RAF want very much to have the US Air Forces tarred with the morale bombing aftermath which we feel will be terrific.' Library of Congress, Manuscript Division: Henry H. Arnold Papers, Box 48. I am indebted to Dr Melden E. Smith for helping me find this.

105 Arnold to General Spaatz, 29 September 1944, reporting what Portal had said to him; in Henry H. Arnold Papers, Box 48.

106 Earlier, less staggering instances of his defiantly going his own way are mentioned by Middlebrook in Carver (ed.), *The War Lords: Military Commanders of the Twentieth Century*, Boston, 1976, pp. 326, 327–8.

107 What were the purposes and explanations of the Dresden raid?
The explanation included a growing impatience, especially among
Americans, to get the European war over and done with, and an
urge to find something for the already huge but ever-growing
bomber forces to do. There was a general purpose, which may at
best be called political, to step up the indiscriminate bashing of
a foe who was continuing to fight more stoutly than had been
expected six months before and who was still giving the allies a
bad time and nasty surprises: e.g. the V2's were still hitting
London and Antwerp; new U-boats still being launched; the
allies' ground offensive had bogged down. There was an intention,
neither more nor less reasonable than morale-breaking talk had
been for the past three years, to terrify the Germans out of the
idea of guerrilla resistance, of which Goebbels had been making
much. Two of the better-looking purposes at first announced were
not true. Dresden was not an important industrial centre (see, e.g.,
the apologetics in Craven and Cate, vol. 3, p. 371), nor had the
Russians specifically asked for Dresden to be 'neutralized' or
'paralysed' (see Webster and Frankland, vol. 3, p. 113 and note),
although they had asked for such to be done to the transportation
means of Berlin and Leipzig, and they had welcomed suggestions,
latterly much made by Churchill, ('Dresden bombing was due to
W[inston] C[hurchill] – wanted to make biggest splash to impress
Stalin', noted Liddell Hart on a letter from the official historian,
16 December 1960: Liddell Hart Papers LH.1/296) that Anglo-
American air power could help them in that kind of way. So far
as that generally was among the purposes, the seriousness with
which it had been thought out may be judged from the fact that
the railway was working again, through the desert which now
was central Dresden, within three or four days (Calvocoressi and
Wint, *Total War*, London, 1972, p. 534; David Irving, *The
Destruction of Dresden*, London, 1963, end of Part 3, ch. 4). A
legitimate object of the raid (not that destroying the city was a
good way to achieve it) was to prevent the railway which passed
through Dresden (and many other places) from delivering certain
important reinforcements to strengthen the Germans' eastern
front. Before it was too late to call the raid off, RAF Intelligence
had learnt that the vital trains were going by a different route.
(Calvocoressi and Wint, same page, confirmed by former Intelligence officer in Max Ophüls's documentary film *The Memory
of Justice*, first shown on BBC2, 7 November 1976.) The raid
however went on, as, considering its main terror purpose and its
other explanations, was not surprising.
108 In fact nearby Chemnitz (another virgin city on Harris's list) was

heavily raided just afterwards. But it was much less 'successful', and at once fell into Dresden's shade. The diminishing series of area raids thereafter attracted less attention.

109 The most distinguished, in the UK, were the Bishop of Chichester, George Bell, and the former Archbishop of Canterbury, Lord Lang; see especially their speeches in the House of Lords, 9 February 1944; Parliamentary Debates, House of Lords, 5th series, vol. 130, cols. 737–46, 747–50. But even they were driven thereafter to give up.

110 Churchill's volte-face was signalled in his Minute of 28 March 1945 to the Chiefs of Staff Committee and the Chief of Air Staff in particular, which he withdrew at Portal's quiet insistence, and replaced by a less embarrassing one on 1 April. See Webster and Frankland, vol. 3, pp. 112–17 *passim*. There is a good chapter (chapter 4) on Churchill's ambivalence vis-à-vis Trenchardism in Ronald Lewin, *Churchill as Warlord*, London, 1973.

111 See e.g. his address at the commemoration of the collaboration of RAF Bomber Command and US 8th Bomber Command at High Wycombe, 8 September 1976, and the BBC Radio 4 programme 'The Bombers' (script by Norman Longmate) partly reproduced in *The Listener*, 6 April 1978.

112 *Inside the Third Reich*, wherein he first expressed these views, came out in 1970. Much mileage has been got by ardent bombers out of them and his repetitions of them; see e.g. Sir Arthur Harris, in the sources cited in the previous note, and his old comrade-in-arms General Ira E. Eaker (to whom I am much indebted for comments and criticisms) and the American businessman-strategist Arthur G. B. Metcalf in *Air Force*, April 1977, pp. 53–7.

113 Op. cit., New York, 1968, p. 181. Even so fine and discriminating a historian as Professor Wright here puts a foot in the undiscriminating mud which is the normal medium of so many writers on this matter. When he says 'mass bombing', he means all strategic bombing, both 'precision' and 'area'. He has no doubt which sort in fact did the more good.

114 It is dedicated to Trenchard's memory, and the author (forty-two other books by whom are listed) was for four years 'Leverhulme Research Fellow at the RAF Museum'; whose own Trustees 'sponsored the project'.

115 For this, see mainly Frankland, 1965, p. 97. Incidental evidence of the same is in Irving, op. cit., Part 1, ch. 2.

116 My round figure, from Webster and Frankland, vol. 3, pp. 286–7.

117 Telford Taylor in his closing statement, 13 February 1948, *Trials of War Criminals before the Nuremberg Military Tribunals under Control Council no. 10*, Washington, DC, 1949, vol. 4, pp. 369–83

at p. 381. 'Dresden' and 'Hiroshima' were used by several defendants in these trials. Taylor was of course justified in pointing out that Germany itself had conducted indiscriminate bombardments (though his particular examples of Warsaw and Rotterdam were not happily chosen) and, above all, that the programme of Jewish extermination could seem comparable with bombing of enemy civilians only to murderously perverted minds.

Chapter V

1 In the signing of the Final Act of the 1907 Hague Conference the only States not either European (including Russia and Turkey) or American (north, central and south together) were China, Japan, Persia, and Siam. List in Schindler and Toman, p. 56.

2 Forty-eight States signed the final act of the 1929 Geneva conference which produced the Conventions of that year – see Schindler and Toman, p. 245. Partly because some of the 1907 signatories were not present, the ostensibly non-European and non-American proportion was higher; but merely to list that group's membership is to indicate its actual cultural and political composition: Australia, Canada, Egypt, India, Japan, New Zealand, Persia, Siam and South Africa.

3 For 1949, Schindler and Toman, pp. 479–82 (following the list of 1945/50 signatures). For 1977, *Official Records*, vol. 1, p. 4, says 126 States were there at the 1974 start and 109 stayed the course. But only 102 seem to have signed at the end.

4 That is not to be understood as saying that christianity historically has been *particularly* supportive of the law of war, or that non-christian religions or ideologies may not be found to be more supportive.

5 I refer primarily to the writings of our contemporary international lawyers, who besides naturally writing with close professional attention about the main events of their own lifetime and the actual making of the greater part of the law which it is their business to understand, have also in some cases taken the opportunity of their own participation in that making to record their impressions of it: e.g. many articles by the Harvard jurist R. R. Baxter, and the Leyden one F. Kalshoven. Forsythe's *Humanitarian Politics*, 1977, includes much recent history. Many large books by or edited by Richard Falk include coverage of all the recent ground. R. I. Miller, 1975, does the same within a single pair of covers.

6 The succession of meetings was as follows: the 19th meeting of the governors of the League at Oxford, 8–20 July 1945; a 'Preliminary conference' of national Red Cross societies . . . in Geneva,

26 July–3 August 1946; a government experts conference, 14–26 April 1947; the 17th international Red Cross conference, at Stockholm, 1948; and at last the diplomatic conference of the summer of 1949.

7 USA, 2 August 1955; UK, 23 September 1957.

8 No States opposed the Human Rights Declaration, but eight *abstained*: Czechoslovakia, Poland, Yugoslavia, the USSR and its Byelorussian and Ukrainian echoes, South Africa, and Saudi Arabia. (From Brownlie, ed., 1971, p. 106.)

9 For a terse summary of what happened up to 1972, see Bailey, pp. 48–9.

10 IMT, *Trial of the Major War Criminals*, 42v., Nuremberg, 1947–9, vol. 19, p. 424.

11 Cited by Koessler, pp. 90–1.

12 I am not sure if that is true of trials in the USSR's sphere of influence.

13 The British and American manuals were prudently modified in this respect before the trials began. Lewy, 1961, is a good short guide to this great question; the main books now seem to be: Société Internationale de Droit Pénal Militaire et de Droit de la Guerre, vol. 1 of the proceedings of its 5th congress at Dublin, published at Strasbourg, 1971; and Green, 1976.

14 It is worth remarking that in the major case of the former kind, US v. List and others, General Rendulic was acquitted of that portion of the charge alleging that he had overdone his destructions; the court basing its decision on the accused's perception of the facts at the time. I am indebted to Mr W. Hays Parks for reminding me of this and for pointing out that it has been used as a sort of precedent for several important military States' interpretation of Articles 48–58 of Additional Protocol I.

15 That insistent phrase comes in the first Article common to all four Conventions. Its effect is to 'eliminate the plea of military necessity' as accepted, to so considerable an extent, in the war-crimes trials: see e.g. Draper, 1958, pp. 96–7.

16 As usual I have to make clear that the basis for my judgement necessarily excludes Soviet and east European material.

17 1961, pp. 428, 445. Similar concern was expressed by another supreme exponent of humanitarian principle: Boissier, pp. 122–9. Kalshoven takes him to task, pp. 335–9.

18 Krafft, in 1951, cited by McDougal and Feliciano, p. 684n.

19 See Forsythe, 1977, p. 169, for an exact statement of the situation.

20 Veuthey, 1976, pp. 193–4, cites the astoundingly restrictive terms of recognition proposed by Britain.

21 *Summary of Report of the Work of the Conference of Govern-*

ment Experts . . . 1947 (English trans., typed; copy in American Red Cross headquarters library), p. 39.

22 For the various Russian ventures, see first of all Durand, chs. 3 to 5 *passim*. For Spain, the same, ch. 8, part 2, and Junod, chs. 7, 8 and 9.

23 Knitel, p. 54; more about the incident in Durand, pp. 12–13.

24 In the first Convention, Article 47; in the second, 48; in the third, 127; in the fourth, 144. There were insignificant verbal variations between the first and second pairs. Article 127 of the third Convention reads thus:

> 'The High Contracting Parties undertake, in time of peace as in time of war, to disseminate the text of the present Conventions as widely as possible in their respective countries, and, in particular, to include the study thereof in their programmes of military and, if possible, civil instruction, so that the principles thereof may become known to all their armed forces and to the entire population. . . .'

25 V stood not, as most Britons thought, for some German version of Victory, but for *Vergeltung*, reprisal.

26 This was said especially of civilian bombing.

27 That is what it looked like to the Russians and almost everyone else. Yet the American chiefs of staff felt *they* were the disadvantaged ones through 1945–8! See David Alan Rosenberg, 'American Atomic Energy and the Hydrogen Bomb Decision', in *J. American Hist.*, vol. 66, 1979, pp. 62–88.

28 For a concise summary and assessment of these contentions, see Mallison, pp. 168–71.

29 My summary of Soviet approach to international law etc. rests partly on Baade; G. I. Tunkin, *The Theory of International Law*, trans., Cambridge, Mass., 1974; E. A. Korowin, *Das Völkerrecht der Übergangzeit*, trans., Berlin, 1929; Miller, 1975, ch. 7; W. E. Butler, 'Soviet Attitudes towards Intervention', in J. N. Moore (ed.), *Law and Civil War in the Modern World*, Baltimore, 1974; F. Przetazuik, 'L'attitude des états socialistes à l'égard de la protection internationale des droits de l'homme', in *Revue des droits de l'homme*, vol. 7, 1974, pp. 175 ff; and of course Korovin, Krylov et al., *International Law, A Textbook for Use in Law Schools*, Moscow, n.d.

30 For N. Korea and China, see especially Miller, chs. 4 and 8; Forsythe, *passim*, but esp. pp. 134–6; I. C. Y. Hsu, *China's Entrance into the Family of Nations*, Cambridge, Mass., 1960; Suzanne Ogden, 'Sovereignty and International Law: the Perspective of the People's Republic of China', in *N.Y. University J. of Internat. Law & Pol.*, vol. 7, 1974, pp. 1–32; Jerome A.

Cohen, ed., *China's Practice of International Law*, Cambridge, Mass., 1972; Cohen and Chiu, *People's China and International Law*, 2v., Princeton, 1974; CICR, *Le Comité de la C-R et le Conflit de Corée*, Geneva, 1952; William H. Vatcher, jr., *Panmunjon: the Story of the Korean Military Armistice Negotiations*, New York, 1958; and Walter G. Hermes, *Truce Tent and Fighting Front*, Washington, DC, 1966.

31 For the legal ramifications of the Algerian war I have relied mainly on Fraleigh's long chapter in Falk, ed., 1971, and Mohammed Bedjaoui, *Law and the Algerian Revolution*, Brussels, 1961. There is a lot about it in Veuthey and Forsythe.

32 I refer especially to what Bedjaoui describes (p. 216 n. 20) as its establishing, in 1957, 'a permanent delegation in Geneva attached to the CICR', and to its sending to Bern in 1960 or 1961 notice of its accession to the 1949 Conventions. 'The Swiss Federal Government circulated the instruments to other Parties in its capacity as depository, but as itself a Party to the Conventions objected to the accession of Algeria at that stage, that is, before obtaining independence' (UN Gen. Assembly papers, 1970, A/8052, para. 215).

33 From the 'Struggle of peoples for freedom and self-determination' section (paras. 28, 29) of the rapporteur's report from the 'Commission on International Humanitarian Law' of the 22nd International Conference of the Red Cross, Tehran, 1973; conference paper P/7/b.

34 *Official Records . . . 1974–7*, vol.5, p. 120, reporting the 12th plenary meeting, 6 March 1974 (conference paper CDDH/SR. 12).

35 Ibid., p. 123.

36 Ibid., vol. 4, pp. 177–88, being Annex III, conference paper CDDH/41, dated 12 March 1974.

37 Ibid., p. 180.

38 Ibid., p. 188.

39 Ogden points to China's suppression of the Tibetan independence movement and its denial that the Bangladesh national liberation movement was anything other than an India-inspired coup. Since then Vietnam's aggressive policies towards Laos and Cambodia tell the same old tale.

40 Jean Pictet, 'The Need to restore the Laws and Customs relating to Armed Conflicts', in *Review of the International Commission of Jurists*, March 1969, p. 31. The draft rules may be seen in Schindler and Toman, pp. 79–85.

41 Baxter, 1975, p. 3.

42 This resolution is in Schindler and Toman, pp. 187–8.

43 This 'note' is reproduced by Pictet in the article cited in n. 40 above, at pp. 37–42.

44 For Vietnam, about which I have said nothing because it raised few new questions of principle, see first of all Lewy.

45 For the Nigerian civil war, see first of all Forsythe, esp. pp. 181–96.

46 The amount of writing about the Arab-Israeli conflict is by now enormous, and exceptionally controversial. A compendious review of it may be had in John Norton Moore (ed.), *The Arab-Israeli Conflict*, 3v., Princeton, 1974–5. Forsythe of course often refers to it, *passim*.

47 This *Report of the Secretary-General on Respect for Human Rights in Armed Conflicts* came out in three stages: UN. GA. A/7720, dated 20 November 1969; UN. GA. A/8052, dated 18 September 1970; and UN. GA. A/8370, dated 2 September 1971. Important parts of the first and second are printed by Friedman, vol. 1, pp. 701–31, 732–54.

48 Since what is really meant is 'humanitarian principles in armed conflicts', it can be argued that the introduction of the concept of 'human rights', however historically explicable, is intellectually confusing. See esp. Keith D. Suter, 'An Inquiry into the Meaning of the phrase "Human Rights in Armed Conflicts" ', in *Revue de Droit Pénal Militaire et de Droit de la Guerre*, vol. 15, 1976, pp. 393–430.

49 The *Official Records* were published by the Swiss Federal Government in 1978 – see Bibliography under Switzerland.

50 Article 2, common to all four, simply said: '. . . all cases of declared war or of any other armed conflict which may arise between two or more of the High Contracting Parties, even if the state of war is not recognized by one of them. The Convention shall also apply to all cases of partial or total occupation of the territory of a H.C.P., even if the said occupation meets with no armed resistance.'

51 It goes on: '. . . as enshrined in the Charter of the UN and the Declaration on Principles of International Law concerning Friendly Relations and Co-operation among States in accordance with the Charter of the UN.'

52 It is worth observing, that there were no comparable caveats about sovereignty in the 1949's common Article 3.

53 No systematic study seems yet to have been made of this crucially important theme. It goes back at least to the meeting of the Institute of International Law at Zürich in 1877, when (– how characteristic of the epoch!) it was proposed that military attachés should by international agreement be constituted as a 'jury of honour' to report on infractions of the law.

54 Article 90. From a Commission of 'fifteen members of high moral

standing and acknowledged impartiality', five who are 'not nationals of any Party to the conflict' are to be appointed by the President 'on the basis of equitable representation of the geographical areas, after consultation with the Parties', and they are to be joined in a Chamber of Inquiry by 'two *ad hoc* members, not nationals of any Party ..., one to be appointed by each side'.

55 Draper, 1972, at pp. 46–7. See also Forsythe, 1977, pp. 116–17. The relevant treatise is A. Janner, *La Puissance protectrice en droit internationale*, Basel, 1948.

56 Paras. 1 to 4 maintain a superficially imperative tone through their ordaining of the (very complicated) series of things that 'shall' be done to get a Protecting Power or a substitute into place; but the last prescribed stage of action collapses at: 'The functioning of such a substitute is subject to the consent of the Parties ...'.

57 Forsythe, pp. 115–17, 120–1.

58 Article 50 (1, 2).

59 Article 50 (1) last sentence, Article 52 (3).

60 Articles 51 (1, 2), 52 (1).

61 Article 54 (1, 2, 3).

62 Articles 51 (6), 52 (1), 53 (c) which concerns the special category of 'cultural objects and places of worship', 54 (4), and 55 (2) on the 'natural environment'.

63 Article 51 (2).

64 Article 51 (4, 5).

65 Article 54. Para. 5 makes an exception of devastation of your own territory 'where required by imperative military necessity'. Unless my eyes fail me, that is the only express mention of military necessity in the whole Protocol; though its sense is approached in several references to what is 'feasible' in Arts. 41 (3), 57 (2a), and 58, in the expression 'unless circumstances do not permit' in Article 57 (2c), and so on. The US and its NATO allies have, I am informed by one who should know, agreed to define *feasible* thus: 'that which is practicable or practically possible, taking into account all circumstances at the time, including those relevant to the success of military operations'.

66 Article 52 (2). 'Attacks shall be limited strictly to military objectives. In so far as objects are concerned, military objectives are limited to those objects which by their nature, location, purpose or use make an effective contribution to military action and whose total or partial destruction, capture or neutralization, in the circumstances ruling at the time, offers a definite military advantage.'

67 Article 57 constitutes nearly the whole of Chapter IV, 'Precautionary Measures'.

68 Article 58.

69 It may be worth noting that this means *any* party to the conflict; an insurgent or liberationist party equally with an established one.
70 Chapter VI, comprising Arts. 61–7. Arts. 68–71 are on 'Relief in favor of the civilian population'.
71 Arts. 59 and 60. Spaight, 1911, p. 178, records an *ad hoc* example of this near Ladysmith. '*Localités et zones sanitaires*' and '*zones de securité*' figured among the *voeux* of the final act of the 1929 Geneva diplomatic conference. The wars of the later thirties quickly stimulated interest in them. See e.g. R. Debeyre in *Revue générale de droit international public*, vol. 13, 1939, pp. 600–15, the CICR '*Memorandum sur les possibilités d'accords destinés à apporter ... certaines ameliorations au sort des victimes de la guerre ...*', 21 octobre 1939, and its pamphlet *Rapport relatif aux localités et zones sanitaires et de securité*, Geneva, May 1946. In 1949 the ICRC's hope of making them an 'obligatory norm' was disappointed; see the Civilians Convention, Arts. 14 and 15.
72 A British author finds it worth mentioning that his own government accompanied its signature of the first Protocol with a declaration that, 'in relation to Article 1, . . . the term "armed conflict" of itself and in its context implies a certain level of intensity of military operations which must be present before the Conventions or the Protocol are to apply to any given situation, and that this level of intensity cannot be less than that required for the application of Protocol II, by virtue of Article 1 of that Protocol, to internal conflicts.'
73 Article 44 (3), first sentence. The text becomes tortuous here, reflecting the enormous difficulty of reconciling the traditional with the guerrilla positions, and the intensity of the arguments about it. The second sentence reads: 'Recognizing, however, that there are situations in armed conflicts where, owing to the nature of the hostilities an armed combatant cannot so distinguish himself, he shall retain his status as a combatant, provided that, in such situations, he carries his arms openly (a) during each military engagement, and (b) during such time as he is visible to the adversary while he is engaged in a military deployment preceding the launching of an attack in which he is to participate.' A clear and, so far as the report allows one to judge, acceptable explanation of what that means in practice was offered by the United States chief delegate, Mr Aldrich:
    '. . . it was the understanding of his delegation that situations in which combatants could not distinguish themselves through their military operations could exist only in the exceptional circumstances of territory occupied by the adversary or in those armed conflicts described in Article 1, paragraph 4, of draft

Protocol I. In those situations, a combatant who failed to distinguish himself from the civilian population, though violating the law, retained his combatant status if he lived up to the minimum requirements set forth in that sentence. On the other hand, the sentence was clearly designed to ensure that combatants, while engaged in a military operation preparatory to an attack, could not use their failure to distinguish themselves from civilians as an element of surprise in the attack. Combatants using their appearance as civilians in such circumstances in order to aid in the attack would forfeit their status as combatants. That meant that they might be tried and punished for acts which would otherwise be considered lawful acts of combat. That was justified because such combatants necessarily jeopardized the civilian population whom they are attempting to serve.

'. . . As regards the phrase "military deployment preceding the launching of an attack", . . . his delegation understood it to mean any movement towards a place from which an attack was to be launched. In its view, combatants must distinguish themselves from civilians during the phase of the military operation which involved moving to the position from which the attack was to be launched.'

Official Records . . . , vol. 6, p. 150 (conference paper CDDH/SR. 41).

74 Article 37 (1c).
75 Article 43 (1).
76 Article 46, 'Spies', para. 3 is further suggestive. It protects from the charge of espionage a member of a recognized armed force who in his own territory 'gathers or attempts to gather information of military value' about an occupying armed force, 'unless he does so through an act of false pretences or deliberately in a clandestine manner'. This presumably means that he may go about looking like a civilian, but he must own up to not actually being one if asked.
77 See above, pp. 316–17.
78 Article 51 (4, 5).
79 Article 35 (1, 2).
80 Article 35 (3).
81 *Official Records* . . . , vol. 1, pp. 215–16.
82 Citing again the declaration on signing, 12 December 1977, communicated to the Houses of Parliament on 14 December 1977; see Lord Goronwy-Roberts on p. 2223, Mr Luard on p. 236.
83 Article 47. It says 'a mercenary shall not have the right to be a combatant or a prisoner of war' but leaves a Party free to accord

such status if it wishes. The definition of a mercenary is drawn so tight that hardly anyone, actually, will be so definable. Countries which have to get outside help are thus left generally free to do so. A learned friend has commented to me, that 'any mercenary who cannot exclude himself from this definition deserves to be shot – and his lawyer with him!'

Bibliography

This Bibliography includes only books etc. particularly important for the subject or referred to in the Notes.

Abell, Francis, *Prisoners of War in Britain, 1756 to 1815*, Oxford, 1914

Anderson, Frank Maloy, *The Constitutions and other Select Documents illustrative of the History of France, 1789–1907*, 2nd edn., Minneapolis, 1908

Angeberg, Comte d', *Recueil des traités, conventions, etc., concernant la guerre franco-allemande*, 5v., Paris, 1873

Appleman, John Alan, *Military Tribunals and International Crimes*, Indianapolis, 1954

Ariga, N., *La guerre russo-japonaise au point de vue continental et de droit international . . .*, Paris, 1908

Arnold, Thomas, *Introductory Lectures on Modern History*, London, 1842

Aulard, F. V. A., *Recueil des actes du comité de Salut Public . . .*, Paris, 1889–

Baade, H. W. (ed.), *The Soviet Impact on International Law*, Dobbs Ferry, NY, 1965

Badeau, Adam, *Military History of Ulysses S. Grant*, 3v., New York, 1882

Bailey, Sydney B., *Prohibitions and Restraints in War*, London, 1972

Baratier, Anatole, *L'intendance militaire pendant la guerre de 1870–1: justification, réorganisation*, Paris, 1871

Basdevant, Jules, *La révolution française et le droit de la guerre*, Paris, 1901

Batchelder, Robert C., *The Irreversible Decision, 1939–50*, Boston, 1962

Baxter, R. R., 'The Duty of Obedience to the Belligerent Occupant', in *British Year Book of International Law*, vol. 27, 1950, pp. 235–66.

—— 'So-called "Unprivileged Belligerency": Spies, Guerrillas, and Saboteurs', in ibid., vol. 28, 1951, pp. 323–45

—— 'The Geneva Conventions of 1949', in *Naval War College Review*, no. 5, 1956, pp. 59–

—— 'Forces for Compliance with the Law of War', in *Proceedings of the American Society of International Law*, 1964, pp. 82–99

—— 'The Law of War', in Maarten Bos (ed.), *The Present State of International Law and Other Essays*, Deventer, 1973, pp. 107–24

—— 'Humanitarian Law or Humanitarian Politics? The 1974 Diplomatic Conference on Humanitarian Law', in *Harvard International Law Journal*, vol. 16, 1975, pp. 1–26

—— 'Modernising the Law of War', in *Military Law Review*, No. 78, 1977, pp. 165–83

Bell, A. C., *A History of the Blockade of Germany . . .* , privately printed for the British HMSO, 1937

Bernard, Henri, *La guerre et son évolution*, Brussels, 1955–7

Bernard, Montague, 'The Growth of Laws and Usages of War', in *Oxford Essays*, Oxford, 1856, pp. 88–136

Best, Geoffrey, and Wheatcroft, Andrew (eds.), *War, Economy and the Military Mind*, London, 1976

Best, Geoffrey, 'How right is might? Some aspects of the international debate about how to fight wars and how to win them, 1870–1918', in Best and Wheatcroft (eds.), *War, Economy and the Military Mind*, London, 1976, pp. 120–35

—— 'Britain and Blockade, 1780–1940', in Duke and Tamse (eds.), *Britain and the Netherlands*, vol. 6, 'War and Society', The Hague, 1978, pp. 141–67

—— 'Restraints on War by Land before 1945', in M. Howard (ed.), *Restraints on War: Studies in the Limitation of Armed Conflict*, Oxford, 1979, pp. 17–37

Birnbaum, Karl E., *Peace Moves and U-Boat Warfare*, Stockholm, 1958

Biro, S. S., *The German Policy of Revolutionary France*, 2v., Cambridge, Mass., 1957

Bluntschli, Johann Caspar, 'Les lois de la guerre sur terre. Lettres de M. le comte de Moltke et de M. Bluntschli', in *Revue de droit international*, vol. 13, 1881, pp. 79–84

—— 'Droit de guerre et coutume de la guerre, a propos des attaques du Colonel von Rustow contre le droit des gens', in Revue de droit international, vol. 8, 1876, pp. 663–72

Boissier, Pierre, *L'epée et la balance*, Geneva, 1953

—— *De Solférino à Tsoushima. Histoire du Comité International de la Croix-Rouge*, t. I, Paris, 1963

Bonfils, Henry, et Fauchille, Paul, *Manuel de droit international public (droit des gens)*, 6th edn., Paris, 1912

Bourdoncle, René, *De l'influence des ruses sur l'évolution du droit de la guerre*, Paris, 1958 (= Annales de l'Université de Lyon, 3e série, Droit, fascicule 17)

Brenet, Amadée, *La campagne de 1870–1 étudiée au point de vue du droit des gens*, Paris, 1902

Bricard, *Journal du Canonnier Bricard, 1792–1802*, 2nd edn., Paris, 1894

Brownlie, Ian (ed.), *Basic Documents on Human Rights*, Oxford, 1971

Buondelmonti, Giuseppe, *Ragionamenti sul diritto della guerra giusta*, 2nd edn., Florence, 1757

Busch, Moritz, *Bismarck and the Franco-German War 1870–71*, 2v., London, 1879

Butler, Geoffrey, and Maccoby, Simon, *The Development of International Law*, London, 1931

Chareton, V., *Les corps francs dans les guerres modernes. Les moyens à leur opposer*, Paris, n.d. but c. 1900

Clausewitz, Carl von, *On War*, ed. and trans. by Michael Howard and Peter Paret, Princeton, 1976

Corbett, Julian, *Some Principles of Maritime Strategy*, London, 1911

Corbett, P. E., *Law and Society in the Relations of States*, New York, 1951

Craig, Gordon A., *The Politics of the Prussian Army, 1640–1945*, 1st edn., Oxford, 1955

Creveld, Martin van, *Supplying War*, Cambridge, 1977

Crousse, Franz, *Invasion du Danemark en 1864*, Paris, 1866

Davidson, Basil, *Partisan Picture*, Bedford, 1946

Deltenre, Marcel, *Recueil général des lois et coutumes de la guerre . . .*, Brussels, 1943

Derschau, C. F. von, *Über Verminderung der Kriege*, Dessau, 1782

Draper, G. I. A. D., *The Red Cross Conventions*, London, 1958

—— 'The Geneva Conventions of 1949', in *Recueil des cours de l'académie de droit international*, vol. 114, 1965 (I), pp. 61–165

—— 'Implementation of International Law in Armed Conflicts', in *International Affairs*, vol. 48, 1972, pp. 46–59

—— 'Military Necessity and Humanitarian Imperatives', in *Rev. de droit pénal militaire et de droit de la guerre*, vol. 12, 1973, pp. 129–42

Dukacinski, Joseph, *Les règlements militaires des grandes puissances* ... , Bordeaux, 1912

Durand, André, *De Sarajévo à Hiroshima. Histoire du Comité International de la Croix-Rouge*, t. 2, Geneva, 1978

Edmonds, J. E., and Oppenheim, L. F. L., 'The Laws and Usages of War on Land', = ch. 14 of *The British Manual of Military Law*, 1914. (Originally *Land Warfare. An Exposition of the Laws and Usages of War on Land for the Guidance of Officers* ... , London, HMSO, 1912)

Falk, Richard A., *Legal Order in a Violent World*, Princeton, 1968

—— (ed.), *The Vietnam War and International Law*, 4v., Princeton, 1968–76

—— *The International Law of Civil War*, Baltimore, 1971

Fantin Des Odoards, General, *Journal*, Paris, 1895

Farrer, James Anson, *Military Manners and Customs*, London, 1885

Ferrand, Georges, *Droit public des réquisitions militaires*, Paris, 1891

Fezensac, Duc de, *Souvenirs militaires de 1808 a 1814*, Paris, 1863

Forsythe, David P., *Humanitarian Politics: The International Committee of the Red Cross*, Baltimore and London, 1977

François, *Journal du Capitaine François, 1792–1830*, ed. Grolleau, Paris, 1903

Frankland, Noble, *The Bomber Offensive against Germany. Outlines and Perspectives*, London, 1965

—— *Bomber Offensive: The Devastation of Europe*, London, 1969

Frankland, see Webster and Frankland

Franklin, Benjamin, *Writings*, collected and edited by Albert H. Smyth, 10v., New York, 1907

Frederick III, *The War Diary of*, London, 1927

Friderici, Christoph C. W., *Gründliche Einleitung in die Kriegswissenschaft, worinnen die Lehre vom Kriege und Frieden aus dem Natur- und Völker-Rechte vorgetragen* ... *wird*, 2v., Breslau, 1763–4

Friedman, Leon (ed.), *The Law of War. A Documentary History*, 2v., New York, 1972

Galpin, W. F., *The Grain Supply of England during the Napoleonic Period*, New York, 1925

380 *Bibliography*

Garner, J. W., *International Law and the World War*, 2v., London, 1920

Gibson, Hugh, *A Journal from our Legation in Belgium*, London, 1917

Gilbert, Felix, *To the Farewell Address. Ideas of early American Foreign Policy*, Princeton, 1961

Glahn, Gerhard von, *The Occupation of Enemy Territory*, Minneapolis, 1957

Graber, Doris A., *The Development of the Law of Belligerent Occupation, 1863–1914. A Historical Survey*, New York, 1914

Graf, Daniel W., 'Military Rule behind the Russian Front', in *Jahrbücher für Geschichte Osteuropas*, vol. 22, 1974, pp. 390 ff

Green, L. C., *Superior Orders in National and International Law*, Leyden, 1976

Guichard, L., *The Naval Blockade 1914–18*, trans. C. R. Turner, London, 1930

Gurlt, Ernst, *Zur Geschichte der internationalen und freiwilligen Krankenpflege im Kriege*, Leipzig, 1873

Hahlweg, Werner, *Guerilla: Krieg ohne Fronten*, Stuttgart etc., 1968

Hall, W. E., *A Treatise on International Law*, 8th edn., by A. Pearce Higgins, Oxford, 1924 (1st, 1880)

Halleck, 'Retaliation in War' [1864], in 6 *American Journal of International Law*, 1912, pp. 107–16

Heffter, A. G., *Le Droit international de l'Europe*, first trans. from the German, 1844, by Bergson; 4th edn. by F. H. Geffcken, Berlin and Paris, 1883

Helbing, René, *La levée en masse*, Paris, 1911

Henderson, G. F. R., *The Science of War*, London, 1905

Higgins, A. Pearce, *War and the Private Citizen*, London, 1912

—— and Colombos, C. J., *The International Law of the Sea*, 2nd edn., London, 1951 (1st, 1943)

Hinsley, F. H., *Power and the Pursuit of Peace*, Cambridge, 1967

Holland, T. E., *Letters to 'The Times' upon War and Neutrality*, 2nd edn., London, 1914

—— *Elements of Jurisprudence*, Oxford, 1880

—— *Studies in International Law*, Oxford, 1898

Holtzendorff, Franz von (ed.), *Handbuch des Völkerrechts, auf Grundlage Europäischer Staatspraxis*, 4v., Berlin and Hamburg, 1888–9

Howard, Michael, *The Franco-Prussian War*, London, 1961

—— (ed.), *Restraints on War*, Oxford, 1979

Huber, Max, 'Die kriegsrechtlichen Verträge und die Kriegsraison', in *Z. fur Völkerrecht*, vol. 7, 1913, pp. 351–74

Hubner, Martin, *De la saisie des bâtiments neutres ou du droit qu'ont les nations belligérantes d'arrêter les navires des peuples amis*, The Hague, 1759

Hufeland, Gottlieb, *Lehrsätze des Naturrechts*, Jena, 1790

Hyde, H. Montgomery, *British Air Policy between the Wars*, London, 1976

Johnson, James Turner, *Ideology, reason, and the limitation of war. Religious and secular concepts, 1200–1740*, Princeton, 1975

Jones, Neville, *The Origins of Strategic Bombing. A Study of the Development of British Air Strategic Thought and Practice up to 1918*, London, 1973

Junod, Marcel, *Le troisième combattant*, Lausanne, 1947

Kalshoven, Fritz, *Belligerent Reprisals*, Leyden, 1971

—— 'Droits de l'homme, droit des conflits armés et représailles', in *Rev. Internat. Croix-Rouge*, 1971, pp. 205–15

—— 'Geneva Conventions: Conference of Government Experts, 24 May–12 June 1971', in *Netherlands Year Book of Int. Law*, 1971, pp. 68–90

—— 'The position of guerrilla fighters under the law of war', in *Rev. Droit Pénal Militaire et Droit de la Guerre*, vol. 11, 1972, pp. 55–90

—— *The Law of Warfare, a Summary . . .*, Leyden, 1973

Kant, Immanuel, *Kant's Political Writings*, ed. Hans Reiss, Cambridge, 1970

Karsten, Peter, *Law, Soldiers and Combat*, Westport, Conn., 1978

Kennedy, Paul, *The Rise and Fall of British Naval Mastery*, London, 1976

Kitchen, Martin, *A Military History of Germany from the Eighteenth Century to the Present Day*, Bloomington, 1975

Knitel, Hans G., *Les délégations du CICR*, Geneva, 1967 (= Etudes et Travaux de l'Institut Universitaire des Hautes Etudes Internationales, no. 5)

Koessler, Maximilian, 'American War Crimes Trials in Europe', in *Georgetown Law Journal*, vol. 39, 1950–1, pp. 18–112

Kossoy, Edward, *Living with Guerrillas. Guerrilla as a Legal Problem and a Political Fact*, Geneva, 1976 (= Univ. de Genève, Institut Universitaire des Hautes Etudes Internationales, thèse no. 287)

Kriegsbrauch im Landkriege, 1902: see Morgan, ed., 1915

Kuhn, Josef L., 'The Geneva Conventions of August 12, 1949', in G. A. Lipsky, ed., *Law and Politics in the World Community*, Berkeley and Los Angeles, 1953

Lampredi, Giovanni, *Del commercio dei popoli neutrali in tempo di guerra trattato*, Florence, 1788

Lawrence, T. J., *The Principles of International Law*, London, 1895

Lewy, Guenter, 'Superior Orders, Nuclear Warfare, and the Dictates of Conscience', in *Am. Pol. Sci. Rev.*, vol. 55, 1961, pp. 3–23 (partially reprinted in Wasserstrom, 1970, pp. 115–34)

—— *America in Vietnam*, New York, 1978

Lorimer, James, *The Institutes of the Law of Nations*, 2v., Edinburgh, 1884

Louter, Jan de, *Le droit international public positif*, New York, 1920

Lueder, C., *Den Genfer Convention. Historisch und kritisch-dogmatisch mit Vorschlägen zu ihrer Verbesserung . . .*, Erlangen, 1876

—— 'Krieg und Kriegsrecht im Allgemeinen', = Holtzendorff, vol. 4, pp. 169–367

McDougal, Myres, and Feliciano, F., *Law and minimum world public order*, New Haven and London, 1961

Maclean, Fitzroy, *Disputed Barricade*, London, 1957

Macpherson, W. G., 'The Geneva Convention', in *Journal of the Royal Army Medical Corps*, November 1910, pp. 607–28

Mallison, W. T., Jr., *Submarines in General and Limited Wars*, Washington, 1968 (= Naval War College, International Law Studies, vol. 58, 1966)

Marcus, Geoffrey J., *The Age of Nelson* (= A Naval History of England, vol. 2), London, 1971

Marder, Arthur J. (ed.), *Fear God and Dread Nought; the correspondence of Admiral . . . Lord Fisher . . .*, 3v., London, 1952–9

—— *From the Dreadnought to Scapa Flow: The Royal Navy in the Fisher Era, 1906–1919*, 5v., London, 1961–70

—— *The Anatomy of British Sea Power: a History of British Naval Policy in the pre-Dreadnought Era, 1880–1905*, New York, 1940

Martens, Georg Friedrich, *Summary of the Law of Nations, founded on the treaties and customs of the modern nations of Europe . . .*, trans. from the French trans. of the 1st, 1789, ed. by W. Cobbett, Philadelphia, 1795

—— *Recueil des principaux traités d'alliance, de paix, de trève, de neutralité, [etc.] conclus par les puissances de l'Europe . . . depuis 1761 jusqu'à present*, Göttingen, 1791–1801

Martens, F. de, *La paix et la guerre*, trans. from the Russian by N. de Saucé, Paris, 1901

Medlicott, W. N., *The Economic Blockade*, 2v., London, 1952, 1959

Meyrowitz, Henri, 'Réflexions à propos du centénaire de la Déclaration de Saint-Petersbourg', in *Revue Internationale de la Croix-Rouge*, 1968, pp. 541–55

—— *Le principe de l'égalité des belligérants devant le droit de la guerre*, Paris, 1970

Midgley, E. B. F., *The Natural Law Tradition and the Theory of International Relations*, New York, 1975

Miller, Richard I. (ed.), *The Law of War*, Lexington, Mass., 1975

Moltke, Helmuth von, *Letters to his Wife, et al.*, 2v., London, 1895

Monod, G., *Allemands et Français: souvenirs de campagne*, Paris, 1872

Morgan, J. H. (ed. and trans.) *The German 'War Book'* [i.e., *Kriegsbrauch im Landkriege*], London, 1915

Morvan, Jean, *Le soldat impérial, 1800–1814*, 2v., Paris, 1904

Moser, Johann Jakob, *Versuch des neuesten Europäischen Völkerrechts in Friedens- und Kriegs-Zeiten . . .* , 10 parts, Frankfurt, 1777–80

—— *Beiträge zu dem neuesten Europäischen Völkerrecht in Kriegszeiten*, 8v., Frankfurt-am-Main, 1778–81

Müller-Meiningen, Ernst, *Der Weltkrieg 1914–15 und der 'Zusammenbruch des Völkerrechts'*, 3rd edn., Berlin, 1915

Napier, William (General Sir), *Life of*, ed. H. A. Bruce, 2v., London, 1869

Nussbaum, Arthur, *Concise History of the Laws of Nations*, New York, 1950 (1st pub., 1947)

Nys, Ernest, *Le droit international. Les principes, les théories, les faits*, 3v., Brussels and Paris, 1904

O'Brien, William V., 'The Meaning of "Military Necessity" in International Law', in *World Polity*, vol. 1, 1957, pp 109–76

—— 'Legitimate Military Necessity in Nuclear War', in ibid., vol. 2, 1960, pp. 35–120

—— 'Biological/Chemical Warfare and the International Law of War', in *Georgetown Law Journal*, vol. 51, 1962, pp. 1–63

—— 'The Law of War, Command Responsibility and Vietnam', in ibid., vol. 60, 1972, pp. 605–64

Occupants, Occupés 1792–1815, Colloque de Bruxelles, 29–30 January 1968.

Paskins, B. and Dockrill, M., *The Ethics of War*, London, 1979

Percy, Pierre-François, *Journal des Campagnes du Baron Percy, Chirurgien-en-chef de la Grande Armée*, ed. E. Longin, Paris, 1904

Phipps, R. W., *The Armies of the First French Republic . . .* , 5v., Oxford, 1926–39

Pritchard, R. John, 'The Historical Experience of British War Crimes Courts in the Far East, 1946–48', in *International Relations*, vol. 6, 1978, pp. 311–26

Randall, J. H., and Donald, David, *The Civil War and Reconstruction*, 2nd edn., Lexington, 1969

Rayneval, Gérard de, *Institutions du droit de la nature et des gens*, 2v., Paris, 1832 (1st edn., 1803)

Risley, John S., *The Law of War*, London, 1897

Riste, Olav, *The Neutral Ally: Norway's relations with belligerent powers in the first world war*, Oslo, 1965

Ritter, Gerhard, *The Sword and the Scepter*, trans., 4v., Coral Gables, Fla., 1969, 1970, 1972, 1973

Roberts, Adam, and Guelff, R. K., *Basic Documents on the Laws of War*, expected Oxford, 1981

Rolin, Albéric, *Le droit moderne de la guerre*, 3v., Brussels, 1920–1

Rolin-Jaequemyns, G., Articles on the Franco-Prussian War, in *Revue de droit international*, vol. 2, 1870, pp. 643–718; vol. 3, 1871, pp. 288–384; vol. 4, 1872, pp. 481–525

—— Article on the Brussels Conference, in *Revue de droit international*, vol. 7, 1875, pp. 87—111

Röling, B. V. A., 'The Law of War and the National Jurisdiction since 1945', in *Recueil des Cours de l'Académie de Droit National*, val. 100, 1960 (II), Leyden, 1961, pp. 325–456

—— *International Law in an Expanded World*, Amsterdam, 1960

Root, Elihu, "The Real Significance of the Declaration of London', in *American Journal of International Law*, vol. 6, 1912, pp. 583–94

—— 'Francis Lieber', in ibid., vol. 7, 1913, pp. 453 ff

Rüstow, W., *The War for the Rhine Frontier, 1870*, trans., 3v., London, 1872

Schimsewitsch, Lydie, *Portalis et son Temps . . .* , Paris, 1936

Schindler, Dietrich, and Toman, Jiri, *The Law of Armed Conflicts: a collection of Conventions, Resolutions etc.*, Leyden, 1973

Schmid, Jürg H., *Die völkerrechtliche Stellung der Partisanen im Kriege*, Zürich, 1956

Schmidt-Ernsthausen, M., *Das Prinzip der Genfer Convention ... und der freiwilligen nationalen Hülfsorganisation für den Krieg*, Berlin, 1874

Schoell, Maximilian, *Recueil des pièces officielles. Destinées à détromper les Français, sur les évènements, qui se sont passés depuis quelques années*, 9v., Paris, 1814–16

Schwarzenberger, G., 'Military Necessity: a Misnomer', in *Mélanges Seferiades*, Athens, 1961, pp. 13–21

Scott, James Brown (ed.), *Reports to the Hague Conferences of 1899 and 1907*, New York, 1917

—— *The Hague Peace Conferences of 1899 and 1907*, 2v., New York, 1972 (1st, 1909)

—— (ed.), *Proceedings of the Hague Peace Conference of 1899*. Translation of the Official Texts, New York, 1920

—— (ed.), *Proceedings of the Hague Peace Conference, 1907*. Translation of the Official Texts, 3v., New York, 1920–1

Sherman, William T., *Memoirs, written by himself*, 2v., London, 1875

Slade, Adolphus (Rear-Admiral Sir), *Turkey and the Crimean War*, London, 1867

Spaight, J. M., *War Rights on Land*, London, 1911

—— *Air Power and War Rights*, London, 1924 (Also 1933, 1947)

Stone, Norman, *The Eastern Front, 1914–1917*, New York, 1975

Strupp, Karl, *Das Internationale Landkriegsrecht*, Frankfurt-am-Main, 1914

—— (ed.), *Wörterbuch des Völkerrechts und der Diplomatie*, 3v., Berlin, 1924–9

Switzerland, Federal Political Dept., *Official Records of the Diplomatic Conference on the Reaffirmation and Development of International Humanitarian Law Applicable in Armed Conflicts, 1974–7*, 17v., Bern, 1978

Tarle, Eugene, *Napoleon's Invasion of Russia, 1812*, New York, 1971 (Reprint of 1942 edn.)

Taylor, Telford, *Nuremberg to Vietnam: an American Tragedy*, Chicago, 1970

Tetens, Johannes Nikolaus, *Considérations sur les droits réciproques des puissances belligérantes et des puissances neutres sur mer, avec les principes du droit de guerre en général,* Copenhagen, 1805

Thoumas, General Charles Antoine, *Les transformations de l'armée française* . . . , 2v., Paris, 1887

Trainin, I. P., 'Questions of Guerrilla Warfare in the Law of War', in *Am. J. Internat. Law,* vol. 40, 1946, pp. 534–62

Trimble, E. G., 'Violations of Maritime Law by the Allied Powers during the World War', in *Am. J. Internat. Law,* vol. 24, 1930, pp. 79–99

Tucker, Robert W., *The Law of War and Neutrality at Sea* (= Naval War College, International Law Studies, vol. 50, 1955), Washington, 1957

Uhler, Oscar M., *Der völkerrechtliche Schutz der Bevölkerung eines besetzten Gebietes gegen Massnahmen der Okkupationsmacht,* Zürich, 1950

Vagts, Alfred, *A History of Militarism, Civilian and Military,* Rev. edn., London, 1959 (1st, 1937)

Vattel, Emmerich de, *Le droit des gens ou principes de la loi naturelle, appliqués à la conduite et aux affaires des nations et des souverains,* first published in Neuchatel, 1758. I have used the translation by C. G. Fenwick, done as vol. 3 of the Carnegie Institution's edition, Washington, 1916

Verrier, Anthony, *The Bomber Offensive,* London, 1968

Völkerrecht im Weltkrieg. Dritte Reihe im Werk des Untersuchungsausschusses, unter Mitwirkung von Dr Eugen Fischer, Dr Berthold Widmann, and Dr Johannes Bell, 4v., Berlin, 1927

Wachholz, Friedrich Ludwig von, 'Auf der Peninsula 1810 bis 1813', in *Militär-Wochenblatt:* Beihefte, 1907

Waddilove, Alfred, 'The Effect of the recent Orders in Council in relation to English, Russian, and Neutral Commerce', in *Journal of the Statistical Society of London,* vol. 18, 1855, pp. 21 ff

Wartensleben, H. von, *Operations of the 1st Army under General von Manteuffel,* London, 1873

Wasserstrom, Richard A. (ed.), *War and Morality,* Belmont, Cal., 1970

Waxel, Platon de, *L'armée d'invasion et la population. Leurs rapports pendant la guerre, étudiées au point de vue du droit des gens naturel,* Leipzig, 1874

Webster, Charles, and Frankland, N., *The Strategic Air War against Germany, 1939–45,* 4v., London, 1961

Werner, Robert, *L'approvisionnement en pain de la population du*

Bas-Rhin et de l'Armée du Rhin pendant la révolution, 1789–1797, Strasbourg and Paris, 1951

Westlake, John, *International Law. Part II, War,* 2nd edn., Cambridge, 1913 (1st, 1907)

—— *Collected Papers,* ed. Oppenheim, Cambridge, 1914

Wheaton, Henry, *History of the Law of Nations in Europe and America from the earliest times to the Treaty of Washington, 1842,* New York, 1845

—— *Elements of International Law,* R. H. Dana's 1866 edition ed. by G. G. Wilson, Washington, 1936 (1st edn., 1836)

Whitlock, Brand, *Belgium under the German Occupation,* 2v., London, 1919

Whittuck, E. A., *International Documents. A Collection of International Conventions and Declarations of a Law-Making Kind,* London, 1908

Wright, J. W., 'Sieges and Customs of War at the opening of the 18th century', in *Am. Hist. Review,* vol. 39, 1934, pp. 629–44

Zorn, Albert, *Das Kriegsrecht zu Lande in seiner neuesten Gestaltung,* Berlin, 1906

Index

DATE DUE

FEB 13 '96			
MAR 01 '96			
	261-2500		Printed in USA